THE
AFRICAN AMERICAN EXPERIENCE
A HISTORY
SECOND EDITION

CONSULTANTS

Stephen Middleton
North Carolina State University

Charlotte M. Stokes
Prince George's County Public Schools

GLOBE FEARON EDUCATIONAL PUBLISHER
Upper Saddle River, New Jersey
www.globefearon.com

ABOUT THE COVER ARTIST

Self-taught artist Synthia Saint James sold her first commissioned paintings in 1969 at the age of twenty. Today, she is an internationally recognized fine artist. She has completed more than twenty commissions for major collectors, organizations, and corporations. She also has designed more than forty book covers. In 1997, she created the first Kwanzaa stamp for the U.S. Postal Service. Synthia Saint James is also the author of six children's picture books, has her own clothing line, and a signature line of clocks.

ABOUT THE COVER

Synthia Saint James's painting "Legacy II" uses the power of triangular forms and bold colors to portray African American culture. Her free-flowing style delivers meaning to every figure. Surrounding the painting is a border of kente cloth, a traditional West African fabric created by stitching together hand-woven strips of materials.

Cover Design Jennifer Visco
Interior Electronic Design Black Dot, Jennifer Visco
Photo Research Jenifer Hixson, Marty Levick, and Omni-Photo Communications, Inc.
Maps Mapping Specialists Limited

Printed in the United States of America   10 9 8 7 6 5 4 3 2 02 01 00 99

ISBN 0-835-92326-6

GLOBE FEARON EDUCATIONAL PUBLISHER
Upper Saddle River, New Jersey
www.globefearon.com

CONSULTANTS

Stephen Middleton is Associate Professor of History at North Carolina State University. He received his Ph.D. from Miami University, Ohio. His particular field of interest is the history of African Americans in pre-Civil War Ohio, an area in which he has written and edited many articles and books.

Charlotte Stokes is Supervisor of Social Studies, K-12, for the Prince George's County, Maryland, School District. She received degrees in history at the University of Chicago and North Carolina A&T State University.

REVIEWERS

Lawrence D. Broughton
Instructor of African American History
North Chicago Community
High School
North Chicago, Illinois

Dr. Cora Charles
Project Administrator for The African and
African American
Curriculum Infusion Project
Atlanta Public Schools
Atlanta, Georgia

Booker T. Coleman, Jr.
Staff Developer/Curriculum Writer
Community School District 9
Bronx, New York

Dr. Stanley E. Denton
Director of Office of Multicultural
Education
Pittsburgh Public Schools
Pittsburgh, Pennsylvania

Dr. Dorothy J. Fields
Historian and Education Specialist
Dade County Public Schools
Miami, Florida

Mildred Fryer
Department Head, Humanities
Snowden International High School
Boston, Massachusetts

Dr. Carolyn Holmes
Supervisor of African and African
American Studies
School District of Philadelphia
Philadelphia, Pennsylvania

Sylvia Hooker
Assistant Principal
Central Middle School
Newnan, Georgia

Nadolyn Y. Hoskins
Social Studies Chair
Northern High School
Detroit, Michigan

Hester G. McFaddin
Social Studies Instructor
Pender High School
Burgaw, North Carolina

Barbara G. Moses
Curriculum Coordinator
School District of Philadelphia
Philadelphia, Pennsylvania

Thandiwe M.C. Peebles
Principal, Whitney C. Young
Jr. Academy
New York City Board of Education

Akua Scott Rahsaan
Instructor, African American Studies
Thomas J. Rush Middle School
Dallas, Texas

Dr. Clyde Robertson
Director of Africana Studies
New Orleans Public Schools
New Orleans, Louisiana

Michael Salem
Social Science Teacher
Small Necessary High School
Oakland, California

Madeleine T. Schmitt
Social Studies Supervisor
St. Louis Public Schools
St. Louis, Missouri

Dahia Shabaka
Director, Office of Social Studies
and African-Centered Education
Detroit Public Schools
Detroit, Michigan

Kenneth F. Smith
Social Studies Instructor
Oliver High School
Pittsburgh, Pennsylvania

THE AFRICAN AMERICAN EXPERIENCE 2nd Edition

▼▼▼▼▼▼▼▼▼▼▼▼▼▼▼▼▼▼▼▼

TABLE OF CONTENTS

▼▲▼ GALLERIES ▼▲▼

▾▴▾ INCORPORATED BIOGRAPHIES ▾▴▾

▾▲▾ FOCUS ON ▾▲▾

▾▲▾ BUILDING SKILLS ▾▲▾

▼▲▼ MAPS ▼▲▼

▼▲▼ CHARTS ▼▲▼

Henry Louis Gates, Jr. Introduces
The African American Experience

▲▽▲▽▲▽▲▽▲▽▲▽▲▽▲▽▲▽▲▽▲▽▲▽▲▽▲▽▲▽▲▽▲

When I was in the eleventh grade, I was leafing through our American history textbook on the first day of school. I liked to skim the final chapters of our history and geography textbooks, because we almost never reached these pages during the course of the academic year. There, in a very brief section entitled "The Achievements of Negro Americans"—just before the appendices, charts, and maps—I encountered the serene and self-confident countenance of a magnificently elegant and intelligent-looking black man. I can never forget his portrait. He looked to be in his mid-fifties, and he was dressed in a three-piece pinstriped suit, his gold watch chain just visible near the bottom of the frame. How intelligent he looked! This man was a scholar, I said to myself. I hurriedly searched for his name: "William Edward Burghardt Du Bois," the caption read, "author of *The Souls of Black Folk* and the founder of the NAACP."

To say that I was startled is to say almost nothing at all. I was mesmerized. The year was 1966, and the Civil Rights Movement was near its peak. Almost each evening for the past several years, my parents and I had watched African Americans engaging in protest marches in an attempt to end segregation. Hungry for more and more knowledge about the Civil Rights Movement, political and social leaders in the black community, and great moments in black history, I began to search as diligently as I could for any facts about the Negro and our history. But in the textbooks that we used in our school system, there were none. Encountering Du Bois's face (and the one paragraph of description in our textbook), however, led me to begin a quest to discover the facts of black history in this country. Unfortunately, however, my high school and its textbooks were not of much help.

High school students today, I am pleased to be able to say, need not confront the dilemma that I faced more than a quarter century ago. Readers of this textbook, *The African American Experience*, are able to trace the development of African American culture from its complex origins in Africa to the new forms that it took as it blended with European and Native American cultural elements in the Americas. The history of the oppression of Africans and African Americans—first as slaves, and then as the victims of legal segregation and discrimination—is charted in great detail in this volume. But the many wonderful and compelling achievements that persons of African descent have made, individually and collectively, as creators and bearers of culture and the arts in the United States are here as well.

For who can imagine an "American" culture without the myriad contributions of African Americans? The accomplishments and struggles of black Americans are fundamental to the very meaning of the United States itself. Until the facts of the African American experience are known by every high school and elementary student in this country, we will not be able even to begin to realize the true promise of the United States. When these facts are known, the dream of creating a common public "American" culture out of the many multicolored strands of the people from throughout the world who have shaped this nation may come to pass. It is, in part, to assist in bringing about this great goal that the authors of *The African American Experience* have written this book.

The Roman writer Cicero once noted that a people without a written history are a people destined to remain in the infancy of civilization. Precisely to keep African Americans ignorant of their great historical past, many people either denied that blacks had a major part in creating this nation or asserted that the achievements of individual blacks were not important enough to be honored as important historical events. Individual black historians such as George Washington Williams, Carter G. Woodson, Rayford W. Logan, Mary Frances Berry, John W. Blassingame, John Hope Franklin, Neil Painter, and of course, W.E.B. Du Bois himself fought against this deprivation or denial of black history. But it is only in the recent past that junior and senior high school textbooks have begun to face this challenge squarely.

The African American Experience brings vividly to life the joys and triumphs, the frustrations and disappointments, of persons of African descent. Using the thoughts, words, and feelings of black people themselves—as expressed in music, art, literature, speeches, and all sorts of formal documents—the authors of this textbook have brought the history of millions of black Americans vividly to life. To read this book is to be transported into the vital black past, and to be made to feel what it was like to be, as Du Bois put it, at once "a Negro and an American."

I only wish that my own generation had been able to use such a textbook. Thank goodness that my own children will never be forced to wonder if African Americans had a history.

Henry Louis Gates, Jr.

W.E.B. Du Bois Professor of the Humanities

Harvard University

UNIT

Rock art in the Sahara.

THE AFRICAN HOMELAND

(Beginnings—1900s)

Obelisk from Ancient Axum.

Bustling modern day Nairobi.

An African American Speaks

African ancestors were among the major benefactors of the human race. Such evidence as survives clearly shows that Africans were on the scene and acting when the human drama opened. For a long time, in fact, the only people on the scene were Africans.

—Lerone Bennett, Jr., Author and Journalist

Human history started in Africa. As the birthplace of humanity, Africa witnessed many "firsts," including history's first great human **migration**, or movement from one region or country to another. Hundreds of thousands of years ago, ancient Africans made their way to what is now Europe and the Middle East—places where no humans yet lived. Their pioneering journeys ensured the spread of human culture to other parts of the world.

Unit 1 tells the history of ancient Africa and the accomplishments of the people who lived there. In Africa, humans made their first tools, planted some of their first gardens, tamed some of their first animals, and rode in some of their first wheeled carts. The inventions of early Africans paved the way for the civilizations that you will read about in the first three chapters of this book. These civilizations include Nubia, Egypt, Ghana, and Zimbabwe.

Birthplace of Humans. A very small museum marks a huge discovery on a stretch of **savanna**, or sweeping grasslands, in modern Tanzania (tan-zuh-NEE-uh). In a place called Olduvai (OHL-duh-peye) Gorge, **anthropologists** Louis and Mary Leakey found the remains of a skull and stone tools that are nearly 2 million years old. Anthropologists are scientists who study the origins of human beings and the development of their ways of life.

The 1959 discovery by the Leakeys led other scientists to dig deeper into Africa's past. Today, scientists believe that East Africa gave birth to humans nearly 1 million years earlier than the date suggested by the Leakeys. In the mid-1990s, for example, scientists found evidence that ancient Africans in present-day Ethiopia chipped pieces of rock to form the earliest known human tools—stone knives for cutting and scraping—some 2.5 million years ago.

The ability to fashion tools from stone opened the door to what has become known as the Old Stone Age—a period beginning about 2.5 million years ago and lasting until about 10,000 B.C. Throughout this vast expanse of time, humans shaped knives, axes, and spear points out of stone and fashioned needles and fishhooks out of bone. They studied the sky and developed ways of making mathematical calculations. They lived as hunters and food gatherers, moving from place to place, as they followed herds of animals across the grassy plains in Africa and elsewhere.

The Changing African Landscape. During much of the Old Stone Age, Africa

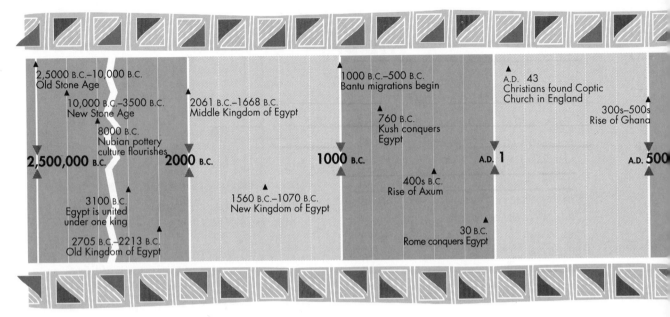

2,5000 B.C.–10,000 B.C.
Old Stone Age

10,000 B.C.–3500 B.C.
New Stone Age

8000 B.C.
Nubian pottery
culture flourishes

2061 B.C.–1668 B.C.
Middle Kingdom of Egypt

1000 B.C.–500 B.C.
Bantu migrations begin

A.D. 43
Christians found Coptic
Church in England

300s–500s
Rise of Ghana

760 B.C.
Kush conquers
Egypt

2,500,000 B.C.   **2000 B.C.**   **1000 B.C.**   A.D. 1   A.D. 500

3100 B.C.
Egypt is united
under one king

1560 B.C.–1070 B.C.
New Kingdom of Egypt

400s B.C.
Rise of Axum

30 B.C.
Rome conquers Egypt

2705 B.C.–2213 B.C.
Old Kingdom of Egypt

looked very different from the way it looks today. Between 2 million and 10,000 years ago, Earth experienced four long periods of cold climate known as the Ice Ages. During each Ice Age, temperatures dipped below freezing across much of Earth, and huge glaciers spread from the polar ice caps. The middle **latitudes**—an area marked by imaginary lines running east and west on both sides of a central line called the equator—remained warm during these periods. In the middle latitudes of Africa, early humans thrived.

During the Ice Ages, there was no Sahara Desert, only fertile plains. In 1981, scientists aboard the space shuttle *Columbia* used special radar instruments to peer deep below the Sahara to see how these plains might have looked. The radar scan revealed the remains of a huge network of waterways and river valleys. Later excavations in southern Egypt and northern Sudan turned up **artifacts**, or objects fashioned by humans, along the banks of these ancient rivers. Scientists now believe

that for hundreds of thousands of years, humans lived in and hunted on what is now the Sahara.

Between the Ice Ages, climates warmed overall—until the next Ice Age began. When the last Ice Age ended, between 12,000 and 10,000 years ago, the climate patterns of today began to appear. The well-watered plains of what is now the Sahara began to dry up. People and animals, such as those in the rock painting on page 2, began to migrate to other parts of Africa. Scientists think, for example, that the ancestors of the ancient Egyptians may have once lived in the central Saharan region.

Rainfall patterns throughout Africa changed. The wettest and most humid zones lay close to the equator. In areas where rainfall was less predictable, people were forced to move near the major river systems that drained the continent—the Nile, Zambezi, Limpopo, Orange, Congo, and Niger—and those that flowed into Africa's largest lakes.

4

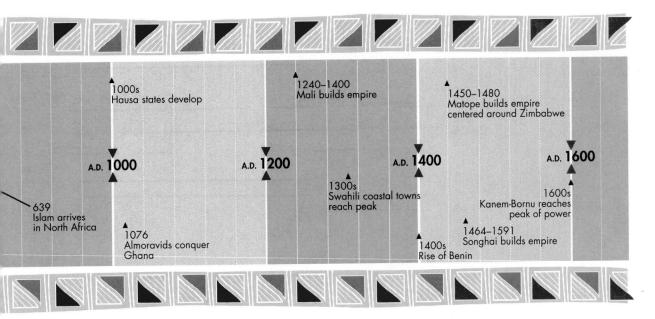

A.D. **1000**

A.D. **1200**

A.D. **1400**

A.D. **1600**

639
Islam arrives
in North Africa

1000s
Hausa states develop

1076
Almoravids conquer
Ghana

1240–1400
Mali builds empire

1300s
Swahili coastal towns
reach peak

1450–1480
Matope builds empire
centered around Zimbabwe

1400s
Rise of Benin

1464–1591
Songhai builds empire

1600s
Kanem-Bornu reaches
peak of power

A Diverse Physical Landscape. All the things that make up a people's way of life—their skills, beliefs, customs, and arts—compose that people's culture. The cultures created by ancient Africans varied with the landscape. Africa offered an immense number of these landscapes. Consider its size. Africa is the second largest continent on Earth. Only Asia is larger. The continent lies along the equator and extends about 4,800 miles (7,680 kilometers) from north to south and 4,500 miles (7,200 kilometers) from east to west at its widest point. All of the following present-day countries could fit into Africa with room to spare: China, the United States, India, and Argentina.

Within this vast expanse of land, climates and land surfaces vary dramatically. Many people mistakenly think of Africa as a land of thick, hot, steamy **rain forests**. But Africa has more desert and dry grasslands than rain forests. The Sahara occupies almost a third of the continent and is the world's largest desert.

Rain forests lie on both sides of the equator, which runs through the middle of Africa. These green belts give way to the sweeping grasslands of the savannas. The savannas are the homes of most of Africa's large animals, including elephants and lions. Most African farms and pasture lands are also found on the savannas, as they have been since the end of the last Ice Age.

A prominent feature of the continent is the **Great Rift Valley**. This deep cut in the Earth's surface extends for more than 3,700 miles (6,000 kilometers), from Syria in Southwest Asia to Mozambique (moh-zuhm-BEEK). It varies in width from 20 miles (32 kilometers) to 60 miles (96 kilometers) and branches into eastern and western sections. A series of long finger-like lakes are found in the Rift Valley. Between the branches of the Rift Valley is Lake Nyanza, the major source of the Nile River. The Nile is the world's longest river, flowing north for more than 4,000 miles (6,400 kilometers).

A narrow plain runs along the coasts. Few natural harbors interrupt these flat coastal lands. Not far inland, the land rises

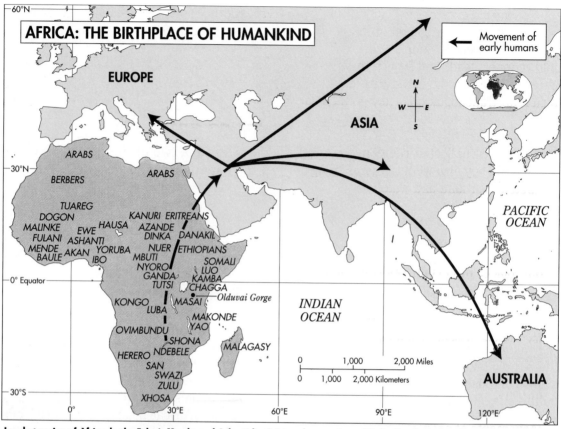

AFRICA: THE BIRTHPLACE OF HUMANKIND

EUROPE

ASIA

Movement of early humans

ARABS

BERBERS   ARABS

TUAREG
DOGON   KANURI ERITREANS
MALINKE   EWE HAUSA AZANDE
FULANI ASHANTI   DINKA DANAKIL
MENDE AKAN YORUBA NUER ETHIOPIANS
BAULE   IBO   MBUTI
NYORO   SOMALI
GANDA   KAMBA LUO
TUTSI   CHAGGA
KONGO   MASAI —Olduvai Gorge
LUBA
MAKONDE
OVIMBUNDU   YAO
SHONA
HERERO NDEBELE   MALAGASY
SAN
SWAZI
ZULU
XHOSA

PACIFIC
OCEAN

INDIAN
OCEAN

AUSTRALIA

N
W   E
S

0   1,000   2,000 Miles
0   1,000   2,000 Kilometers

60°N
30°N
0° Equator
30°S

0°   30°E   60°E   90°E   120°E

In what region of Africa do the Fulani, Mende, and Ashanti live? Into what continent did the first humans to leave Africa move?

sharply up to an **escarpment**, or steep cliff. The greater part of Africa south of the Sahara rises from this escarpment to a high flat plain called a **plateau**.

Most rivers in Africa begin in the interior of the continent. Those that flow to the oceans and seas that surround Africa plunge over the escarpment in waterfalls and rapids. Because of these wild, tumbling waters, it is difficult to navigate these rivers very far inland. However, great rivers such as the Nile have fertilized the soil and enabled Africans to farm along their banks for thousands of years.

Invention of Farming. Africans learned to become resourceful in dealing with the features of the land on which they settled. At

first, they hunted and gathered whatever the land and seasons offered. Then, at different times and in different places, humans developed one of the greatest inventions in history. They learned to farm.

Between 10,000 B.C. and 3500 B.C., people in parts of Africa, Asia, the Middle East, and the Americas discovered how to cultivate the seeds and roots of wild plants and how to **domesticate**, or tame, animals. Some of the world's earliest farming villages began to appear along Africa's Nile River in about 5000 B.C.

The rise of farming triggered the start of what is called the New Stone Age. During this period, one revolution after another took place in the ways people lived. Once people learned to farm, they set up villages. Within villages, the pace of technology quickened. People learned to hammer gold, copper, lead, and iron into weapons and jewelry. They invented the wheel and used it for transportation. They created calendars to measure the seasons and determine when to plant crops. They developed more complicated religions and governments. They also went to war as villages competed over land and water.

Varied Civilizations and Cultures large number of civilizations and cultures emerged as African peoples began in one place. In certain **regions**, with similar physical features, similar ways of life developed. Some of the regions include: North Africa, the East African coast, West Africa, Central Africa, and Southern Africa below the Zambezi River. But even within each of these regions, hundreds of different peoples created distinct cultures and histories.

Movements of peoples among regions— through trade, conquest, or migration— increased cultural diversity as people came in contact with one another. They exchanged new ideas, which in some cases led to the development of entirely new cultures. One example is the Swahili culture that formed along the eastern coast of Africa. The Swahili culture included African, Arab, Persian, Indian, and even Chinese influences. However, the people of this culture were African.

From this rich and varied continent came the ancestors not just of today's African Americans but of all people. Most of the millions of Africans who came to live in the Americas arrived in chains and against their will. Although they were

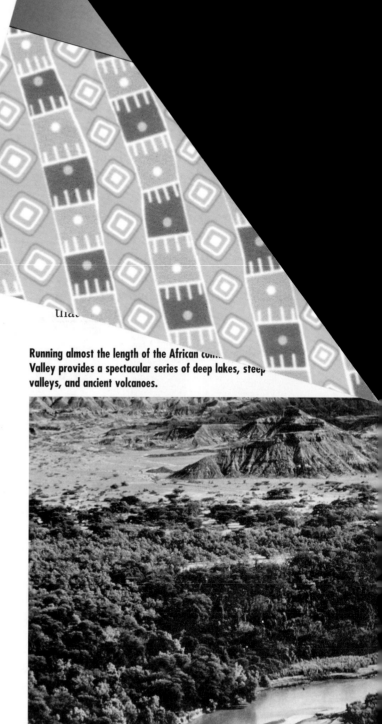

Running almost the length of the African continent, the Great Rift Valley provides a spectacular series of deep lakes, steep valleys, and ancient volcanoes.

The pyramids at ancient Meroë.

Ancient African Civilizations

(c. 8000 B.C.—A.D 800)

THINKING ABOUT THE CHAPTER

How did the ancient civilizations of Northeast Africa interact with one another?

First one beautifully carved slab of stone turned up, then another, and another. United States archaeologist Timothy Kendall found a total of 25 slabs. He moved the pieces around in the sand like a giant jigsaw puzzle. Once fitted together, the slabs formed a picture of a dazzling blue sky filled with golden stars. Vultures wearing magnificent crowns flew through the sky on a journey. But to where?

After years of working in the deserts of present-day Sudan, Kendall believed he knew the answer. The vultures, he guessed, once decorated the ceiling of a passageway leading into a temple dug into a 300-foot (90-meter) hill. That hill is known today as Jebel Barkal (JEHB-ul bar-KAHL). Rubble at the site suggested that the temple was buried nearly 2,000 years ago in an earthquake. In late 1997, Kendall prepared to solve this mystery.

In doing so, he would uncover the ruins of buildings constructed by one of the world's oldest civilizations: Nubia (NOO-bee-uh).

Many archaeologists feel the temple is one of the most important archaeological finds of the 20th century. Ancient treasures inside the temple show that Nubia created one of Africa's most impressive early civilizations. The temple also offers new clues about the complex relationship that developed between Nubia and Egypt, the land that was known as Kemet in ancient times.

Egypt was Africa's other great ancient civilization.

1 THE NUBIAN ACHIEVEMENT

▼ How did the location of Nubia affect its history?

The Nubians lived in a land that followed the twists and turns of the Nile River. As the map below shows, the land stretched from the First Cataract, in what is now Egypt, to Khartoum (kar-TOOM), the capital of modern Sudan. A series of

How did the location of ancient kingdoms in Northeast Africa encourage cultures to mix?

ANCIENT KINGDOMS OF NORTHEAST AFRICA, 3,000 B.C.–A.D. 100

----- Border between ancient Egypt and Nubia

——— Border between present-day Egypt and Sudan

� Cataracts

• Ancient cities and temple sites

✸ Present-day capital

c. 8000 B.C.	Nubian pottery culture flourishes.
c. 3100 B.C.	Egypt is united under its first dynasty.
1759 B.C.	Hyksos invade Egypt.
760 B.C.	Kush conquers Egypt.
591 B.C.	Meroë is built.
A.D. 43	Christians found the Coptic Church of Egypt.
324	King Ezana of Axum converts to Christianity.
350	Axum conquers Kush.

cataracts—strong rapids and waterfalls—made it difficult to travel into Nubia by water. Deserts that lay on either side of the lower Nile also hindered travel to Nubia. As a result, the ancient Nubians had little contact with non-African peoples.

Early Growth of Nubia. The earliest Nubians lived in the fertile plains along the

Nubian artifact.

Nile. These plains were usually less than a mile (1,600 meters) wide. It was along the banks of the Nile that the Nubians learned to build houses out of reeds and to bake mud into pottery. The earliest pottery made by the Nubians dates to before 8000 B.C. That's about 5,000 years before Egypt was first united under one ruler.

At first, the Nubians hunted animals such as giraffes and gathered food from wild grasses and trees along the Nile. Then, as early as the 3000s B.C., they discovered how to grow crops of grain such as wheat and millet and to tame animals such as goats. Around this time, the Nubians began to trade with the Egyptians, who lived downstream.

Recent evidence shows that, along with trade items, the Nubians may have carried a new idea into Egypt—the idea of kingship. Drawings on Nubian relics dated about 3100 B.C. show a king with a crown like that worn by later Egyptian rulers. The contents of Nubian tombs—fine pottery, stone statues, and jewelry—also point to the early existence of a ruling class.

It was around 3100 B.C. that a strong leader named Menes (MEE-neez) united Egypt under its first **dynasty** (DEYE-nuhs-tee), or ruling family. More than 30 dynasties would rule Egypt over a nearly 3,000-year period. Some of these dynasties lasted only a few years; others lasted 250 years.

Both Nubia and Egypt began to flourish after 3100 B.C. Their peoples developed trade, learned to work in copper, and built huge works of art such as the **pyramids**, which served as tombs for their rulers.

Because of Egypt's location—at the northeastern corner of Africa—it had far more contact with the civilizations of Europe and Asia than most other ancient African civilizations. Accounts of Egypt can be found in the writings of the Persians, Hebrews, Greeks, Romans, and other peoples. Knowledge of Nubia came mainly through the Egyptians, who tried for most of their history to control or conquer their southern neighbor. Until recently, when non-Africans talked of ancient African civilizations, they spoke only of Egypt.

Taking Another Look

1. How did the location of Nubia limit its contact with the non-African world?

2. What contacts did Nubia have with Egypt?

3. **Critical Thinking** How do you think isolation might affect a country's development?

2 EGYPT'S CONTRIBUTIONS
▼ What were some of the accomplishments of the Egyptians?

The Greek historian Herodotus called Egypt "the gift of the Nile." The part of the Nile that nourished the growth of Egypt was its broad, triangular **delta**, a low-lying plain at the mouth of a river. Each year the Nile overflowed its banks and flooded the plain. As the floodwaters receded, they left deposits of fertile soil that burst into bloom—first with wild flowers, later with crops planted by farmers.

The lands of the delta were known as Lower Egypt. The lands on the Nile between the delta and the first cataract to the south, were known as Upper Egypt. In the delta, the Nile forked into several branches that kept settlements apart. In Upper Egypt, on the other hand, the river formed a single travel route, which made it easier for a single government to control villages.

3,000 Years of Splendor. Egypt, like Nubia, boasted a history far longer than either Greece or Rome, the two best known ancient European civilizations. Historians generally divide Egypt's history into three main periods, or kingdoms. These kingdoms include:

Old Kingdom, 2705–2213 B.C.
Middle Kingdom, 2061–1668 B.C.
New Kingdom, 1560–1070 B.C.

Each time a kingdom ended, Egypt entered a period of confusion that lasted until a new dynasty restored order. The Egyptians recorded many of their accomplishments in a form of writing based on picture-like symbols known as **hieroglyphics** (heye-ruh-GLIF-iks). The Egyptians carved hieroglyphics into stone tablets and monuments and wrote them on **papyrus** (puh-PEYE-ruhs), a kind of paper made from the papyrus plant.

Developing a system of writing enabled Egyptian **scribes**, or record keepers, to keep track of business matters, such as taxes. This system also allowed Egyptians

Egyptian hieroglyphics could not be understood in modern times until the discovery of the carved object, known as the Rosetta Stone. It contains the same text in hieroglyphics, in another ancient Egyptian language, and in Greek.

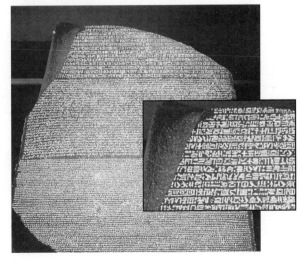

to pass their wisdom and learning on to the next generation.

The Old Kingdom. The rulers of all three kingdoms claimed to be gods. These god-kings stood at the center of Egypt's religion and its government. They expected to rule in both this life and the next. Because life on Earth passed quickly, rulers in the Old Kingdom lived simply. They lived in palaces made of mud bricks, slept on wooden beds, and wore plain linen robes. They believed, however, that the afterlife went on forever. So rulers made elaborate preparations for their death by building huge tombs filled with luxuries for their eternal comfort.

Because Egyptians believed that people needed their bodies as homes for their souls in the next world, they preserved the bodies of their dead. The preserved body is called a **mummy**. Most mummies were laid in painted or gold-encrusted cases that bore a likeness of the person in his or her youth. This was the state in which they believed they would spend their afterlife.

In about 2650 B.C., a ruler named Zoser ordered his chief advisor Imhotep (ihm-HOH-tehp) to design his tomb. Imhotep, a brilliant architect and engineer, built a structure made of six stone platforms. The building rose more than 200 feet (60 meters) and formed Egypt's first pyramid. Hieroglyphics explained its purpose:

During which Kingdom did the Egyptians control Jerusalem?

THE GROWTH OF EGYPT

Mediterranean Sea

Nile Delta

PALESTINE

PHOENICIA

Jerusalem

LOWER
EGYPT

Nile River

Thebes

UPPER
EGYPT

First Cataract — LOWER
NUBIA

Red Sea

Second Cataract

UPPER
NUBIA

Third Cataract — Kerma

Fourth Cataract

Fifth
Cataract

KUSH

AXUM

☐ Extent of Old Kingdom

▨ Extent of Middle Kingdom

▬ Extent of New Kingdom

0   200   400 Miles

0   200   400 Kilometers

A staircase to heaven is laid for him [the king] so that he may climb up to heaven thereby.

Today the so-called Step Pyramid, located at Saqqara (sah-KAH-rah), is the oldest standing building in the world.

After Zoser, the pyramids became bigger and more elaborate. The largest of these stone mountains was the Great Pyramid of Giza, built by King Khufu (KOO-foo). (For more on this pyramid, see page 20.) Near this monument, Khufu's son built his own massive pyramid. To guard it, he ordered construction of the Great Sphinx—a gigantic stone sculpture with the body of a lion and the face of a human.

The stone monuments of the Old Kingdom drained Egypt of its wealth. A series of droughts further weakened the control of Old Kingdom rulers. Low floods led to crop failures. In one 20-year period, no fewer than 20 kings sat on the throne. In the chaos, the Old Kingdom ended.

The Middle Kingdom. The dynasties that restored order learned from past mistakes. During the Middle Kingdom, rulers planned for droughts by digging irrigation systems that piped water from the Nile into storage basins. They also cut trails around the first and second cataracts to set up forts on the Nubian frontier.

Even the most careful efforts, however, could not protect the dynasties of the Middle Kingdom from a group of people known as the Hyksos (HICK-sohz), or "rulers of foreign lands." These warlike newcomers swept into Egypt, probably from present-day Israel and Syria, in the 1700s B.C. They rolled into the Nile delta in revolutionary vehicles—two-wheeled chariots drawn by horses. The soft copper weapons used by the Egyptians were no match for Hyksos's weapons of **bronze**, a metal forged from copper and tin.

Badly outmatched, the Egyptians offered little resistance. For the next 100 years, Hyksos kings ruled Lower Egypt and demanded **tribute**, or forced payment, from Upper Egypt.

The New Kingdom. The rulers of Upper Egypt learned from the Hyksos. They began to use chariots and work in bronze. They then used chariots and bronze weapons to drive out the Hyksos and to reunite Egypt under the New Kingdom.

The New Kingdom saw some of the best-known rulers of Egyptian history, some of whom are listed in the table on this page. These rulers stopped building pyramids, which were too visible and easily robbed.

Which of these pharaohs was a great military leader?

THE 18TH DYNASTY

Some of the best-known Egyptian rulers came from the remarkable 18th Dynasty. The dynasty ruled from 1570 to 1293 B.C. Some of its pharaohs include:

Hatshepsut (haht-SHEHP-soot) She ruled as Egypt's first woman pharaoh.

Thutmose (thoot-MOH-suh) III He led Egypt in its greatest period of empire-building, pushing into Nubia in the South and present-day Syria to the east.

Amenhotep (ah-muhn-HOH-tehp) III He ushered in a long period of peace and constructed huge works of art, such as the Temple of Luxor at Thebes.

Akhenaton (ah-kuh-NAH-tahn) He introduced the idea of **monotheism**– the belief in one god. This god was know as Aton, or the sun god.

Tutankhamen (toot-ahnk-AH-muhn) He returned Egypt to its traditional religious beliefs before dying at age 17.

13

Instead, they built their tombs beneath desert cliffs in the Valley of Kings, near Thebes (THEEBZ) in Upper Egypt.

Unlike the rulers of the Old Kingdom, the rulers of the New Kingdom did not wait until the afterlife to live in comfort. They built beautiful palaces for themselves.

These palaces were called **pharaohs** (FAIR-ohs) or "Great Houses." In time, the Egyptian people began to use the title "pharaoh" for their rulers as well.

The pharaohs raised the money to pay for these luxuries from many sources. Peasants who worked lands protected by the pharaohs paid taxes, while conquered peoples paid tribute. One of the richest sources of tribute flowed out of Nubia—a target of Egyptian conquest throughout the New Kingdom.

Taking Another Look

1. Describe one major accomplishment during each of the three main periods of Egyptian history.

2. Why were the Hyksos able to defeat the Egyptians?

3. **Critical Thinking** Which of the three ancient Egyptian kingdoms do you think had the greatest achievements? Explain your answer.

3 KUSHITES AND EGYPTIANS
▼ How did the relationship between Kush and Egypt change over time?

Nubia lacked the rich farmland of the Nile delta. But access to the grazing lands of the upper Nile valley allowed the Nubians to develop a prosperous cattle industry.

Over time, a number of cultures took shape in Nubia. One of these centered on a city named Kerma that grew up near the grazing lands. Kerma, the oldest African city outside of Egypt, was a thriving place by 2000 B.C. The kingdom that developed around Kerma became known as Kush. Kush became Nubia's most powerful kingdom.

Egypt Marches into Kush. The presence of a strong kingdom along Egypt's southern frontier led rulers of the Middle Kingdom to move into the area. Shortly after 2000 B.C., the Egyptians built a string of forts that stretched to the second cataract. These massive forts, with their moats and drawbridges, looked something like the medieval castles that would appear in Europe nearly 3,000 years later.

As the Egyptians clung to their forts, the Kushites built a thriving trade network that reached into the African interior and to the Red Sea. At coastal ports, they traded with people from as far away as the Greek island of Crete.

When Hyksos conquerors rolled into Lower Egypt in 1759 B.C., the Kushites formed an alliance with them. Egyptian soldiers in Kush either abandoned the forts or asked for protection from the Kushites. Some moved to the city of Kerma, where many married Kushite women.

Shifting Tides of Empire. While the Egyptians struggled under Hyksos rule, Kush entered a time of glory. Rulers built royal tombs filled with wealth. Kings were laid to rest on gold-covered beds. The finest objects of gold, bronze, and ivory were placed beside them. Followers dressed in their best clothes were buried alive so that they could serve the king in the afterlife.

As soon as the rulers of the New Kingdom drove the Hyksos from Egypt, they tried once again to add Kush to the

Egyptian empire. One of the rulers who wanted to govern the Kushites was Hatshepsut.

Hatshepsut was the granddaughter and daughter of conquerors. When her husband died, she ruled in the name of her 12-year-old stepson, Thutmose III. Then she proclaimed herself "king" in her own right.

Hatshepsut's father had pushed south into Kush past the fourth cataract. She vowed to extend her dynasty's rule even farther. To secure this goal, Hatshepsut organized a land-and-sea expedition into Punt—a region along the Red Sea that reportedly supplied Kush with its wealth.

The expedition set out from Thebes in Upper Egypt around 1495 B.C. Oxcarts carried ship parts to the Red Sea, where workers assembled five vessels. Rowers drove these ships across the waters of the Red Sea until they reached Punt. Here the Egyptians spent months loading their ships with exotic goods and animals. The ships also carried several officials from Punt who traveled to Egypt to honor the ruler who had "set all the lands beneath her sandals."

Egyptian Rule. Thutmose III fulfilled the Egyptian dream of conquering Kush. Control of Kush made Egypt wealthier and more powerful than ever before. Kushite mines produced about 48 tons (40,000 kilograms) of gold a year, a level of world production not reached again until the A.D. 1800s. Captives from Kush became soldiers for Egypt's army as well as workers who helped build some of the country's monumental works of art.

Egyptian pharaohs celebrated their dominance over Kush. King Tutankhamen, for example, ordered pictures of Kushites embroidered on the soles of his sandals so that he could trample them every day. Ramses II, one of the most ambitious builders of the New Kingdom, ordered construction of the rock-cut temple of Abu Simbel, which was located deep in Kushite territory. Kushites, for the most part, accepted this dominance until the 700s B.C., when the tides of empire shifted once again.

Kushite Pharaohs. Starting around 1080 B.C., the power of the New Kingdom declined. This turmoil allowed Kushite kings to grow stronger. By the 700s B.C., a Kushite king named Kashta vowed to lead armies northward. "I will take it [Egypt] like a flood of water," boasted Kashta. Around 760 B.C., Kush turned the ancient world upside down by capturing the Egyptian throne.

Egyptian wall paintings show the conquests of Kushite Pharaohs

For almost 100 years, Kushite pharaohs ruled Egypt under the 25th Dynasty. They oversaw an empire that stretched some 1,200 miles (1,930 kilometers) along the Nile. Kushite rule extended to almost a quarter of the African continent. Their rule brought together the cultures of Egypt and Nubia. The blend sparked an outpouring of art that matched the New Kingdom at its peak.

Kushite rule was short-lived. In the 600s B.C., the Kushite pharaohs faced an invasion led by King Esarhaddon (AY-suhr-HAD-un) of Assyria. Although the Kushites and the Egyptians fought bravely, their bronze weapons proved no match for the Assyrians' iron swords and armor. The Kushites retreated south in 667 B.C., leaving Esarhaddon to boast, "I tore up the root of Kush."

An Empire of Iron. The Kushites retreated to Meroë, which was founded about 591 B.C. The location of Meroë had a number of advantages. First, it was beyond easy reach of Egypt. Second, the city lay near rich deposits of iron. Third, because the land was so fertile, fewer people had to spend time raising food. Fourth, caravans carrying goods for trade could travel between Meroë and ports on the Red Sea in just a few weeks.

At Meroë, the Kushites followed the example of the Assyrians and turned to iron-making. Meroë became the first African center of iron manufacturing. At this time, iron was so precious that one ruler had iron spearheads wrapped in gold foil and placed in his tomb.

With iron spears to protect trade routes and conquer neighboring peoples, the Kushites built another powerful kingdom. The influence of Egypt remained strong at Meroë. However, as time went on, the spir-it of southern Africa grew more important. Lions and elephants—animals rarely seen in Egyptian art—appeared in Kushite murals, or wall paintings. Human figures began to look more like Kushites than Egyptians.

The Fall of Kush. The Kushite empire at Meroë flourished for more than 800 years. During this time, Egypt was held together by a series of foreign powers—Assyria, Persia, Greece, and finally Rome, which conquered Egypt in 30 B.C.

More than 300 years after the fall of Egypt, Kush also fell. It was succeeded by Axum, an empire that had little interest in taking over Kush's iron-making skills. Instead, Axum wanted to take over Kush's network of trade, expanding an already large trading empire.

Taking Another Look

1. How did the Egyptians profit from their control of Kush?

2. What were some of the unique features of the Kushite kingdom of Meroë?

3. **Critical Thinking** Suppose you were a Kushite scribe. How would you describe the accomplishments of the Kushite pharaohs?

4 ▼ RELIGIOUS DIVERSITY IN NORTHEAST AFRICA

▼ What were some of the religious influences on people in Northeast Africa?

The location of Northeast Africa's empires and kingdoms brought them into contact with the ideas and religions of many people. Axum, the nation that conquered Kush, for example, felt the influence of the

This detail from an ancient Ethiopian painting shows the visit of the Queen of Sheba.

world's three important monotheistic religions: Judaism (JOO-day-ihzm), Christianity, and Islam. How did these three religions come to Axum and elsewhere in Northeast Africa?

Contact with Judaism.

The kingdom of Axum had its roots in the land along the Red Sea known to the ancient Egyptians as Punt. One of the independent kingdoms there, known as Sheba, sought to open trade with the Hebrews in what is today Israel. The Queen of Sheba paid a personal visit to Jerusalem in the 900s B.C. Accompanying her were many leading nobles carrying gold and other valuable gifts.

While in Jerusalem, Sheba met with King Solomon and converted to Judaism— the religion of the Hebrews and the first major world religion founded on the belief in one God. She later bore Solomon's son, Menelik (men-AY-lick) I. Menelik lived for a time with his father before taking Sheba's throne. As the art on this page shows, the people of what is now Ethiopia came to take great pride in this story.

A Christian Kingdom.

About A.D. 300, Christianity, a religion based on the teachings of Jesus, was well established in the Mediterranean regions of Europe. By then, Axum had become one of the most powerful kingdoms in Punt. Punt's rulers followed their own traditional African beliefs. In 324, however, King Ezana (eh-ZAH-nah) came in contact with Christianity, either through Christian missionaries or traders. He converted to the new Christianity and proclaimed it the official religion of Axum.

About 350, Ezana invaded Meroë and other Kushite cities. As a result of King Ezana's invasion, Kush nearly disappeared from history—until excavations in the late 1900s began to piece together the story of its past. Axum, on the other hand, grew into an important trading empire and became the second great ancient African civilization south of Egypt. It controlled most of the caravan routes from the interior of Africa to the Red Sea. The Red Sea port of Adulis (ah-DOO-lis) was one of the gateways into Africa for merchants from India and the Mediterranean world.

The Coming of Islam.

For a time, it seemed that Egypt might also become a Christian kingdom. About 43 A.D., followers

A Christian church in Ethiopia.

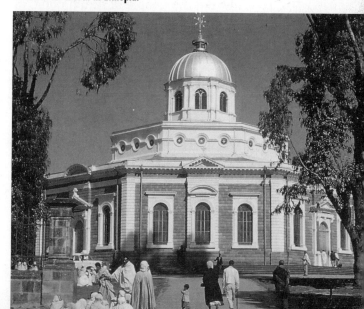

of Jesus founded a Christian church known as the Coptic Church in the Egyptian city of Alexandria.

By the 300s A.D., Alexandria was the leading center of Christian learning in the world. In the 600s, however, another monotheistic religion swept over northern Africa. This religion was **Islam**, which was founded on the teachings of Muhammad.

Although the Coptic Church survived into the present, many people in Northeast Africa converted to Islam. The people of Axum, however, clung to their Christian beliefs. In the 1100s, King Lalibela (lah-lee-BAY-luh) helped preserve Christianity by carving ten churches out of solid rock in the inland mountains of Axum.

When Europeans arrived in Axum during the 1400s, the practice of Christianity amazed them. Although the people of what is now Ethiopia followed teachings of the Bible, their religion also reflected the culture of Northeast Africa, where the influences of traditional African beliefs remained strong. Today, Ethiopians live in the world's oldest Christian nation. They consider Lalibela a saint, and they call his churches the "Jerusalem of Ethiopia."

Taking Another Look

1. How did the people of Axum come in contact with Judaism?

2. How did King Ezana and King Lalibela help establish Christianity in what is now Ethiopia?

3. **Critical Thinking** How did the geographic location of Egypt, Axum, and Kush affect religious practices?

5 A FAR-REACHING HERITAGE
▼ What were some of the contributions of ancient Africans?

In the mid-1900s, African American historian W.E.B. Du Bois wrote:

Ancient Egypt was the first great experiment in human civilization.

Today, the world owes a debt to the African peoples who lived along the Nile, both in Egypt and in the civilizations south of Egypt. Yet for many years the ideas and accomplishments of these peoples were unknown or ignored by people of European backgrounds.

In the case of Nubia, geographic location explains some of the neglect. But prejudice, or an intolerance of racial or ethnic groups other than one's own, played a part, too. Even the ancient Greeks questioned the accomplishments of the Nubians.

The Genius of Ancient Africa. Between 5,000 and 6,000 years ago, the peoples of ancient Africa developed ideas that are important to the modern world. To predict the flooding of the Nile, for example, they measured the passage of time by

Sphinx-like figures on the stage of the Madame C.J. Walker Theater in Indianapolis show the influence of ancient Egypt on the styles of American decoration.

watching the movements of the sun and stars. These observations led the Egyptians to divide a day into 24 hours and a year into 365 days. The result was a calendar much like the one we use today.

The flooding of the Nile sparked other ideas. Because the Nile floods washed away many of the markers used to show land boundaries, the Egyptians developed skillful ways to survey, or measure, land. To control flooding, they designed dams and irrigation ditches.

The need to solve other problems led to more inventions. To figure out fair exchanges for trade, the Egyptians devised a system of weights and measures. To record business transactions, they developed an early system of numerals. The system was based on powers of 10: 1, 10, 100, and so on. Using it, Egyptians could add and subtract even large numbers. Hieroglyphics have been found for numbers larger than 10,000. To build great works like the pyramids, the Egyptians created **geometry**—a branch of math that studies the relationship of points, lines, planes, and surfaces of figures in space. To draw architectural plans, they created graphs.

The list of accomplishments goes on—from the development of dentistry to the use of chemicals to **embalm**, or preserve, the dead. If archaeologists working in Sudan today are right, the list will grow even longer as they dig through the rubble covering Kushite sites.

A Source of Pride. The glory of ancient Africa has inspired generations of African Americans and contributed greatly to the cultural diversity of the United States. When a civil rights movement began to take shape in the 1900s, African Americans fought to have African history and achieve-ments taught in their children's schools. In the 1930s, African American educator Mary McLeod Bethune declared:

> We must let them [our children] hear of the pharaohs and African kings and the brilliant pageantry of the Valley of the Nile.

As a result of African Americans' study of their own heritage, African civilizations have emerged from the shadows of prejudice to be admired by people around the world.

Taking Another Look

1. List three accomplishments of the Nile civilizations.

2. What impact have the accomplishments of the ancient Nile civilizations had on African Americans?

3. **Critical Thinking** Imagine you are Mary McLeod Bethune and write a brief statement in which you state why the teaching of African accomplishments is important.

LOOKING AHEAD

The empires of Northeast Africa—Egypt, Kush, and Axum—had longtime relationships with one another. Even though these relationships were not always peaceful, each kingdom learned from its neighbors and strengthened its own civilization. While these kingdoms were rising and falling, other empires were developing across the continent in the west. From these kingdoms came other diverse achievements that would later serve as a source of pride to today's African Americans.

They called themselves by such names as the "Vigorous Gang" and the "Craftworker Gang." Starting about 2600 B.C., thousands of workers toiled in the blazing sun to carve out huge blocks of stone weighing an average of 2.5 tons (about 1,350 kilograms). The stone-cutting crews competed with one another and took pride in being part of a great building project in honor of their pharaoh.

Having cut millions of stone slabs, the workers began the job of moving the slabs to a site at Giza, near what is today the city of Cairo, Egypt. After 20 years, the product of their labor, the Great Pyramid, was completed. It covers more than 13 acres (5.26 hectares) and soars 481 feet (147 meters) above the desert.

More than 2,000 years later, Greek travelers who visited Egypt gazed in awe at the Great Pyramid and other nearby smaller pyramids. The structures so impressed the Greeks that they listed them among the "Seven Wonders of the Ancient World." Of the seven, only the pyramids still stand. They provide enduring evidence of the extraordinary contributions that the Egyptians made to world culture.

CLOSE UP: CHAPTER 1

The Who, What, Where of History

1. **Where** have archaeologists uncovered new information about ancient Africa?
2. **What** is a cataract?
3. **Who** created some of the earliest pottery in Northeast Africa?
4. **What** is a dynasty?
5. **What** was the reason for the building of the pyramids?
6. **Where** was the most fertile part of Egypt?
7. **What** are hieroglyphics?
8. **What** is a scribe?
9. **Who** were the Hyksos?
10. **Where** did many of the kings of the New Kingdom build their temples?
11. **Who** was Hatshepsut?
12. **What** kingdom conquered Kush?
13. **Who** was the Queen of Sheba?
14. **Who** proclaimed Christianity the official religion of Axum?
15. **What** religion swept over much of northern Africa in the A.D. 600s?

Making the Connection

1. What was the connection between the use of the chariot, the use of bronze, and the end of the Middle Kingdom?
2. What is the link between the Assyrian conquest of Egypt and the rise of the Kushite kingdom of Meroë?
3. How was flooding of the Nile connected to the Egyptian invention of each of the following: a calendar, a system of surveying, and irrigation?

Time Check

1. Which of these peoples invaded Egypt *first:* the Assyrians, the Hyksos, or the Kushites?

2. Place the following events in the order in which they happened: king of Axum converts to Christianity; Islam sweeps over northern Africa; Queen of Sheba converts to Judaism; Christians found the Coptic Church in Egypt.

What Would You Have Done?

1. Suppose you could choose to live in one of the three ancient kingdoms: Egypt, Kush, or Axum. Which would you choose? Explain.

2. Imagine that you were a Kushite king at the time the Hyksos were beginning to move against Lower Egypt. A Hyksos leader sends you a message asking you to form an alliance against Lower Egypt. How would you respond? Explain.

Thinking and Writing About History

1. Imagine you are a wagon maker in Upper Egypt some time after the arrival of the Hyksos. Write an advertisement explaining why every Egyptian soldier needs a chariot.

2. An unknown Greek sailor in the A.D. 100s wrote this description of Adulis, Axum's main Red Sea trading port:

There are imported into [Axum] . . . cloth made in Egypt; robes from Arsinoe [modern Suez]; cloaks of poor quality dyed in colors; double-fringed mantles; many articles of flint glass . . . made in Diospolis [probably the Greek city of Thebes]; . . . wine of Laodicea [on the Syrian coast] and Italy; . . . and imported Indian cloth called monache.

a. What imports were in demand in Axum?

b. What can you conclude about Axum's trading network from this description?

c. Imagine you are a Greek trader reading this description. Would you invest in an expedition to Axum? Why or why not?

Building Skills: Comparing Maps

When you look at photographs of a place taken over time, you may notice changes in its appearance. For example, what differences would you expect to see in photos taken of your community today and photos taken 150 years ago? Would your community even have existed then?

If you compare maps of geographic regions drawn at different times, you will notice changes, too. Find out what changes have taken place in Africa over time by comparing the maps on pages 12 and 426. Then answer the following questions.

1. Which map fits the definition of a historic map—a map that shows an area as it was many years ago?

2. On the map on page 428, find the area that is shown on page 9. How have political boundaries in this region changed over the years?

3. Which ancient sites lie in modern-day Egypt?

4. Based on a comparison of these maps, what generalizations can you form about the historical links between present-day Egypt and Sudan?

14th century map of Mali shows Mansa Musa and extensive trading networks.

CHAPTER 2

West African Empires and Kingdoms

(500s–1600s)

THINKING ABOUT THE CHAPTER

What were some of the accomplishments of the diverse empires and kingdoms of West Africa?

The news of a golden empire southwest of the Sahara traveled north with the camel caravans of the Berbers. The Berbers, some of the earliest settlers of North Africa, charted the first routes across the Sahara more than 2,500 years ago. To get lost in the Sahara's shifting sands meant certain death. Few but the Berbers risked the journey.

When Arab conquerors intent on spreading the Islamic religion swept into North Africa in the 600s, Berber accounts of a "land of gold" seemed unbelievable. "[There's] a country," wrote one Arab, "where gold grows like plants in the sand in the same way as carrots do, and is plucked at sunset." Even the king's dogs, wrote another Arab, "wear collars of gold."

Where did this gold come from? Gold mines, you might say. But the West African land the Berbers and Arabs called Ghana did not have any gold mines. What it did have was a network of trade.

1 EMPIRES BUILT ON TRADE

▼ How did the locations of Ghana, Mali,
▼ and Songhai contribute to their wealth?

People in the "land of gold" called their home Wagadu, their capital Kimbu, and themselves the Soninke (soh-NIHN-kah). They lived in an area that included parts of modern Mauritania, Senegal, and Mali—not in the country that is now called the Republic of Ghana.

Their empire was governed by a strong king. He ruled over lesser kings who controlled surrounding territories. This system provided protection for the people and for the empire's trade. The strong king lived in the capital and was known by the title of *ghana,* meaning "warrior chief." Visitors mistakenly applied the title of *ghana* to the empire itself.

Wealth Through Trade. Ghana rose to power between A.D. 300 and 500. It was the first of three empires to take advantage of a location that lay at a "crossroads of trade," a place where trade routes came together. At the heart of the trade were two items: salt and gold. The salt came from the Sahara and North Africa. The gold came from an area south of Ghana called Wangara (won-GAH-rah). For the salt and gold traders to meet, one or both of them had to pass through Ghana. Passage came at a price: taxes paid to the king.

How did Ghana gain enough power to demand and receive these taxes? First, like the Kushites, the Soninke knew how to make iron tools and weapons. They used iron swords to conquer their neighbors, who possessed only wooden weapons. They also used these weapons to extend their control over a large area (as shown in the map on page 24). Second, Ghana had a centralized government with a king. The surrounding territories gave the king their loyalty as well as taxes and soldiers. In exchange, they demanded protection and the right to rule in their own local areas.

Through its weapons and system of government, Ghana offered traders many benefits. The king used his army to keep the peace and ensure safe trade. He also kept the value of gold high by maintaining tight control over the supply of gold through a system of taxation.

"Master of the Gold." After crossing the Sahara, salt traders headed into the capital, where they paid a tax on salt and any other goods they brought into Ghana. The tax was paid in a certain weight of gold or goods of equal value. The salt traders then went to a point along the Niger River and deposited blocks of salt in piles. The traders beat a drum to announce the start of trade and left.

The gold traders then approached. For the people of Wangara, salt was worth its weight in gold. Like people in other hot climates, they sweated away body salts and had to replace them by adding salt to their food. They also used salt to preserve foods. The gold traders estimated the value of salt and other goods and left gold beside each pile. Then they, too, left.

The salt traders returned. If they accepted the payment, they beat the drum, signaling an end to trade. If not, they retreated once again. This so-called "silent trade" continued until a price was set. Neither side ever saw the other.

The salt traders then went back to the capital, where they paid a tax on the gold before leaving Ghana. All gold paid to the government of Ghana went into the royal treasury, which limited the supply and kept gold's value high. Taxes also enriched the king and enabled him to build bigger armies, pay more officials, and maintain the beautiful courts that led the Soninke to give their kings a new title—*kaya maghan* (kye-uh mah-GHAN), which means "master of the gold."

Arab Caravans on the Desert. Islam, the religion founded in 622 by an Arab merchant named Muhammad, swept into North Africa in the 600s and early 700s. Followers of Muhammad, called **Muslims**, believed they had a duty to spread Islam, peacefully if possible, or by a holy war, called a **jihad** (jee-HAD), if necessary.

Conquerors out of the Arabian Peninsula pushed into lands held by African peoples such as the Berbers and a Berber people called the Tuaregs (TWAR-egz), who mined much of the salt in the Sahara. From what is now Morocco, Muslim Arabs fought their way into Spain, Portugal, and southern France. Accompanying them were Muslim Africans. Europeans called these people **Moors**. Meanwhile other Muslim conquerors seized huge parts of the present-day Middle East.

Muslim merchants greatly increased trade across the Sahara by opening up new markets for African goods. So much gold flowed into Europe from Muslim nations

Name three cities that were involved in the trade in gold.

EMPIRES AND KINGDOMS OF WEST AFRICA, A.D. 500–600

24

along the Mediterranean that several rulers there adopted gold as their currency. By the late Middle Ages, most European gold came out of West Africa—a place little known to Europeans.

The Slave Trade Across the Sahara. The trade across the Sahara had always included a number of captive Africans. Slavery, the system of owning people, had existed for hundreds of years and in most parts of the world, including Greece and Rome. For the most part, Africans enslaved other Africans they captured during wars. Africans were also enslaved when they broke a law or fell into debt. Enslaved Africans often worked as servants, farm laborers, or miners. The Tuaregs, for example, used enslaved Africans in the salt mines of the Sahara.

With Arab conquests, the demand for enslaved Africans increased dramatically. Muslims already traded slaves captured in jihads, including Christians from Europe. They now added Africans taken in jihads or purchased through trade networks. Muslim traders carried many enslaved Africans outside Africa in what people now refer to as the **African Diaspora** (deye-AS-puh-ruh), the forced scattering of Africans to other parts of the world, particularly the Americas.

All slavery deprives people of rights. However, the slavery practiced by Africans allowed enslaved people to earn or purchase their freedom. Muslim law eased some of the pains of slavery by extending the hope of freedom to certain captives. It also denied slaveholders the power of life and death over their human property and forbade them from separating children from enslaved mothers until age 7.

As you will read in later units, the situation was very different for captive Africans carried into the Americas, especially English-speaking America. Although there were exceptions, as a rule neither conversion to Christianity nor the laws of government provided hope of escape from slavery.

Muslim Empires in West Africa. Trade with the Muslims across the Sahara enriched Ghana. The king of Ghana allowed the practice of Islam within the empire, and a Muslim merchant town near the capital had a total of 12 **mosques**, as Muslim places of worship are called. But most of the people of Ghana continued to practice traditional African religions.

In the 1000s, Muslim Berbers from North Africa known as the Almoravids (ahl-MOH-rah-vihdz) launched a jihad against Ghana. The battles exhausted Ghana's power. In its place, two empires arose—Mali (MAH-lee) and Songhai (SONG-heye). The empire of Mali ruled from about 1240 to 1400. Songhai flourished from about 1464 to the late 1500s. Both empires took over and expanded Ghana's profitable trading network. The leaders of both of these empires were Muslim. The history of these two empires can be told in part by the story of a city called Timbuktu (tihm-buhk-TOO).

Mansa Musa and the Rise of Timbuktu. Under Mali and Songhai, Islam remained largely a religion of cities, towns, and market centers. In rural areas, most Africans continued to practice the traditional religions. In the towns and cities where people practiced Islam, however, centers of learning grew up that were based on the study of the **Koran**, the Muslim holy book. One of the most fabled of these cities was Timbuktu.

Timbuktu owed much of its fame to Mansa Musa (MAHN-suh MOO-suh). In 1324, Mansa Musa set out on a **hajj**, a pilgrimage to the Muslim holy city of Mecca, in Arabia. While in Mecca, Mansa Musa persuaded some of Islam's finest architects, scholars, and other professionals to return with him to Mali. These Arab Muslims enlarged and enriched Timbuktu. They constructed handsome buildings, opened Islamic schools, and laid the groundwork for what would become great universities. In describing the city, one Muslim traveler wrote:

> There are many judges, professors, and holy men, all being generously helped by the king, who holds scholars in much honor. Here, too, they sell many handwritten books from North Africa. More profit is made from selling books in Timbuktu than from any other branch of trade.

In 1468, a fierce Songhai warrior named Sunni Ali (SOO-nee AH-lee) conquered Timbuktu and added it to the Songhai empire. Sunni Ali saw Arab Muslims as foreigners and paid them less honor than Mansa Musa had. Sunni Ali angered the city's Arab Muslims by practicing both Islam and the traditional Songhai religion. He allowed conquered African peoples to retain their religious beliefs, too.

When Sunni Ali died, a power struggle brought a devoted Muslim, Askia Muhammad (AHS-kee-uh moo-HAHM-uhd) to the throne. Askia Muhammad began a 35-year reign that brought both the Songhai empire and Timbuktu to the heights of their power. Under Askia Muhammad, scholars from surrounding African states, as well as from Arabia, journeyed to Timbuktu to study literature, law, and science.

Decline of Empire. Askia Muhammad's sons, who lacked their father's wisdom, split Songhai apart as they battled for control of the empire. They even exiled their aged, blind father for a short time.

Timbuktu as it looked in the 19th century. Who was responsible for making Timbuktu a great city?

After the sons died, rivalry continued to plague the empire. The final blow to Songhai, however, came from invaders.

In 1591, an army from Morocco marched into West Africa in search of gold. Although the army had only 4,000 soldiers, it possessed a fearsome new weapon, the harquebus (HAHR-kwuh-buhs). This was an early type of gun. With this weapon, the Moroccans defeated a Songhai force of more than 18,000 cavalry and 9,700 foot soldiers. "From that moment on," wrote one Muslim observer, "everything changed. Danger took the place of security; wealth gave way to poverty. Instead of peace came distress, disasters, and violence."

Taking Another Look

1. What was the basis for the wealth of Ghana, Mali, and Songhai?

2. How did arrival of the Muslim Arabs affect the practice of slavery in Africa?

3. What were the reasons for Timbuktu's fame?

4. **Critical Thinking** How did trade affect the development of Ghana, Mali, and Songhai?

2 ▼ KINGDOMS OF THE GRASSLANDS AND FORESTS

▼ Who were some of the diverse peoples who lived in the savanna and coastal forests of West Africa?

From the upper bend in the Niger River—the heart of West Africa's three great trading empires—the sweeping grasslands of the savanna stretch eastward across the basin of Lake Chad to the Nile River valley. In the west, the grasslands follow the Niger south until they reach a nearly unbroken belt of rain forest.

The rain forest runs along the southern coast of West Africa from modern-day Senegal in the west to the Congo River basin in the east. The only break is in present-day Togo and Benin, where the grasslands dip down toward the Atlantic.

Within the vast expanses of grasslands and forests lived a great variety of peoples. Captives from these two regions would swell the flood of people in the African Diaspora. Some would travel to slave markets on the other side of the Sahara or on the east coast of Africa. Most found themselves on a horrible journey to the Americas. The next part of this section gives a sampling of some of the cultures from this region that existed before the Europeans arrived in West Africa.

Hausa City-States. The Hausa (HOW-zuh) people lived mainly in present-day Nigeria. There they formed **city-states**, self-ruling states made up of a city and its surrounding territory. These city-states started as small fortified towns in the 1000s or earlier. As the towns grew, the Hausa built bigger enclosures. By the 1100s, some towns were encircled by mud walls

Mosque dominates a Hausa walled town.

up to 15 feet (4.5 meters) high and 8 to 9 miles (13 to 14 kilometers) in circumference. Wooden gates bound with iron opened for trade and closed for defense.

Goods from surrounding areas flowed into the capital of each city-state—meat, animal skins, honey, cotton fiber, bars of iron, and more. Inside the cities, thousands of **artisans**, or skilled workers, fashioned items for trade. Smiths forged iron tools and weapons. Weavers made wool and cotton blankets. Leather workers produced leather from brown goats that is still widely valued in Morocco and Europe today.

Although the Hausa city-states were important trade centers, they never united under a central government as the merchant empires to the northwest did. Songhai, the largest of these merchant empires, expanded into Hausa territory and demanded taxes and tribute. But the Hausa states still governed themselves for the most part.

When the Songhai empire collapsed, Hausaland, as the region is sometimes called, entered a time of great growth. The disorder led traders and scholars to bypass Songhai for Hausaland. Market towns such as Katsina (kat-SEE-nah) and Kano (KAH-noh) became major centers of commerce and learning. Each had populations of about 75,000.

The success of these centers drew the interest of Kanem-Bornu (KAY-num BOR-noo), an empire to the east. When soldiers and horses clad in armor charged into Hausaland from Kanem-Bornu, the Hausa states, torn apart by competition over trade, failed to offer unified resistance.

Kanem-Bornu. The empire of Kanem-Bornu centered around Lake Chad. Made up of the dual kingdoms of Kanem and Bornu, the empire lay at the geographic heart of Africa. It sat on routes out of the Sahara to the north and the forest lands to the south. The trade routes connecting eastern trade along the Nile with western trade along the Niger also passed through it.

Trade carried Islam into the area along with Muslim caravans. As in the merchant empires of Ghana, Mali, and Songhai, Islam became well-established in the cities and trading centers of Kanem-Bornu. Contact with Muslim merchants also increased trade, which was the empire's source of power.

Kanem-Bornu traded in items similar to the other merchant empires of West Africa, except for gold, which was less plentiful. The empire made up for the lack of gold by exporting thousands of captive Africans seized in wars fought with weaker peoples to the south.

The armies of Kanem-Bornu were forces to reckon with. Soldiers wore iron armor and iron helmets. They fought with lances and swords from the backs of galloping horses. Until the 1600s, the plunder of war—including captive Africans—flowed largely across Saharan trade routes. However, with the arrival of Europeans on the Atlantic coast, the traffic in enslaved Africans switched directions and headed toward the Atlantic. This change disrupted century-old trading patterns throughout the region.

Benin. The horse-mounted soldiers of the savanna might thunder across the grasslands in conquest. But they could not easily push into the dense rain forests of the southern coast. Protected by the forest, peoples such as the Yoruba (YOHR-uh-buh), Bini (BEE-nee), and many others, lived in thriving kingdoms and states such as Ife (ee-FAY) and Oyo (oi-YOH) in the 1400s and 1500s.

Benin bronze work.

Benin, which dominated a large region around the Niger delta, was among the best known of these kingdoms. Its traditional history extended back as far as the 1100s, when the people of Benin asked the *oni,* or king, of Ife to send one of his sons to rule their land. The king agreed and since that time the ruler of the Benin has been known as the *oba.*

Stories passed down from generation to generation recall the accomplishments of a powerful oba named Ewuare (eh-WOO-ah-ray) who greatly expanded the size of Benin. In recalling the triumphs of Ewuare, a modern-day Benin chief has written:

> He fought against and captured 201 towns and villages. . . . He took their rulers captive and caused their people to pay tribute to him. He made good roads in Benin City. . . . In fact the town rose to importance and gained the name "city" during his reign.

Within Benin City, Ewuare set up a strong government. He appointed chiefs to govern districts within Benin. Other officials collected taxes and managed trade. Ewuare also encouraged goldsmiths and bronze workers to produce beautiful works such as those on this page. The government of Benin so impressed the Portuguese explorers who first visited there that they urged the oba to establish relations with Portugal. An ambassador from Benin visited Portugal in the early 1500s and soon Portuguese missionaries and traders were sailing to Benin.

Kongo.   South and east of Benin, in a stretch of rain forest in West Central Africa, lay another well-organized empire called Kongo. Kongo consisted of a number of small kingdoms ruled by a powerful leader known as the *manikongo* (mah-nee-KOHN-go). The ruler could be either a man or

Helmet mask of the Kuba people of the Kongo.

29

300s–500s	Rise of Ghana.
600s	Islam sweeps into North Africa.
1000s	Hausa city-states are founded.
1076	Almoravid invaders conquer Ghana.
1240–1400	Mali builds its empire.
1400s	Rise of Benin.
1464–1591	Songhai builds its empire.
early 1500s	King of Kongo protests European slave trade.
1591	Moroccans invade Songhai.

woman. By the 1400s, the manikongo ruled over a population of more than 4 million people.

The Bakongo, as the people of Kongo called themselves, knew how to smelt copper and iron. From palm trees, they produced oil, vinegar, and a type of bread. They also wove a beautiful fabric from the fibers of palm leaves that looked to the Portuguese like velvet and satin.

The Portuguese reached Kongo in the late 1400s. By the early 1500s, Christian missionaries had converted a manikongo to Christianity. His son, who took over the empire, also accepted Christianity and took the Christian name of Afonso. Afonso saw the start of the Atlantic slave trade—and the undermining of his empire. He wrote letters pleading for an end to the practice. His pleas, however, went unheeded.

Taking Another Look

1. Why were the Hausa states unable to resist takeover by Kanem-Bornu?

2. How did the location of Kanem-Bornu contribute to the empire's power?

3. **Critical Thinking** How were the systems of government in Benin and Kongo alike?

3 WEST AFRICAN HERITAGE
▼ What traditions developed in West Africa before the arrival of the Europeans?

About 400 years after the arrival of the first Europeans along the coast of West Africa, a U.S. missionary named R.H. Stone climbed a high rock to catch his first glimpse of the Yoruba, people from the area that is now Nigeria and Benin. Stone had come to convert the Yoruba to Christianity. Many of his ideas about Africans were born of racial prejudice. After watching the Yoruba, Stone wrote:

> What I saw disabused [rid] my mind of many errors in regard to . . . Africa. . . . The men are builders, blacksmiths, iron-smelters, carpenters, calabash [wood] carvers, weavers, basket-makers, hat-makers, mat-makers, traders, barbers, tanners, tailors, farmers, and workers in leather. . . . [W]omen . . . spin, weave, trade, cook, and dye cotton fabrics.

Stone wrote these words some 400 years after Europeans had enslaved the first West Africans. The activities that he observed were part of the rich and varied cultures developed by West Africans long before Europeans arrived in Africa. Captive Africans would carry memories of these cultures with them to the Americas. Traditional customs and practices kept alive by enslaved Africans became their gift to the Americas. Many of these customs and practices are reflected in U.S. culture today.

West African Families. "A child is like a rare bird," declared a Yoruba poem. The Yoruba, like other West African peoples, deeply valued family ties. Many believed that a family's children represented the reborn spirits of their deceased ancestors. Thus children linked the generations—both past and present—of a family.

West African peoples developed several different forms of marriage. In one, the groom or the groom's family was expected to give the parents of a bride gifts or money, known as **bridewealth**, to pay for the loss of a daughter's labor. At the time of the marriage, the bride went to live with her husband's family.

As a rule, West African people such as the Yoruba lived in **extended families**— families made up of parents, unmarried children, married sons and their families, and, sometimes, grandparents, aunts, uncles, and cousins. Men usually made major decisions, but women played important roles. They made the clothes, farmed alongside the men, and in a few societies, served as warriors. Olaudah Equiano (oh-LOW-duh ek-wee-AH-noh), the son of an Igbo chief, described the things he learned from his mother. Equiano, who was carried to the Americas in the 1700s, wrote:

> [M]y mother . . . used to take particular care to form my mind. I was trained up from my earliest years in the art of war: my daily exercise was shooting and throwing javelins [spears]; and my mother adorned me with emblems [designs], after the greatest warriors.

A Well-Ordered Life. Outside the great market cities of West Africa, most people lived in farming villages. The land belonged to the community, not to individual members, and almost all people worked as **subsistence farmers**. That is, they grew only enough food for their own needs.

Within villages, each person had a rank, or position. The top rank consisted of elders, men who had gained the respect of others through age and experience. Groups of elders formed the local village governments. Farmers and craftworkers, who made up the majority of people, were the middle class of society. Captives taken during wars formed the lowest class. Although the treatment of these captives varied, some enslaved members of a village lived on an equal footing with others. Equiano, after suffering the harsh bondage of the Americas, wrote of slavery in Africa:

> [Enslaved people did] no more work than other members of the community, even their master. Their food, clothing, and lodging were nearly the same (except that they were not permitted to eat with those who were free-born).

Importance of Religion. Missionaries such as Stone believed the Africans either had no religion or had little concept of a single all-powerful God. They were wrong on both counts. In rural West Africa, religion formed a part of every aspect of life, and almost every traditional religion included a belief in a kind of all-powerful, ever-present creator. Equiano described the Creator as one who lived in the sun, wore a tight belt around his stomach so that he might never eat or drink, and smoked a pipe—the favorite luxury of Equiano's people.

West Africans understood the concept of the Christian and Muslim God, but they accepted the presence of a number of lesser gods and goddesses who were responsi-

Modern-day West African griot passes down the history of his people to villagers.

ble for different tasks such as farming or natural phenomena such as rain. The people of Dahomey, for example, organized their gods and goddesses into the categories of sky, earth, and thunder. Two of these were Mawu, the moon goddess, and her husband, Lisa, the sun god. They were the parents of other gods and goddesses. Many Africans who accepted Christianity or Islam also continued to honor the lesser gods and goddesses.

To West Africans, religion was not something apart from other aspects of life. It was life itself. The social group in which they lived was also a religious community. When people died, their spirits remained part of the community. As a result, most West Africans practiced **ancestor worship**. They prayed to ancestors for protection against evil forces or for help in solving the problems of everyday life. They uttered the names of their ancestors frequently or named children after ancestors so that the souls of the dead would always be connected to their village.

Music, Art, and Literature. "We are almost a nation of dancers, musicians, and poets," remarked Equiano. He might have added artists to the description, too, for West African cultural achievements spanned almost all the art forms.

32

The craftworkers and artisans of West Africa worked in leather, ivory, wood, and metals. Some of their metal works can be seen in this chapter and in "The Artist's View" on pages A1 and A2. These artisans also created beautiful fabrics, such as the brilliantly colored **kente** (KEHN-tee) cloth still woven by the Ashanti (uh-SHAHN-tee) of present-day Ghana.

The musical instruments that accompanied song and dance—drums, whistles, horns, guitars, flutes, and other instruments—were also works of art. For West Africans, music was a form of religious expression.

Dances were elaborate events, with women and men in separate lines swaying, leaping, and clapping their hands to the sound of beating drums. West Africans used dances to celebrate important events such as birth, marriage, and even death, which marked a journey to a spiritual homeland.

Song went hand-in-hand with many activities, such as working in the field. A favorite type of vocal music had a **call-and-response** pattern. The leader sang out a short bit of music and the people sang it back, accompanied by drums or other percussion instruments.

The origin of these and other practices were preserved in **folktales**, the traditional stories handed down from generation to generation. The retelling of these stories was entrusted to **griots** (GREE-ohz), people who memorized and recited important cultural and historical events. The stories told by the griots often had morals that taught lessons. Particularly popular were stories of tricksters in the form of spiders, tortoises, or rabbits who defeated bigger and stronger animals.

A Source of Strength. As Africans experienced the agonies of slavery in the Americas, they held on to the traditions of their homelands. The folktales they told mirrored those of Africa. African musical instruments also took new forms. For example, the banza, which is made from a hollowed-out gourd, became the banjo. The call-and-response patterns of work songs and spirituals recalled the singing patterns of West Africa.

Although nearly all slaveholders in North America forbade legal marriages among enslaved Africans, enslaved people held marriage ceremonies nonetheless. Under the most horrible conditions, they struggled to preserve a sense of family. They honored the names of African ancestors and called out in anguished song and prayer the names of children and loved ones torn from them by slave traders.

Taking Another Look

1. What role did religion play in most West African societies?

2. What were some of the art forms practiced by West Africans?

3. **Critical Thinking** Folktales involving tricksters were popular among enslaved Africans in the Americas. Why do you think this was so?

LOOKING AHEAD

Just as the peoples of West Africa developed their own unique and varied traditions, so too did the many peoples in eastern and southeastern Africa. Although fewer enslaved people from these regions traveled to the Americas, their cultures touched on West Africa through the vast trading networks that spanned the continent.

The peoples of East Africa also created ancient civilizations. These, like the civilization of Kush, were neglected by non-African historians until recently. Some of the traditions that grew up along the East Coast, such as use of the Swahili language, attracted the attention of many African Americans. These African Americans sought strong ties not just to their individual homeland, but also to the African continent as a whole.

WHAT'S IN A NAME ?

"A child's behavior and personality resemble so much his name-bearer," declares an African proverb. In keeping with this saying, many West African peoples had special naming ceremonies for their children. A Hausa child, for example, received two names—a secret, real name whispered by his or her mother and a public name for daily use. Other West African peoples also gave their children two names: one for good times, one for bad; or one temporary, one permanent.

As a result of the Civil Rights Movement of the 1960s, some African Americans are reclaiming their heritage by taking African names for themselves and their children. Some of these names include:

Female

Ainka:	The cherished one
Menjiwe:	The trustworthy
Sowo:	Medicine woman
Mirembe:	Peace
Wamuiru:	The beautiful black one
Yakiri:	Truth, certainty
Barkara:	Blessing, prosperity

Male

Oba:	King
Seve:	Hawk, aggressive person
Ola:	Noble man
Mwangi:	One who conquers
Chiri:	One with a lot of money
Manani:	The beneficent one
Uwezo:	Power

CLOSE UP: CHAPTER 2

The Who, What, Where of History

1. **What** is the African Diaspora?
2. **Where** were Ghana, Mali, and Songhai?
3. **What** is a "crossroads of trade"?
4. **What** was the "silent trade"?
5. **What** is a jihad?
6. **Who** was Mansa Musa?
7. **Where** were the Hausa states located?
8. **What** is an artisan?
9. **Who** was Ewuare?
10. **Where** was the Kongo empire?
11. **Who** belongs to an extended family?
12. **What** does the term *subsistence farming* mean?
13. **What** is ancestor worship?
14. **What** is a call-and-response pattern?
15. **What** is *kente* cloth?

Making the Connection

1. How were gold and salt connected in ancient Ghana?
2. What was the relationship between the spread of Islam and an increase in the trade across the Sahara?
3. What was the connection between religion and daily life in West Africa?

Time Check

1. Which of these events happened *last:* the founding of Mali, the arrival of Islam in North Africa, the rise of Hausa cities such as Katsina?
2. In which century did Kanem-Bornu reach its power?

What Would You Have Done?

1. Suppose you lived in the Mali empire. If you had a choice of working as a trader or as a teacher at a university in Timbuktu, which would you have chosen? Explain.

2. If you could travel back in time to either Ghana, Kanem–Bornu, Benin, Hausaland, or Kongo at the peak of its greatness, which would you visit? Explain.

Thinking and Writing About History

1. Imagine you were a griot. In 100 words, describe the "silent trade" to the people of your village.

2. Imagine that you were a student who had traveled to Timbuktu in the 1300s to study. Write a letter giving your impressions of the city.

3. Suppose you were Afonso of the Kongo. What would you have included in your letter to the Portuguese king to convince him to end the trade in enslaved Africans?

Building Skills: Making Comparisons

Every day you make comparisons. When you go shopping for a new shirt, you might find 15 shirts on the rack in your size. You might choose to try on three. You might choose only one. How would you narrow your selection from 15 to one?

First, you compared the shirts. What did you compare? Several things, probably—style, price, fabric, color, and fit. When you tried on three shirts, you probably concentrated on style, fit, and color.

Whether you are shopping or studying, making comparisons is a way of organizing information. You place things in categories, then you look for similarities and differences—that is, you compare them. This chapter gives you information about some of the diverse empires, kingdoms, and states of West Africa. To organize and compare some of this information, complete the following steps.

1. Copy the chart on a separate sheet of paper. Then use information from your textbook to complete it.

2. Add other categories to your chart and fill in the information.

3. Compare your categories and answer these questions:

   a. What were some of the things that these empires and kingdoms had in common?

   b. What were some of the features that made the empires and kingdoms different from each other?

Kingdom	Location	Major Religion	Source of Wealth
Ghana			gold and salt trade
Mali		Muslim	
Songhai			
Kanem-Bornu			
Benin			
Kongo	rain forest and South of Benin		

Modern-day drawing of life in ancient Zimbabwe.

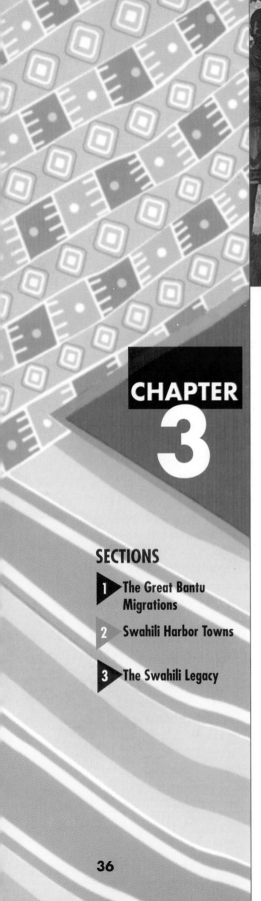
East African Trading States

(1000s–PRESENT)

THINKING ABOUT THE CHAPTER

How did the Bantu and Swahili cultures differ from one another?

Perched on top of a huge granite hill, the ruins can be seen from miles away. Massive walls enclose gigantic pillars of stone and the remains of ancient buildings. Many people say the ruins look like the Greek Acropolis—a beautiful temple atop a hill in Athens, Greece. These ruins, however, form part of what is known as Great Zimbabwe (zeem-BAH-bway). Nicknamed the Zimbabwe Acropolis, the ruins are located near Masvingo (mahs-VING-oh) in present-day Zimbabwe.

The other ruins that form Great Zimbabwe sprawl across a valley at the base of the hill. Here a huge wall forms an oval more than 800 feet (240 meters) long. It rises 32 feet (10 meters) high and is up to 17 feet (5 meters) thick. Nearly a million blocks of granite form the wall. The blocks fit together so precisely that the builders used no mortar to hold them together. The so-called Great Enclosure is the largest single ancient structure outside of Egypt.

When Europeans first saw the ruins of Great Zimbabwe in the 1800s, they refused to believe that African peoples outside of Egypt could have built them. They called the ruins a "mystery" and came to the conclusion that ancient Phoenicians, Arabs, Romans, or Hebrews were the builders. But archaeologists later proved that the builders of Great Zimbabwe were Africans. They credited this impressive engineering feat to the Shona (SHOW-nah), one of the many Bantu-speaking peoples who settled the southern half of Africa.

The Congo River and its tributaries have provided natural highways for migrating Africans.

built Great Zimbabwe and civilizations along the eastern coast of Africa.

Into the Congo Basin. Scientists think the original Bantu speakers may have lived along the present-day border of Nigeria and Cameroon. At some point between 1000 and 500 B.C., the farming peoples of West Africa began expanding into new lands to support their growing populations. The Atlantic Ocean blocked the Bantu speakers from expanding to the southwest, and farming peoples already occupied lands to the north and east. The need to find new farmland pushed a few adventurous pioneers south into the rain forests of the Congo Basin.

The Congo River's many **tributaries**— smaller rivers and streams that feed into a larger river—provided natural highways through the dense rain forests. Using canoes fashioned from the giant trees of the forest, a small number of Bantu speakers made their way to a lightly wooded grassland near what is now Katanga (kuh-TANG-guh). This region, which the Bantu settled around 100 B.C., provided the center from which smaller groups of people would fan out in all directions. You can trace some

1 THE GREAT BANTU ▼ MIGRATIONS

▼ What were some of the areas settled by Bantu-speaking peoples?

Today most Africans living south of the equator speak one of several hundred Bantu languages. The word for human in many of these languages is *ntu*. The prefix for more than one human is *ba* (or *wa* or *ma* or *ama*). Speakers of Bantu languages often identified themselves to foreigners as *bantu,* meaning "the people." Non-Africans who heard this phrase mistakenly applied it to the many diverse peoples who occupy nearly one third of the African continent— an area about the size of the continental United States, including Alaska.

People speaking early forms of Bantu started moving south of the equator about 2,500 years ago. They spread out across what is now central, eastern, and southern Africa in one of history's great human migrations. Descendants of some of these people founded the Kongo empire. Others of these movements on the map below.

Bantu-speaking peoples began a second wave of migrations that continued from roughly A.D. 100 to 1000. They carried with them skills learned in their original West African homeland: mining, ironmaking, goldsmithing, pottery making, and more. These migrants adapted themselves, when necessary, to each new environment, forming varied patterns of life. Hunting cultures they encountered offered little resistance to the Bantu migrants, and the two groups often intermarried.

Between about 400 and 1000, the southward wave of Bantu-speaking peoples pushed into present-day Zimbabwe. Here they discovered gold mines that fueled a profitable trade along the eastern coast. The wealth from this trade helped build several powerful kingdoms centered around Great Zimbabwe.

Great Zimbabwe. The structures that form Great Zimbabwe cover about 1,779 acres (720 hectares). The name of the site comes from the Shona word *dzimbabwe,* meaning "houses of stone." Archaeologists believe that the Great Enclosure and the smaller circular enclosures that surround it were once the capital of a great empire. Based on the remains of mud huts in the area, archaeologists think that

From an original homeland in the Cameroon–Nigeria area, Bantu speakers began moving South about 500 B.C. Where was their Cradleland? In what directions did they fan out from the Cradleland?

12,000–20,000 people may have lived in Great Zimbabwe between 1000 and the 1800s.

The Shona stone masons who built Great Zimbabwe left no written records. However, archaeologists have pieced together the story of the Shona peoples past through artifacts and Shona oral histories. Archaeologists believe that the Shona people built upon the accomplishments of earlier Bantu migrants in the area. They believe, too, that the Shona included a number of **clans**, or groups of people related to one another. Among these clans were the Karanga (kuh-RANH-guh) and the Rozwi (RAHZ-wee).

An East African Empire. Bantu migrants introduced two important ideas to the region around Zimbabwe. First, they developed a religion centered on the belief in one supreme God, called Mwari (em-WAHR-ee). To honor Mwari, they built sites where the people in the community could worship together. At these sites, chiefs prayed for the people. Over time, the chiefs became accepted as the religious leaders, paving the way for the second idea—kingship.

One of the kings in the lands around Great Zimbabwe, a ruler named Mutota (moo-TOH-tuh), began a war of conquest around 1440 to bring the region under his control. Within 10 years, he extended his rule over lands reaching between the Zambezi and the Limpopo rivers. He seized most of the gold mines in the area and trade routes leading to the East African coast.

Like the rulers of Ghana, Mutota demanded tribute from subject peoples, who called him *Mwene Mutapa* (em-WAY-nay moo-TAH-tuh), meaning "Master of the Ravaged Land." He also imposed taxes on

These brass animals were used to weigh gold.

all goods entering or leaving the empire.

When Mutota died in 1450, his son Matope (mah-TOH-pay) followed in his footsteps. Over a 30-year period, Matope extended his control as far as Mozambique and into the Swahili harbor towns that you will read about in the next section. By the time of his death around 1480, Matope ruled one of the largest empires ever created in Africa south of the equator. It rivaled the West African kingdoms in size and wealth.

Not all the Shona peoples willingly submitted to rule by Matope. A leader of the Changa people called the Changamire (CHAN-guh-meer) challenged Matope and Matope's son and successor. Although the Changamire was killed in battle, his son held onto the southern half of the empire—an area that included Great Zimbabwe.

Decline of an Empire. When the Portuguese arrived along the coast of Mozambique in the early 1500s, they learned of the two powerful inland kingdoms. They called the kingdoms by the names of their rulers: Changamire and Mwene Mutapa, which the Portuguese mispronounced as Monomotapa (moh-noh-MOO-tah-puh).

At first, the Portuguese left these kingdoms alone. They focused instead on driving out the Arabs along what is known today as the Swahili coast. That done, they took control of Monomotapa, installing a hand-picked ruler in 1629. Changamire, however, outlasted Portuguese dominance in East Africa. It grew in power, largely from trade with the Portuguese, and thrived into the 1800s. At that time, the pressures of European conquest drove waves of Bantu-speaking invaders into Changamire.

The invaders cut a path of destruction through Changamire as they fought for new homelands. Great Zimbabwe fell into ruins, and a sad chapter dominated by white British rule began. The British renamed the country Rhodesia, after Cecil Rhodes, an empire builder. This name stuck until 1980, when descendants of the Bantu empire-builders regained power. They renamed their nation Zimbabwe in honor of the great achievements of their ancestors.

Taking Another Look

1. Why did Bantu-speaking people originally migrate south of the equator?

2. What ideas did the Bantu-speaking settlers of Great Zimbabwe introduce to the region?

3. **Critical Thinking** How did migrations both benefit and harm the Bantu-speaking peoples of East Africa?

2 SWAHILI HARBOR TOWNS
▼ What was the link between trade and the Swahili culture?

The harbor towns of East Africa blossomed between 1000 and 1700. Like commercial centers all over the world, they experienced a variety of foreign influences. Some 1,200 years ago, for example, Arab traders moved into the towns, bringing the Islamic religion with them. They married

and built homes there. Other influences came from Persia, or present-day Iran, and from India and China.

The strongest influence by far, however, was that of the Bantu-speaking people who arrived on the coast between 200 and 900. Bantu-speakers not only farmed the land along the coast. They also conducted much of the trade with the inland empires. The earliest Muslim visitors to the coast of East Africa referred to the entire region stretching from Mogadishu (maw-gah-DEE-shoe) in the north to Sofala (so-FAH-lah) in the south as the "empire of Zanj," meaning the "empire of blacks." Use the map scale on page 38 to estimate the length of this coastal region.

The Swahili Culture. The term *Swahili* comes from an Arabic word meaning "people of the coast." The Swahili culture takes in the African Islamic peoples who live on African islands and lands along the Indian Ocean. They speak about 14 **dialects**, or variations of a language known as KiSwahili or simply, Swahili. The blend of Bantu and Muslim influences has come to form what we know today as the Swahili culture.

The Swahili harbor towns reached their height in the 1300s. Some towns grew large enough to be considered city-states. Each town had several mosques. Most towns were governed by rulers known as **sultans**. Many of the sultans traced their origins to Persia, or modern-day Iran. They called themselves Shirazi (she-RAH-zee), after the Persian city of Shiraz. They had arrived as invaders to take over Bantu trading centers. Over time, the newcomers married with the local people. Within a few generations, Swahili sultans claimed both Persian and African ancestors.

The upper class in Swahili towns enjoyed comfortable lives. They lived in houses built from pieces of coral stone cemented with mortar. These houses rose several stories and were decorated with ornately carved wooden beams and doors fashioned from African teak or the wood of breadfruit trees. People filled their homes with Persian carpets, African baskets, and occasionally, rare vases from China. They ate foods flavored with local coconut milk and saffron from India.

Descriptions of these cities captured the interest of Ibn Battuta (IB-uhn bah-TOO-tah), an Islamic Berber from North Africa.

Ibn Battuta was born in 1304 in what is now Tangiers, Morocco. He left home at age 21 and for close to 30 years traveled through the Islamic world of his day. He traveled by foot, by ship, and by horse and camel. His combined African and Islamic heritage drew him to the Swahili coast and later to the West African kingdoms. By the time he died at age 65, Ibn Battuta had traveled lands reaching from Spain to China and nearly all of Islamic Africa. He covered far more land than even the famed European explorer Marco Polo.

Ibn Battuta, a devoted Muslim, found much to admire in the Swahili harbor towns. In January 1331, he wrote:

After one night in Mombassa, we sailed on to Kilwa, a large city on the coast whose inhabitants are black. A merchant told me that a fortnight's [two-week] sail beyond Kilwa lies Sofala, where gold is brought from a place a month's journey inland called Yufi. The city of Kilwa itself is among the finest and most substantial [greatest] in the world.

Many scholars believe that Yufi may have been Zimbabwe—the source of most of the gold, copper, and other wealth that enriched Sofala. Other sources of Sofala's wealth included ivory, timber, and, in increasing numbers, enslaved Africans.

The East Coast Slave Trade. From as early as the 800s, Muslim traders carried enslaved Africans from Zanj across the Persian Gulf into lands in the present-day Middle East. In the 800s, for example, large numbers of captives from Zanj drained the marshes where the Tigris and Euphrates rivers meet, in what is now lower Iraq. Harsh treatment led some of these captives to revolt in 869. By 871, the rebels had captured several towns and set up a capital in a new rebel state. From here, they launched raids into present-day central Iraq, seizing property and freeing other enslaved captives from Zanj.

The revolt was put down in 883, but it left many Muslim rulers badly shaken. For a time, the trade in captives from Zanj dropped sharply. When it resumed, Muslims generally tried to avoid the large-scale use of captive Africans. Nonetheless, Muslim merchants still took thousands of captive Africans into North Africa or other Muslim lands each year. From about 650 until the Muslim slave trade ended in the late 1800s, more than 8 million Africans were enslaved in either the trade across the Sahara (see Chapter 2) or the trade along the Swahili coast.

41

1000–500 B.C.	Bantu migration out of West Africa begins.
A.D. 100–1000	Bantu-speaking people fan out through southern Africa.
200–900	Bantu-speakers move into lands and islands on the East Coast of Africa.
869	Enslaved Africans revolt in present-day Iraq.
1300s	Swahili harbor towns reach their peak.
1331	Ibn Battuta visits Swahili coast.
1450–1480	Matope builds one of the largest African empires south of the equator.
1540s	Swahili merchants curb the trade with Portuguese invaders.
late 1800s	East Coast slave trade ends.
1980	Descendants of Bantu builders of Zimbabwe take power in Rhodesia.

Arrival of the Portuguese. When the Portuguese arrived along the Swahili coast, the sight of Muslim mosques infuriated them. For centuries, the Muslims had stood between Europeans and the wealth of Asia. Portuguese ships blasted their way into Swahili harbors and attacked the towns.

The Swahili people, who were merchants rather than soldiers, were not prepared to meet the challenge of the armor-clad Portuguese. Portuguese swords and primitive guns killed many Swahili.

The Swahili then struck back with the only weapon they had. They convinced people in inland kingdoms to stop trading with the Portuguese. By 1550, the bustling commerce of the Swahili coast had slowed to a trickle.

Taking Another Look

1. What were the sources of wealth for the Swahili harbor towns?

2. What were some of the features of the Swahili culture that emerged in these towns?

3. **Critical Thinking** What part do you think the Swahili language might have played in building up the wealth of the Swahili coastal towns?

3 THE SWAHILI LEGACY

▼ What is life like in present-day Swahili islands and towns?

Subira ni ufunguo wa peponi. "Patience is the key to paradise," declares this Swahili proverb. For centuries, the Swahili patiently awaited the end of foreign rule— first the Portuguese, then the Turks, and later, still other Europeans who wanted to carve up Africa. When the nations of East Africa achieved independence, pockets of Swahili culture were still alive up and down the coast—a source of unity in a region made up hundreds of peoples. A key center of this Swahili culture is Zanzibar.

The Zanzibar Archipelago. Zanzibar is the name of a city, an island, and an **archipelago** (ar-kuh-PEL-uh-go), or string of islands. About 50 islands make up the Zanzibar archipelago, which is named after the largest island in the group. Some 800,000 people live on these islands, most of them Swahili. Arab ships called *dhows* (DOWZ) sail between the islands and the mainland much as they did 1,000 years ago.

To step onto an island in the Zanzibar archipelago is to step into the past. Many people, especially on the smaller islands, still wear traditional clothes. Some Muslim women dress in *buibui* (bwee-bwee)—

black sleeveless garments that cover the body from head to toe. Others wear the *khanga* (kahn-GAH)—two pieces of colorful cloth that are often printed with Swahili sayings. One piece ties around the waist and extends to the ankles, the other covers the head and the top of the body.

Towns still have open-air *bazaars,* the Arab word for "market." These markets are filled with the smell of the spices that have made the islands famous: nutmeg, pepper, cinnamon, cardamom, ginger, and cloves—the islands' leading export.

In rural areas, people still live in traditional homes fashioned from the trunks and leaves of palms. Here, in addition to spices, people grow crops of yams and bananas—foods brought to Africa by traders from Malaysia and later grown by Bantu-speaking peoples throughout the region. "You who will travel in the archipelago," say the people of Zanzibar, "will know how to appreciate the Swahili."

Reaching Out to Africa. An appreciation for Swahili culture blossomed in the United States with the Civil Rights Movement of the 1960s. At the peak of the movement, African American students pressured schools, especially colleges and universities, to begin African studies programs that would encourage unity among people of African descent—people of the African Diaspora. Student activist Ron Karenga (kah-RANG-uh) recommended seven principles that could be used to organize these programs. He keyed each principle to a Swahili term. These seven terms later became the basis for the African American holiday of Kwanzaa (KWAHN-zuh).

In 1970, only about 80 colleges and universities in the United States offered courses in African studies. Even fewer offered programs in Swahili. Today hundreds of African studies programs are available.

Taking Another Look

1. What evidence of the different cultures that make up Swahili culture is visible in Zanzibar?

2. Why did African Americans take an interest in the Swahili culture?

3. **Critical Thinking** How do you think the island location of Zanzibar has helped preserve the Swahili culture?

LOOKING AHEAD

Africans forced to travel to the Americas faced a nearly impossible battle: to preserve their diverse cultures. To forget the pains of slavery, however, they often turned to activities that reminded them of their homelands. The act of remembering helped enslaved Africans to survive as a people.

An open-air bazaar in Tanzania.

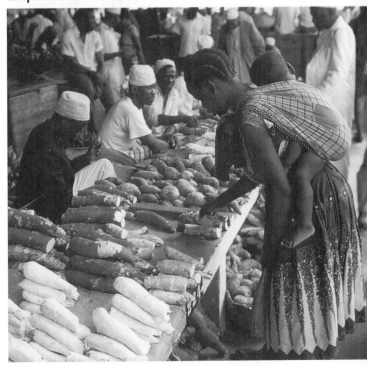

Today an estimated 50 million people speak Swahili, most of them in East Africa—the birthplace of the Swahili culture. On a continent with some 1,000 languages, Swahili is spoken more widely than any other language. Using Swahili, a person from the Congo can speak with someone from Rwanda, Zimbabwe, or Burundi. Swahili is also a symbol of African nationalism. When the nations of Kenya, Tanzania, and Uganda shook off foreign rule, they adopted Swahili as their official language.

Swahili, a Bantu language, has borrowed words from other languages, including Arabic, Persian, Portuguese, German, and English. See if you can recognize these English words borrowed by Swahili: *pensili, mashine, komputya,* or *basikeli.* (They are in order: pencil, machine, computer, and bicycle.)

In recent decades, Swahili words have been heard more often in the United States. When the popular series *Star Trek* came to television screens in the late 1960s, one of the leading characters aboard the starship *Enterprise* was Lieutenant Uhura. In Swahili, *uhuru* means "freedom." More recently, millions of school children learned two Swahili words when they watched the popular movie *The Lion King* and met the characters Simba, meaning "lion," and Rafiki, meaning "friend."

CLOSE UP: CHAPTER 3

The Who, What, Where of History

1. **What** is Great Zimbabwe?
2. **Where** was the homeland of the earliest Bantu-speaking people?
3. **Who** were the Karanga and Rozwi?
4. **Who** was Matope?
5. **What** was the Changamire?
6. **Where** was the land the Arabs called Zanj?
7. **Who** was Ibn Battuta?
8. **Where** was Zanzibar?
9. **What** is an archipelago?
10. **What** is a khanga?

Making the Connection

1. What was the link between trade and the Swahili culture?
2. How did the arrival of Europeans help lead to the destruction of Great Zimbabwe?
3. What is the connection between Swahili and the modern day independence movements?

Time Check

1. Which of these events happened *first:* Bantu migration into the Congo Basin, population growth in West Africa, or the arrival of the Portuguese in Africa?
2. When did enslaved Africans rise up in revolt against Muslims in present-day Iraq?
3. Explain the significance of these two dates to the history of present-day Zimbabwe: 1440 and 1980.

What Would You Have Done?

1. You are a Bantu-speaking farmer in West Africa during the 500s B.C. Good farmland in West Africa is in short supply. You have just heard about new farmland located somewhere in the dense rain forests to the east. Would you set out with your family to try to find this land? Why or why not?

2. A Swahili merchant has just traveled inland to ask people in your village to stop trading gold and ivory with the Portuguese. This trade has enriched your village in the past, but you dislike the Portuguese destruction of Swahili towns. What would you do? Explain.

3. You have been taken captive and sent from Africa to labor in the marshes of Iraq. You participated in the revolt of 869, which led to an independent state for the formerly enslaved Africans. Now a friend urges you to return to your original home in Africa. What would you do? Explain your decision.

Thinking and Writing About History

1. You are a leader of the enslaved Africans who have revolted against harsh conditions in which they are forced to work along the Tigris and Euphrates rivers. Write a letter to Arab leaders in Baghdad. State your grievances and what actions leaders should take to end the revolt.

2. Imagine you are a professor of an African studies course on Swahili culture. List some of the topics students will study. Then write a description encouraging students to sign up for the course.

Building Skills: Interpreting Visual Evidence

The archaeologists who studied the remains at Great Zimbabwe had to piece together the story of the site based on the visual evidence they found. They looked at the overall scene and sketched and measured the layout of the ruins. Then they took a closer look at the details. They examined the way the rocks were put together. They studied artifacts that they found on the ground or dug up during excavations. Based on the examination of these details, the archaeologists formed conclusions about the ancient people who built the structures.

You follow much the same procedure whenever you examine visual evidence, such as photos, drawings, charts, diagrams, or maps. First, you look at the big picture to identify the main subject or topic of the visual evidence. Then you identify the important details and decide what these details tell you about the subject or topic.

Practice interpreting visual evidence by examining the drawing on page 36.

1. What is the drawing's main topic?
2. What are the most important details in the drawing?
3. How do the details support the main topic of the drawing?

UNIT 2

Enslaved ~~Africans~~ Golfers and ~~overseer~~ caddie

AFRICANS IN THE AMERICAS

(1500s–1760s)

European slave trader and African captive

Processing sugar in the West Indies

THE BIG PICTURE

Unit 2 tells the story of Africans who were brought to the Americas against their will, first by Europeans and then by Americans. The first European settlers came to the Americas in search of freedom and a better life. Africans traveled to the Americas in chains.

For nearly 400 years, people who traded in enslaved people shoved Africans aboard overcrowded ships in the largest forced movement of people in history. According to some historians, the slave trade cost Africa almost 40 million people. Many died from harsh treatment and filthy conditions in cargo holds. Others died resisting bondage, either through rebellion or by taking their own lives.

An African American Speaks

At the time we came into this ship, she was full of black people, who were all confined in a dark and low place in irons. . . . [M]any of us died every day. . . . When our prison could hold no more, the ship sailed.

Account of the Middle Passage by an Enslaved African

The nearly 20 million enslaved Africans who survived the **Middle Passage,** as the terrible journey across the Atlantic came to be called, shaped the course of history in the Western Hemisphere. Although they were deprived of basic human rights, enslaved Africans and their descendants helped build the Americas through their labor, their ways of life, and their ongoing struggle for freedom.

Expanding the Horizons of Europe. The Atlantic slave trade had its roots in the Crusades, a series of wars waged by Europeans between 1095 and the late 1200s to seize control of the Holy Land from the Muslims. During the Crusades, Europeans took an interest in Arab trade with India and China. People in Europe wanted exotic spices to preserve and flavor their foods, fine porcelain to serve the foods in, and shimmering silks to dress the wealthy.

After two centuries of Crusades, the Europeans had failed to break Muslim control of either the Holy Land or the land routes into Asia. To bypass the Arabs who controlled trade with Asia, Europeans began to search for all-water routes to India and China. Their search led them into the uncharted waters of the Atlantic, known to sailors as the "green sea of darkness."

In the early 1400s, Prince Henry of Portugal, nicknamed Henry the Navigator, financed voyages down the western coast of Africa. As Portuguese sea captains headed farther and farther south, they convinced Africans to sail with them as guides and interpreters. Six Africans sailed with Bartholomeu Dias when he rounded the southern tip of Africa in 1488. Africans also traveled with Vasco da Gama when, in 1498, he sailed around Africa and across the Indian Ocean to India.

Da Gama and other Portuguese set up trading posts along this route, and Portugal became one of the great trading countries of Europe. Portugal not only traded with countries in Asia, but also with kingdoms in West Africa and city-states along the coast of East Africa.

1488
Dias rounds the
tip of Africa.

1502
First Africans arrive as slaves
in the Americas.

1444
First Africans are sold
as slaves in Europe.

1492
Columbus arrives in
the Americas.

1513
Balboa sights the
Pacific Ocean.

1400

1450

1500

1550

1498
Da Gama crosses
the Indian Ocean.

Face to Face in Africa. Only a narrow waterway, known as the Strait of Gibraltar, separates Portugal from North Africa. However, Portugal's knowledge of Africa stopped at the northern edge of the Sahara until explorers began moving south along the coast of West Africa.

The first Portuguese encounter with a large group of Africans came in 1444. That fateful year, Portuguese sailors attacked a West African village. They carried about 200 men, women, and children back to Portugal and sold them at a public auction.

Start of the African Slave Trade. The Portuguese saw possibilities for trade in Africa. As they pushed along the western coast, they renamed parts of the continent after the leading product from each region: the Grain Coast (named after pepper, the "grains of paradise"), the Ivory Coast, and the Gold Coast. They called one region the Slave Coast, making clear that the European–West African trade included traffic in human beings.

African rulers saw an economic advantage in the slave trade. Slavery—the practice of owning human beings as property—had existed in Africa, as it had in other places in the world, for hundreds of years. Although slavery differed across the continent, until this time, most slaves in Africa were people who had been captured during wars. These slaves worked as servants, farmers, or soldiers. Most could earn or buy their freedom after time. The Portuguese, however, expanded the African slave trade by introducing valuable new items for exchange: cloth, guns, and European manufactured goods. African **slave-raiders** now rounded up captives expressly for export at slave-collecting stations along the coast.

At first, the Portuguese accepted the Africans as equal trading partners. For their part, African nobles from such great centers as Benin saw themselves as being on equal footing with, or even a step above, the Europeans. African rulers traveled to Lisbon, Portugal, or to Rome, Italy, to

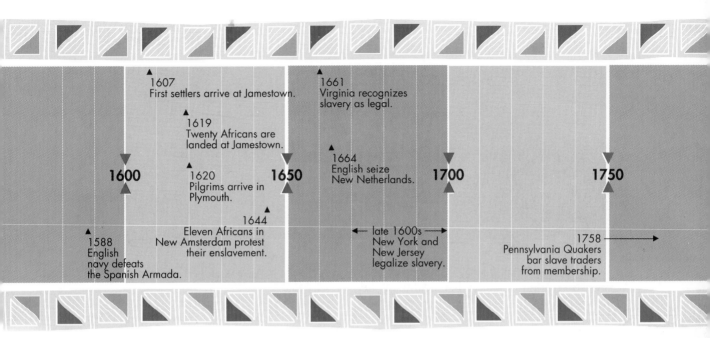

1607
First settlers arrive at Jamestown.

1619
Twenty Africans are
landed at Jamestown.

1600

1620
Pilgrims arrive in
Plymouth.

1644
Eleven Africans in
New Amsterdam protest
their enslavement.

1650

1661
Virginia recognizes
slavery as legal.

1664
English seize
New Netherlands.

1700

1750

1588
English
navy defeats
the Spanish Armada.

← late 1600s →
New York and
New Jersey
legalize slavery.

1758 →
Pennsylvania Quakers
bar slave traders
from membership.

study. In 1518, for example, a king from the Kongo (now spelled Congo) visited the Vatican and spoke to the pope in Latin. While European traders bought and sold enslaved Africans, missionaries tried to convert Africans to Christianity.

Africans in the Americas. By the time da Gama reached India, Christopher Columbus had already made three trips to the Americas, returning with news that turned world history upside down. Spain and Portugal quickly realized the wealth that was to be had in the new lands across the Atlantic. Spain sent **conquistadors** (kahn-KEES-tuh-dawrs), or conquerors, to establish outposts in the Americas. One conquistador was frank in stating his reasons for going to the Americas: "We came here to serve God and the king, and also to get rich."

From the start, descendants of the first African slaves in Portugal and Spain took part in the expeditions that opened the Americas. At least 30 Africans stood with Vasco Núñez de Balboa (bal-BOH-uh) when he sighted the Pacific Ocean in 1513. Still others accompanied the Spanish conquistadors into what are now Peru, Mexico, Florida, and the southwestern United States.

However, European discovery of the Americas created a whole new demand for labor. The number of Europeans who came as workers did not meet the growing demand. The Spanish tried enslaving Native Americans to work in the mines of Peru and Mexico and the sugar **plantations,** or large farms, of the Caribbean islands. After the Native American slaves died by the thousands, Europeans bought enslaved Africans to take their place. From the Caribbean islands, slavery spread to the American mainland. In the

The West Indian economy was based on the labor of African slaves. This is an indigo plantation.

300 years following Columbus's first voyage, the trade in enslaved Africans swelled into the millions. Ships carrying enslaved Africans flew the flags of many nations— among them Portugal, Spain, England, France, Sweden, and the United States. Over time, many people in the Americas came to associate slavery with race, laying the basis for deep-rooted racial prejudice against Africans and their descendants.

English Colonization. In 1588, an event occurred that opened the way for the spread of slavery to what would one day become the United States. In that year, the English navy smashed the Spanish Armada in the English Channel, ending Spain's control of the Atlantic. In the next century, England planted 13 **colonies** up and down the Atlantic seaboard of North America. A colony is a settlement in another land that remains under the control of the home country.

Most of the settlers in these colonies came from England, many in search of religious freedom for themselves. From Germany, Holland, and Sweden came settlers who sought simply to escape poverty. These European **immigrants,** as settlers who move from one country to another are known, established farms, villages, and towns. As they did so, the new arrivals pushed Native Americans, the first American settlers, off their lands.

The majority of colonists who seized Native American lands worked as farmers. However, the importance of farming to a colony's **economy**—the systems of producing, distributing, and using goods and services—depended on its location.

In New England, the name for the northernmost colonies, long winters and rocky soil encouraged subsistence farming. Like the farmers of West Africa, most New England farmers grew only enough for their own families. In time, New Englanders developed other economic activities, such as fishing, manufacturing, shipbuilding, and commerce, or trade. New England merchant ships sailed to England, the West Indies, and Africa. After 1698, many of these ships carried enslaved Africans.

In the Middle Colonies, farmers enjoyed a more temperate climate and more fertile soil than in New England. Here many farmers produced **cash crops,** crops raised for sale rather than for a farmer's personal use. The Middle Colonies, with large crops of wheat, corn, and rye, were called the "breadbasket colonies." Some large farms hired laborers on a regular basis. The owners of a few large estates in the Hudson Valley of New York used enslaved Africans, first brought into the region by the Dutch. In addition to the sale of cash crops, the Middle Colonies profited from commercial activities centered around the bustling ports of New York and Philadelphia.

In the Southern Colonies, the plantation that raised tobacco, rice, or indigo (a blue dye) became the symbol of farming, although in reality most farms were small. Trade and industry played little part in the Southern **economy**, the system of producing, distributing, and using goods and services. Crops were shipped to England in New England vessels, and manufactured goods were bought from England.

Plantations had heavy demands for labor. At first, landowners tried **indentured servants**, people who exchanged a period of work for payment of their passage to the Americas. But every few years, when the servants received their freedom, a new group had to be trained. Eventually, plantation owners found it more practical and profitable to use slaves as their main source of labor. At first, they enslaved Native Americans and then, later, Africans.

From their arrival in the first colony, at Jamestown, in 1619, as indentured servants, Africans played a part in the English settlement of what would one day become the United States of America. Soon, enslaved Africans would be used as workers in both New England and the Middle Colonies. However, the largest number of African slaves were taken to the colonies that ran from Delaware south to Georgia.

The Issue of Slavery. Few American colonists gave much thought to the question of slavery. For the most part, they worried more about earning a living in a new land and winning favorable treatment from England. In addition, most whites looked on Africans as less than human. They did this to justify the mass enslavement of Africans. Explained one British critic of slavery in the 1700s, "If they believe them [Africans] to be of human kind, they cannot regard them . . . as no better than dogs or horses."

Slavery had its opponents. The Quakers of Pennsylvania objected strongly to slavery and banned slave traders from membership in 1758. A few colonies limited slavery by imposing heavy taxes on enslaved Africans imported into the colony. But it was not until the colonies struggled for their own liberty in the late 1700s that slavery began to sting the conscience of some colonial leaders.

Taking Another Look

1. How did the Portuguese and African peoples regard each other when they first began trading?

2. Why did Europeans carry enslaved Africans to the Americas?

3. What conditions kept most colonists from looking critically at slavery?

4. **Critical Thinking** How did geography influence the distribution of enslaved Africans in the 13 colonies?

Africans on a slave ship

The Atlantic Slave Trade

(1500–1760s)

THINKING ABOUT THE CHAPTER

How did the Atlantic slave trade rob Africans of their most basic human rights?

In 1493, a strange parade made its way through Seville, Spain. Christopher Columbus proudly marched through the city's streets displaying objects from his first voyage across the Atlantic—colorful parrots, exotic plants, and people he called Indians. A 19-year-old student, Bartolomé de Las Casas (bahr-toh-loh-MAY de lahs KAH-sahs), watched the procession with great interest.

In 1502, Las Casas himself traveled to the Americas as a conquistador. His bloody conquests in the Caribbean won him a huge estate and the labor of many Native American slaves. Ten years later, he became the first Roman Catholic to be ordained a priest in the Americas. In 1514, Las Casas read a passage in the Bible that convinced him "that everything done to the Indians thus far was unjust." He spent the rest of his life trying to end the enslavement of Native Americans.

However, Las Casas did not oppose the idea of slavery completely. In 1517, in order to help Native Americans, he persuaded the king of Spain to substitute African labor for Native American labor in the Americas.

When Las Casas died at 92 in 1566, he left behind a book called *History of the Indies*. It remained unpublished for more than 300 years. When people finally read it, they learned that Las Casas had repented his decision to enslave Africans. By that time, however, the Atlantic slave trade had changed the history of three continents.

1 ▼ SLAVE RAIDS IN WEST AFRICA
▼
How were West Africans rounded up for sale as slaves?

Just before dawn broke, wooden drums sounded the alarm. Enemies had surrounded the village. Warriors grabbed their weapons, but it was too late. Intruders armed with heavy wooden clubs, spears, and bows and arrows overran the compound. Some villagers fled. Others fought back. Most fell stunned by well-aimed blows to the head. When the battle ended, the invaders joined the captured villagers together neck to neck with heavy logs and ropes.

The villagers had fallen victim to African slave-traders from the Atlantic coast. The traders marched them barefoot over mountains, through forests, and along rivers. Those who rebelled were killed. Those who fell ill were left to die along the trail. Near the end of the journey, the slave traders fattened the survivors with yams, melons, and dried fish. They covered bruises on the captives with powder and rubbed palm oil into their skin until it glistened.

The African slave-traders marched their captives to a slave-trading station along the coast. Here a silent trade began. White slave-traders examined the captives and piled up bundles of red and blue cotton cloth in payment. The African traders pushed these goods away. The white traders added a few guns, some gunpowder, and a keg of rum. When there was enough, the deal was sealed.

Profit in Enslaved People. Starting about 1500, such cooperation between African and European slave-traders took

African slave traders march captives toward the coast for sale. What European trade item in the picture made it easier to round up captives?

1492–1493 Columbus makes his first voyage to the Americas.

1502 Atlantic slave trade begins.

1517 Bartolomé de Las Casas asks Spain to replace Native American labor with African labor.

1624 Queen Nzinga begins battle against Portuguese slave-raiders.

1700–1800 Atlantic slave trade reaches its peak.

place time and time again in the Atlantic slave trade. At first, the Portuguese and Spanish controlled much of the European side of the trade. But other nations wanted a share of the profits, too. Soon, the English, the Dutch, the French, the Prussians, the Swedes, and other Europeans entered the slave trade.

By the 1600s, merchants from all over western Europe had formed slave-trading companies. Their agents built what became known as **"slave factories"** in harbors along the West African coast. The factories were made up of supply warehouses, living quarters for Europeans, and pens for the captured Africans.

Africans from thousands of villages passed through these factories. They included Yorubas, Mandingos (man-DING-gohs), Hausas, Fantis (FAHN-tees), Asantes (uh-SAHN-tees), Dahomeans (duh-HOH-mee-uhns), Binis (BEE-nees), and more. All had been seized in savage raids that destroyed villages, killed resisters, and broke up families forever.

While European merchants liked to fill their ships quickly, they feared transporting a large number of Africans who spoke the same language. People who could communicate could also make plans. To prevent rebellions, they tried to keep captives from the same region in separate holding pens, whenever possible. Whip-carrying guards terrorized captives and sometimes branded them with hot irons before loading them on ships for the next leg of their journey to the Americas—the Middle Passage.

Taking Another Look

1. How were West Africans captured for the Atlantic slave trade?

2. What happened to African captives at the factories along the Atlantic coast?

3. **Critical Thinking** The Atlantic slave trade helped cause wars both between European nations and between African peoples. Explain why this might have been so.

2 THE MIDDLE PASSAGE

▼ What were some of the cruelties experienced by Africans during the Middle Passage?

The men who fastened irons on the mothers took the children out of their hands and threw them over the side of the ship into the water. Two of the women leaped overboard after the children. . . . One of the two women . . . was carried down by the weight of her irons before she could be rescued; but the other was taken up by some men in a boat and brought on board. This woman threw herself overboard one night when we were at sea.

This loading plan of a slave ship shows how the greatest number of Africans were squeezed onto a ship to make the transatlantic voyage as profitable as possible.

This was only one of the horrors described by an African who survived the Middle Passage—the long, nightmarish trip across the Atlantic. Other Africans recalled equally terrible scenes: brutal whippings, forced feedings, and the smell of death and filth in disease-ridden cargo holds. Hundreds of Africans lay wedged together, bound by chains, and praying that death would come to them, too.

The Cruelty of the Voyage. The holds of most merchant ships measured only about 5 feet (1.5 meters) high. But this space was cut in half by a shelf that extended about 6 feet (1.8 meters). The Africans were chained by the neck and legs to the shelf or to the deck below and had only about 20 to 25 inches (50 to 64 centimeters) to sit up. On storm-tossed seas, they banged into one another, and the chains cut deeply into their flesh.

Sanitary facilities were crude. The foul odor of a ship carrying enslaved Africans could be smelled for miles downwind.

Diseases—hookworm, dysentery, malaria, smallpox, yellow fever, and the like—swept through the ships. Some ships lost half their human cargo during the Middle Passage. The death rate averaged between 13 and 20 percent. Amid the suffering, many Africans went mad. Some killed each other fighting and clawing for breathing space.

To run a successful business, ship captains needed to deliver a majority of live captives to buyers in the Caribbean islands and the mainland Americas. Accordingly, the crews brought the Africans on deck in shifts for fresh air and food and forced exercises. They fed the captives cornmeal, bean pulp, or stewed yams. Next, came the "dancing of the slaves." A piper or fiddler played a tune, while sailors with whips

55

made the Africans dance around deck to strengthen their battered legs and arms.

Resistance and Rebellion. Africans did not submit easily to such brutality. From the start of the voyage to the end, they fought back, preferring death to the inhumanity of the Middle Passage. Some threw themselves overboard when they came up to be fed. Others refused food and medicine. Sailors pried open clenched jaws or broke teeth to pour food down the throats of resisting Africans. But some of them still managed to starve themselves to death.

The crew aboard most slave ships lived in constant fear of rebellion. "If care not be taken," wrote one sailor, "they [the Africans] will mutiny and destroy the ship's crew." Ship diaries document 55 uprisings aboard ship by Africans between 1699 and 1845 and mention hundreds of attempted uprisings.

Taking Another Look

1. How did the Middle Passage brutalize Africans?

2. How did Africans resist the Middle Passage?

3. **Critical Thinking** What lasting effect do you think the experience of the Middle Passage had on Africans after they came to the Americas?

3 WEST AFRICA AFTER THE ▼ SLAVE TRADE
How did the Atlantic slave trade affect the development of West Africa?

The Portuguese slave-traders described her as an Amazon—a member of a mythological ancient race of female warriors. The people of Matamba saw her as a hero. Her name was **Queen Nzinga.** She came to power in 1624 and ruled the state of Matamba, in what is now Angola, until 1663. She used her power to launch a war against the Portuguese for enslaving her brother. She battled slave-traders for nearly 30 years and greatly disrupted the inland slave trade. In 1656, the Portuguese negotiated a treaty with her. It remained in effect until Nzinga's death at 83.

Other West African leaders tried to fight slavery, too. But European guns and the greed of African slave-raiders defeated them in the end. By the 1700s, most West Africans found themselves victims of a system that spelled tragedy for West Africa's future.

The Weakening of West African Society. For more than 300 years, the slave trade plundered West Africa. The area suffered an enormous loss of population. At least one African died for every one who reached the coast alive. Estimates for the total number of Africans lost to the West African slave trade ranged from 25 to 50 million. Slave traders showed no respect for rank or skills. Noble and peasant, artisan and laborer—all might find themselves lashed together in the Middle Passage.

African slave traders eager for profit from European trade captured more and more people over the years. Local warfare spread, and standing armies expanded. Wars were fought for the purpose of gaining captives to sell as slaves. By the mid-1700s, gunsmiths in Birmingham, England, were making more than 100,000 guns a

European goods were brought to West Africa through slave factories and trading forts like this one.

year for the trade with Guinea (GIN-ee) alone. The splendor that was Africa under Ghana, Mali, and Songhai was destroyed.

Effects on West African Economies. The large scale exchange of humans for manufactured goods created a vicious cycle of economic dependence in Africa. Europeans used their profits from African slave labor to invest in trade and industry in their own countries. The cheap goods that Europeans exchanged for slaves discouraged West Africans from developing further their own manufacturing and from seeking commerce beyond the slave trade. As a result, when European interest in enslaved Africans declined in the late 1800s, West Africans no longer had the economic strength to stop Europeans from stripping the region of its natural resources. More than 300 years of European domination left the region economically undeveloped and financially bankrupt.

Taking Another Look

1. What were the effects of the Atlantic slave trade on West Africa?

2. How did the Atlantic slave trade disrupt West African economies?

3. **Critical Thinking** Why do you think Europeans in the slave trade might want to consider their victims as "something less than human"?

LOOKING AHEAD

The white view that Africans were something less than human grew out of the whites' need to justify the African slave trade. Wrote one British author in the 1700s: "The Africans are . . . little better than the lions, tigers, leopards, and other wild beasts, which that country produces in great numbers." Such racist ideas about Africans were part of the most evil legacy of the slave trade.

CLOSE UP: Chapter 4

A woman applies a paste made of red clay and water to repair the wall of her family compound in a Soninke village in Mauritania. Another woman rushes to work in a modern office building in downtown Accra, capital of Ghana. Young boys in a rural village in Togo learn to make spearheads. A student takes a physics course at Lagos University in Nigeria. Such scenes—a mixture of past and present—typify the West Africa of today.

West Africa bears the cultural marks of its thousands of years of history. Once the home of ancient African kingdoms, West Africa fell prey to European conquerors in the 1800s. After World War II, West African colonies shook off European rule and formed 16 independent nations (see map, page 428). Official languages include French, English, and Portuguese. But hundreds of African dialects can be heard across the region—Twi, Hausa, and Fanti, for example. Religions are equally diverse, with people practicing Islam, forms of Christianity, and many African religions.

Today, about 200 million people live in West Africa. Once stripped of its people by the slave trade, the region now faces overpopulation in some areas. It also faces the struggle of trying to modernize while not giving up its traditions.

The Who, What, Where of History

1. **Who** was Prince Henry the Navigator?
2. **Where** was the Slave Coast?
3. **Who** were the conquistadors?
4. **What** does the term *indentured servant* mean?
5. **Who** was Bartolomé de Las Casas?
6. **Where** were most European slave factories located?
7. **What** was the Middle Passage?
8. **Who** was Queen Nzinga?

Making the Connection

1. What was the connection between the death of large numbers of Native American laborers and the Atlantic slave trade?
2. What was the connection between the slave trade and later European domination of Africa?

Time Check

1. When did the Atlantic slave trade begin?
2. During what years did the Atlantic slave trade flourish?

What Would You Have Done?

1. If you had been an African trader, how would you have responded to a request by a European merchant to become partners in the slave trade?
2. If you had been Queen Nzinga, what terms would you have demanded from the Portuguese in a treaty?

3. Imagine you are an English sailor in 1701. You have agreed to sail on a ship going to Africa and then the Americas. Just before the ship sails, you learn it will carry enslaved Africans. What will you do? Explain.

Thinking and Writing About History

1. Imagine that you are an African noble visiting Spain in 1517. Write a letter to the Spanish king giving your reactions to Bartolomé de Las Casas's idea of using more African labor in the Americas.

2. Imagine that you are an African who was captured and brought to the Americas as a child. After many years, you have gained your freedom. A newspaper that opposed slavery asks you to describe your voyage across the Atlantic. Write a brief account of your Middle Passage.

3. Imagine you are a West African historian teaching at a university in present-day Ghana. Write a brief lecture on the effect of the slave trade on the region.

Building Skills: Understanding Cause and Effect

Most things that occur in your life happen for a reason or reasons. Sometimes it's very easy to see why an event takes place. The fire alarm goes off because someone pulls it. The pulling of the handle is the *cause;* the alarm is the *effect.*

When events take place over a long period of time, it is sometimes harder to identify causes and effects. One day you notice that a classmate looks different.

What are the *causes* for the *effect* of your classmate's appearance? He explains that it has been a gradual process. For about four months, he's been eating only healthful foods, drinking lots of water, and exercising every day. He's also gotten a new haircut. These several causes created the effect of his appearance.

Some effects in history had very obvious causes. Bartolomé de Las Casas suddenly began to work against the use of Native Americans as slaves. The *cause* was a passage he read in the Bible; the *effect* was a change of opinion.

Other events in history occur because of several causes working together. Below is a list of possible causes for this effect: West Africans were unable to resist European domination in the 1800s. On a separate sheet of paper write the numbers of the items that were not causes of this effect.

1. West Africans lacked armies.

2. Some Africans organized rebellions aboard slave ships.

3. West Africa suffered enormous population loss because of the slave trade.

4. The slave trade destroyed the order of society in West Africa.

5. Queen Nzinga battled the Portuguese and their slave traders for nearly 30 years.

6. Africans fought each other to acquire more captives to sell as slaves.

7. In the 1500s, Europeans searched for an all-water route to Asia.

8. West Africans became dependent on European goods.

African slaves taking sugar to market

The West Indies, First Stop for Africans

(1500–1760s)

THINKING ABOUT THE CHAPTER
Why did the plantation system make slavery profitable in the Caribbean?

In northwest Jamaica, one of the West Indian islands, lies a rugged region called the Cockpit Country, after the Jamaican word for pothole. In the 1600s and 1700s, Cockpit Country was home to the **Maroons**, Africans who had escaped bondage. The first Maroons fled Spanish slave holders on the island in the 1500s. After the English took Jamaica in 1655, they tried to subdue the Maroons for more than 75 years. Finally, in 1739, they signed a peace treaty granting the Maroons independence.

As a result of the British West Indian experience with the Maroons, colonists took brutal measures against enslaved Africans.

60

escaped slaves (maroons)

Chapter 5 describes the system of slavery that emerged in the English-speaking islands of the West Indies—a system that spread in the late 1600s to what would one day become the United States.

1 EMPIRES BUILT ON SUGAR

▼ How did sugar become "king" in the West Indies?

On a Sunday morning in July 1631, Sir Henry Colt joined his crew in early morning prayer aboard the *Alexander*. As sailors knelt on the deck, a cannon shot rang out. Off in the distance, the crew saw 20 Spanish ships bearing down on them under full sail.

Colt ordered his crew to fight. When the smoke cleared, the English had triumphed, and the Spanish were sailing away. But the danger had not passed. Colt raced back to alert the colonists on St. Christopher Island (St. Kitts), which the English had colonized in 1623, that the Spanish were coming to push the English out of the Caribbean.

A Taste for Sugar. The Spanish had taken possession of the West Indies in the early 1500s, colonizing Puerto Rico in 1508, Jamaica in 1509, and Cuba in 1511. But once other European countries—France, England, the Netherlands, and Denmark—learned of the riches there, they challenged Spain's hold on the islands. For over 200 years, from the late 1500s to the early 1800s, the waters of the Caribbean were an almost constant battleground.

The West Indies offered many cash crops for sale—dyewoods, cotton, and spices. But what Europeans wanted the most was sugar and molasses. The English shipped the molasses to New England where it was made into rum.

Sugar and Slavery. The story of sugar in the Caribbean goes hand in hand with the story of slavery. As the demand for sugar grew, so did the demand for slaves. Huge plantations devoted to the production of sugar were set up. Like Spain, other countries tried to enslave Native Americans to work the plantations, but they died by the thousands.

A few European countries tried using the forced labor of white prisoners. England, for example, used Irish prisoners to work in the islands, but they too died. Europeans generally did not use the forced labor of other Europeans because there was opposition to enslaving fellow Christians. West Indian plantation owners, called **planters,** soon turned to enslaved Africans as their major source of labor.

By the mid-1600s, European ships were carrying some 10,000 enslaved Africans a year to the West Indies—and at an extraordinary profit. Company agents in the 1600s paid the equivalent of about $25 each for African captives in West Africa, and then sold the captives in the West Indies for more than $150 each. Slave holders expected the labor of enslaved Africans to repay their cost in less than two years. They barely fed the Africans, and they worked them so hard that many died from the cruel treatment within two years. Plantation owners had to keep buying African captives to maintain their supply of workers at the same level.

The labor of enslaved Africans fueled almost the entire sugar industry. They planted and harvested the sugar cane. They turned the huge rollers that ground up the stalks and stirred the giant, boiling copper vats that melted sugar into molasses. The sweat of African workers produced two of the West Indies' most valuable products—sugar and molasses.

1508	Spanish colonize Puerto Rico.
1509	Spanish colonize Jamaica.
1511	Spanish colonize Cuba.
1625	English colonize Barbados.
1631	Spain tries to take Caribbean islands from the English.
1655	English take over Jamaica.
1739	English sign treaty with Jamaican Maroons.

Triangular Trades. With Barbados, colonized in 1625, and Jamaica among its West Indian holdings, England became one of the leading nations in the sugar-slave trade of the 1600s and 1700s. This trade rested on a number of three-legged routes known as the **triangular trades.** These routes began in West Africa, crossed to the West Indies, went north to the English colonies on the mainland, and then either returned to Africa or continued to Europe. The slave trade formed a vital part of the English economy until the late 1700s.

How many triangular routes do you see on the map? What was shipped on the Africa-Americas triangle?

England's interest in the Americas began to shift from the Caribbean to the mainland in the mid-1600s, and the islands started sending Africans to English colonies on the Atlantic Seaboard. As part of this process, enslaved Africans were brought to the islands for an introduction to life under slavery. This process was known as seasoning. Then they were shipped to plantations in the South.

Taking Another Look

1. How did the growing of sugar cane help promote the Atlantic slave trade?

2. What regions were involved in the triangular trades?

3. **Critical Thinking** Do you think sugar could have become so important in the West Indies without the use of enslaved Africans? Explain.

2 ▼ PATTERNS OF WEST INDIAN SLAVERY
▼ How were enslaved Africans treated in the English West Indies?

In 1756, a British slave ship docked at the West Indian island of Barbados. Among those on board was an 11-year-old African, Olaudah Equiano, whom you met in Unit 1. That evening, a group of white merchants who had financed the voyage examined the human cargo, poking and prodding. "There was much dread and trembling among us," wrote Equiano years later, as a free man, "and nothing but bitter cries."

After the slave merchants set a price for each African, they herded them into the shipyard. At the sound of a drum, the

Why was African slave labor so important to the sugar economy of the West Indies?

scramble began. Buyers raced to tag the healthiest Africans for purchase. The sight of a mass of whites swarming toward them left the Africans panic-stricken.

Worse was yet to come. After the buyers paid for the Africans, they dragged them to waiting wagons, often ripping them from the arms of sobbing family members. "In this manner," wrote Equiano, "without scruple [misgiving], are relations and friends separated, most of them never to see each other again."

The Africans who were sold in Barbados faced a severe life. Most were marched off to work in blazing-hot sugar fields or in mills that sometimes ground up people as well as raw sugar.

A System Based on Racism. The cruelty suffered by Africans in the West Indies grew out of **racism.** Racism is the unjust treatment of a people by others who falsely believe that their race is by nature superior to another and who have the political, economic, and military ability to enforce their attitude. A racist attitude allowed the English to deny enslaved Africans their rights as human beings.

Racism existed among other Europeans in the West Indies, as well. But racism was the most severe among the English. The Spanish and the French, for example, sometimes married Africans. The English almost never did. The Spanish often gave Africans freed from bondage the same rights enjoyed by people born in freedom. The English restricted the rights of all Africans—free and enslaved. In most of the West Indies, a person's standing in society was related to the color of his or her skin. But nowhere was color as important as it was in the English West Indies by the late 1600s.

Taking Another Look

1. What awaited Africans after they arrived in the West Indies?

2. What part did racism play in the treatment of Africans in the British West Indies?

3. **Critical Thinking** Reread page 48. Then explain how slavery in Africa differed from slavery in the West Indies.

LOOKING AHEAD

The West Indies introduced Africans to the harsh realities of slavery in the Americas. The racism and hard labor on English sugar plantations set the pattern for the later treatment of Africans in the English colonies. These practices set the stage for the bitter racial divisions that would trouble the United States for some two hundred years.

63

Salsa, reggae, calypso—hear this music and you're listening to the sounds of the Caribbean. Fufu, fried plantains, cassava pone—eat these foods and you're tasting the cooking of the Caribbean. Each of these sounds and tastes is rooted in the region's African heritage, helping to create what some call an Afro-Caribbean culture.

The culture is as rich and varied as the region's people. Some 22 nations and nearly 30 million people make up the Caribbean Islands. Official languages include Spanish, English, Dutch, and French—languages of the nations that first brought Africans there as slaves. Creole, a dialect rooted in African languages, is widely spoken, too.

The end of slavery in the islands during the 1800s fueled feelings of pride in traditional African culture—music, foods, and dialects. These feelings grew as many of the islands gained independence in the 1800s and later.

The transition to independence in most of the islands has been smooth. Today, 11 of the 13 independent island-nations practice democracy. Even islands still tied to a home country have much political freedom. "The Caribbean people," says one expert, "have undoubtedly proven their capacity to govern themselves."

The Who, What, Where of History

1. **Who** were the Maroons?
2. **What** were cash crops?
3. **What** were the triangular trades?
4. **What** is racism?
5. **Where** were sugar, molasses, and rum produced for England?

Making the Connection

1. What was the connection between sugar and slavery in the West Indies?
2. How was the practice of slavery in the West Indies linked to the practice of slavery in the 13 English colonies?

Time Check

1. Which of these Caribbean islands did Spain colonize *first*: Cuba, Puerto Rico, Jamaica?
2. When did the English take over the island of Jamaica?

What Would You Have Done?

1. If you had been an enslaved African in Jamaica, would you have tried to join the Maroons? Explain.
2. Imagine that you are an African on board a ship carrying African captives to the Caribbean. You and a young English person are washed overboard in a storm and have survived by clinging to debris. You wash ashore in Jamaica. The English person says he will get a boat and sail you to safety on any island in the Caribbean you choose. Which island would you choose? Explain your reasons.

Thinking and Writing About History

1. Write a newspaper account of the naval battle described on page 47. Remember to answer the questions *who, what, when, where,* and *why.*

2. Imagine that you are a British ship-owner in the early 1700s. Write an advertisement aimed at attracting people to invest in your ship's next voyage to the West Indies.

3. Imagine that you are the owner of a plantation in the English West Indies. You have just received a letter from an old friend back in England who asks why you use enslaved Africans on your plantation. Write a short letter giving your explanation.

Building Skills: Distinguishing Cause and Effect

Distinguishing cause and effect in history often involves answering the question *why?* To practice identifying the "whys" of history, turn each statement in the column labeled "Effects" into a question beginning with the word *why.* Then determine the answer to this question in the column labeled "Causes."

Effects

1. West Indian colonists brutally restricted their African slaves.
2. Demand for slaves increased in the West Indies.
3. The English denied African slaves their rights as human beings.
4. Africans were the main source of labor in the West Indies.
5. Slave owners barely fed and clothed their African slaves.

Causes

A. Native Americans and Irish people died when forced to work in the West Indies.

B. Slave owners expected the labor of African slaves to repay their cost in less than two years.

C. More people wanted to buy more West Indian sugar.

D. The Maroons, runaway slaves in Jamaica, successfully resisted the English and were granted their independence.

E. Mass enslavement of Africans led many whites to feel a false sense of racial superiority.

F. There were great riches available in the West Indies.

Of course, when you are reading your textbook, causes and effects are not isolated as they were in the exercise above. Read the following paragraph about the decline of the sugar industry in the West Indies. Then write in a sentence one effect and one cause for it that you find in the paragraph.

By the nineteenth century, West Indian slavery had stopped bringing big profits. In fact, by 1807 the typical British West Indian planter was operating at a loss. Other areas of the world now produced sugar, and there was a glut on the market. The price of West Indian sugar fell lower and lower, and the need for slaves decreased along with it.

Arrival of the first Africans in Jamestown, Virginia

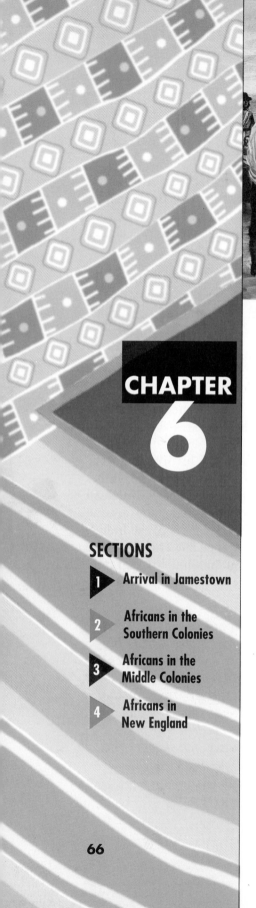

CHAPTER

6

Africans in the Thirteen Colonies

(1619–1760)

THINKING ABOUT THE CHAPTER

How did Africans help settle what would one day become the United States of America?

In 1522, Luis Vasquez de Ayllon, a wealthy Spanish judge on the Caribbean island of Hispaniola (his-puhn-YOH-luh) (where present-day Haiti and the Dominican Republic are located), sailed for Spain. He wanted to convince King Charles I to finance Spain's first permanent colony north of Mexico. Hernando Cortés and his conquistadors had just conquered the rich Aztec Empire in Mexico. Charles, thinking there might be more fabulous wealth in the Americas, agreed to the plan.

In July 1526, six Spanish ships left Hispaniola with 500 men and women aboard, including 100 enslaved Africans. The expedition put ashore along the marshy Pee Dee

River near present-day Georgetown, South Carolina. Here Ayllon ordered the Africans to build a settlement.

The colony, San Miguel, lasted a year. Over half the Spanish died, including Ayllon. The Africans rebelled and set fire to the settlement. The 150 Spanish who survived fled back to Hispaniola.

To this day, the fate of the Africans at San Miguel remains a mystery. Perhaps they built a new settlement, or perhaps they went to live among the Native Americans. They were the first non–Native Americans, however, to live permanently in what is today the United States.

Other Africans played a role in the country's early history, too. In the late 1530s, an African named Estevanico (es-tay-vah-NEE-koh) trekked with a handful of Spanish through much of the present-day U.S. Southwest. In 1565, African slaves helped the Spanish build St. Augustine, Florida, the oldest permanent city founded by Europeans in the United States. In the 1600s, the English also used the forced labor of Africans to build their colonies in North America.

1 ARRIVAL IN JAMESTOWN
▼ Who were the first Africans to arrive in the Virginia Colony?

In August 1619, a Dutch ship sailed up the James River to the struggling English settlement at Jamestown, Virginia. The captain of the ship offered to trade 20 Africans for much-needed food. Many of the Africans had Spanish-sounding names—Pedro, Isabella, Antoney, Angelo—so the English suspected that the Dutch had stolen them from a Spanish merchant ship headed for the West Indies. The English also suspected that the Africans had been baptized as Christians, as was the Spanish

custom. As a result, the English took them as indentured servants.

The Africans amazed the English colonists with their farming abilities—talents they had learned in their farming villages in Africa. Two of the Africans—Antoney and Isabella—married, and in 1624, Isabella gave birth to a son whom they named William. He was the first child of African descent born in English America. William escaped the fate of later generations of African American children—he was not automatically born into slavery.

A Taste of Freedom. By the time the first Africans arrived in Jamestown, the settlement, founded in 1607, had weathered drought, starvation, and disease. The terrible winter of 1609–1610, when nearly nine out of ten colonists starved to death, was only a memory. In 1612, John Rolfe, one of the colonists, had helped change the colony's fortunes by successfully growing tobacco. Virginia now had a profitable cash crop for sale in Europe.

However, the colony faced a severe labor shortage. To promote settlement, the colony offered settlers 50 acres of land (about 20 hectares) for each indentured servant they brought to Virginia. The colony also promised settlers the same rights they enjoyed in England. In 1619, shortly before the arrival of the first Africans, the colony had established the House of Burgesses, the first legislative assembly in the Americas. Here, male property-owners voted on day-to-day affairs in the colony.

During the early years of struggle, Virginia welcomed the labor of all workers—both Africans and Europeans. Indentured servants, both African and European, who finished their contracts could become

1526	West Africans become first non–Native Americans to live permanently in the present-day United States.
1619	First Africans arrive at Jamestown.
1638	First Africans arrive in Massachusetts.
1641	Massachusetts legalizes certain forms of slavery.
1641	Mathias De Sousa elected to Maryland's General Assembly.
1644	Africans in New Netherlands sue for their freedom.
1660s	Virginia passes its first slave laws.
1663	Maryland makes all Africans in the colony slaves for life.
1750	Georgia legalizes slave trade.

settlers. For a time, Africans enjoyed a measure of freedom they would not know again until the mid–20th century. Individual African males acquired property, voted, and testified in court. One such person was Anthony Johnson.

Anthony Johnson arrived in Jamestown in 1621 as an indentured servant. He married a woman named Mary, and the two gained their freedom sometime in the 1630s. In 1651, the Johnsons bought the indentures, or contracts, of five servants—some European, some African—and were granted 250 acres of land. In the following years the Johnsons' children acquired more land. A third-generation Johnson named his plantation "Angola," perhaps in memory of his grandfather's African homeland.

Slavery Amid Freedom. By the mid-1600s, large landowners in Virginia and farther south had found steady markets for their major crops: tobacco, rice, sugar cane, and indigo. For maximum production, the planters were growing their crops on huge plantations similar to those in the West Indies.

A shortage of workers made planters take a hard look at enslaved Africans. Assured of an income for crops, planters now saw several advantages to slavery. The initial cost of buying and supporting an enslaved African was about the same as an indentured servant, but the investment in an enslaved African was for life, not just a few years.

Unlike enslaved Africans, European indentured servants could appeal to sympathetic people in the home country for protection against neglect or mistreatment. Enslaved Africans would find it difficult to escape because they could be identified by skin color. European indentured servants could fade into the general population.

Legalizing Slavery. In the 1660s, Virginia passed its first laws regulating slavery. According to a 1660 law, planters could hold enslaved Africans to a lifetime of bondage. Even baptism no longer protected Africans from slavery. Declared a 1667 law: "Baptism does not alter the condition of the person as to his bondage or freedom." Another law held that children born in the colony would have the same status as their mothers. In other words, if a mother was enslaved, her children would also be enslaved.

There were only about 300 Africans in Virginia in the 1660s. By the end of the 1600s, Africans were being brought to the colony at the rate of about 1,000 a year. By 1756, of Virginia's 293,000 people, more than 120,000 were of African descent. Of this number, only about 3,000 lived as free people.

Racism. Less than a century after the arrival of the first Africans in Virginia, racism had come to distinguish how the colonists treated Africans and those of African descent, just as it did in the West Indies. By the late 1600s, English men and women began to refer to themselves as *white* and to Africans as *black*.

The liberty enjoyed by the Anthony Johnsons of the past had disappeared. In 1691, the House of Burgesses—symbol of freedom in English America—banned marriages between English and Africans. It also denied free Africans the vote and the right to testify against whites in court. Most Africans could no longer boast, as an African farmer in the 1640s had, "I will work when I please and play when I please." By the 1700s, most Africans in English America lived according to the will and whip of white slave holders.

Taking Another Look

1. What rights did free Africans enjoy in Virginia before 1660?

2. Why did plantation owners turn to the system of slavery as a labor source?

3. **Critical Thinking** Why did most white Virginians overlook the contributions of African indentured servants?

2 AFRICANS IN THE SOUTHERN ▼ COLONIES
How did slavery spread in the South?

In 1634, Cecilius Calvert, Lord Baltimore, sent 200 settlers from England to what is now the state of Maryland. Cal-

THE THIRTEEN BRITISH COLONIES

How many Southern colonies were there? Which region had the fewest colonies?

vert hoped to establish a refuge for England's Roman Catholics, persecuted because of their religion. Among those who landed on the Maryland shore were three African indentured servants—John Price, Francisco Peres, and Mathias De Sousa.

After he completed his term of service, De Sousa built a thriving trade with the Native Americans of the region. In 1641, the colonists elected him to serve in the General Assembly, the colony's lawmaking body. Within about 20 years, however, Maryland followed the lead of Virginia. The word *slave* crept into the colony's laws, and Africans lost their voice in colonial affairs.

Durante Vita. Like the Virginians, the colonists of Maryland found the soil and climate around Chesapeake Bay well suited to growing tobacco. They, too, turned to enslaved Africans as labor. In 1663, Maryland passed a law allowing

69

Tobacco was colonial Virginia's main crop. These drawings show enslaved Africans preparing the tobacco leaves for drying, curing, and storing. Where did the colony sell most of its crop?

enslavement of Africans and their children *durante vita,* or for life.

Soon enslaved Africans became the backbone of Maryland's labor force. They cleared forests, tended fields, and harvested and processed tobacco. Africans also worked as servants in the elegant homes of planters, doing everything from cooking to caring for children.

The Slave Trade. Maryland and Virginia became known to European slave traders as good markets for selling African captives. To prevent colonists from buying Africans from rivals such as the Dutch, England formed the Royal African Company in 1663. The company built eight forts in West Africa. Between 1663 and 1698, it forcibly carried some 120,000 Africans to English America.

At first, most Africans were shipped to the West Indies to be "seasoned," or broken in, on sugar plantations (see page 62). English slave traders then sold the Africans to colonists along the Atlantic coast. By the 1700s, however, most Africans were shipped directly from Africa to the mainland.

70

The Carolinas. In 1663, King Charles II of England granted eight nobles a huge tract of land south of Virginia. The colony's owners asked English philosopher John Locke to draw up a plan of government. Locke believed that government existed to protect the life, liberty, and property of the people. Because Locke considered enslaved Africans as "property," he gave them no rights. His plan declared: "Every freeman of Carolina shall have absolute power and authority over his negro slaves."

The owners of Carolina saw the colony as a business. They dreamed of cash crops suitable to warm climates—olives, citrus fruits, tea, and more. Eventually, only rice provided the profits they sought—that is, when farmed by enslaved Africans. Four of Carolina's founders were members of the Royal African Company, and they gave land to all settlers who bought enslaved Africans for use in the colony.

In 1729, Carolina split into two colonies—North Carolina and South Carolina. North Carolina's economy was more varied than South Carolina's and it had a larger number of small farmers. In South Carolina, slavery and rice plantations became a way of life. By 1763, Africans accounted for 70 percent of the colony's population. Almost all were enslaved.

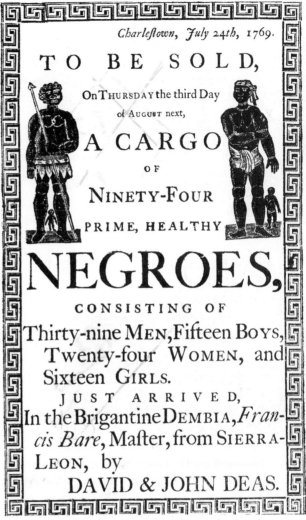

Posters like this one were used to announce the sale of newly arrived Africans.

Georgia. The founders of Georgia pictured a colony without slaves. Led by James Oglethorpe, they wanted to establish a haven for people who had been imprisoned for their debts. All settlers were to start on an equal footing, without great differences in wealth.

In 1733, Great Britain agreed to the plan. It hoped that Georgia would act as a buffer between its colonies and Spanish Florida to the south. Planters in South Carolina favored the plan for the same reason. Georgia's colonists opposed the ban on slavery. "All unanimously agree," wrote one leader, "that without Negroes Georgia can never be a colony of any consequence [importance]." To get around the rule, they "hired" Africans from South Carolinians on 100-year terms. Finally, slavery was allowed in 1750. By 1760, enslaved Africans made up one third of Georgia's population.

Taking Another Look

1. Why was slavery established in Maryland?

2. What did the founding of Carolina reveal about English attitudes toward Africans by the 1660s?

3. **Critical Thinking** Compare the different ways slavery became established in Maryland, the Carolinas, and Georgia.

3 ▼ AFRICANS IN THE MIDDLE COLONIES

▼ What conditions discouraged the widespread use of slavery in the Middle Colonies?

In 1644, 11 African indentured servants petitioned the Council of New Netherlands for their freedom. The Africans had helped the Dutch build the colony's first village—New Amsterdam—18 years before. They had been "promised their freedom on the same footing as other free people in New Netherlands." Yet they remained bound to the Dutch West India Company, the trading firm that had financed New Netherlands.

The council ruled in the Africans' favor. Each person named in the petition— Manuel de Gerrit de Rens, John Francisco, Little Anthony, John Fort Orange, Simon Congo, Big Manuel, Little Manuel, Paul d'Angola, Anthony Portuguese, Gracia, and Peter Santome—received a grant of land in the area that is now New York City's Greenwich Village. Here, they took up life with the same legal rights as the Dutch.

New York and New Jersey.

Because New Netherlands never attracted a lot of settlers, the Dutch West India Company encouraged the use of enslaved Africans. Africans held in bondage had almost the same rights as other non-citizens in the colony. The Dutch allowed enslaved Africans to hire themselves out for wages, sue in courts of law, and to shoulder arms in times of danger. No laws kept Africans from mixing with whites; in fact the two groups often socialized.

When the English seized the sparsely settled Dutch colony in 1664, the lives of Africans changed. King Charles II gave the New Netherlands to his brother James, the Duke of York, who renamed it New York. James awarded what is now New Jersey to two friends. In the late 1600s, both New York and New Jersey legalized slavery. The two colonies also restricted the rights and movements of Africans, who they feared might rebel, which they did in 1712 (see page 125).

Even though the Royal African Company imported thousands of Africans into the two colonies, the region's climate discouraged the rapid growth of slavery. Because few people wanted to feed and clothe large numbers of farm laborers all winter, the number of enslaved Africans in New York and New Jersey lagged far behind those in the Southern Colonies.

Pennsylvania and Delaware.

In 1681 and 1682, William Penn received grants from the English king for the lands that now make up Pennsylvania and Delaware. Penn founded Pennsylvania as a religious haven for Quakers and other Christians seeking religious freedom. He generally treated Native Americans more fairly than other colonial founders had. But since enslaved Africans already lived along the Delaware River on lands once held by the Swedes and the Dutch, Penn allowed slavery to continue.

Most farms in New Jersey were small. How does this help account for the few enslaved Africans in the colony?

Not all of Pennsylvania's colonists shared Penn's tolerance of slavery. In 1688, members of the German Quakers issued the first antislavery protest in North America. The document declared, "Negroes are brought hither against their will. . . . Have these poor Negroes not as much right to fight for their freedom as you have to keep them as slaves?"

The protest fell on deaf ears. Even so, Africans in Pennsylvania managed gradually to win more rights than Africans in other colonies. By the mid-1700s, Pennsylvania claimed the largest number of free Africans in any of the 13 colonies. It would be these people and their descendants who would give voice to the antislavery movement of the late 1700s and the 1800s (see Units 3, 4, and 5).

Africans in Delaware were less successful. Delaware's location made tobacco production on plantations profita-

ble. Some settlers bought enslaved Africans—first from the Dutch, then from the English. When Penn gave Delaware its own legislature in 1703, the lawmakers made it more difficult to free Africans. By the mid-1700s, Delaware had allied itself more closely with slaveholding colonies to the south than with its neighbors to the north.

Taking Another Look

1. How did their location affect slavery in the Middle Colonies?

2. Why did the Royal African Company stand to benefit from the English takeover of New Netherlands?

3. **Critical Thinking** Suppose the Dutch had kept New Netherlands. How might the lives of Africans there have been different?

4 AFRICANS IN NEW ENGLAND
▼ How did New Englanders help promote the African slave trade?

In February 1645, the *Rainbow* left Boston, Massachusetts, intending to trade for Africans along the Guinea coast. When the ship reached Guinea, however, James Smith, the captain, found no Africans for sale, and he took matters into his own hands. He ordered his crew to attack several villages. They set one village ablaze, killed perhaps 100 people, and kidnapped a handful of others.

Smith had hoped to sell his human cargo in the West Indies, but a strange twist of events took him back to Boston. Never before had a Massachusetts ship carried West Africans directly to the colony. Colonial leaders charged Smith with "man-stealing" and ordered the Africans to be returned. Little did anyone know that Massachusetts ships would soon be sailing regularly to Africa for human cargoes.

"A Model Community." Massachusetts started as a haven for religious dissenters who were unhappy with the Church of England. The Puritans (from *purify*) wanted to make the church stricter and simplify its services. The first group of Puritans arrived in what is now Plymouth, Massachusetts, in 1620. They called themselves Pilgrims—people on a holy mission. By the end of the 1630s, over 16,000 men and women had arrived in the colony.

In building their model Christian community, the Puritans struggled with the question of whether to allow slavery. The question first arose in 1638 when a Massachusetts ship, the *Desire,* landed a shipment of Africans from the West Indies. Because the captain had bought the Africans, rather than kidnapped them, he was allowed to sell them.

In 1641, the question came up again when the Puritans drafted a code of laws. The code prohibited slavery except for "lawful captives taken in just wars" and those who would "sell themselves or are sold to us." By this wording, the Puritans tried to distance themselves from the "man-stealing" in West Africa.

The New England Slave Trade. Eventually, economics settled the question. The rocky soil and cool climate of Massachusetts made farming difficult, so many settlers turned to the sea for their livelihood. Fishing and trade with England

During which 10-year period were the most Africans brought to the colonies? During which 10-year period did the greatest increase occur?

NUMBER OF ENSLAVED AFRICANS BROUGHT TO THE THIRTEEN COLONIES 1701–1775	
Years	Enslaved
1701–1710	9,000
1711–1720	10,800
1721–1730	9,900
1731–1740	40,500
1741–1750	58,500
1751–1760	41,900
1761–1770	69,500
1771–1775	15,000
Total	255,100

Source: R.C. Simmons, *The American Colonies: From Settlement to Independence* (New York: David McKay Company, Inc.). Copyright 1976 by R. C. Simmons. Reprinted by permission of Harold Matson Co., Inc.

became the basis of New England's economy. Then, in 1698, the Royal African Company licensed New England merchants to allow them to participate in the Atlantic slave trade.

New Englanders built, sailed, and financed many of the vessels involved in the Middle Passage. While New Englanders owned few enslaved Africans themselves, they sold thousands to planters in the Southern Colonies. The colonial slave trade, in which New England participated, grew so rapidly that the number of Africans in the colonies soared from 59,000 in 1714 to nearly 300,000 by 1754.

Treatment of Africans. There were far fewer enslaved Africans in New England than in either the Southern or Middle colonies. Yet, even here, laws called **slave codes** limited the rights of Africans, although they were not as harsh as laws elsewhere. Enslaved Africans in New England were better able to win their freedom than Africans in other colonies. In time, Africans—free and enslaved—in New England would take up the cause of liberty for people of African descent.

Eventually New Englanders banned slavery for two reasons. The first was the contributions of Africans during the American Revolution and the early years of the new nation. The second was the fact that slavery had no important place in the economy of the region.

Taking Another Look

1. How did Puritan laws help ensure the future of slavery in Massachusetts?

2. How did New Englanders become involved in the Atlantic slave trade?

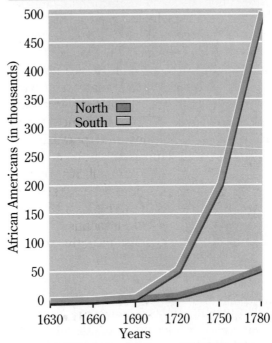

▶▶ **GROWTH OF AFRICAN POPULATION NORTH AND SOUTH, 1630–1780**

Source: U.S. Department of Commerce, Bureau of the Census, *Historical Statistics of the United States, Colonial Times to 1970, Part 2* (Series Z 1–19), p. 1168

How many more people of African descent lived in the South than the North in 1720? in 1750? in 1780?

3. **Critical Thinking** How did geography influence the spread of slavery in the Southern, Middle, and New England colonies?

LOOKING AHEAD

By the 1700s, the English colonies had two separate populations—one free and one in chains. In colony after colony, lawmakers established ways to hold Africans in bondage. Meanwhile, Africans struggled to find ways to survive the day-to-day humiliations of enslavement—and to resist slave holders.

FOCUS ON THE AFRICAN BURIAL GROUND

Stop digging! In 1992, New York City's first African American mayor, David Dinkins, halted excavation of a parking lot between the corner of Duane and Reade streets. Just 16 to 28 feet below street level lay a cemetery known in colonial times as the Negroes Burial Ground—a five-to-six acre plot where some 10,000 to 20,000 people, both African and white, are believed to be buried.

The cemetery had its start in a 1697 English ruling that placed New York City burial grounds off-limits to Africans. Africans chose instead to bury their dead at a spot outside the city. During the 1600s, Duane and Reade streets were located outside of the city's limits.

Africans lost this burial ground as the city expanded. By the end of the 1800s, pavement covered the area and the burial grounds were all but forgotten to New Yorkers.

In 1991, it was revealed that builders had found African graves just two blocks from City Hall. African Americans demanded an end to all construction. They also demanded that African Americans be given the deciding voice in preserving this piece of their heritage.

African American protest reached the White House. In October 1992, President George Bush approved long-term study of the site as well as $3 million for construction of a museum honoring the contributions of Africans to colonial New York City.

CLOSE UP: Chapter 6

The Who, What, Where of History

1. **Where** was San Miguel?
2. **Who** was Estevanico?
3. **Where** in the Virginia Colony did the first Africans arrive?
4. **Who** was the first child of African descent born in the Virginia Colony?
5. **What** was the House of Burgesses?
6. **Who** was Anthony Johnson?
7. **Who** was Mathias De Sousa?
8. **What** does the phrase *durante vita* mean?
9. **Who** drew up a plan of government for the Carolinas?
10. **Who** was James Oglethorpe?

Making the Connection

1. What was the connection between the cultivation of tobacco in Virginia and the growth of slavery there?
2. What was the connection between climate and slavery in the 13 colonies?

Time Check

1. When did the first Africans arrive at Jamestown?
2. When did Maryland make all Africans slaves for life?

What Would You Have Done?

1. Imagine that you are an African living in Maryland. You came to the colony as an indentured servant, but have completed your term of service. Now the colony has passed a law enslaving Africans for life. What will you do?

2. If you had been James Oglethorpe, how would you have argued against slavery in Georgia?

Thinking and Writing About History

1. Write a story that explains what happened to the Africans of San Miguel.
2. Write a letter from the daughter of John Fort Orange to the king of England explaining how her father obtained his freedom and protesting the legalization of slavery in New York.

Building Skills: Identifying Relevant Information

A friend of yours has moved to a new part of town. You ask for directions to her house and she tells you the following:

[1] You go down Washington Street, then turn right at Garvey. [2] Go down Garvey past the video store. [3] They've got the new tape I was telling you about there. [4] Go three blocks on Garvey and take a left on Wheatley. [5] Angie Thomas, who used to be in our class, lives in the first yellow house on the left. [6] I'm in the fourth house on the right.

Which of the sentences in her directions are *not* necessary to help you find her house?

The sentences you listed are examples of *irrelevant* information. They do not have any significant, or relevant, information about what you are trying to find out—how to get to your friend's house. They may contain true or interesting information, but not information directly related to the subject

The skill of recognizing relevant information is an important one to develop. It can help you focus your reading and think more clearly about a topic.

Each of the questions below has three facts listed after it. On a separate sheet of paper, write an *R* next to the letter of the fact if it is relevant to the topic. Write an *I* next to the letter of the fact if it is irrelevant to the topic.

1. What was the economy of colonial Virginia like?
   a. Tobacco was successfully grown there in 1612 for sale in England.
   b. William, the son of Antoney and Isabella, was the first child of African descent born in English America.
   c. In its early years, the colony faced a severe shortage of workers.

2. What were conditions like for Africans in New Netherlands?
   a. In 1644, 11 African indentured servants won their freedom.
   b. In 1664, the English seized the Netherlands.
   c. The Dutch Reformed Church married African couples in New Netherlands.

3. How did the British colony at Georgia develop?
   a. James Oglethorpe wanted to establish a haven for debtors.
   b. The Royal African Company brought many enslaved Africans to British America.
   c. James Oglethorpe died in 1785.

UNIT 3

A Revolutionary War soldier

AFRICAN AMERICANS AND A NEW NATION

(1768–1840s)

Benjamin Banneker

Preamble to the Constitution of the United States

We the People *of the United States* insure domestic Tranquility, provide for the common defence, promote the general and our Posterity, do ordain and establish this Constitution for the United States of

78

THE BIG PICTURE

Unit 3 traces one of the great debates in U.S. history—the debate over African American* rights and freedoms. The unit explores how discussions of liberty during the American Revolution and the early years of nationhood raised the question of slavery. Slavery was no longer a British problem, but a problem for the new United States.

In an effort to win passage of a new **constitution**—a document containing the basic principles and laws of government—leaders temporarily set aside the question. Each time the nation pushed westward, however, the troubling question reemerged: Would slavery grow along with the nation?

The Seeds of Conflict. The question of independence, both for the 13 British colonies and for African Americans, became sharper in the years following the French and Indian War. This nine-year conflict between Great Britain and France was fought over control of much of the North American continent. When the war ended in 1763, a victorious Britain took possession of Canada and most of the land from the Atlantic coast west to the Mississippi. The colonists were happy with Britain's victory. But the war had been expensive for the British and they felt it was time for the colonists to help pay the

costs of empire. Beginning in 1764, the British imposed a series of heavy taxes on the 13 colonies. When the British moved to collect the new taxes, howls of protest went up throughout the colonies.

Many colonists claimed that since they were not represented in Parliament, the British law-making body, Great Britain had no right to **levy,** or impose, taxes on them. From Massachusetts to Georgia, these colonists rallied behind a single cry: "No taxation without representation!"

Calls for Independence. The protest over taxes led some colonists to speak openly of independence from Britain. African Americans wondered what liberty would mean to them. Would it mean an end to slavery? Would it mean increased rights?

Some white Americans, such as Benjamin Franklin, Patrick Henry, and Thomas Paine, called for **abolition,** or ending of slavery. But most colonists considered such views too extreme. Southern slaveholders feared that African Americans held against their will might revolt if they heard talk of freedom. Many white

---

*Beginning with this unit, the term *African American* is used to indicate people of African descent even though the rights of citizenship were not yet available to them. This was also true at this time for both Native Americans and women.

An African American Speaks

That liberty is a great thing we know from our own feelings, and we may likewise judge so from the conduct of the white people in the late war [Revolution].

—Jupiter Hammon,
Enslaved African American,
New York, 1787

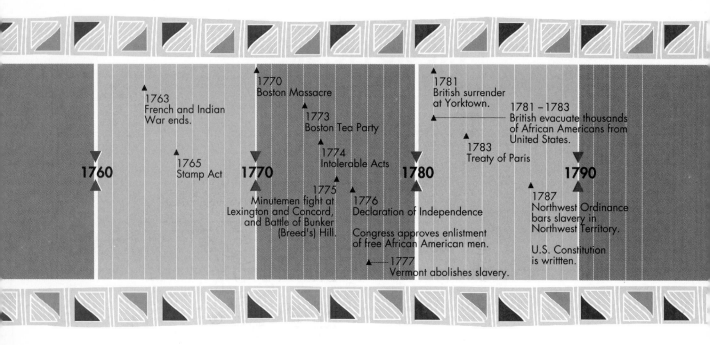

1763
French and Indian War ends.

1765
Stamp Act

1770
Boston Massacre

1773
Boston Tea Party

1774
Intolerable Acts

1775
Minutemen fight at Lexington and Concord, and Battle of Bunker (Breed's) Hill.

1776
Declaration of Independence

Congress approves enlistment of free African American men.

1777
Vermont abolishes slavery.

1781
British surrender at Yorktown.

1781–1783
British evacuate thousands of African Americans from United States.

1783
Treaty of Paris

1787
Northwest Ordinance bars slavery in Northwest Territory.

U.S. Constitution is writtten.

1760   1770   1780   1790

Northerners also rejected the idea of equality for African Americans. Some of these Northerners profited richly from the slave trade. Yet others were influenced by the false ideas of racial prejudice.

Backing Liberty. However, the spirit of liberty led some free African Americans to become **Patriots,** the name given to colonists who favored independence. Free African Americans, for example, helped force the repeal of the Stamp Act. This act placed a tax on every kind of paper, from marriage licenses to playing cards, and was one of the most hated taxes. Free African Americans joined other colonists in anti-British **boycotts,** refusing to buy goods from Great Britain. They also took part in the riots against the Stamp Act in Boston. African Americans and whites threatened tax collectors and held protest meetings, gathering around huge bonfires, crying "Liberty and Property!"

As the 1770s unfolded, ties between the colonists and Great Britain weakened. About one third of the colonists remained loyal to Britain, and about one third supported neither side.

Patriots began to arm themselves. Laws generally forbade African Americans from owning guns. Many white colonists, especially in the South, feared that armed African Americans might try to stage slave rebellions. In the North, some free African Americans loaded muskets and trained as **Minutemen**—Patriots ready to fight at a minute's notice.

When war finally came, African Americans took part in every major battle. Some were volunteers; others were drafted, or taken for military service. Most were from the North. On the whole, African Americans fought side by side with white Americans. This practice changed in later wars, when African Americans were forced to serve in separate army units.

1803
Louisiana
Purchase

1808
United States
ends slave trade.

1812–1815
War of 1812

1816–1843
Seminole Wars

1800

1810

1820

1830

1819
United States acquires Florida.

1800s–1840s
Mountain Men trap and trade in western territories.

Promises of Freedom. At the start of the American Revolution, the British were short of soldiers and eager to undercut the colonial army. They offered freedom to any enslaved African American who would join them. On November 7, 1775, Lord Dunmore, royal governor of Virginia, declared all African Americans "free, that are able and willing to bear arms . . . [in] his Majesty's troops." African Americans by the thousands joined the British as soldiers, laborers, teamsters, cooks, orderlies, and even spies.

Countless more African Americans, however, were swayed by the words of the Declaration of Independence. Signed on July 4, 1776, this document captured the Patriots' belief in liberty. "All men are created equal," it boldly proclaimed.

These words inspired many African Americans to place their faith in an independent United States. They believed liberty for the nation could mean liberty for them, too. Throughout the war, African American soldiers displayed individual acts of valor. As Lemuel Haynes, a young African American soldier from Massachusetts put it: "Shall a man's color be the decisive criterion [standard] whereby to judge . . . his natural right?"

Debating Slavery. As the Revolution raged, other African Americans asked this question of the new state governments created by the Declaration of Independence. Typical of the pleas to end slavery was a petition sent to the New Hampshire assembly in 1779. "From what authority do [slave holders] assume to dispose of our lives, freedom and property?" demanded a group of 19 African Americans.

These words echoed the earlier Declaration of Independence. What African Americans did not know, however, was that a debate over slavery had nearly prevented the Continental Congress from approving the document. When Thomas Jefferson first wrote the Declaration, he

African American soldiers stood by the nation during some of the darkest hours of the war. Here they are with Washington at Valley Forge in the bleak winter of 1778–1779.

listed British abuses of colonial rights. Among them, he charged, the British king had "waged cruel war against human nature itself, . . . in the persons of a distant people [Africans]; . . . captivating and carrying them into slavery in another hemisphere." Angered at the attack on slavery, Southern delegates, most of whom were slave holders, forced the Congress to drop this clause.

After American troops defeated the British in 1781, the nation faced a dilemma. Asked one white soldier, "What is to be done with these [African American] soldiers who have shed their best blood in its [the nation's] defense?"

One by one, state governments in the North answered the question by ending slavery. However, slavery remained firmly established in the South.

A New Law of the Land. Differences between the North and South over slavery created a crisis in 1787. Delegates from the new states met in Philadelphia and decided to create a new constitution for the United States.

Many delegates to the **Constitutional Convention,** as the meeting was later called, feared for the future of a democratic nation that allowed slavery to continue. However, they feared the danger of a disunited nation even more. Some Southern delegates threatened to walk out if any antislavery measures were adopted. Eventually, each side gave up some of its demands in order to reach a **compromise.** The Constitution recognized slavery. But it permitted Congress to end the Atlantic slave trade in 1808. It would take a bloody civil war and a constitutional **amendment,** or change, in the 1860s to end slavery within the United States itself.

Defending the Nation. In the years following 1787, the United States took steps to strengthen itself in the eyes of the world. In 1812, the nation fought another war against Great Britain. This time it fought to prevent the British from violating United States rights at sea and from arming Native Americans in the Northwest Territory. In 1819, the United

States also acquired Florida from Spain to protect its southeastern border.

Expanding the Nation. Even before the colonies won their independence, some colonists were leaving their homes along the East Coast and heading inland. After independence, U.S. territory extended as far as the Mississippi River. Some of the settlers going west and south were slave holders who took enslaved African Americans with them. However, in one area slavery was forbidden. This was the Northwest Territory, a large region that lay north of the Ohio River and east of the Mississippi. The **Northwest Ordinance,** passed by Congress in 1787, barred slavery in the territory. Here some free Africans built homes.

The Northwest Territory had vast amounts of rich farmland. Farmers in the territory shipped their products to market down the Mississippi River to New Orleans. From New Orleans, their goods were sent to the East Coast and overseas. However, France owned New Orleans, as well as the whole region from the Mississippi River to the Rocky Mountains. U.S. farmers wondered what would happen if France chose to close the port of New Orleans to them. President Thomas Jefferson eased their fears by buying the entire territory from France in 1803.

This **Louisiana Purchase** doubled the size of the United States and gave its people an enormous new territory in which to make their homes. The fact that Native Americans already lived on the land was of little concern to the thousands of settlers who began pouring into these lands. Among them were Southerners who established plantations and ran them with the forced labor of enslaved African Americans.

THE NORTHWEST TERRITORY, 1787

Some free African Americans made their homes in the Northwest Territory. Which rivers and lakes were included in this territory? What states were made from this territory?

The expansion of the country stepped up the debate over slavery. Expansion brought Americans face to face with a question that had troubled them since the Revolution. Could a democratic nation exist part slave and part free?

Taking Another Look

1. Why did some African Americans choose to side with the British in the American Revolution, while others sided with the Patriots?

2. How did the members of the Constitutional Convention compromise on the question of slavery?

3. How was the Northwest Ordinance favorable to African Americans?

4. **Critical Thinking** List three ways African Americans helped further the freedom of what would become the United States of America.

Washington Crossing the Delaware, by Emmanuel Leutze

The American Revolution: Liberty for All?

(1768–1783)

THINKING ABOUT THE CHAPTER

How did the Revolution affect the lives of African Americans?

On Christmas night, 1776, amid a blinding snowstorm, a band of ragged colonial troops dragged rowboats toward the Delaware River. Some men wrapped strips of blankets around their feet to keep their torn boots from falling apart.

George Washington, commander of the Continental Army, hoped to score a desperately needed victory against the British stationed on the opposite shore. As Washington's troops slid the boats into the ice-clogged river, Washington climbed into one of them. An enslaved African named Prince Whipple was one of those who pulled at the oars of Washington's boat.

Prince Whipple's wealthy African parents had sent him to America at age ten to receive an education. But a treacherous slave trader seized the boy and sold him to William Whipple of New Hampshire. When war came to the 13 colonies, Captain Whipple served as an aid to General Washington. He brought Prince with him.

On the morning of December 26, Prince Whipple took part in a stunning victory over the British at the Battle of Trenton in New Jersey. He traveled with Captain Whipple to fight in other battles of the American Revolution. By summer 1777, Captain Whipple noticed that Prince's spirits had fallen. He asked why. Said Prince: "Master, you are going to fight for your liberty, but I have none to fight for."

Captain Whipple later freed Prince for his bravery. Many other enslaved African Americans remained in bondage despite their service. In this chapter, you will learn why and how African Americans, enslaved and free, took part in the American Revolution.

1 FROM PROTEST TO WAR
▼ What role did African Americans play on the road to war?

In September 1768, drums rolled as two regiments of red-coated British soldiers marched up King Street in Boston. The **Redcoats,** as the British troops were called, set up camp on the Commons, a park in the center of the city. The sight of British troops on the Commons angered the Patriots. Passersby hurled insults. "You lobster-backs! You bloody-backs!" they shouted.

African Americans were among those who resented the presence of British troops in Boston to protect British cus-

Crispus Attucks, who worked as a sailor on a whaling ship, was the first colonist killed by the British army. How did Attucks help advance the cause of liberty?

toms officers. The customs officers were sent to stop smuggling, so that Britain could collect its new taxes.

The Boston Massacre. During the next year, African Americans joined with white Patriots in regularly harassing the Redcoats. Tensions reached a peak in the winter of 1770. On the snowy evening of March 5, violence erupted. A mob ran down King Street, shouting, "Let us drive out these [Redcoats]; they have no business here!"

The leader of the group was Crispus Attucks, a 47-year-old African American who had fled slavery. Attucks was well known in Boston as a strong opponent of British rule. That night he told the crowd: "Don't be afraid. They dare not fire."

The crowd pelted the troops with snowballs, pieces of ice, and anything else they could find. The British struck back, and a fight broke out. An enslaved African American named Andrew later described what happened next:

This stout man [Attucks] held [a] bayonet with his left hand, and twitched it and cried kill the dogs. . . . The people then crowded in, and . . . I turned to go off, when I heard the word fire. . . .

British bullets killed five people. The first person to fall in the cause of liberty was Attucks, a man who was himself not free. Patriots named the sad event the **Boston Massacre.**

The Coming of War. News of the Boston Massacre set off a storm of outrage throughout the 13 colonies. The victims' funeral, the largest ever held in Boston, drew thousands of mourners.

The incident moved many people, including an enslaved African named Phillis Wheatley. She wrote a poem entitled "On the Affray [Fighting] in King Street on the Evening of the 5th of March 1770."

At the time **Phillis Wheatley** wrote that poem, she was one of the best-known poets in the colonies. Wheatley arrived in the colonies from Africa aboard a slave ship in 1761. She was only about seven or eight years old. She stood on the slave block clutching a piece of carpet around her. The young girl caught the attention of John Wheatley, a rich merchant. He bought the child and took her home to his wife, Susanah. Within 16 months, Susanah had taught the girl, whom she named Phillis, to read and write. By her teens, Phillis was an accomplished poet. In 1773, a London publisher agreed to print her poems. Phillis

Wheatley was the first person of African descent in the 13 colonies to publish a book, and only the second woman to do so.

In 1773, events quickened. The British passed the Tea Act, giving the East India Company a **monopoly,** or total control, over tea sold in the colonies. Patriots struck back by dumping hundreds of pounds of tea into Boston harbor, an act known as the **Boston Tea Party.** In late 1773, the British responded with the Intolerable Acts, which among other things put Boston under martial, or military, law. Patriots now united against the British. In 1774, the Continental Congress declared a boycott of the profitable British slave trade. The time had come, the colonists decided, to stand together.

Taking Another Look

1. List events that increased tension between Britain and the colonies.

2. What role did Crispus Attucks play in the fight against the British?

3. **Critical Thinking** If you had been a free African American in Boston during the 1770s, would you have joined the Patriots? Explain.

2 FIGHTING THE WAR
▼ How did African Americans help win the Revolutionary War?

On the evening of April 18, 1775, some 700 British troops, under the command of Major John Pitcairn, tried to slip out of Boston. Pitcairn had learned through spies that the Patriots had collected a store of guns and powder in Concord, a village about 20 miles (32 kilometers) away. Pitcairn decided to search Concord and make an example of it.

Opening Battles of the War. As the sun rose on April 19, 1775, the British marched into Lexington, a village on the road to Concord. There 77 Minutemen, alerted by Patriots Paul Revere and William Dawes, stood ready to block the British advance. One was an African American, Prince Estabrook. Someone shouted "Fire!" and shots rang out. Eight Minutemen fell, mortally wounded. The rest scrambled for cover.

In a jubilant mood, the British broke into song and began the march to Concord. While they searched the village for arms, Minutemen from nearby towns quietly took up positions behind trees and stone walls. On spotting the Minutemen, British guards on Concord's North Bridge panicked and opened fire. The Minutemen returned the shots. Several African Americans, both enslaved and free, joined the battle that followed. Among these were Lemuel Haynes, Peter Salem, Pomp Blackman, Cuffe Whitemore, Cato Woods, and Prince Estabrook. By day's end, the British dead and wounded totaled more than 250, while colonial casualties numbered less than 100. The British had little choice but to make a hasty retreat to Boston.

Digging in at Boston. Two months later, on June 17, 1775, the British and the Patriots met again. That day, the British repeatedly stormed the Patriots' stronghold on Breed's Hill, overlooking Boston harbor. On one charge, two veterans of Concord—Peter Salem and Major Pitcairn—faced each other. As Pitcairn cried out, "The day is ours!" Salem cut him down.

The Battle for Bunker Hill, as it was called, was one of the bloodiest battles of the war. Although the colonists lost, they proved they could stand up to the better-trained British troops. African Americans distinguished themselves. Salem Poor, for example, was commended by 14 white officers as a "brave and gallant soldier." Others cited Cuffe Whitemore for "fighting to the last."

Enlisting African Americans. In 1775, hundreds of African Americans stood ready to join the Continental Army. At first, a debate raged in Congress over whether to enlist African Americans. Some members doubted the loyalty of armed African Americans. Slave holders feared the loss of valuable property. "I hope none of [ours] enlist," wailed one Southerner. "The price if paid . . . is not equal to their value."

This situation changed, however, when many African Americans accepted the British promise of freedom if they joined the British army. George Washington worried that this move might dangerously increase the size of the British army. Faced with a severe shortage of troops, Washington asked Congress to approve enlistment of African Americans into the Continental Army. This reversed a 1775 order stating that "neither [African Americans], boys . . . nor old men unfit to endure the fatigues of the campaign are to be enlisted."

Washington entered the winter of 1777-1778 at Valley Forge with only 9,000 troops. He now welcomed any able-bodied soldier into his ranks—African American or white, free or enslaved, young or old. By the end of the war, 5,000 African Americans from all 13 colonies, except South Carolina, served in the army. Another 2,000 served in the navy, which accepted African Americans from the start.

REVOLUTIONARY WAR HONOR ROLL

Colonel Middleton—Commanded a company of African American volunteers from Massachusetts

Caesar Tarrant—Served four years in Virginia navy as a pilot on the armed ship *Patriot*

George Latchom—Under British attack, dragged his colonel out of waist-high mud and carried him to safety

Quaco–Fled from British colonel and provided the Patriots with valuable military information.

John Peterson—Launched attack that prevented British spy Andre from escaping

Saul Matthews—Spied for Virginia militia

James Armistead—Acted as double agent to spy on British officers, helping Patriots win Battle of Yorktown

James Armistead

Liberty and Independence African Americans entered the service for many reasons. Some believed the words of the Declaration of Independence, signed July 4, 1776, which said "All men are created equal." Many African Americans served because the people that held them in bondage took them to war or sent them in their place. Still others hoped to win their freedom in return for serving in the Patriots armed forces.

No matter what led African Americans into the Revolution, they served with honor. They fought in almost all the important battles of the war, and their presence in some helped to turn the tide. In commenting on one battle, a white soldier said: "Had they [African Americans] been unfaithful, or even given way before the enemy all would have been lost."

In 1781, the Continental Army finally defeated the British at the Battle of Yorktown. The battle meant independence for the United States. But what did the future hold for African Americans?

Taking Another Look

1. How did the Battle of Bunker Hill win respect for African Americans?

2. Why did Washington and Congress finally enlist African Americans?

3. Why did some African Americans decide to join the Continental Army?

4. **Critical Thinking** If you had been a free African American in 1781, what arguments would you have used to convince your state to end slavery?

3 SEEKING LIBERTY
▼ What changes did the Revolution
▼ bring to African Americans?

In 1783, the United States and Great Britain signed the Treaty of Paris, officially ending the American Revolution. Nearly 20,000 African Americans who had sided with the British during the Revolution decided to leave the United States. True to their word, the British ferried them to freedom in Jamaica, in England, or in Nova Scotia, Canada. "We cannot," said one British official, "in justice abandon [them] to the merciless resentment [displeasure] of their former masters." The British also returned some enslaved African Americans to the people who had held them and sold yet others into bondage in the West Indies.

Freedom in the North. Thousands of African Americans in the North also found freedom. Slavery died in the North for many reasons. For one thing, slavery was never widespread, since the geography of the region made plantation farming and the use of enslaved Africans impractical. Efforts by African Americans and white Patriots during the war helped speed the end of any slavery that did exist there. In 1777, Vermont became the first Northern state to pass a law ending slavery. New Jersey was the last state, in 1804.

Slavery in the South. A different fate awaited enslaved African Americans in the South. Some slave holders freed African Americans to reward their bravery during the war. In 1783, Virginia passed a law giving freedom to ex-soldiers, but most slave holders refused to obey the law. Instead many slave holders in the Upper South sold African American veterans to plantation owners farther south, where they were less likely to run away. "I didn't like to sell a man who fought for his country," said the owner of one slave ship. "[But] if I didn't do it, I never could get a bale of cotton, . . . nor anything, to carry from or to any Southern port."

Taking Another Look

1. What happened to enslaved African Americans who joined the British?

2. How did the Revolution affect slavery in the new United States?

3. **Critical Thinking** In what ways do you think the United States benefited by allowing African Americans to join the Continental Army?

LOOKING AHEAD

The Revolution had mixed results for African Americans. The number of free African Americans in the United States reached 60,000 by 1790. A decade later, the number topped 100,000. Even so, nearly 700,000 African Americans remained enslaved.

Some leaders of the war changed their ideas on slavery. In 1786, George Washington, a wealthy Virginia slaveholder, wrote: "I can only say that there is not a man living who wishes more sincerely than I do to see some plan adopted for the abolition of [slavery]."

The French called them the Volunteer Chasseurs (sha–SERS)—the Volunteer Infantry. They came from the Caribbean island of Santo Domingo and included 545 free Africans. They had signed up with the French rulers of Santo Domingo to help the Patriots fight for their freedom from Great Britain.

The Volunteer Chasseurs joined a larger French unit sent to drive the British out of Savannah, Georgia. On October 9, 1779, the French troops needed every bit of bravery they could summon. As they charged into battle, the British rained murderous fire upon them.

French commander Count D'Estaing ordered a retreat. The British followed, determined to wipe out the French. Then the Volunteer Chasseurs swung into action and held the French rear line against the British assault. The Volunteer Chasseurs refused to break ranks and run, preventing a breakthrough by the British troops.

After this battle, D'Estaing, who was twice wounded, and his weary troops set sail from Savannah, leaving the war behind. Sailing with the fleet was Henri Christophe, a 12-year-old Volunteer Chasseur. In the battle, Christophe had glimpsed the sacrifices required for freedom. In later years, he would help Haiti to shake off French rule and to emerge as the independent Republic of Haiti in 1804.

CLOSE UP: Chapter 7

The Who, What, Where of History

1. **Who** were the Redcoats?
2. **Who** was Crispus Attucks?
3. **What** were the Intolerable Acts?
4. **Who** was the first person of African descent in the colonies to publish a book?
5. **Who** were the Patriots?
6. **What** was the Boston Tea Party?
7. **Who** were the Minutemen?
8. **Where** were the opening battles of the Revolution fought?
9. **What** did the British promise to enslaved African Americans who joined the British army?
10. **What** was the Treaty of Paris?
11. **Who** was Salem Poor?
12. **Where** was slavery first officially ended in the North?

Making the Connection

1. What was the connection between the Boston Tea Party and the Intolerable Acts?
2. What was the connection between the Declaration of Independence and the decision of many African Americans to become Patriots?
3. What was the connection between the policies of the British and Continental armies on using African Americans as fighting troops?

Time Check

1. In what year did the Boston Massacre occur?

2. Which event happened *last:* the writing of the Declaration of Independence, the end of the French and Indian War, the battles at Lexington and Concord?

3. In what year did the first Northern state end slavery?

4. Which of the following came *first:* the writing of the Declaration of Independence or the British offer of freedom to enslaved African Americans who joined the fighting on their side?

What Would You Have Done?

1. If you had been an African American who decided to serve in the Continental Army or the navy, what would have been your main reason for deciding to join? Explain.

2. If you had been an enslaved African American during the American Revolution, would you have fought with the British, with the Patriots, or with neither side? Explain.

Thinking and Writing About History

1. Imagine that you are going to interview Prince Whipple 25 years after the Battle of Trenton. Write at least three questions that you would like to ask him.

2. Imagine that you are an African American who fought with the British during the Revolution. Now you are leaving North America for a new life in Great Britain. Write an entry in your diary explaining why you are leaving the new United States.

Building Skills: Skimming and Scanning

At different times, you may read for different reasons. For example, you may want to get a general idea of the kind of information that is presented in a chapter before you read the chapter carefully. At other times, you may need to find information quickly. Skimming and scanning will help you to do both of these.

When you skim, you skip words in order to read rapidly and get a quick overview of the text. When you scan, you read quickly in order to locate a specific piece of information. Skim and scan Chapter 7 in order to answer the questions below.

1. What is the title of this chapter?

2. Answer the question in the title.

3. List the titles of the three sections in this chapter.

4. By skimming and scanning, find which chapter section contains each of the following:
   a. discussion of the departure of some African Americans with the British after the Revolution;
   b. actions of the British that convinced many colonists to seek independence;
   c. a chart listing the names of some African American heroes of the Revolution.

5. Each section of the chapter begins with a question. Skim each section and write a statement that answers the question.

Richard Allen (left) and Absalom Jones (right)

Forging a New Constitution

(1787–1799)

THINKING ABOUT THE CHAPTER

What did the Constitution say about the rights of African Americans?

Benjamin Banneker's habits seemed strange to many people. This African American astronomer, farmer, mathematician, and surveyor spent nights wrapped in a cloak under a pear tree, watching the stars and planets. At dawn, he slept for a few hours and then took care of his garden or observed his bees. Most afternoons, Banneker huddled over a large oval table, reading through his books and papers and working with mathematical instruments.

Born a free African American in 1731, Banneker lived all his life on a farm near Baltimore, Maryland. He learned to read and write at a small private school for whites and free African Americans. But Banneker taught himself mathematics and astronomy from books that were lent to him by a Quaker neighbor.

In 1791, when the nation's new capital city, Washington, D.C., was being planned, Secretary of State Thomas Jefferson recommended Banneker to help with the survey. The next year, Banneker asked Jefferson to read an **almanac** he had written. An almanac is a book that contains weather forecasts and astronomical information. Banneker also sent a letter to Jefferson, reminding him of the writing of the Declaration of Independence:

> Sir, suffer [allow] me to recall to your mind that time, in which the arms and tyranny [unfair rule] of the British crown were exerted . . . in order to reduce you to a state of servitude [enslavement] . . . This, Sir, was a time when you clearly saw into the injustice of a state of slavery.

Banneker also pointed out that Jefferson had written the words "all men are created equal." He then criticized Jefferson for allowing African Americans to suffer "under groaning captivity and cruel oppression." Banneker and other African Americans realized that liberty still lay beyond their grasp.

1 ▼ AFRICAN AMERICANS ORGANIZE
▼ What were the aims of the Free African Society?

By the first census in 1790, some 60,000 free African Americans lived in the United States, about a third in the Northern states. Pennsylvania had a larger African American population than any other Northern state. Most African Americans in Pennsylvania lived in Philadelphia.

The word *Philadelphia* means "City of Brotherly Love," and the city followed its name in the 1700s by welcoming people from many nations and of many religions. It was also the city where the Declaration of Independence had been signed. In 1787, six years after the Revolution, Philadelphia was the site of another important meeting. This one was organized to improve the lives of African Americans and to deal with the questions of prejudice, or intolerance, against them.

Promoting Self-Help. Although Philadelphia had the reputation of a friendly city, some white Philadelphians were **prejudiced** against African Americans. Some schools barred African American children from attending. Most social clubs prohibited African Americans from becoming members. Many churches forced them to sit in separate pews.

Realizing that they had to take matters into their own hands to improve their situation, Richard Allen, Absalom Jones, and six other African American Philadelphians met to form the **Free African Society.** Both Allen and Jones had purchased their freedom from bondage.

The Free African Society committed members to work for African Americans' freedom and to live "an orderly and sober life . . . to support one another in sickness, and for the benefit of their widows and fatherless children." Education for African Americans was another important goal. Similar societies soon formed in New York City, Boston, and Newport, Rhode Island.

Support for Liberty. In 1793, a yellow fever epidemic struck Philadelphia, claiming the lives of thousands of people. The members of the Free African Society joined in a round-the-clock fight to help both African American and white victims of the plague.

1787	Free African Society is founded.
	Constitutional Convention is held.
	Northwest Ordinance bars slavery in Northwest Territory.
1788	U.S. Constitution is ratified.
1790	First U.S. Census: African Americans account for 19 percent of U.S. population.
1791	Benjamin Banneker is part of land survey commission for Washington, D.C.
	Benjamin Banneker begins his almanac.

What African Americans did during the epidemic impressed many whites and inspired them to join African Americans in calling for the abolition of slavery. In fact, Philadelphia was to become a stronghold for the powerful abolition movement of the 1800s.

Taking Another Look

1. Why did Richard Allen, Absalom Jones, and six others form the Free African Society?

2. What did the Free African Society hope to accomplish?

3. How did the Free African Society influence white Philadelphians?

4. **Critical Thinking** How might Allen and Jones have reacted to the letter written by Benjamin Banneker to Thomas Jefferson (see page 93)? Explain.

2 COMPROMISES OVER SLAVERY

How did the writers of the Constitution deal with the issue of slavery?

In 1787, one month after the founding of the Free African Society, another important meeting took place in Philadelphia. Fifty-five leading citizens of the United States arrived for what became known as the Constitutional Convention. Some traveled by horseback, others by stagecoach, and a few by ship. All were white men who owned property. Sixteen of them counted as property the African Americans they held in bondage.

Congress had called the meeting to revise the **Articles of Confederation,** the plan of government drawn up during the Revolution. The delegates soon decided to write an entirely new constitution. The document they wrote set up a democratic government that has endured for over 200 years. However, it did not abolish slavery.

Slavery Untouched. The men who met in Philadelphia came to build a strong and united nation. Government under the Articles of Confederation had proved too weak. So they created the **federal system** that we have today—a system that divides power between the national government and state governments. They also divided the government into three branches—executive, legislative, and judicial—each with power to check, or control, the other branches. This is known as the system of **checks and balances.** The legislative was further divided into the Senate and the House of Representatives.

In hammering out this form of government, the delegates compromised on many issues. No issue caused more disagreement than slavery. Sometimes tempers soared as high as the blistering summer heat. The delegates spent hours arguing thorny questions. Should slavery be abolished? Should the national government have the power to regulate the slave trade? Should enslaved African Americans be taxed as property? Should they be counted in determining a state's representatives in the House?

To ensure support for the Constitution from Southern slave holders and from slave traders in both the North and the South, delegates agreed to the following:

1. Slavery itself would not be abolished.
2. The Atlantic slave trade would continue until 1808, after which time Congress could abolish it if it wished. Meanwhile, a tax of up to $10 could be imposed for each African captive brought into the country.
3. Three-fifths of the number of enslaved African Americans would be counted in determining a state's representation in the House.
4. All states were required to return African Americans who fled bondage.

Delegates never used the word *slave* in the Constitution. Instead, they used phrases such as "persons held to servitude or labor."

While the Constitutional Convention was meeting, Congress passed the Northwest Ordinance, banning slavery in the Northwest Territory. This action supported the view of many that slavery would remain limited to the South. "Slavery in time," said one Northern delegate, "will be but a speck in our country."

African American Reaction. African Americans were not content to wait for slavery to become that "speck in our country." On December 30, 1799, 74 members of the Free African Society sent a petition "to the President, Senate, and House of Representatives." It called for an immediate end to the slave trade and for the protection of free African Americans against kidnapping by slave catchers. The petition also asked that African Americans "be allowed to partake of the liberties" to which they were entitled.

The House of Representatives debated the petition briefly, then rejected it by a vote of 85 to 1. This was a chilling glimpse of the struggle facing African Americans.

Taking Another Look

1. How did the Constitution affect slavery in the United States?
2. Why did antislavery delegates agree to these provisions?
3. **Critical Thinking** In five Northern states, African American men voted in the process that ratified the Constitution. If you had been one of these voters, would you have voted for or against the Constitution? Explain.

LOOKING AHEAD

When the Constitution went into effect in 1789, the United States had a new form of government, but slavery was untouched. As the 1700s drew to a close, slavery began to move beyond the South. In 1803, the United States added the vast Louisiana Territory. Unlike the Northwest Territory, much of this area was suitable for growing cotton, the South's most valuable crop. Southern plantation owners, free under the new Constitution to continue slavery, extended their cotton kingdom into the new lands. As a result, slavery increased, and African Americans and antislavery whites would have an even harder struggle to abolish it.

FOCUS ON GLOBAL ANTISLAVERY

In 1767, a white Englishman named Granville Sharp came upon a badly injured man lying in a London street. The injured man, an enslaved African named Jonathan Strong, told Sharp that he had traveled to London with a West Indian planter. In a fit of rage, the planter had savagely whipped Strong and left him in the street.

Sharp helped Strong escape from the control of the brutal slave holder. He then resolved to take the issue of slavery before the British courts. In 1772, Sharp presented his case to Lord Chief Justice Mansfield, who ruled: "Is not a Negro a Man? . . . As soon as any slave sets foot on English soil he shall be free."

Sharp next took aim at the slave trade, helping to organize the British Anti-Slavery Movement. Its members pleaded the antislavery cause before Parliament. In 1807, Parliament voted to halt Britain's slave trade, but it did not end slavery in British colonies.

In all but a few of the British possessions in the Americas, slavery came to an end as the colonies gained their independence from Great Britain. One of the countries that did not follow this pattern was the United States. It took nearly 100 years of independence and a bloody civil war to unlock the chains of slavery here.

The Who, What, Where of History

1. **Who** was Benjamin Banneker?
2. **What** was the Free African Society?
3. **What** is an almanac?
4. **Who** was Absalom Jones?
5. **Who** was Richard Allen?
6. **What** is abolition?
7. **What** was the purpose of the Constitutional Convention?
8. **Where** was the Free African Society founded?
9. **What** is meant by a federal system of government?
10. **What** was the Northwest Territory?

Making the Connection

1. What was the connection between the yellow fever epidemic of 1793 in Philadelphia and support for the abolition of slavery?
2. What was the connection between the treatment of slavery in the Constitution and the desire of many delegates to the Constitutional Convention to have a new plan of government for the United States?
3. What was the connection between the Northwest Ordinance and slavery in the Northwest Territory?

Time Check

1. Which of these events happened *first*: the founding of the Free African Society, the adoption of the Articles of Confederation, the adoption of the Constitution?
2. When did the U.S. Constitution go into effect?

What Would You Have Done?

1. If you had been a member of the House of Representatives or the Senate in 1799, how would you have voted on the petition from the Free African Society? Explain.

2. If you had been a newly freed African American in 1804, would you have settled in Philadelphia or the Northwest Territory? Explain.

Thinking and Writing About History

1. Write an advertisement for the Free African Society urging other African Americans to join.

2. Imagine that you are an African American veteran of the Revolution. Write a letter to one of your white comrades, explaining your reactions to the new Constitution.

Building Skills: Main Ideas and Details

Just as chapters and chapter sections contain main ideas, paragraphs also have main ideas. Usually there is a single sentence in a paragraph that tells what the paragraph is about. The rest of the sentences in the paragraph give details that support the main idea. Keeping track of the main ideas as you read will help you to understand and remember the points that the author is making.

In the following paragraph, the first sentence gives the main idea:

Benjamin Banneker's habits seemed strange to many people. This African American astronomer, farmer, mathematician, and surveyor spent nights wrapped in a cloak under a pear tree watching the stars and planets. At dawn, he slept for a few hours and then took care of his garden or observed his bees. Most afternoons, Banneker huddled over a large oval table reading through his books and papers and working with mathematical instruments.

1. Read the paragraph that follows and then write the sentence that states the main idea.

Although Philadelphia had the reputation of a friendly city, some white Philadelphians were prejudiced against African Americans. Some schools barred African American children from attending. Most social clubs prohibited African Americans from becoming members. Many churches forced African Americans to sit in separate pews.

2. The main idea is not always contained in the first sentence of a paragraph. Read the paragraph below and then write the sentence that states the main idea.

The men who met in Philadelphia came to build a strong and united nation. Government under the Articles of Confederation had proved too weak. So they created the federal system that we have today—a system that divides power between the national government and state governments.

Toussaint L'Ouverture (right) with French officers

Expanding the Nation
(1779–1840s)

THINKING ABOUT THE CHAPTER

How did African Americans contribute to the new nation's growth?

In 1760, a ship sailing from the West Indian island of Haiti sank in storm-tossed waters off the coast of New Orleans. The ship's captain, Jean Baptiste Point Du Sable (jon ba-TEEST pwan doo SAH-buhl), managed to get ashore with his life. But he lost everything he owned, including papers proving he was a free man. Without such papers, Du Sable knew he faced the constant threat of being seized and sold into slavery. He decided to head up the Mississippi River into safer territory.

Du Sable's parents, a French sailor and an African woman living in Haiti, had sent him to France for an education. The six-foot, elegant Du Sable spoke French, English, and Spanish fluently. He also learned to speak several Native American languages.

In 1779, Du Sable and his Native American wife, Catherine, settled in the Illinois Territory. They chose a spot on the southwestern edge of one of the Great Lakes and not far from a river that flowed into the Mississippi. Believing that this would be a natural crossroads for trade between Native Americans and fur traders, they built a trading post.

The business flourished after the Revolutionary War. Visitors to the Du Sables' home gazed in amazement at their elegant collection of European paintings, crystal mirrors, and French furniture. In 1800, the Du Sables sold their holdings and moved on. The area they left behind is known today as Chicago, and Chicagoans honor Du Sable as their city's founder.

Du Sable was one of the many people of African descent who helped the new nation expand. Like Du Sable, some explored the interior of the continent. Others fought in a war with Great Britain to defend the United States' freedom at sea. Still others fled slavery and built new lives with Native Americans.

What present-day states or parts of states did the Louisiana Purchase include?

1 ▼ INCREASING THE NATION'S SIZE

Why was the purchase of the Louisiana Territory important to the future of the United States?

On a steamy August night in 1791, more than 100,000 enslaved Africans revolted in the French colony of Haiti. Their leader, Toussaint L'Ouverture (too-san-loo-ver-TYOOR), vowed to drive the French from Haiti. Napoleon Bonaparte, the powerful emperor of France, sent tens of thousands of French troops into Haiti to put down the revolt. However, bullets and yellow fever nearly wiped them out.

In 1803, Napoleon tricked Toussaint, who called himself the "Black Napoleon," into surrendering. Toussaint died a year later in a French prison. However, his followers fought on until they won independence for Haiti in 1804.

The Louisiana Purchase. President Thomas Jefferson knew that Napoleon was involved in two costly wars—the one with Haiti and another with Great Britain. Hoping to ensure that New Orleans would remain open to farmers in the Northwest Territory, he asked Napoleon to sell the port city to the United States. Napoleon, worn out by the revolt in Haiti, decided to give up his plans for building an empire in North America. In 1803, he astounded Jefferson by offering to sell to the United States for $15 million the entire Louisiana Territory, which stretched from the Mississippi River to the Rocky Mountains.

1779 Jean Baptiste Point Du Sable founds Chicago.

1791 Toussaint L'Ouverture leads revolt on Haiti.

1803 Louisiana Purchase

1803–1806 Lewis and Clark explore Louisiana Territory, with York as guide.

1808 James P. Beckwourth heads west as Mountain Man.

1812–1815 War of 1812

1813 African American sailors fight in Battle of Lake Erie.

1815 African Americans fight in Battle of New Orleans.

1816–1843 African Americans and Native Americans fight the United States in Seminole Wars.

1819 United States acquires Florida.

Jefferson quickly accepted Napoleon's offer. In doing so, he made one of the best bargains in U.S. history. For what amounted to four cents an acre, the United States bought a territory that nearly doubled the nation's size.

Into the Unknown. Jefferson decided to send an expedition into the vast Louisiana Territory to find out who lived there and what the land was like. To head the expedition, he chose two 23-year-old army officers, Meriwether Lewis and William Clark.

The exploring party consisted of about 45 people, including an enslaved African American held by Clark named York. York contributed to the expedition's success by winning the friendship of many Native Americans and trading with them for sup-

plies. Peoples such as the Flathead trusted York more than the white explorers. Explained one Flathead, "Those who had been brave and fearless, the victorious ones in battle, painted themselves with charcoal." Thus, they believed that the African American "must have been the bravest of his party."

Another valuable member of the expedition was a Native American woman named Sacajawea (sak-uh-juh-WEE-uh). Just 17 years old, Sacajawea served as a guide and a translator for the explorers and helped them pass safely through Native American lands.

Upon the expedition's return, Clark freed York. York's final days remain a mystery, but some stories say he returned west and died a chief among the Crow people he had met on the journey.

Importance of the Expedition. For over two years, the Lewis and Clark expedition surveyed and mapped the Louisiana Territory and the land beyond it. Their work opened up these western lands to people living in the eastern United States. Before long, this area would become the center of a heated debate over slavery that would eventually lead to the Civil War.

Taking Another Look

1. Why did Napoleon sell the Louisiana Territory to the United States?

2. **a.** How did York contribute to the success of the Lewis and Clark expedition? **b.** What were some of the results of the expedition?

3. **Critical Thinking** How might events in Haiti have affected the way U.S. slave holders treated African Americans? Explain.

2 SECURING INDEPENDENCE

How did African Americans help win the War of 1812?

On January 1, 1813, a British warship opened fire on a small U.S. vessel. Two African American sailors fell. As one of them, John Johnson, lay dying, he called out to the rest of the crew, "Fire away, my boys!" The other sailor, John Davis, asked only that he be moved out of the way. The captain of the ship later wrote, "When America has such tars [sailors], she has little to fear from the tyrants of the ocean."

What did Andrew Jackson say about the African American troops who fought in the Battle of New Orleans?

The War of 1812. The sea battle you have just read about was part of the War of 1812. The war was fought to prevent the British from arming Native Americans in the Northwest Territory and searching U.S. ships at sea for British sailors.

When the war began, African Americans were willing to set aside their own struggle for liberty and fight again for their homeland. In Philadelphia, for example, Richard Allen and Absalom Jones (see page 93) rallied more than 2,000 African Americans to help fortify their city against the British. Other African Americans fought in battles along the frontier and in Canada.

Most African Americans, however, served at sea, where they made up at least one out of every six members of the U.S. Navy. At first, one naval officer, Captain Oliver Hazard Perry, objected to having African Americans assigned to his ship. But his commander assured him, "[They] are not surpassed by any seamen we have in the fleet!" When African American sailors helped Perry win the Battle of Lake Erie in 1813, he agreed. "They are absolutely insensible [indifferent] to danger," said Perry.

The Battle of New Orleans. The most famous battle of the war took place in New Orleans. Free African Americans who had already formed their own unit were pressed into service with the state militia. Another African American unit formed by Joseph Savory of Santo Domingo joined them. These troops were placed under the command of General Andrew Jackson.

On a cold, foggy night of December 23, 1814, Jackson led his troops against the British as they tried to sneak into the city through the swamplands to the east. Brutal hand-to-hand fighting forced the British to withdraw.

On January 8, 1815, the British stormed the city directly. Jackson's troops, including two African American units, crouched behind a huge earthen wall. As the British headed directly toward this wall, they were mowed down by U.S. sharpshooters and cannon. More than 1,500 British fell dead or wounded. Only 13 of Jackson's soldiers were killed.

Because of the slow communications of that time, Jackson did not know that two weeks before the battle, Great Britain

101

William Flora—Fought in Revolutionary War and War of 1812; in latter, was a marine on a gunboat

Charles Forneret—Commanded a company of 41 men of the Company of People of Color, Louisiana Militia

Vincent Populus—Second Major, ranking African American officer of First Battalion of Free Men of Color, Louisiana Militia

Joseph Savory—Major, Second Battalion (D'Aquin's) Free Men of Color, Louisiana Militia; fought with distinction at Battle of New Orleans

John Vashon—Seaman on *USS Revenge;* after war became active in the fight to end slavery

and the United States had agreed to end the war.

The Battle of New Orleans again showed the ability of African American soldiers to fight. Said Jackson to his African American troops:

> I expected much from you. . . . I knew that you could endure hunger and thirst and all the hardships of war. I knew that you loved the land of your nativity [birth]. . . . But you surpass my hopes. I have found in you. . . that noble enthusiasm which impels [drives one] to great deeds.

Florida and the Slavery Issue. The praise given to African Americans during the War of 1812 was soon forgotten.

Slave holders had a new complaint. They demanded loudly that the government stop enslaved African Americans from fleeing into Florida—a territory owned by Spain at the time.

The swamps and marshes of Florida were home to Native Americans who called themselves Seminoles, meaning "runaways" in their language. The Seminoles had fled government efforts to relocate them west of the Mississippi. They sympathized with the runaway African Americans and allowed them to build villages among them. Some Seminoles and African Americans intermarried.

Georgia slave holders saw the villages as a threat to the whole slave system and asked the government to **annex,** or take over, Florida. From 1816 to 1843, the U.S. fought a series of three wars to subdue the Seminoles and to force African Americans back into bondage.

These Seminole Wars started after about 1,000 African Americans and Seminoles took over an abandoned British fort not far from the Georgia border. Troops led by Andrew Jackson attacked the fort. A cannonball fired by his soldiers landed in an ammunition dump. The entire fort burst into flames, killing more than 300 men, women, and children.

Ignoring Spain's rights, Jackson took more territory. Finally, to avoid war, the United States in 1819 bought Florida from Spain for $5 million. By 1843, the federal government had forced many Seminoles onto reservations west of the Mississippi. Among them were Black Seminoles, people of mixed Seminole and African American descent.

Taking Another Look

1. How did African Americans play an important role in battles waged by the United States during the War of 1812?

2. Why did some enslaved African Americans flee into Florida?

3. **Critical Thinking** Why might the Seminoles have sided with African Americans who fled slavery?

3 LOOKING WESTWARD

▼ How did African Americans open up new territory?

Writer Washington Irving called him "powerful in frame and fearless in spirit." This is how he described Edward Rose, one of the first **Mountain Men**. Mountain Men were rough-and-tumble fur trappers who helped open the lands beyond the Mississippi. Native Americans simply named Rose "Cut-Nose," for the huge slash that ran across his nose.

Most Mountain Men looked as rugged as the Rocky Mountains they explored. Many of them were more comfortable living with Native Americans than with the city folk back East.

Building the Fur Trade. In the early 1800s, most people who headed across the Mississippi were interested in furs, not settlement. Edward Rose, an African American, led his first group of fur traders west in 1806. He later became the guide and interpreter for three of the largest fur-trading companies in North America.

One of the best-known Mountain Men was **James P. Beckwourth,** who had been born into slavery. Beckwourth's career as a Mountain Man started in 1808, when he got into a fist fight and punched a white blacksmith in St. Louis, Missouri. The 19-year-old Beckwourth decided to run away rather than face a whipping—or worse.

For the next 50 years, Beckwourth swept across the continent hunting for furs, running a trading post, and serving as an army scout. On a trip through the Sierra Nevada, Beckwourth found a mountain pass that became one of the most important routes into California in the mid-1800s. It bears his name today.

Beckwourth spent most of his adult life with Native Americans. The Crow named him "Morning Star" and made him a chief. One story claims the Crow poisoned him to keep his spirit with them forever. In reality, Beckwourth died of food poisoning on a journey to one of the Crow villages he called home.

In the 1840s, the fur-trading days ended. Many of the Mountain Men now turned to guiding settlers westward.

Taking Another Look

1. How does James P. Beckwourth's name live on today?

2. **Critical Thinking** Why do you think the life of a Mountain Man appealed to some African Americans?

LOOKING AHEAD

While Beckwourth and others explored the lands beyond the Mississippi, cotton became "king" in the South. Slaveholders looked to the Louisiana Territory as a place where they could start new cotton plantations. Soon more African Americans would arrive in the lands west of the Mississippi, but most of them would come in chains or at the end of a whip.

FOCUS ON: NEW ORLEANS TRADITIONS

The French called them the *gens de couleur*. They were free "people of color"—part African and part Spanish or French. The *gens de couleur* came to form an important part of New Orleans' Creole population, the people whose ancestors were the original settlers of what is today Louisiana. The term *Creole* comes from the Spanish *criollo* meaning "native to the place."

The first Africans came to New Orleans in bondage. Children of these Africans who also had a Spanish or French parent were often set free, becoming the *gens de couleur*. When New Orleans became a center of the U.S. slave trade in the 1800s, the *gens de couleur* also experienced the burden of prejudice. As a result, they often were forced to live in separate communities or neighborhoods in New Orleans.

It was in these communities that many traditions associated with New Orleans took root and grew. These traditions include musical styles such as jazz and zydeco, foods such as gumbo (a hearty soup made of vegetables, and meat or fish), and the Creole dialect. It was the *gens de couleurs* who built many of the Spanish-style churches and lacy iron balconies that tourists have come to admire in the part of New Orleans known as the Old City.

CLOSE UP: Chapter 9

The Who, What, Where of History

1. **Who** is considered the founder of Chicago?
2. **Who** was Toussaint L'Ouverture?
3. **What** was the Louisiana Purchase?
4. **Who** was York?
5. **What** was the most famous battle of the War of 1812?
6. **Where** did the Seminoles live?
7. **What** does it mean to annex a territory or country?
8. **Who** were the Black Seminoles?
9. **Who** were the Mountain Men?

Making the Connection

1. What was the connection between the revolt in Haiti led by Toussaint L'Ouverture and the Louisiana Purchase?
2. What was the connection between the slave system of the South and the purchase of Florida?

Time Check

1. Which event happened *last:* the purchase of Florida, the Louisiana Purchase, the War of 1812?
2. When was the Battle of New Orleans fought?
3. Which of the following events happened *first:* the Lewis and Clark expedition, Toussaint L'Ouverture's revolt in Haiti, or the beginning of the Seminole wars?

What Would You Have Done?

1. Imagine that you are an enslaved African American. Major William Clark has asked you to join the expedition

he and Meriwether Lewis will lead into the Louisiana Territory. Clark has explained that the expedition will be dangerous and that you do not have to go. Explain your reasons for deciding to accept or reject Clark's invitation.

2. If you had been an enslaved African American in New Orleans in 1814, would you have volunteered to fight the British? Explain.

Thinking and Writing About History

1. Imagine that you are part of a committee designing a memorial to Jean Baptiste Point Du Sable. Write the words for a plaque explaining his role in Chicago's history.

2. Imagine you are an African American who has heard about James Beckwourth. Make a list of the pros and cons of becoming a Mountain Man. Think about what life might be like and what skills you might need.

3. Write a short, two-character play set in Florida in 1816 in which a fleeing enslaved African American asks a Seminole leader for shelter.

Building Skills: Distinguishing Fact From Opinion

As you study history, you will often be asked for your opinion about the people and events that you read about. At other times, you will be asked to give the facts about a person or an event. Opinions and facts are different, but they are connected.

A fact is a statement that can be checked or tested to see whether it is true. The statement "James P. Beck-wourth was an African American slave" is a fact. You can check it in reference books to see whether it's true or not.

An opinion is a person's attitude or thoughts about something. An opinion cannot be checked or tested to see whether it's true. It is what someone believes about a subject. The statement "James P. Beckwourth was the greatest of all the Mountain Men" is an opinion. Someone else might think that Edward Rose was by far the greatest of all Mountain Men.

Facts and opinions are related because we form opinions based on facts. A person might hold the opinion that Beckwourth was the greatest Mountain Man because of the following facts: he lived in the mountains for 50 years, he discovered an important pass through the Sierra Nevada, and he became a Crow chief. Some of the sentences below are facts and some state opinions. On a separate sheet of paper, write the numbers of the sentences that state opinions.

1. Jean Baptiste Point Du Sable was a ship captain who became a trader.

2. Jean Baptiste Point Du Sable had a more exciting life than any of the Mountain Men.

3. Toussaint L'Ouverture called himself the "Black Napoleon."

4. Sacajawea was the most valuable member of the Lewis and Clark expedition to map the Louisiana Territory.

5. The Battle of New Orleans was fought after the treaty ending the War of 1812 had been signed.

6. Andrew Jackson took over territory in Florida that legally belonged to Spain.

UNIT 4

Eli Whitney's cotton gin

FREE AND ENSLAVED
(1619–1860)

Mary Jane Patterson, first African American graduate of Oberlin College

Enslaved Africans seize the ship *Amistad*.

Death of Capt. Ferrer, the Captain of the Amistad, July, 18..

Don Jose Ruiz and Don Pedro Montez, of the Island of Cuba, having purchased fifty-three slaves at Havana, recently imported from Africa, on board the Amistad, Capt. Ferrer, in order to transport them to Principe, another port on the Island of Cuba. After being out from Havana four days, the African captives on board, in order to obtain their freedom, and return to Africa, armed themselves with cane knives, and rose Captain and crew of the vessel. Capt. Ferrer and the cook of the vessel were killed; two of the crew escaped; Ruiz and Montez were made

Unit 4 is the story of how Africans and their descendants lived in the years between 1619 and 1860, first in the 13 English colonies and later in the United States of America. Despite the attempts of slave holders to dehumanize them, Africans and their descendants forged a new culture from their experiences. Much of it was based on African traditions. As life under slavery worsened in the 1800s, enslaved African Americans fought back. Resistance and rebellions occurred more often. The pressure against slavery was mounting, but profits from slave labor blinded Southern leaders to abolition.

From Colonies to Nation. In Unit 2, you read about how Africans were brought to the Americas in chains and forced to work in the colonies. Unit 3 discussed the war for independence that the 13 English colonies waged against Great Britain and the role of African Americans in that war. Six years after the war ended, the Northwest Ordinance forbade slavery in the territories that the new United States had won from Great Britain. One by one, the Northern states abolished slavery. By 1800, however, slavery was solidly established in the Southern states.

As the nation expanded across the continent, three regions developed after 1800—the industrial Northeast, the agricultural Midwest, and the Cotton Kingdom in much of the South. These three areas developed different interests and different needs.

The United States in 1800. As the 1800s dawned, the United States was still a small nation. It had fewer than 5 million people. Most lived in the states along the Atlantic coast, from Maine to Georgia. Much of the land between the Appalachian Mountains and the Mississippi River was inhabited by Native Americans.

As U.S. settlers pushed west of the Appalachians, they asked for government protection against the Native Americans. In reality, they wanted the Native Americans' land. With government support, they took it. In the 1790s, there were enough settlers to petition for statehood for Kentucky and Tennessee. In 1803, Ohio became a state, and soon the rest of the Northwest Territory (see map, page 83) was rapidly settled.

Improved   Transportation. Four important improvements sped transportation from region to region and within regions during the first decades of the 1800s. One was the steamboat. Robert Fulton proved that a boat could travel upstream against a river's current by using a steam engine. In 1807, his boat the *Clermont* steamed up the Hudson River from New York to Albany. Soon, steamboats were carrying large cargoes of corn, wheat, and cotton quickly and cheaply along many rivers. Among the most important river routes were the Ohio and the Mississippi.

An African American Speaks

Seen in this perspective [of slavery], theirs [African Americans'] has been one of the great human experiences and one of the great triumphs of the human spirit in modern times, in fact, in the history of the world.

—Ralph Ellison,
author

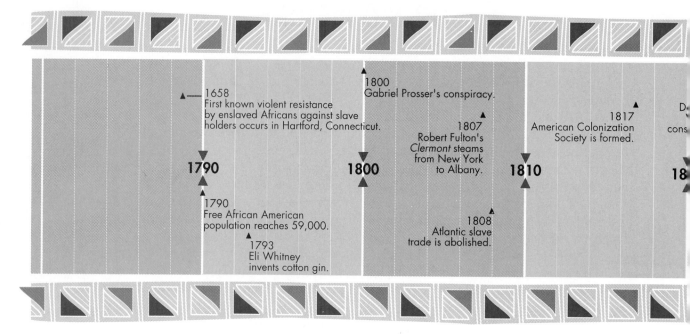

1658
First known violent resistance by enslaved Africans against slave holders occurs in Hartford, Connecticut.

1800
Gabriel Prosser's conspiracy.

1807
Robert Fulton's *Clermont* steams from New York to Albany.

1817
American Colonization Society is formed.

1790
Free African American population reaches 59,000.

1793
Eli Whitney invents cotton gin.

1808
Atlantic slave trade is abolished.

1790   **1800**   **1810**   **18**

Up to the early 1800s, most roads were dirt tracks. Traveling on them by wagon or carriage was slow, expensive, uncomfortable, and dangerous. In the early 1800s, however, new methods made it possible to build roads that would carry goods and people more quickly, cheaply, and with some comfort.

Like the steamboat, the new roads made it easier for settlers to move west and for products grown or made in one part of the country to be sold in another. One of the most important roads was the National Road across the Appalachians, connecting the Potomac and Ohio rivers.

The building of canals also sped the transportation of people and goods. The first important canal was built across New York State, linking the Hudson River at Albany with Lake Erie, 350 miles (560 kilometers) away. The canal was completed in 1825. By 1840, canals connected the Great Lakes with the Ohio and Mississippi rivers. It was now possible to travel by water from New York City through the Great Lakes to New Orleans.

The first U.S. railroad opened for business in 1830. By 1860, the Northeast and Midwest were covered by a network of railroads. Fewer railroads were built in the South because of the availability of water routes to ship people and goods.

Improved Communication. With improvements in transportation came improved communications. In 1800, a letter took a week to travel the 200 miles (320 kilometers) from New York to Washington, D.C. In 1860, a letter covered the same distance by train in a few hours.

Even faster communication was made possible by the invention of the telegraph by Samuel F. B. Morse in 1844. The telegraph used electricity to send messages over wires. Within 15 years, a network of telegraph lines covered the eastern half of the nation. In 1861, a telegraph line reached all the way to California.

The Growth of Factories in the Northeast. Before 1800, almost everything made in the United States was made

1825
Erie Canal opens.

1830
First U.S. railroad begins service.

1830
Free African American population reaches 319,000.

1840s
European immigrants begin to enter United States in large numbers.

1860
Free African American population reaches 488,000.

Nearly 75 percent of enslaved African Americans work in cotton fields.

1830

1840

1844
Telegraph is invented.

1850

1860

1829
David Walker publishes his *Appeal.*

1831
Nat Turner's rebellion.

by hand in small workshops. The first factory appeared in 1790 in Pawtucket, Rhode Island. By the 1820s, factories had become an important part of the nation's economy.

The first factories were spinning and weaving mills that used fibers such as cotton and wool to turn out finished cloth. The majority of factories were built in the Northeast, particularly in New England. There, a number of small villages like Lowell, Massachusetts, grew into industrial cities. Other factories, mainly making farm equipment, were established in the Midwest in the 1830s and 1840s.

The Arrival of European Immigrants. At first, the factories in New England employed girls and young women from nearby farms. By the 1840s, owners had cut wages, and working conditions in the mills had worsened. The women were replaced by immigrants from Europe, who came to settle in the United States and who were willing to work for less money and under poor conditions.

Most of these immigrants were farmers from Ireland, where a disease had destroyed the potato crop, their major source of food. In the terrible famine that followed, millions of Irish were forced either to leave or to starve. Most Irish immigrants settled in the factory cities of the Northeast.

Large numbers of German immigrants also came to the United States in the 1840s and 1850s. Most moved to the cities and farms of the Midwest. Few European immigrants moved to the South because there were few factories. Enslaved African Americans already provided most of the nonplantation labor needed in the South.

Cash Crops in the Midwest. Most of the early settlers in the Midwest were subsistence farmers. They grew only enough for their own needs. They bought few goods and sold few goods. But in the first decades of the 1800s, farmers began to plant cash crops, such as corn and wheat. The improvements in transportation made it possible for the farmers to move crops cheaply from the Midwest to the ports and cities of the Northeast.

Now that crops could be shipped easily and cheaply, a large market for them developed. The growing market, in turn, encouraged more settlers—farmers, shopkeepers, and doctors and the like—to move to the Midwest to farm the land and set up towns. Farms in the Midwest were generally family-run operations. Slavery, as you have read, had been forbidden by the Northwest Ordinance.

Cotton in the South. In much of the South, cotton was the cash crop. It became so profitable that most Southerners felt no need to invest in factories. They could always sell their raw cotton to the factories of the Northeast or to Great Britain. But cotton required large numbers of workers. In the South, that meant enslaved African Americans.

During the 1700s, most enslaved African Americans in the South had worked on plantations that raised tobacco, indigo, sugar, or rice. Beginning in 1793, however, several factors combined to turn cotton into the main crop and slavery into big business. In that year, Eli Whitney

How was the invention of the cotton gin, shown here, related to the claim, "cotton is king"?

invented the **cotton gin**. Until then, the seeds of the cotton plant had to be separated from the cotton fibers by hand. Because it was hard to do, a person could clean only a few pounds of cotton a day. With the cotton gin, one person could clean 50 times as much in a day. Within one year, Southern cotton production had increased 12 times. Within eight years, it had increased more than 250 times.

To produce such large crops, plantation owners devoted more land to growing cotton. They expanded to new land in Alabama, Mississippi, Louisiana, and Texas, where they grew cotton on thousands of acres. Soon Southerners were proclaiming, "Cotton is king."

The Internal Slave Trade. To raise so much cotton, huge numbers of laborers were needed. The nation officially ended the Atlantic slave trade in 1808. But by 1820, a booming trade in enslaved African Americans had developed within the nation. It was centered in the states of the Upper South: Maryland, Virginia, Kentucky, North Carolina, and Tennessee. In these states, tobacco production had worn out the soil, and fewer field hands were needed.

By the 1830s, these states were selling about 80,000 African Americans a year to the **Cotton Belt.** This was the band of cotton-growing states that stretched from Virginia to Texas (see map, page 117). With the Atlantic slave trade legally closed, slave traders in the Upper South packed African Americans aboard ships in voyages similar to those of the Middle Passage (see Chapter 4). They unloaded the enslaved African Americans in port cities, such as Charleston, South Carolina, and New Orleans, Louisiana, and marched them inland to plantations.

The cabins to the right of the huge mansion housed enslaved African Americans. Their labor allowed the planter's family to lead a rich and comfortable life.

Southern Slave Holders. When many people think of the South before the Civil War, they think of a huge white mansion and rows of slave cabins, such as in the picture above. In reality, few Southern whites owned such estates. But most whites in the South dreamed of joining the handful who did. The key to wealth, they believed, was holding enslaved African Americans. Even if a white family held only one African American in bondage, it considered itself socially better than the family that held none.

How many Southerners actually held enslaved African Americans? By 1860, some 8 million white people lived in the South. About 385,000 individuals held enslaved African Americans. But only 12 percent of these people held more than 20 enslaved African Americans and fewer than 3,000 held over a hundred. Still, this minority of planters dominated the economy, politics, and society of the Cotton Belt. No one felt their iron-fisted rule more heavily than the 2 million African Americans who labored under King Cotton.

Taking Another Look

1. How did transportation in the United States change after 1800?

2. **a.** What were the cash crops in the Midwest? **b.** in the South? **c.** Who worked the farms in each region?

3. What effects did changes in Southern agriculture have on enslaved African Americans?

4. **Critical Thinking** There were few factories in the South. How would this affect the development of the South in the long run?

Working in the cotton fields

The Tyranny of Slavery

(1619–1860)

THINKING ABOUT THE CHAPTER

**How did African Americans survive
the cruelty of slavery?**

CHAPTER 10

Several inches of snow lay on the ground that February. Harriet Jacobs silently thanked her grandmother, an African American who had been freed from bondage, for giving her a new pair of shoes. The old ones were so tight that they cut into her feet. But the slave holders, Dr. and Mrs. Flint, had little sympathy for the young teenager.

As Jacobs walked past Mrs. Flint, her new shoes squeaked. The sound annoyed her owner. "Take them off," Mrs. Flint ordered, "and if you put them on again, I'll throw them into the fire."

Jacobs knew that Mrs. Flint would whip her if she disobeyed, so she took off the shoes. When Mrs. Flint sent her on an errand, Jacobs walked barefoot through the snow and got sick. As she lay in bed, she wished for death rather than to spend the rest of her life with the Flints. As Jacobs later recalled, "What was my grief in waking up to find myself quite well."

Eventually, Jacobs escaped to the North and wrote the story of her life. Her story, published in 1861, shocked her readers. She told of enslaved African Americans working in the fields from dawn to dusk. She revealed how African American women were forced to have children fathered by white planters or by enslaved African Americans whom they did not love. She described children ripped from their mothers' arms to be sold. She recounted the brutal treatment any enslaved man or woman received who dared to say no to a white.

In this chapter, you will read about how Africans and their descendants were enslaved. You will also read how they developed defenses against the cruelties of slavery and managed to keep alive traditions that tied them to the African homeland.

1 THE EARLY YEARS OF SLAVERY
▼ What was life like for enslaved Africans from 1619 to the early 1800s?

> For you must both . . . bear in mind that you remain . . . your Master's Property, and therefore it will be justly expected, both by God and Man, that you behave and conduct yourselves as Obedient and faithful Servants toward your respective Masters & Mistresses.

These words form part of a marriage ceremony written by a white New England minister in the early 1700s. Some slave holders allowed enslaved Africans to marry, but they reserved the right to separate husbands from wives and sell either. Children, too, could be sold. This was one of the most brutal aspects of slavery, especially to the West African peoples who placed a high value on extended families. Yet, against all odds, enslaved people from all over West Africa drew together and forged a culture that made life more bearable.

The First Generations. The first generations of Africans to arrive in English America in the 1600s and 1700s came from many different West African cultures. Until about the mid-1700s, they spoke the many different **dialects**, or forms of language, of the regions of West Africa from which they came. When Africans from different places had to work together on the same farms or plantations, they often had difficulty communicating with one another at first. Only after two or three generations did English become the common language. Over time, some African words crept into English— tote, okra, mumbo jumbo, goober, yam, and gumbo, to list a few.

Ship captains and planters often gave Africans English names. Renaming Africans was an attempt to strip them of their identities as individuals. But most new arrivals continued to use their African names regardless of what owners called them. An ad in a Georgia newspaper reflected this fact:

> Run aways . . . TWO NEW NEGRO YOUNG FELLOWS; one of them . . . calls himself Golaga, the name given him here Abel; the other . . . calls himself Abbrom, the name given him here Bennet.

Many first-generation Africans gave their children African names. However, slave holders usually respelled the names to make them sound more familiar to English ears. For example, the African names Quashee, Cudjo, Abbe, and Cuffee became Squash, Joe, Abby, and Cuff.

1793	Eli Whitney invents cotton gin.
1808	Congress bans Atlantic slave trade.
1820s	Internal slave trade booms.
1845	Solomon Northup is kidnapped and sold into slavery.
1860	Nearly 75 percent of enslaved African Americans are working in cotton fields.

As Africans picked up English, they sometimes pretended, when it served their purposes, not to understand the English spoken by whites. They also developed pronunciations and sayings that had meaning only to them.

Daily Life. During much of the 1600s, enslaved Africans and most white colonists struggled to survive. Except for the very wealthy, colonists generally had little more than a few pieces of furniture, an iron pot or frying pan, and some animal skins or straw for floor covering. But as time passed, differences between the living conditions of Africans and Europeans widened. By the 1800s, most Europeans lived in board or brick houses, while enslaved Africans continued to live in shacks with very few conveniences.

Since slave holders bought Africans to earn profits, they tended to spend as little as possible on their upkeep. They clothed them in the cheapest material available—usually a coarse fabric known as Negro cloth. They fed them rice, corn, beans, salt pork, and molasses.

Africans turned some of these foods into dishes they had enjoyed in Africa. They pounded corn into meal and made hoe cakes or mush similar to African fufu or kenkey. Some dishes, such as spoon bread, a puddinglike dumpling, also made their way to the tables of slave holders.

Working Conditions. Most Africans came from farming villages and adapted quickly to farming in the Americas. But as enslaved workers, they faced grueling hours in the fields. A 1740 South Carolina law passed to "protect" Africans gives a glimpse of their working conditions.

> [I]f any owner of slaves . . . shall work or put such slave or slaves to labor more than fifteen hours in twenty-four hours . . . every such person shall forfeit [give up] a sum not exceeding twenty pounds nor under five pounds of current money.

Officials rarely collected such fines.

Owners of large plantations worked enslaved Africans in gangs. They did not leave enough hours in a day for the laborers to tend to their own garden plots and to spend time with their families. But Africans had ways to resist bad working conditions. They worked slowly, broke tools, or, in a few cases, set fire to farm buildings.

Defenses Against Slavery. To forget the pains of slavery, Africans often turned to activities that reminded them of their homeland. In the "slave quarters," the area that housed enslaved Africans, they sang West African songs. Craftsworkers made drums or fashioned three-string banjos similar to those used in West Africa. Africans also brought their dances to English America. The dances involved hand-clapping, singing, and moving to complicated rhythms.

Like West Africans' words and foods, their dances slipped into the culture of white colonists. In the mid-1700s, one English visitor was shocked at the sight of

During the limited hours when enslaved African Americans were not working, they created their own dances, songs, and other forms of recreation. Many were based on African traditions.

Southern colonists swaying to "Congo minuets" and dancing African-style "jigs."

Storytellers, similar to West African griots, told folktales that recalled their African homeland. These tales have since become part of the African American heritage. Some tales described the deeds of African ancestors or clever enslaved workers. Many tales involved weak, helpless animals who defeated larger, stronger animals. Especially popular were the Brer Rabbit stories, in which the clever rabbit outsmarted such enemies as Brer Fox.

Work Songs. Singing was a way to get through the long day. There were special songs for picking cotton, for doing the laundry, and for many other tasks. Most songs, however, expressed a deep longing for freedom. Said one song:

Rabbit in de briar patch,
Squirrel in de tree,
Wish I could go huntin',
But I ain't free.

Family Life. By far the strongest defense against the cruelties of slavery was the family. Enslaved Africans recognized marriages among themselves even when whites did not. According to tradition, a couple married by "jumping over the broomstick." It was bad luck to stub your toe on the broom, so most couples, said one African, tried to fly over the broomstick "like a cricket." Africans created a sense of closeness by calling one another "brother," "sister," "aunt," "uncle," and so on, even when they had no family relationship.

Religion. Some planters required enslaved Africans to attend church. Here white ministers pounded home one message—obedience. From these ministers, enslaved Africans learned about Christianity. But they mixed these teachings with their own spiritual beliefs taught by their own preachers.

The early generations of Africans in English America believed that their souls returned to Africa when they died. Some

115

Africans buried bodies with items needed for the journey—a bow and arrows, a small canoe and paddle, and some food. But by the mid-1700s many began to adopt the Christian idea of heaven.

Some enslaved Africans in the South even viewed death as a positive event. One African, known as Uncle Silas, asked a white preacher, "Us slaves gonna be free in heaven?" The preacher ignored the question, but Silas and most other enslaved Africans believed it was true.

Many slave holders searched the Bible for passages that they could use to convince Africans that slavery was God's will. But Africans had another view of the Bible stories. In their eyes, they were the Israelites (IZ-ree-uh-lyts), who suffered enslavement at the hands of Egyptian pharaohs. Christianity taught about a gentle Jesus who suffered persecution—and was set free—on the cross. Where they could, Africans gathered together in "invisible churches" to hold their own services. These were places away from the eyes of slave holders.

Taking Another Look

1. What African ways entered into the lives of white colonists?

2. How did Africans try to soften the cruelties of slavery?

3. **Critical Thinking** Why might hymns with titles like "We Are the People of God" have given enslaved Africans hope?

2 ▼ AFRICAN AMERICANS IN ▼ THE COTTON KINGDOM
▼ What was life like for enslaved African Americans after 1800?

An African American child named Stephen huddled with his family in the corner of a slave-trading yard. The planter who held them had just died, and his relatives wanted to sell off Stephen's family. As the slave trader approached, Stephen's mother clung to him and his two sisters, Mary and Jane. She begged the trader not to break up the family.

This drawing shows a slave auction in New Orleans in the 1850s. No other aspect of slavery was dreaded more by enslaved African Americans than the possibility of being sold and separated from their families.

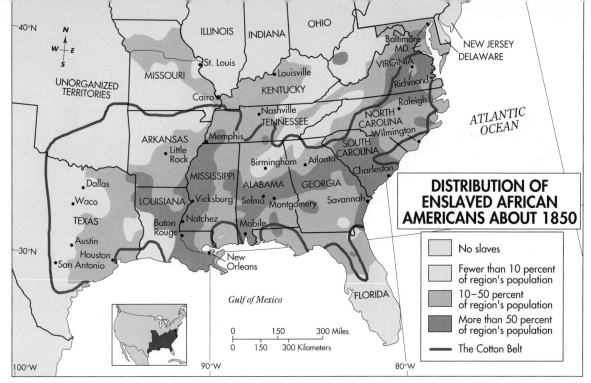

40°N

N
W—E
S

ILLINOIS   INDIANA   OHIO

Baltimore   NEW JERSEY
MD.   DELAWARE

St. Louis   VIRGINIA

MISSOURI   Louisville   Richmond

UNORGANIZED   Cairo   KENTUCKY   Raleigh

TERRITORIES   Nashville   NORTH   ATLANTIC
TENNESSEE   CAROLINA   OCEAN

ARKANSAS   Memphis   Wilmington

Little   SOUTH
Rock   CAROLINA

Birmingham   Atlanta   Charleston

MISSISSIPPI   ALABAMA   GEORGIA

Dallas

Waco   LOUISIANA   Vicksburg   Selma   Savannah
Montgomery

TEXAS   Baton   Natchez   Mobile
Rouge

Austin

Houston   New   30°N
San Antonio   Orleans

Gulf of Mexico   FLORIDA

0   150   300 Miles

0   150   300 Kilometers

100°W   90°W   80°W

DISTRIBUTION OF ENSLAVED AFRICAN AMERICANS ABOUT 1850

No slaves

Fewer than 10 percent of region's population

10–50 percent of region's population

More than 50 percent of region's population

The Cotton Belt

Which states had the highest percentage of enslaved African Americans? How many of these states were in the Cotton Belt? What does this tell you about the relation between slavery and cotton?

But the trader had other ideas. To him, the slave trade was a business. He bought enslaved African Americans from plantation owners who no longer needed them or who needed money more, and sold them at a profit to other slave holders. He did not care that in the process of buying and selling he broke up families.

Bullwhip in hand, the trader grabbed Mary and shoved her toward a well-dressed plantation owner. The trader's words stuck in Stephen's mind. "Here's jes' the girl you want for a nurse," said the trader.

Stephen never forgot the slave-trading yard. He vividly recalled the scene in his later life.

I was jes' a little chap, . . . but I can remember that place like it happened yesterday—husbands sold away from wives, and children taken away from mothers. A trader, them days, didn't think no more of selling a baby or little child away from its mother than a little calf away from a cow.

Breaking up families by selling members to distant planters was much more common after 1793 than before. With the invention of the cotton gin that year, cotton became the major crop of the South. As a result, cotton plantations needed the labor of more and more enslaved African Americans. Thus slavery became big business and the life of those who were enslaved, which had never been easy, became much harder.

How did it feel to be enslaved on the cotton plantations of the South? In the 1930s, interviewers put this question to former enslaved African Americans, many of whom were 75 to 100 years old. Some still bore deep scars on their backs from the lash of the whip. To be enslaved meant to have no rights at all. "Once they whipped my father," said elderly Roberta Mason, " 'cause he looked at a slave they killed and cried."

117

Enslaved African Americans who worked on the plantations of the Cotton Kingdom spent their whole working lives planting and picking the crop that brought the South its great wealth in the years before the Civil War. How many people benefited from the labor of African Americans in the pre-Civil War South?

Compare the figures for 1820 and 1860 in the graph below. In which year did the average enslaved African American produce more cotton? African American women and children as well as men worked in the cotton fields.

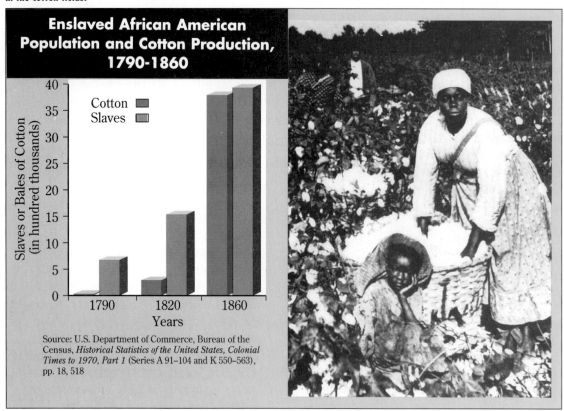

Enslaved African American Population and Cotton Production, 1790-1860

Cotton ▮
Slaves ▮

Slaves or Bales of Cotton (in hundred thousands)

Years: 1790, 1820, 1860

Source: U.S. Department of Commerce, Bureau of the Census, *Historical Statistics of the United States, Colonial Times to 1970, Part 1* (Series A 91–104 and K 550–563), pp. 18, 518

From Sunrise to Sunset. Slavery varied from state to state and from owner to owner. But the worst conditions existed on the "cotton factories" of the Deep South, the lands that extended west from Georgia through Alabama, Mississippi, Arkansas, and Louisiana to Texas. Nearly every enslaved African American dreaded the thought of being "sold down the river" (the Mississippi) to plantations in Louisiana or Texas. One free African American who was sold down the river was Solomon Northup.

Solomon Northup was a free African American from New York. In 1841, while he was visiting Washington, D.C., slave traders grabbed Northup and shipped him to a slave market in New Orleans. There, a cotton planter bought him and forced him to work in the cotton fields for 12 years. After Northup's freedom was secured by a family friend in 1853, he published the story of his years on a southern plantation. The book sold widely and helped whip up antislavery feeling throughout the North.

Northup wrote how, as a typical field hand on a cotton plantation, he worked from sunrise to sunset:

> The hands [workers] are required to be in the cotton field as soon as it is light in the morning, and with the exception of ten or fifteen minutes, which is given them at noon to swallow their allowance of cold bacon, they are not permitted to be a moment idle until it is too dark to see and when the moon is full they often times labor till the middle of the night.

On larger plantations, white **overseers** stood constant watch. Assisting them were **slave drivers,** often enslaved African Americans themselves, who snapped the whip at any worker who lagged behind the others. Although hated by other enslaved African Americans, slave drivers feared the anger of plantation owners even more. A slave driver could find himself sold away from his family or put to work in the fields. So, as Northup wrote, "The lash flew from morning to night."

Each evening weary field workers trudged home to unload cotton bags and do the planter's chores—chop wood, feed mules, and so on. Then they built fires in their cabins and threw potatoes or some ash cakes—patties of corn meal and water—onto the coals to cook. After they ate, they tumbled into bed. An hour before dawn, a horn or bell awoke them to another day of labor.

Skilled Workers. By 1860, nearly 75 percent of all enslaved African Americans worked in the cotton fields. A few, however, worked in the planter's mansion, called the "big house." They were skilled craftworkers, tailors, butlers, maids, cooks, and nurses for the owners' children. Some house servants and planters developed close personal ties. But even the kindest slave holders rarely freed African Americans until they were old and no longer able to work.

Some holders, both on plantations and in Southern towns and cities, trained African Americans in various skills such as blacksmithing. Then, they hired them out,

receiving pay for their work. Some slave holders gave the workers a part of what they earned, allowing African Americans in the South occasionally to buy their freedom and that of their families.

Enslaved African Americans worked at a variety of jobs, ranging from ship pilot to carpenter to factory worker. They preferred city work to working on a plantation because they had more freedom and the hope of earning money. Also, with greater freedom came the opportunity to escape, as you will read in Chapter 14.

Cultural Changes. The closing of the Atlantic slave trade in 1808 and the rise of the Cotton Kingdom brought about great changes among enslaved African Americans in the 1800s. Because slave holders could not buy any more Africans, they created an interregional trade in the enslaved. By now, most had been born in the United States. All or almost all spoke English.

Reliance on the Extended Family. As families were increasingly under the threat of being broken up by slave holders

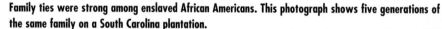
Family ties were strong among enslaved African Americans. This photograph shows five generations of the same family on a South Carolina plantation.

in the 1800s the extended family became especially important. Because slave holders could sell off one or both parents, children were thought of as belonging to the whole community. Everyone took part in the care of children. It was the extended family that saw children through their early years. Harriet Jacobs fondly recalled the role of her grandmother in raising her. She wrote:

> It has been painful to me . . . to recall the dreary years I passed in bondage. . . . Yet . . . with those gloomy recollections come tender memories of my good old grandmother, like light, fleecy clouds floating over a dark and troubled sea.

A slave holder who had sold a man's wife to a distant plantation might order the man to take another wife. To refuse such an order took courage, but many men did. Henry "Box" Brown (see page 159) gave this reason for his refusal to obey his owner: "Marriage was a sacred institution binding upon me."

Strengthened Religion. The religious beliefs African Americans had developed in the 1700s grew stronger in the 1800s. Now, almost all enslaved African Americans adopted Christianity, but in a form that included some of their African religious beliefs. They continued to worship at "invisible churches." Despite slave holders' efforts to track them down with savage "slave hounds," the believers refused to give up their meetings. They posted guards to listen for barking dogs. Sometimes, they strung vines through the trees to trip patrols. Other times, they deadened the voices of worshipers with "hush harbors"—shelters built out of tree branches.

As enslaved African Americans were sold throughout the South, religious songs known as **spirituals** spread from plantation to plantation. The spirituals expressed a defiance toward slavery and a belief in equality, even if only after death. The words of one spiritual led officials in Georgetown, South Carolina, to lock up anyone who sang them. The song declared:

> And it won't be long. And it won't be long,
> And it won't be long, Poor sinner suffer here.
> We'll soon be free
> De Lord will call us home.
> . . . .
> We'll fight for liberty
> When the Lord will call us home.

Taking Another Look

1. Describe in a paragraph the life of a field hand.

2. List two ways that lives of enslaved African Americans differed in the 1700s and 1800s.

3. **Critical Thinking** Why do you think slave holders tried to crush "invisible churches"?

LOOKING AHEAD

As the plantation economy of the South boomed with the growth of the Cotton Kingdom, the lives of enslaved African Americans grew harsher. Yet, they were able to build on and strengthen their sense of family and to develop ways of coping with slavery. The will to be free, however, burned brightly in slave quarters. The Cotton Kingdom contained within itself the seeds of its own destruction, and its end loomed on the horizon.

We rose and stood for a few moments in breathless silence . . . afraid that someone might have been about the cottage listening. . . . I took my wife by the hand, stepped softly to the door, raised the latch, drew it open, and peeped out. . . . Everything appeared to be as still as death.

At this moment, the two people held in bondage fled into the night—runaways, risking their lives for their freedom. Would they make it to freedom? To find out, anxious readers turned page after page of slave narratives. These were books published about the lives of enslaved African Americans.

These stories sold quickly in the North and in Great Britain, France, and Germany in the 1840s and 1850s. For example, the British edition of Frederick Douglass's slave narrative sold 4,500 copies in five months in 1845.

Slave narratives undermined foreign support for the South. Southern slave holders claimed that enslaved African Americans enjoyed better lives than factory workers in Europe, but the slave narratives proved otherwise. They described terrible living conditions, brutal whippings, back-breaking labor, and heartbreaking slave auctions. "This fugitive slave literature," said one American, "is destined to be a powerful lever [tool] to help end slavery."

CLOSE UP: Chapter 10

The Who, What, Where of History

1. **Who** was Harriet Jacobs?
2. **What** are dialects?
3. **What** were the slave quarters?
4. **Who** was Solomon Northup?
5. **Who** were the overseers?
6. **What** were "invisible churches"?
7. **Who** were the slave drivers?
8. **Where** was the Cotton Belt?
9. **What** are spirituals?

Making the Connection

1. What was the connection between the system of slavery and the development of a distinct form of the English language?
2. What was the connection between the closing of the Atlantic slave trade, the rise of the Cotton Kingdom, and the role enslaved African Americans attached to extended families?
3. What was the connection between the Biblical story of the Israelites and the feelings of enslaved African Americans about their condition?

Time Check

1. What event in 1793 changed life for people in bondage in the South?
2. When did Congress end the Atlantic slave trade?

What Would You Have Done?

1. Imagine you are an enslaved African American working on a plantation. What arguments would you use to

your owner to allow you to learn a skill such as blacksmithing?

2. Imagine that you are Solomon Northup. You have been captured by slave traders and have just learned that you have been sold to a Louisiana cotton planter. Write a brief passage describing your reaction on hearing where you are being sent.

Thinking and Writing About History

1. Write a paragraph that begins with this sentence: "Of all the cruelties and injustices of the slave system, I think the most brutal feature was _____."

2. Choose one of the following: write a folktale about a small, weak, but clever, animal who outsmarts a large, strong animal; or write a work song that describes a job or chore that you do.

3. Reread the question that Uncle Silas asked the white preacher (see page 116). Write a paragraph explaining why the white preacher might have wanted to ignore his question.

Building Skills: Stating the Main Idea in Your Own Words

Most of us have had a conversation like this more than once in our lives:

Mother: Did you read your history assignment?
You: I sure did and it was kind of interesting, too.
Mother: What was it about?
You: Slavery.
Mother: What about slavery?

You: Lots of things; I can't explain it really.
Mother: Maybe you had better go read it again.

Sound familiar? One way to be sure that you understand and remember the main ideas of what you've read is to put them into your own words.

Here is an example. Read the following paragraph from Chapter 10:

Since slave holders bought Africans to earn profits, they tended to spend as little as possible on their upkeep. They clothed them in the cheapest material available—usually a coarse fabric known as Negro cloth. They fed them rice, corn, beans, salt pork, and molasses.

1. On a separate sheet of paper, write the sentence that states the main idea of the paragraph. Next, try to rewrite the sentence in your own words.

2. Find the main idea of the following paragraph and write a sentence that states it in your own words.

To forget the pains of slavery, Africans often turned to activities that reminded them of their homeland. In the slave quarters, the name given to the area where Africans lived on the farms and plantations, they sang West African songs. Craftsworkers made drums or fashioned three-stringed banjos similar to those used in West Africa. Africans also brought their dances to English America. The dances involved hand-clapping, singing, and moving to complicated rhythms.

The title page from *Walker's Appeal*

Armed Resistance to Slavery

(1658–1860)

THINKING ABOUT THE CHAPTER

What actions did enslaved African Americans take to show their hatred of slavery?

"If I remain in this bloody land," said David Walker of North Carolina, "I will not live long." The son of a freed mother and an enslaved father, Walker knew the pain of slavery from his father's stories. In 1827, Walker left North Carolina for Boston, Massachusetts, where he set up a secondhand clothing store. Within a short time, Walker had taught himself to read and write. Soon he was writing fiery articles for the nation's first African American newspaper, *Freedom's Journal*.

In September 1829, Walker released a booklet entitled *Walker's Appeal, in Four Articles*. In it, Walker urged African Americans to rebel against slavery. "Kill or be

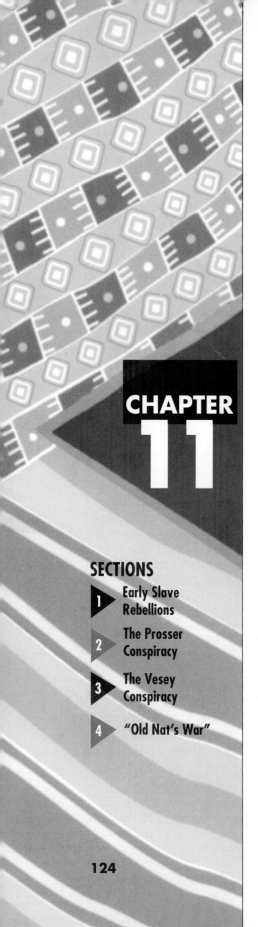

killed," wrote Walker. "Had you rather not be killed than to be a slave to a tyrant, who takes the life of your mother, wife, and dear little children?"

Walker also sent a message to white Americans. "While you keep us and our children in bondage," said Walker, "we cannot be your friends." Resisting change, he warned, might mean violence. "Remember, Americans, that we must and shall be free."

Walker's Appeal sent shock waves through the South. Slave holders recalled earlier slave rebellions and feared that African Americans might take Walker's words to heart. Some slave holders offered a reward for his capture—dead or alive. Several Southern state legislatures held special sessions to discuss Walker's words. A number of Southern mayors demanded that Boston officials arrest Walker and burn his books.

In 1830, Walker mysteriously disppeared. Some said he was murdered. Still the fear he had stirred lingererd in the South. State after state in the South outlawed the *Appeal* and tightened their restrictions on enslaved African Americans.

1 EARLY SLAVE REBELLIONS

▼ Where did slave rebellions take place in the 1600s and early 1700s?

On April 7, 1712, a group of 23 enslaved Africans met in an orchard near a slave holder's home in New York City. They crept up on the house and set it afire. When a group of white colonists tried to put out the blaze, the Africans fell upon them with axes, knives, and guns. In the fighting that followed, nine whites died, and six others were injured.

English soldiers stationed in New York City tracked down the Africans and arrested them. The incident terrorized the city's white population. New York had more enslaved Africans than any other colonial city except Charleston, South Carolina. The failed rebellion showed how difficult it was for enslaved people to win freedom.

Unrest in the 1600s and Early 1700s. The New York uprising was not the first rebellion by people held in bondage. In 1658, enslaved Africans and enslaved Native Americans joined to burn the homes of the families that held them. In 1663, white indentured servants and enslaved Africans in Gloucester County, Virginia, organized a plot, but were betrayed by a spy. In 1708, an enslaved

Why did so many early rebellions, like the "Great Negro Plot," take place in the North?

How did the building of a fort by enslaved Africans in Florida lead to the Stono Uprising?

Native American and an enslaved African killed the family that held them on Long Island, New York. In 1741, 34 people were killed for supposedly taking part in what New Yorkers called the "Great Negro Plot." A wave of fires and thefts had broken out and rumors placed the blame on the city's Africans.

In each case, colonial officials executed the rebels and passed tough slave codes. These laws limited the personal movements of those who were enslaved. Most slave codes prohibited them from meeting in groups of two or more. Codes set curfews and required enslaved people to carry passes when on business. Violations of these laws resulted in severe whippings. Some slave codes gave officials the right to brand offenders on the forehead with a hot iron. In this way, "troublemakers" could be easily spotted.

The Stono Uprising. Throughout the colonies, enslaved people resisted slavery by running away. Some enslaved Africans fled to live with Native Americans. Africans in South Carolina and Georgia escaped whenever they could to live in Spanish Florida.

In 1733, the Spanish king, eager to strike at his enemy Great Britain, offered **fugitives** from the colonies their freedom. In 1739, a group of African runaways built a fort near St. Augustine, Florida, to protect their families from slave catchers. The Spanish helped arm the Africans and their Native American allies, the Seminoles.

The thought of an armed African fort near the Florida border horrified Southern slave holders. News of the fort reached enslaved Africans in South Carolina through ships arriving in Charleston harbor. The number of escaping Africans increased.

On Sunday, September 9, 1739, a group of about 20 enslaved Africans gathered along the Stono River, 20 miles (32 kilometers) from Charleston. Led by an enslaved African named Jemmy, they looted an arsenal for weapons. Then, they headed for St. Augustine.

Along the way, they burned plantations and killed about 20 to 30 whites. One observer recalled the scene: "They called out liberty, marched on with colours displayed, and two drums beating." A colonial militia finally caught up with the rebels and killed or wounded many of them.

Once again, the authorities turned to slave codes, passing even tighter restrictions. The South Carolina assembly also ordered every white male in the colony to carry a gun or pair of horse pistols. Any enslaved African caught without a pass was to be shot on sight.

Taking Another Look

1. Where did slave rebellions occur in the 1600s and early 1700s?

2. How did slave holders respond to rebellions?

3. **Critical Thinking** Many of the slave codes passed after 1700 forbade the education of enslaved Africans. Why do you think that white colonists enacted such laws?

2 THE PROSSER CONSPIRACY

▼ What was Gabriel Prosser's daring rebellion plan?

Gabriel, a 24-year-old enslaved African American who was held by Thomas Henry Prosser of Henrico County, Virginia, was a skilled craftworker. Prosser hired him out to work at nearby plantations and towns. Little did he know that soon Gabriel's name would strike fear in the hearts of most white Southerners. In the spring and summer of 1800, Gabriel began making plans for a revolt.

A Vision of Freedom. Gabriel Prosser drew his inspiration for rebellion from the Bible. He compared the enslavement of African Americans to the enslavement of the Israelites by Egypt. Like the Moses of the Israelites, Prosser dreamed of leading his people to a promised land— an African American state carved out of the heart of Virginia.

Prosser believed that a successful rebellion was possible. In his visits to

SNAPSHOT OF THE TIMES

1658	Enslaved Africans and Native Americans burn owners' homes in Hartford, Connecticut.
1663	Plot by enslaved Africans in Gloucester County, Virginia, is discovered.
1708	Enslaved African and Native American kill slave holder's family on Long Island, New York.
1712	Enslaved Africans revolt in New York City.
1739	Stono Uprising occurs.
1741	"Great Negro Plot" occurs in New York City.
1800	Gabriel Prosser's conspiracy fails.
1822	Denmark Vesey's conspiracy is discovered.
1829	David Walker publishes his *Appeal*.
1831	Nat Turner leads rebellion.

nearby plantations and towns, he learned about the uprising in Haiti under Toussaint L'Ouverture (see page 99). Prosser also listened to white Virginians talk with pride about their own struggle for independence from Great Britain.

Spreading the Word. Prosser convinced his brother Martin and his wife Nanny to join him. At fish fries and barbecues, they asked other enslaved African Americans in Henrico County to rebel on the night of August 30. To prepare, Prosser advised his followers to whittle handmade swords or to steal axes, shovels, knives,

127

MAJOR AFRICAN AMERICAN RESISTANCE, 1712–1839

New York, 1712

Lexington, 1810

Gabriel Prosser's Conspiracy, 1800

Nat Turner's Rebellion, 1831

Stono Uprising, 1739
Denmark Vesey's Conspiracy, 1822

New Orleans, 1811

Amistad Rebellion, 1839

ATLANTIC OCEAN

How many instances of African resistance are shown on the map? What other ones does the text describe?

or anything else that they might use as weapons.

Prosser expected to arm his followers more fully with guns seized from local slave holders. He would then lead his forces in a lightning attack on Richmond, the capital of Virginia. There, enslaved African Americans would put all whites to death except Quakers, Methodists, and any French, groups thought to be friendly to African Americans.

A Failed Uprising. On the night of the raid, more than a thousand supporters gathered outside Richmond. Little did they know that two enslaved African Americans had informed on Prosser. As the rebels advanced, a great thunderstorm struck. It washed out roads and bridges and made it impossible for Prosser's army to march toward Richmond. Their fate was sealed when 600 troops, who had been called out by Governor James Monroe—the future

President of the United States—set out after the rebels.

Prosser tried to escape by sea but was captured. He was put on trial with some 35 other rebels. One of the defendants, perhaps even Prosser, made this moving speech at the trial:

> I have nothing more to offer than what General Washington would have had to offer, had he been taken by the British and put to trial by them. I have adventured my life in endeavoring to obtain the liberty of my countrymen, and am a willing sacrifice to their cause.

On October 7, 1800, Prosser was hanged. The fact that the Prosser plot had failed did not discourage African Americans. Within a year, more plots were reported elsewhere in Virginia and in North Carolina. In 1810, an uprising was put down in Lexington, Kentucky. A year later, a free African American named Charles Deslondes led hundreds of enslaved African Americans in an unsuccessful attack on New Orleans. Meanwhile, a much larger uprising was being talked about in South Carolina.

Taking Another Look

1. What was Prosser's goal?

2. What inspired Prosser to act?

3. **Critical Thinking** Why do you think the defendant at the Prosser trial compared himself to George Washington?

3 THE VESEY CONSPIRACY

▼ How did the Vesey conspiracy further prove African Americans' willingness to resist slavery?

In 1800, the same year that Gabriel Prosser died, an enslaved African American named Denmark Vesey won $1,500 in a lottery. He used $600 to buy his freedom and then opened a carpentry shop in Charleston, South Carolina.

Desire for Revolution. In his spare time, Vesey studied the Haitian and French revolutions. His hatred of slavery grew so intense that he vowed to lead enslaved African Americans in a rebellion to take over Charleston. If threatened with capture, Vesey planned to sail to the island of Haiti—homeland of his hero Toussaint L'Ouverture.

For years, Vesey cornered enslaved African Americans on the streets of Charleston to talk about rebellion. He held meetings in his home to try to persuade others to join him in an attack on Charleston.

In May 1822, one of his recruits, Peter Poyas, helped Vesey organize an elaborate plot. They scouted Charleston and set up seven points of attack that would give them control of most of the city's arsenals and the harbor.

Betrayal. Vesey thought he had guarded against betrayal. He and Poyas had been very careful. For example, only they knew the names of everyone involved in the plot. Still, before they could act, an enslaved African American close to Vesey and Poyas turned in their names and those of several other leaders to the authorities.

Officials arrested some 130 African Americans. Only one of them broke down and confessed. But this confession was enough to sentence Vesey, Poyas, and others to death.

In the end, some 45 of the rebels were executed. Others were sent to islands in the Caribbean. The South Carolina legislature rewarded the informer, Devany Prioleau, with a pension of $50 a year. The legislature also passed laws limiting the rights of free African Americans in the state. No African American, vowed white officials in Charleston, would ever again have the freedom of Denmark Vesey. When the abolitionist leader Frederick Douglass was recruiting African Americans to serve in the Union army during the Civil War, he urged them to "remember Denmark Vesey."

Taking Another Look

1. How were Prosser's and Vesey's plans similar?

2. How did the Vesey conspiracy affect the rights of free African Americans in South Carolina?

3. **Critical Thinking** After the Vesey conspiracy, the South Carolina legislature banned all criticism of slavery. How effective do you think this act might have been as a way of preventing slave uprisings? Explain.

4 "OLD NAT'S WAR"

▼ Why was it said that no Southerner before the Civil War could ever forget Nat Turner?

Nat Turner was an enslaved worker on a plantation in Southampton County, Virginia. People called him the Prophet. From an early age, he had seen visions and heard voices. Turner firmly believed he had a special mission in life. He waited for a message to guide him. In 1825, he felt,

Nat Turner had long dreamed of staging an uprising against slave holders but did not reveal his plans to other enslaved African Americans until he was ready to act. Why were white Southerners shocked by Turner's rebellion?

the message came. Turner later recalled the vision:

> White spirits and black spirits engaged in battle, and the sun was darkened—the thunder rolled in the Heavens, and blood flowed in streams—and I heard a voice saying, 'Such is your luck, such you are called to see, and let it come rough to smooth, you must surely bear it.'

The vision convinced Turner that the Lord wanted him to take revenge on the white planters who enslaved African Americans. He waited for a sign to tell him when to strike.

Judgment Day. The sign came in February 1831 when a total eclipse darkened the sun. Turner took a few people into his confidence about his goal. However, unlike Prosser and Vesey, he did not form an elaborate plan nor did he try to organize large numbers of African Americans.

After months of delay, Turner made his move on August 21, 1831. Along with eight other enslaved African Americans, he set out on a journey of death. The first stop was the home of Turner's owner, where they killed everyone. They then headed for other plantations, picking up about 50 supporters along the way. In all, they killed some 60 whites.

A hastily formed militia combed the countryside looking for Turner. But he escaped capture until the end of October. Meanwhile, as panic gripped whites in the South, dozens of innocent African Americans were seized and put to death. Turner later described his capture:

> I [hid] under a pile of fence rails in a field, where I concealed myself for six weeks. . . .[Two] Negroes having started to go hunting . . . discovered me. . . .On making myself known, they fled. . . . I immediately left my hiding place, and was pursued almost incessantly [endlessly] until I was taken a fortnight [two weeks] afterwards.

To celebrate Turner's capture, guns were fired all over Southampton County. On November 5, 1831, a judge ordered Turner "hung by the neck until you are dead! dead! dead!"

Reaction to Turner. Turner became a legend among enslaved African Americans in Southampton County, who passed on stories of "Old Nat's war." White planters saw him as a devil. Turner's rebellion confirmed fears raised by David Walker's *Appeal.* A number of Southern states strengthened the slave codes and enforced them with a new determination.

For any whites who still believed that enslaved African Americans generally were satisfied with their lives, the Turner rebellion was a shock. Such uprisings continued throughout the South up to and even during the Civil War.

After hiding for almost two months, Turner was captured and later executed.

Taking Another Look

1. How did Turner's rebellion differ from the Prosser and Vesey conspiracies?

2. What actions did the South take after Turner's rebellion?

3. **Critical Thinking** Although none of the slave revolts succeeded, why were they important?

LOOKING AHEAD

The economy of the South was based on slavery. When uprisings and revolts by African Americans in bondage quickened in the 1800s, few Southern whites realized that slavery was in danger of collapse. Instead, they tightened the slave codes and hoped the danger would pass. Meanwhile, free African Americans in the North and South gave the lie to the Southern view that slavery was the "natural" condition for African Americans.

◄ **FOCUS ON** ►
AMISTAD

Amistad is a Spanish word for "friendship." But the 49 men and 4 children who sailed aboard the *Amistad* saw nothing friendly about the ship. It carried them to bondage in one of the blazing sugar fields of Cuba.

One of the Africans was Cinque (SEEN-kay), a 25-year-old rice farmer from a well-to-do family of the Mende ethnic group. Cinque refused to submit without a fight. On July 1, 1839, he led the Mende in a successful takeover of the *Amistad*. He then directed slave traders to sail back to Africa. The traders obeyed by day, but at night they plotted a course toward North America. Two months later, the ship landed at the tip of Long Island. Here an American naval vessel seized the ship and guided it to Connecticut.

For the next 18 months, a legal battle raged over the fate of the rebels. The case went all the way to the U.S. Supreme Court, where former President John Quincy Adams defended the West Africans. James Covey, a Mende sailor aboard a British ship, served as an interpreter for Cinque. In a landmark ruling, the Court decided in favor of the West Africans. In 1841, the 35 captives who had survived the ordeal set foot back in Africa.

The Who, What, Where of History

1. **Who** was David Walker?
2. **What** was *Freedom's Journal?*
3. **What** were the slave codes?
4. **Where** did the "Great Negro Plot" take place?
5. **What** was the Stono Uprising?
6. **Who** was Gabriel Prosser?
7. **Where** did Charles Deslondes and his followers launch their unsuccessful attack?
8. **Who** was Denmark Vesey?
9. **Who** was Nat Turner?

Making the Connection

1. What was the connection between slave revolts and slave codes?
2. Explain the relationship between the king of Spain and the Stono Uprising.
3. What was the connection between Toussaint L'Ouverture and Prosser?

Time Check

1. Which of the following slave revolts or conspiracies happened *last:* the "Great Negro Plot," Turner's rebellion, Vesey's conspiracy?
2. When did the first known slave revolt in the colonies occur?
3. When did David Walker publish his *Appeal?*

What Would You Have Done?

1. If you had been the owner of a bookstore in Charleston in 1831, would

you have carried copies of Walker's *Appeal*? Explain your answer.

2. Imagine that you are a judge who must pass sentence on an enslaved African American who had planned an uprising similar to that of Gabriel Prosser. You strongly believe that slavery is a great evil. However, as a judge, you must uphold the law. What would you do?

3. Imagine that you are a Northern white who opposes slavery. Details of Nat Turner's unsuccessful revolt have just been published in the newspaper. Write a letter to the editor giving your reaction to the event.

Thinking and Writing About History

1. Write a review of Walker's *Appeal* for the newspaper *Freedom's Journal*. In your review, include information about David Walker himself, about the contents of the book, and give your opinion of the book.

2. Write an editorial for a Charleston newspaper giving the paper's reaction to the discovery of the Vesey conspiracy. In the editorial, offer suggestions for measures that might help prevent further conspiracy.

3. Imagine that you are an enslaved African American. Write a very short account of Nat Turner's rebellion that will be smuggled to other African Americans living in bondage throughout the South.

4. What impact do you think Prosser's, Vesey's, and Turner's rebellions had on enslaved African Americans? Write a brief paper explaining why you think such revolts would have

inspired or discouraged African Americans in the South.

Building Skills: Main Ideas in a Chapter Section

In previous chapters, you practiced finding the main idea of a paragraph and stating a main idea in your own words. You have also practiced using the titles and section headings of your textbook to keep track of main ideas. Now try putting these skills together by restating the main ideas from a chapter section in your own words.

Section 1 of Chapter 11 begins on page 125. On a separate sheet of paper, write the title of the section. Next write the question that follows the title. Then write one sentence that states the main idea. If you have trouble, see if you can turn the section-opening question into a sentence.

The sentence you have written probably does state the main idea of the section, but it may be a bit vague. Skim the section and review its content. Now rewrite the main idea sentence, making it stronger and more specific. You may add dates, or give an example.

For instance, suppose you wrote for the main idea: "A number of slave rebellions took place in the late 1600s and early 1700s." You could make that sentence much more specific by writing: "As early as 1658, Africans showed their resistance to slavery by rebellion and by running away."

Follow the same steps for sections 2, 3, and 4 of this chapter. Look at the section title and the question that follows it. Write a sentence that gives the main idea of the section. Then skim the section and rewrite your main idea, making it clearer or more specific.

Prosperous free African Americans in the North

Free African Americans in the North and South

(1700s–1860)

THINKING ABOUT THE CHAPTER

What challenges faced free African Americans in their struggle for success?

"It is well known that the color of one's skin does not prohibit [prevent] one from any place or station that he or she may be capable of occupying." So wrote Nancy Gardner Prince, an African American in the 1820s. But her words described Russia, not the United States.

Prince traveled to Russia with her husband, Nero, a former sailor who took a job as a personal servant to Czar Alexander I, the ruler of Russia. There, Prince opened a dressmaking business. She made elegant dresses for the empress of Russia and other noblewomen.

The cold Russian weather forced Prince to return home for health reasons. When she reached Boston, a stagecoach driver denied her a seat inside the carriage.

CHAPTER 12

"The weight of prejudice," mourned Prince, "has again oppressed me." This chapter tells the story of the obstacles free African Americans faced and how they overcame them.

1 NEITHER ENSLAVED NOR FREE

▼ What hardships did free African
▼ Americans face in their daily lives?

At the time Prince arrived in Boston, all African Americans in New England were legally free. Slavery existed only in the slave states of the South (see map, page 117). Even so, free African Americans everywhere experienced **discrimination.** This is unjust treatment based on a characteristic such as color or religion.

Source: U.S. Department of Commerce, Bureau of the Census, *Historical Statistics of the United States, Colonial Times to 1970, Part 1* (Series A 91–104), p. 14

Compare the rate at which the number of free and enslaved African Americans grew after 1800.

The Free African American Population. The nation's free African American population had steadily increased in the years following the American Revolution. In 1790, free African Americans totaled about 59,000. In 1830, the number had climbed to 319,000. By 1860, it had reached 488,000, or about 11 percent of the total African American population in the United States.

The banning of slavery in the North helped account for this increase, but the number of free African Americans in the South also grew. In 1860, for example, Maryland, a slave state, had more free African Americans than any other state. About half the African Americans there were free.

Routes to Freedom. In 1860, nearly half of all free African Americans lived in the South. Some had bought their freedom. Others were freed by the people who had held them. Many were the descendants of Africans who had won their freedom in the colonial period.

One African American in Mobile, Alabama, Pierre Chastang, was freed by grateful citizens. Whites in the city raised money to buy his freedom because of his service in the War of 1812 and his help during a yellow fever epidemic in 1819.

Thousands of African Americans became free simply by running away. As you will read in Chapter 14, many made their way to freedom in the North on the Underground Railroad.

Limits on Freedom. Fears that free African Americans would aid or organize a slave rebellion led Southern lawmakers to sharply limit the rights of free African Americans. Laws denied them the right to vote, to have a trial by jury, and to testify against whites. African American children

1790	Free African American population reaches 59,000.
1817	American Colonization Society is formed.
1830	Free African American population reaches 319,000.
1830s	Large numbers of European immigrants begin to enter United States.
1860	Free African American population reaches 488,000.

could not attend public schools. Yet, in some places, their parents were expected to pay school taxes.

Free African Americans were not even free to move about in the South. Laws required them to carry passes proving they were free. They were denied the right to reenter a state after they had left it. In some states, free African Americans were not allowed to gather together—even in church—without the presence of a white person.

Free African Americans in the North suffered discrimination, too. In 1840, only four Northern states—Maine, Massachusetts, New Hampshire, and Vermont—granted equal voting rights to African American men. In New York State, all white males over age 21 could vote, but African American men had to own $250 worth of property to vote. All Northern states except Massachusetts barred African Americans from serving on juries. California, Illinois, Indiana, Ohio, and Iowa prohibited them from testifying against whites. Some states did not permit African Americans to sign binding contracts. Often, they had to show a certificate of freedom to obtain work.

Separation of races also existed in the North. Although laws did not keep African Americans and whites apart, custom did. Many white churches in the North required African Americans to sit in separate pews. Public schools were closed to African American children. In many ways, African Americans in the North were neither free nor enslaved.

Earning a Living. Because of the severe limits on free African Americans in the South, it might seem that earning a living there would have been more difficult. But free African Americans in the South were no worse off than those in the North. In fact, in some Southern cities, they did better financially.

A constant labor shortage in the South allowed many free African Americans to build businesses as craftworkers. For example, in 1850, Charleston had among its free African American workers 122 carpenters, 87 tailors, and 30 shoemakers. The city also had more than half a dozen African American innkeepers. A number of free African Americans became wealthy.

THOMAS DAY,
CABINET MAKER,

RETURNS his thanks for the patronage he has received, and wishes to inform his friends and the public that he has on hand, and intends keeping, a handsome supply of

Mahogony, Walnut and Stained FURNITURE,

the most fashionable, and common **BED STEADS**, &c. which he would be glad to sell very low. All orders in his line, in Repairing, Varnishing, &c. will be thankfully received and punctuallo attended to.
Jan. 17.   38

Day, a free African American, was a master craftworker. See "The Artist's View" for a picture of his work.

Some free African Americans were able to own stores and shops where they served whites and African Americans.

In the North, most free African Americans did not do as well. Some worked as furniture makers, barbers, or tailors, or in other skilled crafts. Many were laborers or servants. But in addition to discrimination, African Americans faced competition from the immigrants who flooded the cities of the North beginning in the 1830s.

Many of the new arrivals were poor farmers from Ireland. They usually had fewer skills than free African Americans. However, because they were white, they gradually crowded African Americans out for jobs and housing. Wrote Frederick Douglass in 1853:

> White men are becoming house-servants, cooks and stewards on vessels—at hotels. They are becoming porters, stevedores [dock-workers], . . . brick-makers, . . . barbers, so that the blacks can scarcely find the means of subsistence [support].

Taking Another Look

1. How did laws limit the liberty of free African Americans in the mid-1800s?

2. How did immigration in the 1800s affect job opportunities for free African Americans in the North?

3. **Critical Thinking.** Would you rather have lived in the North or the South as a free African American in the 1800s? Explain your answer.

2 A FRAGILE FREEDOM
▼ How did some free African Americans succeed?

Despite the obstacles that free African Americans faced, there were success stories in both the North and the South. Godfrey Brown of Cincinnati bought the freedom of his family for $2,350, purchased 550 acres [223 hectares] of land, and set up a shoemaking business. Thomy Lafon of New Orleans built a real estate fortune worth $500,000. Aaron Ashworth of Jefferson County, Texas, owned some 2,470 head of cattle and 4,578 acres [1,854 hectares] of land. These are only three of the many free African Americans who became successful business people in the mid-1800s.

Developing Businesses. A number of free African Americans became the managers of restaurants, barbershops, hotels, and other businesses. A few became **entrepreneurs**—people who risk money to earn more money. James Forten, for example, invented a device for handling sails. He then built a sail-making factory in Philadelphia that employed more than 50 African American and white workers. Another successful entrepreneur was Paul Cuffe.

Paul Cuffe, who was born in 1759, went to sea at 16. After an adventurous life at sea, he decided to build his own fishing fleet. By 1806, Cuffe owned three ships, several smaller vessels, and a wharf and warehouse on Connecticut's Westport River. He hired African American crews to sail to Great Britain, the West Indies, Russia, and Africa. Cuffe believed that African Americans would be better off in Africa than in the United States, and he paid the costs of transporting a number of them in his ships.

Many African Americans who earned money in business helped finance the abolition movement that took shape in the 1800s. James Forten, for instance, contributed money to start *The Liberator*, a newspaper run by white **abolitionist** William Lloyd Garrison (see page 145). An abolitionist was a person who worked to end slavery.

Getting an Education.

Many free African Americans realized how important education was to success. In both the North and the South, they paid money out of their own pockets to educate themselves and their children.

Some teachers opened schools to educate African Americans. In 1833, townspeople burned down a Connecticut boarding school for girls when Quaker principal Prudence Crandall admitted African Americans. In spite of the dangers, teachers—African Americans and some whites—continued to set up schools, and African Americans continued to attend.

Free African Americans began attending colleges and universities, and several African American colleges were founded in the North (see map, page 247). Out of these schools came doctors, dentists, teachers, ministers, writers, and poets. They were in the forefront of the battle to abolish slavery.

In the years prior to the Civil War, free African Americans established some 32 newspapers, wrote hundreds of pamphlets and books, and delivered thousands of speeches and sermons. Their ranks included some of the great leaders of the abolition movement, such as Frederick Douglass and Frances Ellen Watkins Harper (see Chapter 13).

Mutual Aid.

As you have read, laws passed in the South during the 1800s prevented free African Americans from meeting together. But in Northern cities, free African Americans formed more than 45 mutual-aid societies to provide help to families in case of sickness or death. They established libraries and reading rooms, and offered lectures. Some of these societies later helped runaway enslaved African Americans resettle in the North.

Threats to Freedom.

As free African Americans became more vocal in their demands for equality, they faced harsh treatment in both North and South. In 1840, white mobs attacked free African American workers in Cincinnati. Frederick Douglass recalled Massachusetts train conductors beating him for sitting in all-white cars. There was also the constant threat of slave catchers waiting to pounce on free African Americans and sell them into slavery in the Deep South.

Migration and Colonization.

Some free African Americans supported migration to Canada. Most African Ameri-

COLORED SCHOOLS BROKEN UP, IN THE FREE STATES.

In places in the North, as this picture shows, some whites were as much opposed to the education of African American children as Southern whites were.

can leaders, however, opposed colonization, a plan to send African Americans back to Africa. In 1817, white Southerners, anxious to remove free African Americans, formed the American Colonization Society to set up a colony in Africa for them. President James Monroe helped negotiate the establishment of Liberia, on Africa's west coast, for this purpose. But few African Americans wanted to resettle in Liberia. The United States was their home.

As soon as the colonization society was founded, a meeting of some 3,000 in Philadelphia denounced these efforts to resettle free African Americans. A statement issued by the meeting mirrored the feelings of many free African Americans at the time.

> Resolved, That we never will separate ourselves voluntarily from the slave population of this country; they are our brethren by the ties of consanguinity [blood], of suffering, and of wrong.

Taking Another Look

1. How did free African Americans support education?

2. Why did most free African Americans oppose colonization in Africa?

3. **Critical Thinking** Imagine you are a free African American in the early 1800s with a good job. Why might you be concerned about African Americans who are still enslaved?

LOOKING AHEAD

Free African Americans in the 1800s lived in the shadow of slavery and the reality of racism. Yet they kept the dream of freedom alive for enslaved African Americans who could not speak for themselves. The presence of free African Americans was a visible reminder of what African Americans could—and did—achieve outside of slavery. When a reform movement took shape in the United States in the 1840s, free African Americans were more than ready to speak out against slavery.

Starting in the 1600s, African Americans went to sea. Working alongside white sailors, they tasted a freedom unknown to most African Americans onshore. Both Crispus Attucks and Denmark Vesey, two famous African American rebels, worked as sailors.

Because of the opportunities found at sea, free African Americans were far more likely to work as mariners, or seafarers, than their white counterparts. Between 1800 and 1820, free African Americans made up about 5 percent of the population in and around Philadelphia. But they accounted for about 22 percent of the city's maritime, or sea-related, workers.

Free African Americans found the greatest chance for profit in the dangerous New England whaling industry. By 1820, African Americans accounted for about one-third of all whalers in Nantucket, Rhode Island, the nation's largest whaling port.

In the period after the Civil War, discrimination against African American sailors increased. Jobs once given to African Americans went to the flood of white immigrants who arrived in the late 1800s. African American sailors still at sea lived in either segregated quarters, or in a few cases, on all-African American ships commanded by white officers. It took the Civil Rights Movement after World War II to restore the freedom of the seas to African Americans.

CLOSE UP: Chapter 12

The Who, What, Where of History

1. **Who** was James Forten?
2. **What** is discrimination?
3. **What** is an entrepreneur?
4. **Who** was Paul Cuffe?
5. **Who** were the abolitionists?
6. **Where** was a colony set up for free African Americans?

Making the Connection

1. What was the connection between immigration and the loss of jobs by free African Americans?
2. What was the connection between discrimination and the efforts to re-settle African Americans in Africa?

Time Check

1. When was the American Colonization Society formed?
2. The free African American population of the United States increased by how much from 1790 to 1860?

What Would You Have Done?

1. If you had been Nancy Gardner Prince, what would you have done after experiencing the incident of prejudice in Boston? Would you have stayed in the United States or would you have tried to make a home in another country? Explain the reasons for your choice.
2. Imagine you are an African American entrepreneur in the 1850s. You want to help other African Americans.

Explain what you would do to be of the greatest benefit to other African Americans.

3. Imagine that you are a free African American in the early 1800s. You have just met Paul Cuffe, who has explained his plan for settling African Americans in Africa. He asks if you would like to take part in the plan. How would you respond to his offer?

4. Imagine that you are a free African American cabinetmaker in the 1840s. If you were offered the chance to open a new shop in either Charleston, South Carolina, or New York City, which would you choose? Be sure to explain the reason for your selection.

Thinking and Writing About History

1. Write a short play in which Nancy Gardner Prince and her husband, Nero, describe the lives of African Americans to some Russian servants of the czar.

2. Make a poster to advertise a meeting of African Americans to protest the efforts of the American Colonization Society.

Building Skills: Stating an Implied Topic Sentence

Darrell was angry at his friend Yolanda. "You said that I wasn't smart," he said. Yolanda denied it. "I never said that you were not smart." "Yes, you did. You said that there were only four smart kids in school—Martin, Kahlil, Lisa, and Tamara. So you implied that I am not smart."

To *imply* something is to say it indirectly. When you look for the main ideas in your reading, you will find that sometimes writers do not clearly state the main idea in a sentence. Sometimes they imply the main idea.

Read the following paragraph from Chapter 12:

A number of free African Americans became the managers of restaurants, barbershops, hotels, and other businesses. A few became entrepreneurs— people who risk money to earn more money. James Forten, for example, invented a device for handling sails. He then built a sail-making factory in Philadelphia that employed more than 50 African American and white workers. Another successful entrepreneur was Paul Cuffe.

The main idea of this paragraph, although not stated in a sentence, is clear: Some African Americans became successful by working for others; others were entrepreneurs who started their own businesses.

Now read the following paragraph. Write what you think is its implied main idea on a separate sheet of paper.

Laws passed in the South during the 1800s prevented free African Americans from meeting together. But in Northern cities, free African Americans formed more than 45 mutual-aid societies to provide help to families in case of sickness or death. They established libraries and reading rooms, and offered lectures. Some of these societies later helped runaway enslaved African Americans resettle in the North.

UNIT 5

CHALLENGES TO SLAVERY
(1800–1860)

Scene from *Uncle Tom's Cabin*

$2,500 REWARD!

RANAWAY, from the Subscriber, residing in Mississippi county, Mo., on Monday the 5th inst., m,

Negro Man named GEORGE.

Said negro is five feet ten inches high, of dark complexion, he plays well on the Violin and several other instruments. He is a shrewd, smart fellow and of a very affable countenance, and is twenty-five years of age. If said negro is taken and confined in St. Louis Jail, or brought to this county so that I get him, the above reward of $1,000 will be promptly paid.

JOHN MEANS.
Also, from Radford E. Stanley,

A NEGRO MAN SLAVE, NAMED NOAH,

Full 6 feet high; black complexion; full eyes; free spoken and intelligent; will weigh about 180 pounds; 32 years old; had with him 2 or 3 suits of clothes, white hat, short blue blanket coat, a pair of saddle bags, a pocket compass, and supposed to have $350 or $400 with him.

ALSO---A NEGRO MAN NAMED HAMP,

Of dark copper color, big thick lips, about 6 feet high, weighs about 175 pounds, 36 years old, with a scar in the forehead from the kick of a horse; had a lump on one of his wrists and is left-handed. Had with him two suits of clothes, one casinet or cloth coat and grey pants.

Also, Negro Man Slave named BOB,

Copper color, high cheek bones, 5 feet 11 inches high, weighs about 150 pounds 22 years old, very white teeth and a space between the centre of the upper teeth Had a blue blanket sack coat with red striped linsey lining. Supposed to have two suits of clothes with him; is a little lame in one uncle.
$1,000 will be given for George—$600 for Noah—$450 for Hamp—$450 for Bob; if caught in a free State, or a reasonable compensation if caught in a Slave State, if delivered to the Subscribers in Miss. Co., Mo., or confined in Jail in St. Louis, so that we get them Refer to

**JOHN MEANS &
R. E. STANLEY.**

ST. LOUIS, August 23, 1852.
(PLEASE STICK UP.)

Reward poster

William Lloyd Garrison's newspaper

THE LIBERATOR.

Unit 5 describes the abolition movement and how it brought the nation closer to war. Abolitionists, both free African Americans and whites, worked to bring an end to slavery by publicizing its evils. Through their newspapers, books, and speaking tours, they worked to influence **public opinion**—the collective beliefs of the people—against slavery. This strategy was similar to what reformers concerned with other problems in U.S. society were doing.

The Spirit of Reform. The years from 1820 to 1860 brought great changes to the United States. The nation was expanding rapidly across the continent. Immigrants were arriving in ever-increasing numbers from Europe. New roads, railroads, and canals carried goods from new factories to market. The nation was alive with economic progress.

Some Americans, however, saw a gloomier side to these years. In drunkenness, illiteracy, and slavery, they saw the nation's weaknesses. In a spirit born of the belief that Americans could accomplish anything they chose to do, these people set out to reform the nation. They formed organizations to end drunkenness, create asylums for the mentally ill, change prisons, promote **women's rights** as equal citizens, and end slavery.

Reform Movements. The temperance movement was one of the earliest attempts to reform U.S. society. By the 1820s, the nation's consumption of liquor was at an all-time high. In 1826, a group opposed to heavy drinking formed the American Society for the Promotion of Temperance. The organization grew rapidly, with many religious leaders, doctors, and business people among its members. They feared the damage that alcoholism was doing to individuals' health, to the family, and to the nation's economy. In its first 15 years, the temperance movement persuaded many Americans to cut back on their drinking or to stop entirely.

The early successes of the temperance movement inspired other reformers. Teacher and writer Dorothea Dix worked to improve the care of the mentally ill. She visited prisons throughout the nation and reported that the mentally ill were imprisoned as criminals. Through her writings, she advocated the building of asylums to care for and treat the mentally ill.

Prisons became another target of reformers. They pushed for the building of new prisons where they hoped prisoners could reform their lives.

Reformers also brought change to the field of education. Up to this time, an elementary school education was available in most parts of the country, only to those who could pay for it. Now, reformers urged that schools be tax-supported and

---

An African American Speaks

Those who profess to favor freedom, and yet deprecate [disapprove of] agitation [stirring people up], are men who want crops without plowing up the ground, they want rain without thunder and lightning. They want the ocean without the awful roar of its many waters.

—Frederick Douglass,
Abolitionist Leader

143

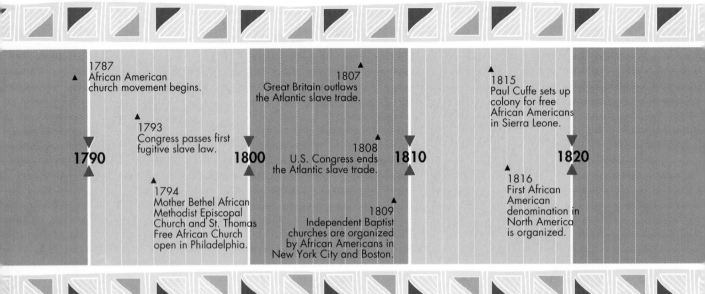

1787
African American church movement begins.

1793
Congress passes first fugitive slave law.

1790

1794
Mother Bethel African Methodist Episcopal Church and St. Thomas Free African Church open in Philadelphia.

1807
Great Britain outlaws the Atlantic slave trade.

1800

1808
U.S. Congress ends the Atlantic slave trade.

1809
Independent Baptist churches are organized by African Americans in New York City and Boston.

1815
Paul Cuffe sets up colony for free African Americans in Sierra Leone.

1810

1816
First African American denomination in North America is organized.

1820

open to all children. Guided by Horace Mann, Massachusetts became the model for other states' reforms. Mann revised the course of study, lengthened the school day, and raised teachers' salaries. Public high schools also appeared during this period.

At the time, these improvements in education, as in other areas of U.S. society, were of little benefit to African Americans. But in years to come, the principle of free public education for all would become central to their fight for justice (see Chapter 30).

Early Antislavery Efforts. Antislavery efforts drew their strength from the reforming spirit of the period. The first antislavery movements did not attack slavery directly. Instead, they hoped to encourage holders to free large numbers of enslaved African Americans.

Before the American Revolution, most white colonists did not object to the idea of holding enslaved African Americans. During the Revolution, however, some

people's attitudes began to change, in the South as well as in the North. The Northwest Ordinance of 1787 barred slavery from the territories north of the Ohio River. By the early 1800s, the Northern states had ended slavery. In 1808, the U.S. Congress forbade traders from bringing enslaved people into the country. The year before, Great Britain had abolished its Atlantic slave trade. To many people, slavery seemed a dying institution that would gradually fade away on its own.

Some early reformers did not believe that African Americans and white Americans could live peacefully together in the United States. They looked to Africa as a place to establish colonies for freed African Americans. In 1815, Paul Cuffe, the wealthy African American sea captain (see page 138), spent his own money in an unsuccessful attempt to set up a colony of African Americans in Sierra Leone, on the west coast of Africa. In the 1820s, the American Colonization Society, founded by Southerners as a way of removing free African Americans from the South, set up

1830s
African American churches in the North increase opposition to slavery.

1831
William Lloyd Garrison publishes first issue of *The Liberator.*

1830

1833
American Anti-Slavery Society and Female Anti-slavery Society of Philadelphia are founded.

1837
First women's national antislavery convention is held.

1840
American Anti-slavery Society splits into several groups.

1841
Frederick Douglass launches abolitionist speaking career.

1840

1843
Henry Highland Garnet calls for enslaved African Americans to revolt.

1830 – 1860
The Underground Railroad helps thousands escape from slavery.

1850
Congress passes Fugitive Slave Law as part of the Compromise of 1850.

Harriet Tubman begins leading African American slaves out of the South.

1850

1852
Uncle Tom's Cabin is published.

1848
Henry "Box" Brown escapes to the North.

First women's rights convention is held at Seneca Falls New York.

1860

the colony of Liberia in West Africa (see page 139).

The trouble with these plans was that hardly any free African Americans wanted to relocate to Africa. By 1830, only about 1,400 African Americans had settled in Liberia. Populated mostly by native Africans, Liberia survived to become one of the few independent African nations of the late 1800s.

William Lloyd Garrison and the Abolitionist Movement. How could slavery be ended? A young white man from Boston thought he had the answer. On January 1, 1831, William Lloyd Garrison published the first issue of a weekly newspaper called *The Liberator.* On the front page of the first issue, Garrison made a promise: "I will not equivocate [beat around the bush]—I will not excuse—I will not retreat a single inch— AND I WILL BE HEARD."

What Garrison wanted was simply stated—the immediate end to slavery. All enslaved African Americans should be set free at once. No money should be given to their "owners" to repay them for their lost property.

Garrison and those who agreed with him were called abolitionists. The main abolitionist organization was the American Anti-Slavery Society. Abolitionists were the most radical arm of the antislavery movement. Other antislavery supporters, called gradualists, opposed slavery and wanted to do away with it. However, they felt a slower, more orderly way should be found.

Most abolitionists were whites, with the greatest number in New England. But as the movement grew, free African Americans joined. In time, former enslaved African Americans, such as Frederick Douglass and Sojourner Truth, also became leading spokespersons.

At first, the abolitionists hoped to advance their cause by persuasion, as the temperance movement had done. By 1840, however, it was clear that something more was needed. At this point, the American Anti-Slavery Society divided

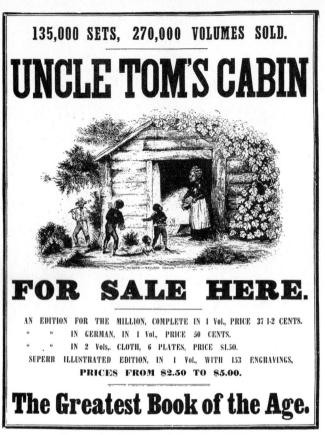

135,000 SETS, 270,000 VOLUMES SOLD.

UNCLE TOM'S CABIN

FOR SALE HERE.

AN EDITION FOR THE MILLION, COMPLETE IN 1 Vol., PRICE 37 1-2 CENTS.
"   "   IN GERMAN, IN 1 Vol., PRICE 50 CENTS.
"   .   "   IN 2 Vols,. CLOTH, 6 PLATES, PRICE $1.50.
SUPERB ILLUSTRATED EDITION, IN 1 Vol., WITH 153 ENGRAVINGS,
PRICES FROM $2.50 TO $5.00.

The Greatest Book of the Age.

Why was the publication of *Uncle Tom's Cabin* important to the abolitionists?

into several groups. The most radical, led by Garrison, urged that people have nothing to do with a government that allowed slavery. He argued, for example, that people should not vote, hold office, or use the courts.

Other people saw political action as the best way to attack slavery. They joined such antislavery parties as the **Free-Soil party**, and the **Liberty party**, which were able to affect the outcome of elections in some states. These parties tended to focus on preventing the spread of slavery to new territories, rather than on abolishing it entirely.

In 1852, the antislavery movement received a tremendous boost with the publication of *Uncle Tom's Cabin*, a novel by white author Harriet Beecher Stowe.

Stowe described the lives of an enslaved African American family, showing in particular the cruelty of the brutal overseer. The novel was a huge success. It was soon turned into a play that was performed around the country—except in the South. More than any other single factor, *Uncle Tom's Cabin* turned large numbers of Americans against slavery.

The Women's Movement. From the beginning, women were part of the abolitionist movement. They wrote booklets, got signatures on petitions, and organized conventions. More than 100 women's antislavery societies were formed. Yet women could not take part in the American Anti-Slavery Society and the other leading abolitionist organizations. Membership in these groups was limited to men. According to custom, women could not even speak before audiences that included men.

Two South Carolina women challenged these practices. Sarah and Angelina Grimké had been born into a wealthy slave-owning family but moved to the North and became abolitionists. In 1837, when Angelina was attacked for speaking before audiences of men and women, Sarah wrote a booklet defending her sister's action. She went on to address other inequalities in the treatment of women. Women, she argued, should not be treated differently from men.

In 1840, three Americans sent to England to represent the United States at an antislavery convention were turned away because they were women. As women, they had to sit in the spectators' gallery, where the wives of the male delegates also sat.

One of the rejected delegates, Lucretia Mott, met another American woman at the convention, Elizabeth Cady Stanton,

Women in the United States in the 1800s had few rights. For example, married women who worked outside the home had no control over the money they earned.

wife of a delegate. As the two women talked about the treatment of women in the United States, they decided that something had to be done. Eight years later, in 1848, Mott and Stanton organized the first women's rights convention at Seneca Falls, New York.

At that time, women had few legal rights. Although single women could own property, married women could not. When a woman married, her husband gained complete control of her property. If she worked, her wages belonged to her husband. She could not make a contract or sue for damages. In a divorce, the husband usually was given custody of any children. It was very difficult for women to attend college, and impossible for them to become doctors or lawyers.

The convention drew up the Seneca Falls Declaration. It spelled out the rights that women did not have but were entitled to. Soon other groups around the country were working for women's rights, and some laws began to change.

Because they also were active in the antislavery movement, most women's rights supporters felt that slavery was the issue that should be attended to first. However, the spirit of reform was not strong enough to end slavery. Instead, as abolitionists worked to end slavery, tensions increased, and the threat of war grew greater.

Taking Another Look

1. What problems of U.S. society did reformers attack in the first half of the 1800s?

2. How did the goal of the abolitionists and gradualists differ?

3. **Critical Thinking**   Besides the antislavery movement, how might the women's rights movement and educational reform have long-term importance for African Americans? Explain.

Pennsylvania Hall set afire by anti-abolitionists

Abolitionists

(1800–1860)

THINKING ABOUT THE CHAPTER

How did African Americans work to end slavery in the United States?

On December 4, 1833, 63 delegates from 11 states walked along Philadelphia's Walnut Street toward Adelphi Hall. Bystanders flung insults at them, and police stood guard to prevent violence. At the request of city officials, the delegates held all their meetings in daylight hours to avoid attacks under the cover of darkness.

Thus began the American Anti-Slavery Society. Its purpose was to coordinate the activities of white and African American abolitionists. For three days, the band of reformers pounded out a program of action. They called for the immediate abolition of slavery and the elevation of the condition of African Americans.

William Lloyd Garrison, the strong-minded, radical white abolitionist leader, dominated the convention. Most of the delegates were white, but African Americans such as James Forten, the Philadelphia businessman and abolitionist; James C. McCrummell, a Philadelphia dentist;

Robert Purvis, a Philadelphia merchant; and James G. Barbadoes, a Boston clothing-store owner, took active roles in the proceedings.

On December 5, a committee of delegates drew up a **Declaration of Sentiments**—a statement of liberation for the more than 2 million African Americans who were held in slavery. The convention unanimously approved it.

Within a short time, dozens of agents of the American Anti-Slavery Society were spreading the word of abolitionism in the North and South. They helped form local groups and raised money for the cause. With that money, antislavery pamphlets and periodicals poured off the presses. Antislavery sentiments, long simmering, were about to boil over.

1 NEW DIRECTIONS
▼ How did African Americans take part in the early abolition movement?

A handful of women—African American and white—attended the opening sessions of the American Anti-Slavery Society. No one asked them to speak. No one asked them to sign the Declaration of Sentiments. But women were ready to join the abolitionist movement as active members, and they started an antislavery society of their own.

On December 14, 1833, the Female Anti-Slavery Society of Philadelphia was born. Seven African Americans were among the 18 women who signed the society's constitution. They included Sarah Douglass, Quaker principal of a school for African Americans, and Harriett, Sarah, and Margarette Forten, the daughters of James Forten.

The women abolitionists of Philadelphia worked with women around the country to form a network of women's antislavery societies. In 1837, they held their first national convention in Boston. More than 100 women from ten states attended. The next year, they held a second convention in Philadelphia's Pennsylvania Hall.

The sight of African American and white women walking together inflamed racial hatred among some whites. Mobs threatened the women and hurled rocks through the windows of Pennsylvania Hall. When the mobs failed to break the women's courage, they set fire to the hall. The delegates responded with a public statement. It read in part:

> Resolved, That prejudice against color is the very spirit of slavery. . . . That it is, therefore, the duty of abolitionists to identify themselves with these oppressed Americans, by sitting with them in places of worship, by appearing with them in our streets, by . . . visting them at their homes and encouraging them to visit us, receiving them as we do our white fellow citizens.

Moving Toward Action. Some antislavery sentiment had existed in colonial times. Two African American New Englanders, Prince Hall and Abijah Prince, and a white New Englander, Samuel Sewall, were among the leading abolitionists in the colonies. The Quakers (see page 73) were the first religious group in the 13 colonies to speak out against slavery. Most early abolitionists were mild in

After 1830, however, with the growth of slavery in the Cotton Belt, abolitionism took on a new spirit. African American and white abolitionists loudly demanded

1833 American Anti-Slavery Society is formed.
Female Anti-Slavery Society of Philadelphia is founded.

1834 Homes of New York City African American abolitionists are burned.

1837 First women's national antislavery convention is held.

1841 Frederick Douglass launches abolitionist speaking career.

1843 Henry Highland Garnet calls for a slave revolt.

that Americans face the slavery question now—not some time in the future. David Walker ushered in the new era with his militant Appeal in 1829 (see page 124). William Lloyd Garrison followed close behind in 1831 with his fiery newspaper, the *Liberator*. The stage was set for a showdown between proslavery and antislavery forces.

Reactions to Abolitionism. The reactions of proslavery white Americans to abolitionists were sometimes violent. White abolitionists risked public insults, the loss of jobs, and worse. In 1836, in Cincinnati, Ohio, the office of James G. Birney's antislavery newspaper was attacked. The next year mobs in Alton, Illinois, killed Elijah P. Lovejoy, publisher of an antislavery newspaper. Mobs had already destroyed his press three times before. The commitment of white abolitionists like Lovejoy earned them high respect among African Americans.

African American abolitionists also faced great risks. In 1834, for example, mobs in New York City burned the homes of 20 of them to the ground. Everywhere,

African American abolitionists might be marked for arrest or even murder—the suspected fate of David Walker.

Differences Among Abolitionists. While all abolitionists agreed that slavery must be ended, they could not agree about how to achieve their goal. One especially important issue was whether the abolitionist movement should be as radical as leaders like Garrison wanted it to be. Although members of the American Anti-Slavery Society called for an immediate end to slavery, Garrison felt they were not militant enough. He attacked the U.S. government for allowing slavery and refused to vote. He criticized churches for not taking a clear stand. He linked abolitionism to the movement for women's rights. He wanted women to hold office in the American Anti-Slavery Society.

By the late 1830s, splits occurred in the abolitionist movement because of these and other differences. Moderates and those who believed in working through political action were at odds with Garrison. On the other hand, abolitionists who advocated the use of force rejected Garrison's emphasis on nonviolent change. Still another group decided to focus on winning certain rights for enslaved African Americans, rather than ending slavery itself.

In the 1840s, new patterns emerged in the abolitionist movement. Joining free African Americans were a group of new leaders—former enslaved African Americans with a powerful message to send to the world.

Taking Another Look

1. How did women contribute to the growth of abolitionism?

2. Why did splits develop within the abolitionist movement?

Why did a mob destroy Elijah P. Lovejoy's newspaper and murder him? Why do you think abolitionists were so hated?

3. **Critical Thinking** Why might many white women have been sympathetic to the struggle to end slavery?

2 NEW VOICES
▼ How did former enslaved African Americans help the cause of abolition?

In January 1842, a strikingly handsome speaker stepped before the annual meeting of the New England Anti-Slavery Society. He stood six feet tall with broad shoulders. In a steady voice, he declared:

I stand before the immense assembly this evening as a thief and a robber. I stole this head, these limbs, this body from my master, and ran off with them.

The speaker was a fugitive from slavery named Frederick Douglass.

Stories to Tell. The tales told by fugitives from slavery such as Douglass horrified audiences. The fugitive slave laws—laws requiring states to return runaways—threatened their very freedom. Yet they spoke. Henry Highland Garnet explained: "I was born in slavery and have escaped, to tell you, and others, what the monster [slavery] has done, and is still doing."

▶ **Henry Highland Garnet** fled slavery in Maryland while he was still a child and made his way to New York City. There he received an education at the African Free School. Garnet later graduated from New York's Oneida Institute and began his career as a minister. In 1843, he became the pastor of a mostly white Presbyterian church in Troy, New York. In 1881, the United States government appointed Garnet as its representative to Liberia, a nation that had been set up in West Africa in

1822 as a way to relocate African Americans to Africa. He died in the capital city of Monrovia a short time after his arrival.

In 1843, the 28-year-old Garnet delivered a fiery speech to a Buffalo, New York, audience. It matched the passion of Walker's *Appeal.* Addressing enslaved peoples everywhere, Garnet cried out:

> Brethren, arise, arise! Strike for your lives and liberties. Now is the day and the hour. Let every slave throughout the land do this and the days of slavery are numbered. Rather die freemen than live to be slaves.

Such strong words shocked and frightened some white audiences. But Garnet spoke for a group of African Americans impatient with the slow pace of change. Not all went as far as Garnet in calling for rebellion. But they wasted no words and spared no feelings in driving home the evils of slavery. "I intend to make full use of you," wrote Frederick Douglass to his former owner, "as a weapon to assail [attack] the system of slavery."

The Orator From Slave Row. When Douglass spoke, people listened. He made them feel the sting of the overseer's whip, the hunger for enough food to eat, and the grief of a mother seeing her child sold away.

Why would the Boston police and anti-abolitionists try to stop Frederick Douglass from speaking?

Frederick Douglass was born Frederick Augustus Washington Bailey, an enslaved African on a Maryland plantation. When refused an education, he tricked white playmates into teaching him the alphabet. Later, he was sold to a slave holder in Baltimore, whose wife helped him with his reading and writing. By age 17, Douglass proved so troublesome that the slave holder sent him to a slave-breaker named Edward Covey. There, recalled Douglass, "I reached the point at which I was not afraid to die." At that moment, he wrestled Covey to the ground. Shame-faced, Covey kept the incident to himself.

At age 21, Douglass was working in a shipyard. He disguised himself as a sailor and ran away to New Bedford, Massachusetts. There, to escape capture, he changed his last name from Bailey to Douglass. In 1841, he began to lecture to audiences about the evils of slavery.

Douglass's fame as a speaker grew. He traveled abroad to speak to huge antislavery audiences in London and the West Indies. He called for justice for all oppressed peoples regardless of their race, nationality, or sex. In 1846, he told a London audience: "You may rely upon me as one who will never desert the cause of the poor, no matter whether black or white."

Women Speakers. After the late 1830s, former slave women began speaking out, too. Perhaps the most effective woman abolitionist was Sojourner Truth.

Sojourner Truth was born Isabella Baumfree in New York State about 1797. Freed by a New York law in 1827, she became deeply religious and changed her name to Sojourner Truth. She traveled to abolitionist meetings throughout the North and Midwest. Although she could neither read nor write, she became one of the most effective women abolitionists. After the Civil War, she became a champion of women's rights.

Other women joined Truth in speaking out. They included Mary Ann Shadd, Mary Bibb, and Sarah Parker Remond, to name a few. They joined with Frederick Douglass, Henry Highland Garnet, and hundreds of others in seeking to bring a swift end to slavery.

Taking Another Look

1. What were two purposes for the founding of the Female Anti-Slavery Society of Philadelphia?

2. List four of the great African American abolitionists of the mid-1800s.

3. How did Douglass and Truth broaden the struggle beyond slavery?

4. **Critical Thinking** Douglass once remarked "justice to the Negro is safety to the nation." Explain what you think he may have meant by this comment.

153

THE NORTH STAR.

FREDERICK DOUGLASS, Editor.   RIGHT IS OF NO SEX—TRUTH IS OF NO COLOR—GOD IS THE FATHER OF US ALL, AND ALL WE ARE BRETHREN   WILLIAM C. NELL, Publisher,
                                                                                                                                    JOHN DICK, Printer.

VOL. I. NO. 1.   ROCHESTER, N. Y. FRIDAY, DECEMBER 3, 1847.   WHOLE

Frederick Douglass published the first issue of his newspaper in 1847.

3 TAKING ACTION

What were some other tactics African Americans used to oppose slavery besides public speaking?

Born free in Baltimore, Maryland, Frances Ellen Watkins faced a difficult life. Orphaned at an early age, she was raised by an aunt and uncle. They sent her to a school for free African Americans so that she could support herself. Beginning at 13, Watkins took jobs as a servant, a seamstress, and a teacher. But her first love was writing.

In the 1840s and 1850s, Watkins turned her pen to the antislavery cause. She wrote under the name F. E. W. Harper (Harper was her married name). By the late 1850s, she was one of the most popular African American poets in the United States. Her verses did much to advance abolitionism. "Bury Me in a Free Land" demanded the title of one poem.

> I could not rest if I heard the tread
> Of a coffle-gang . . .
> And the mother's shriek of wild despair
> Rise like a curse on the trembling air.

The Power of the Pen. Other African Americans also battled slavery with their pens. William Wells Brown wrote African American histories and dozens of antislavery pamphlets. Former enslaved African Americans, such as Frederick Douglass, published their stories in best-selling narratives. Harriet Beecher Stowe,

LADIES' DEPARTMENT.

"Am I not a Woman and a Sister?"

White Lady, happy, proud and free,
Lend awhile thine ear to me ;
Let the Negro Mother's wail
Turn thy pale cheek still more pale.
Can the Negro Mother joy
Over this her captive boy,
Which in bondage and in tears,
For a life of wo she rears ?
Though she bears a Mother's name,
A Mother's rights she may not claim ;
For the white man's will can part,
Her darling from her bursting heart.

From the Genius of Universal Emancipation.
LETTERS ON SLAVERY.—No. III:

William Lloyd Garrison's paper, *The Liberator,* tried to attract women to the abolitionist cause.

the author of *Uncle Tom's Cabin*, benefited from the narratives. She had an audience that was more than ready for *Uncle Tom's Cabin.*

In the North, African American journalists built upon the tradition started by

154

The cover of an abolitionist song sheet shows Frederick Douglass escaping from slavery.

Freedom's Journal (see page 124). In the mid-1800s, antislavery newspapers were being published in 17 African American communities in the North. One of the most famous was *The North Star,* published by Frederick Douglass. Even though most journals failed for lack of funds, while they published, they drove home two themes—equality and freedom for African Americans.

Committees and Raising Money. Following a long tradition of self-help, African American mutual-aid societies formed committees and raised funds to promote antislavery causes. Some organizations sponsored lectures by famous abolitionists. A few groups used the profits to buy freedom for the family members of African Americans who had escaped slavery.

The self-help societies also set up legal committees to defend runaways from being taken under the fugitive slave laws. John Mercer Langston, a lawyer who had been born into slavery, took the struggle further. He argued that African Americans should be given the right to vote.

Legal aid committees and lawyers such as Langston turned the antislavery cause from a moral battle into a political battle. They said that slavery was not only evil, it was contrary to democracy. They demanded more than abolition. They also demanded that African Americans be equal citizens under the law.

Taking Another Look

1. What were some of the ways that African Americans fought slavery?

2. What political demands did African American abolitionists begin to make in the mid-1800s?

3. **Critical Thinking** It has been said that the pen is mightier than the sword. Do you think that abolitionists would have achieved more through armed rebellions than they did through antislavery writings? Why or why not?

LOOKING AHEAD

From the 1830s on, African American and white abolitionists bombarded the nation with meetings, demonstrations, speeches, and newspapers calling for an end to slavery. Meanwhile, the most direct attack on slavery came through committees set up to help enslaved African Americans escape and guide them safely to the North. A Mississippi governor claimed that between 1810 and 1850 the South lost some 100,000 slaves, valued at more than $30 million.

CLOSE UP: Chapter 13

I have ploughed and planted and gathered into barns, and no man could head [do better than] me! And ain't I a woman? . . . I have borne thirteen children, and seen them most all sold off to slavery. . . . And ain't I a woman?

Sojourner Truth spoke these words at a women's rights convention in 1851. As a former enslaved African American, Sojourner Truth saw the connection between slavery and the lack of rights for women. She joined others—African Americans and whites, women and men—in demanding full citizenship and equality for all Americans.

In 1863, a petition to enact what became the 13th Amendment ending slavery was started by the Women's Loyal National League and supported by other abolitionists. But after the Civil War, a split developed within the movement. Feminists felt strongly that women's rights should be included in the 14th and 15th amendments. Others feared that this issue might endanger the passage of these amendments.

About the 14th Amendment, Frederick Douglass counseled: "This hour belongs to the negro." To this, Elizabeth Cady Stanton hotly replied: "Do you believe the African race is composed entirely of males?" The debate over women's suffrage continued until 1920 and passage of the 19th Amendment.

The Who, What, Where of History

1. **Who** was Sarah Douglass?
2. **Who** was William Lloyd Garrison?
3. **What** was *Uncle Tom's Cabin*?
4. **What** was the Declaration of Sentiments?
5. **What** does the term *militant* mean?
6. **Who** was Frederick Douglass?
7. **Who** was Sojourner Truth?

Making the Connection

What was the link between the women's rights movement and the antislavery movement?

Time Check

1. In what year was the American Anti-Slavery Society formed?
2. When did the first women's national antislavery convention take place?

What Would You Have Done?

1. Suppose that you were a middle-class American living in a northern city between 1820 and 1860. Which reform movement would you have worked for? Explain.
2. Would you have supported William Lloyd Garrison in his call for nonviolent change or would you have agreed with his critics? Explain the reasons for your decisions.

Thinking and Writing About History

1. Write your own *Declaration of Sentiments* giving reasons for freeing enslaved African Americans.

2. Imagine that you were in the audience of the New England Anti-Slavery Society when Frederick Douglass spoke in 1842. Write a letter to a good friend or to a relative describing Douglass, his speech, and the effect his words had on you.

3. Imagine that you are an abolitionist in 1835. An important merchant in your town objects to the idea of founding an antislavery organization. He uses the following argument:

[W]e are not such fools as not to know that slavery is a great evil, a great wrong. But it was consented to by the founders of our Republic. It was provided for in the Constitution of our Union. A great portion of the property of the Southerners is invested [in it]; and the business of the North, as well as the South has become adjusted to it. . . . We cannot afford to let you and your associates succeed in your endeavor to overthrow slavery. It is not a matter of principle with us. It is a matter of business necessity.

Write a response to his argument.

Building Skills: Recognizing a Generalization

People who study and write about history are in some ways our official memory. It is their job to help us experience and understand events of the past. However, we don't want them to present us with a book containing every newspaper, every lecture, every debate from a time period—we want a shortened version.

As historians (and other writers) make their decisions about what to put in a book and what to leave out, they *generalize* about the events or trends of the past. A generalization is a broad conclusion that is based on many facts that are related to one another.

Here is an example of a generalization that could be made after reading Unit 4's "The Big Picture": "The nation was alive with progress." The sentences below are examples of some of the facts that support this generalization.

The nation was rapidly expanding its boundaries across the continent. Immigrants were arriving in ever increasing numbers from Europe. New roads, railroads, and canals carried goods from new factories to market.

It is not always easy to recognize a generalization. You should look for *broad* (as opposed to specific) and *summarizing* sentences (as opposed to examples).

On a separate sheet of paper, write the numbers of the sentences below that are generalizations.

1. The homes of New York City African American abolitionists were burned in 1834.

2. William Lloyd Garrison was strong-minded and courageous.

3. Reformers were strong-minded and courageous people.

4. In the 1800s, women in the United States had few of the rights of men.

5. Sojourner Truth worked against slavery and for women's rights.

Harriet Tubman (left) with some of the people she helped

Escaping from Slavery

(1800–1860)

THINKING ABOUT THE CHAPTER
How did enslaved African Americans flee the South?

In 1846, two enslaved African Americans in Macon, Georgia, won permission to marry. The couple—Ellen and William Craft—were skilled workers. Ellen was hired out as a seamstress. The slave holder who held William hired him out as a cabinetmaker. Neither slave holder treated the two badly. But Ellen feared having a child who might be sold away from them, so she plotted a way for the couple to escape.

Ellen was the daughter of a white planter and an enslaved African American mother. Because she was light-skinned, she proposed dressing up as William's male owner and leading them out of the South. Because William was allowed to earn money as a waiter at a local hotel, he had some savings. Ellen persuaded William to use some of the money to buy men's clothes for her to wear. They would still have enough money to pay for their trip to the North.

In December 1848, they were ready. Ellen, who could neither read nor write, put her right arm in a sling so that

CHAPTER 14

she would not be expected to sign her name. She bandaged her jaw so that she could not speak and give herself away. Looking at her, no one could doubt that she was an invalid planter headed north for medical treatment accompanied by a loyal servant.

Ellen acted every inch a planter, walking with a manly swagger. The couple booked first-class passage on boats and trains and stayed at the best hotels. In January 1849, they arrived in Philadelphia. Here, the Crafts met abolitionist William Wells Brown, who guided them to Boston and safety.

From the earliest days of slavery, thousands of African Americans escaped to freedom, by one means or another. Some traveled unaided like the Crafts, but from the 1830s to the 1860s, many more traveled by Underground Railroad.

1 PATH TO FREEDOM

▼ What were the risks for those who ran or used the Underground Railroad?

In 1848, an enslaved African American in Richmond, Virginia, named Henry Brown stepped into a specially made box and had a friend nail it shut. The friend then shipped the box to the office of an antislavery committee in Philadelphia.

Twenty-six hours later, the wooden box arrived at the committee's office. Four abolitionists pried off the lid. One of them, the African American William Still, long remembered Brown's words. Still later wrote: "Rising up in his box, he reached out his hand, saying, 'How do you do, gentlemen?'"

After his spectacular escape, Brown became famous as Henry "Box" Brown. He joined others who had escaped slavery, including Ellen and William Craft, on lecture tours. Their appearances helped abolitionists raise money to bring other African Americans to freedom.

Look for the "Drinking Gourd." Some enslaved African Americans fled the South to avoid the auction block. Others wanted to find a loved one or to escape

What did Henry "Box" Brown's escape from slavery show about African Americans' desire for freedom?

1793 Congress passes a fugitive slave law.

1830-1860s The Underground Railroad helps thousands of African Americans escape to freedom.

1848 Henry "Box" Brown escapes to the North.

1849 Ellen and William Craft escape to the North.

1850 Congress passes Fugitive Slave Law as part of the Compromise of 1850.

Harriet Tubman begins leading enslaved African Americans out of the South.

the whip of a cruel overseer. Most, however, slipped away just to find freedom.

Planters tried to keep enslaved African Americans ignorant of geography, but most knew the magic word *North*. To head north, they searched the evening sky for the "Drinking Gourd," or Big Dipper. In this way, they found the North Star—their guide to the North. On starless nights, they felt for moss on the north side of trees.

Slave holders often used packs of dogs to hunt down runaways. If the runaways refused to halt, their pursuers might shoot them. Some enslaved African Americans chose death over the brutal punishment that awaited them if they were caught.

Runaways knew the dangers that they faced. They had seen fugitives crippled so that they could not flee again. Still, many African Americans fled slavery. "Many of them had no idea where they were going," recalled runaway Edward Lycurgas. "But one and all, they had a good strong notion [desire] to see what it was like to own your own body."

The Underground Railroad. The obstacles faced by African Americans who wished to escape aroused sympathy among some whites. Northern Quakers were the first to shelter runaways. Others joined the Quakers when Southern slave owners convinced Congress to pass a federal fugitive slave law in 1793.

Early in the 1800s, African American and white abolitionists set up an informal network to protect runaways from capture. By the early 1830s, this network had grown into the **Underground Railroad**, a system aimed at helping enslaved African Americans flee the South. The "tracks" of this railroad consisted of country roads, backwoods trails, and rivers. Its "stations" were homes where runaways could receive food and shelter. Its "conductors" were abolitionists, both African American and white, who defied federal and state laws to guide the fugitives to freedom in the North and Canada.

Antislavery societies sent agents into the South to tell enslaved African Americans about the Underground Railroad. The agents posed as peddlers, map makers, and census takers. Some agents were daring runaways on "return runs" to the South to help others. From 1830 to 1860, perhaps 2,500 fugitives a year took the Railroad to freedom.

A Dangerous Operation. From their first stop on the Underground Railroad to their last, slaves were in constant risk of capture. They traveled at night and slept during the day. They waded through streams to cover their tracks. Mothers muffled the cries of their children.

Agents and conductors faced danger, too. White abolitionists who were caught helping runaways escape the South risked being sent to prison. Calvin Fairbanks of Kentucky served over 17 years in jail for

THE UNDERGROUND RAILROAD, 1840–1860

CANADA

Montreal · VT. · ME.

Kingston
Toronto · N.Y. · N.H. · Boston
Albany · MASS.
· R.I.
· CONN.
New York
Philadelphia · N.J.
· DEL.
· MD.

ATLANTIC
OCEAN

0   300   600 Miles
0   300   600 Kilometers

NEBRASKA
TERRITORY

40°N

UNORGANIZED TERRITORY

MINN.   WIS.   MICH.
Milwaukee   Detroit
IOWA   Chicago   Cleveland
Des Moines   IND.   Toledo   PENN.
OHIO
ILLINOIS   Cincinnati
Springfield   VA.
KANSAS   MO.   Evansville   Washington, D.C.
TERRITORY   Topeka   Louisville
St. Louis   Norfolk
Cairo   KY.
N.C.
TENN.   New Bern
INDIAN
TERRITORY   ARK.   S.C.
Charleston
TEXAS   ALA.   GA.
LA.   MISS.
30°N
FLA.

100°W   90°W   80°W   70°W

Legend:
- Slave states
- Free states and territories
- Canada
- Routes of the Underground Railroad
- · "Station" on the Underground Railroad

Why do you think many escapees chose Canada instead of remaining in the North?

delivering fugitives to Levi Coffin, one of the Quaker founders of the Underground Railroad. Elijah Anderson died in a Kentucky prison for the same offense.

African American agents faced higher penalties. Slave holders placed a price on the heads of some. David Ruggles, head of the New York Vigilance Committee, which aided fugitives, regularly changed residence to avoid kidnappers. A judge ordered Samuel Burris, a free African American agent in Delaware, to be sold at auction.

Luckily, the highest bid came from a white abolitionist.

Conductors in the North. From the start, free African Americans in the North took a leading role in sheltering runaways. Two business owners in Pennsylvania—Robert Purvis of Philadelphia and William Whipper of Columbia—kept stations on the Railroad. Purvis hid runaways in a room of his house reached only by a trapdoor. Whipper shipped runaways

Steubenville, Ohio, on the opposite shore of the Ohio River, was a magnet for African Americans fleeing from slavery at this crossing on the river.

north in the false end of a railroad car he owned. Frederick Douglass and Henry Highland Garnet also kept busy stations.

One of the best-known African American conductors of the Underground Railroad was William Still. Some 2,000 fugitives passed through his station.

William Still escaped slavery when his mother fled from Maryland to New Jersey with as many of her children as she could carry. Here, she joined Still's father, and they saved money to buy the rest of their children. At age 23, William Still moved to Philadelphia to find work. He took a leading role in the Philadelphia Society for the Abolition of Slavery. Still helped push the city's Underground Railroad routes farther north and deeper into the South. His activities led him to be described as the "president of the Underground Railroad." In 1872, he published a firsthand account of African American abolitionists in action in *The Underground Railroad.*

Still's book documents one of the most courageous figures of the Underground Railroad—Harriet Tubman. Southerners called her a criminal. Enslaved African Americans called her Moses.

Taking Another Look

1. What risks did enslaved African Americans face in running away?

2. In what ways was the Underground Railroad like a real railroad?

3. **Critical Thinking**   Would you have worked for the Underground Railroad? Explain. Consider the risks and the rewards.

2 A WOMAN CALLED "MOSES"
▼ How did Harriet Tubman earn the title "the Moses of her people"?

One night, around 1860, Thomas Cole set out from an Alabama plantation with bloodhounds on his heels. He shuddered with fear as he heard the howl of dogs behind him. Recalled Cole, "I was hopin' and prayin' all de time dat I could meet up wid dat Harriet Tubman woman. . . . I never did see dis woman, but I thinks she was a brave woman, anyway."

Liberty or Death.   By the time Cole fled the South, Harriet Tubman had become a legend.

Born in 1820, **Harriet Tubman** was one of the 11 children of Harriet and Benjamin Ross —two field hands on a Maryland plantation. She tasted her owner's whip for the first time at age 7. From that time on, she recalled, "[I] prayed to God to make me strong and able to fight." Fight she did, for at 13, she tried to save another enslaved African American from being punished. Her enraged owner hit her on the head with a rock, fracturing her skull.

At 20, Harriet was married to an enslaved man named John Tubman. One day in 1849, Harriet learned that she and several of her brothers were to be sold into the Deep South. That night she fled. Later, Harriet recalled her feelings: "I had reasoned this out in my mind; there was one of two things I had a *right* to, liberty or death; if I could not have one, I would have the other; for no man should take me alive."

Joining the Underground Railroad.

Freedom felt good to Tubman. But she also felt sorrow, for her family remained enslaved. After settling in Philadelphia, she turned to William Still for help. He sent Tubman traveling on the Underground Railroad.

In 1850, Tubman rescued one of her sisters and her two children from being sold at auction. A few months later, she led one of her brothers and two other men out of Maryland. In 1851, she went back for her husband. But John Tubman had taken another wife and refused to see her. Heartbroken, Harriet decided "to drop him out of my heart." She told Still to put her to work full-time saving other enslaved African Americans.

In all, Tubman made 19 trips south. Armed with a gun and a firm belief in God, she delivered more than 300 people to freedom in the North.

Tubman maintained that she never let "a train run off the track," meaning that she had never lost anyone in a rescue operation. But few in her charge dared falter. Those who lagged behind or had second thoughts stared into the barrel of her gun and heard her husky voice order, "Go north or die."

Slave holders who matched wits with Tubman lost. They placed a $40,000 price on her head, but nobody was able to collect it. Not even the Civil War stopped her from rescuing African Americans from slavery. As a scout and spy for the Union army, she once helped free more than 750 slaves. Frederick Douglass later wrote a stirring tribute to the woman called Moses.

The midnight sky and silent stars have been the witness of your devotion to freedom and your heroism. . . . I know of no one who has willingly encountered more perils and hardships to serve our enslaved people than you have.

Taking Another Look

1. How did Harriet Tubman become involved in the Underground Railroad?

2. What risks did Tubman take?

3. **Critical Thinking** Harriet Tubman rescued only a small number of all the fugitives who fled slavery. Why, then, do you think slave holders considered her so dangerous?

LOOKING AHEAD

The conductors of the Underground Railroad were able to rescue as many African American slaves as they did because of the moral, practical, and financial support of dedicated abolitionists. Included among those who supported the Underground Railroad were African American churches. They served as stations and raised money for conductors. They gave shelter to runaways—and fueled the hope that God would one day deliver all African Americans out of chains.

Mary Ann Shadd was the first woman ever to speak before the Colored National Convention. In 1855, Shadd hoped to sway delegates to the 11th annual convention to support the relocation of African Americans to Canada. Of Shadd's speech, a reporter wrote: "The House was crowded and breathless in its attention to her masterly exposition [explanation] of our present condition."

Shadd had moved to Canada after the passage of the Fugitive Slave Law of 1850. In the next decade, more than 15,000 African Americans relocated there. In Canada, African American men could vote and own property, and African American children could go to school.

Shadd settled in Windsor, Canada, a final stop for western Underground Railroad routes. She opened a school in Windsor for fugitives from slavery and also started a newspaper, *Provincial Freeman*. Many African Americans, including Frederick Douglass, believed abolitionists should stay in the United States to fight slavery. Shadd, however, saw more hope of freedom in Canada.

During the Civil War, the U.S. government asked Shadd to recruit African American soldiers in Canada. She convinced hundreds to join the Union army. After the war, Shadd moved to Washington, D.C., to earn a law degree from Howard University and enter a new fight—the struggle for women's rights.

CLOSE UP: Chapter 14

The Who, What, Where of History

1. **Who** were Ellen and William Craft?
2. **Who** was Henry "Box" Brown?
3. **What** was the "Drinking Gourd" to which escaping slaves often referred?
4. **What** was the Underground Railroad?
5. **Who** was Levi Coffin?
6. **Who** was William Still?
7. **Who** was Harriet Tubman?

Making the Connection

What was the connection between the Fugitive Slave Law and the Underground Railroad?

Time Check

Use the time line on pages 144–145 to answer the following questions.

1. During what years did the Underground Railroad operate?
2. Did the year in which Harriet Tubman began to lead enslaved African Americans out of the South come closer to the beginning or to the end of the years the Underground Railroad was in operation?

What Would You Have Done?

1. Suppose you were an enslaved African American who wanted to escape to the North. List some qualities or skills that you think would have helped you to reach freedom safely.
2. Imagine that you are a white farmer in Indiana. One night you hear noises and realize that several fugitive

enslaved African Americans are trying to hide in your farm. You know that if you help them and you are caught, your family may go to prison and you will lose the farm. What course of action would you take? Why?

Thinking and Writing About History

1. Write a short play about an episode in the escape of Ellen and William Craft. Choose a simple event, such as registering at a hotel or eating a meal in the dining car of a train.

2. Write a song or poster about the Underground Railroad using such code words as "tracks," "stations," and "conductors."

Building Skills: Recognizing a Generalization

In the last chapter you learned about generalizations, broad statements based on many related facts. Read this account of the Underground Railroad and answer the question that follows:

[T]he Underground Railroad . . . needed capital [money to operate]. The fugitives required food and clothing, and frequently there were unexpected expenses such as boarding a train in order to evade a pursuing owner, or displaying affluence [wealth] to convey the impression that one had been free long enough to accumulate wealth. Quakers and similar groups raised funds to carry on the work. The vigilance committees . . . solicited [asked for] money. Philanthropists [wealthy people who give to charity] contributed, as did the conductors and other "officials" of the Railroad.

1. Number the sentences in the quotation from 1 to 5. Which of the sentences contain generalizations?

Next, read the following selection and answer the questions.

As a historian attempting to research the Underground Railroad, I have found, with a mixture of admiration and chagrin [disappointment], that [an] atmosphere of secrecy endures. So much is uncertain. Even the origin of the term "Underground Railroad" is obscure. No one knows how many fled from bondage along its invisible tracks. . . . What we do know is a mere fragment of the whole, but it is enough. Ordeals may have gone unrecorded and names have been forgotten, but such records as have survived in the memories of men like my grandfather and the memoirs of those who risked all for freedom and brotherhood make it clear that the flight to freedom on the Underground Railroad was an epic of American heroism.

2. Number the sentences in the quotation from 1 to 6. Which of the sentences contain generalizations?

3. In the last sentence the author indicates that he has based his generalizations on certain kinds of information. What information do you think he used? Explain what kinds of facts would be necessary to tell the story of the Underground Railroad.

166

Philadelphia's Mother Bethel African Methodist Episcopal Church

African American Churches: Agents for Change

(1787–1860)

THINKING ABOUT THE CHAPTER

What part did African American churches play in the struggle for equality?

The day in 1833 when Thomas James was ordained a minister in the African Methodist Episcopal Zion Church was a milestone in the life of this former enslaved African American. As he stood in the pulpit preparing to give his first sermon, he thought of the events that had brought him there.

Born enslaved in upstate New York in 1796, James remembered being auctioned off at 17 "in exchange for a yoke [pair] of steers, a colt, and some additional property." Fleeing slavery, he supported himself by digging canals and chopping wood. Gradually, he made his way to Buffalo, New York, where he discovered a Sunday school that changed his life. The church, he decided, would be his life's work.

Once ordained, in 1833, James frequently used his pulpit to speak out against slavery. On several occasions, white mobs beat him for his strong words. That did not stop him. In 1835, he became an antislavery missionary and went on to found African Methodist Episcopal Zion churches in Syracuse, Ithaca, and Sag Harbor, New York.

In 1839, James left New York State for a post in New Bedford, Massachusetts. In the church where he became pastor, he met a young man who spoke so eloquently that he "licensed him to preach." One night, James was giving an antislavery speech when he spotted the young man in the audience. He called on him to speak. The man was Frederick Douglass. Years later Douglass said that he had found his purpose in life that night—to use his voice against slavery.

Both James and Douglass long credited their antislavery awakenings to the same source—the African American church.

1 THE SEARCH FOR RELIGIOUS ▼ EQUALITY

Why did African Americans organize their own churches?

In November 1787, two months after the end of the Constitutional Convention, African American worshipers filed into the St. George Methodist Episcopal Church in Philadelphia. The church had always allowed them to be seated on the main floor. But church officials had grown uneasy at the large number of African Americans attending services. On that November Sunday, they met African Americans at the door and forced them to climb to the upstairs gallery instead.

Two prominent African Americans, Richard Allen and Absalom Jones, founders of the Free African Society (see page 93), walked up the steps to the gallery with the others. They headed to the front of the gallery and knelt in prayer. Unknown to them, church officials had closed off this spot, too.

"We had not been long upon our knees," Allen later recalled, "before I heard considerable scuffling and low talking." Allen lifted his head from prayer and saw a white usher pulling Jones from his knees. "Wait until prayer is over," pleaded Jones, "and I will trouble you no more." The usher called for help to remove Jones by force.

After prayer had ended, the African American worshipers walked out of the church together. They were furious at the treatment they had received. "We were filled with fresh vigor," said Allen, "to get a house erected to worship God in." Thus began the independent African American church movement in the United States.

New Churches. Richard Allen and Absalom Jones agreed that African Americans had to have their own church. But they disagreed on the direction they should take in founding a new church. In 1794, Allen founded the Mother Bethel African Methodist Episcopal Church in Philadelphia and became its first minister. Still stinging from his treatment by the St. George Methodists, Jones joined the Episcopalians. In 1794, he opened the doors of the St. Thomas Free African Church, also in Philadelphia.

Locally, some **denominations**, or religious groups, especially the Episcopalians and Quakers, did not believe it was wise for African Americans to form separate churches. But Allen and Jones defended the move. They recalled the treat-

1787	African American church movement begins.
1794	Richard Allen founds Mother Bethel African Methodist Episcopal Church. Absalom Jones opens St. Thomas Free African Church.
1809	Independent Baptist churches are organized by African Americans in New York City and Boston.
1816	First African American denomination in North America is organized.
1830s	White Southerners move against African American churches. African American churches in the North increase opposition to slavery.

ment they had received in racially mixed churches. Accordingly, they admitted only members of African descent to their churches. They did, however, organize a number of joint activities with white churches, including Bible readings, picnics, and lectures.

Over the next 20 years, Allen's followers demanded greater freedom from the white Methodist church authorities. In 1816, African American Methodists from various cities met in Philadelphia to set up a new denomination—the African Methodist Episcopal (AME) church. This was the first African American denomination in North America. Trustees of the church elected Allen their bishop.

As African American Methodists moved toward independence, African American Baptists did the same. On May 14, 1809, 13 African Americans organized Philadelphia's first Baptist church for African Americans. That same year, African Americans, under the leadership of Reverend Thomas Paul, organized independent Baptist churches in New York City and Boston. Already active among African Americans in the South, the Baptist church soon competed with the Methodists in importance to African Americans.

Churches in the Mid-1800s. Discrimination in mixed churches continued in the mid-1800s. Once Frederick Douglass stormed out of a church when the minister refused African Americans communion until all white worshipers were served. Douglass called on African Americans to push into white pews, go limp, and force ushers to haul them into the streets. In 1837, the New York *Colored American* called for "stand ins." Do not sit in separate pews, demanded the journal:

> Stand in the aisles, and rather worship God upon your feet, than become a part to your own degradation [humiliation]. You must shame your oppressors, and wear out prejudice by this holy practice.

Separate Sunday school classes, separate pews, separate communion services—these were only some of the practices in many Christian churches in the mid-1800s.

Most free African Americans protested these actions by forming their own **congregations**, or groups for worship. A handful of African American abolitionists, including Frederick Douglass, came to object to this practice. Douglass believed that separate churches made true racial equality hard to attain. Most African

The Reverend Lemuel Haynes, who had fought in the American Revolution, was one of the few African American ministers who preached to white congregations.

American abolitionists, however, felt that the independent churches gave them a freedom to organize protests that might otherwise have been denied them. Thomas James, Douglass's former ally, was among this group. Whether or not Douglass's view had merit, independent churches became vital forces for change. They gave African Americans a place not only to express themselves spiritually but to assemble freely.

Taking Another Look

1. Why did African Americans first form independent churches?

2. How did African American churches serve their people?

3. **Critical Thinking** Why do you think the independent African American church movement took shape in the North rather than in the South?

2 JOINING THE ANTISLAVERY ▼ BATTLE

How did African American churches contribute to the antislavery cause?

In 1855, police burst into a meeting of African American church officials in Washington, D.C. They seized one Bible, two books on morality, and an agreement drawn up for the purchase of an enslaved woman. Of the 24 church members arrested, a judge ordered one to be whipped, four jailed, and the rest fined.

Further Restrictions in the South.
Farther south, white fears of African American assemblies grew. Fear of slave rebellions still gripped the minds of many white Southerners. The fact that both Denmark Vesey and Nat Turner had been preachers strengthened opposition to separate African American churches in the region.

Beginning in the 1830s, African American preachers in much of the South had to be approved by white ministers. In many Southern states, only white ministers could preach to African American congregations. A handful of independent African American churches operated. But most existed in cities—and under the close watch of whites.

Opposition in the North. African American ministers such as Henry Highland Garnet and Samuel Ringgold Ward blasted white church officials for not taking a strong stand against slavery. Even the Quakers, who supported abolition, were attacked for discriminatory practices. "They give us good advice," said Ward of the Quakers. "They will aid in giving us a partial education—but never in a Quaker school, beside their own children. Whatever they do for us savors of pity, and is done at arm's length."

Ward's militant words expressed the new spirit among African American abolitionists in the 1840s. He spoke so eloquently that some said he surpassed Frederick Douglass as a speaker.

African American clergymen were joined by many white ministers, like the owner of this house on the Ohio River, in providing safe havens for runaways from slavery.

Samuel Ringgold Ward was born in 1817 on a Maryland plantation. His enslaved parents escaped and carried him to freedom in New York. There, he received an education and became a minister in a white Presbyterian church in South Butler, New York. But Ward abandoned his ministry in 1839 to become a full-time antislavery agent. His stirring words shook audiences. "If I cannot go to heaven as black as God made me, let me go down to hell and dwell with the Devil forever," declared Ward in one speech. When Congress passed the 1850 Fugitive Slave Law, Ward fled to England and then to the Caribbean island of Jamaica, where he later died.

Places of Protest. African American churches received their funds from African American parishioners, or church members. This permitted them to support antislavery causes without fear of losing membership. In fact, the tradition of self-help went back to the mutual-aid societies of the 1700s (see page 93). It inspired African Americans to dig deeply into their pockets to help the churches in their fight to end slavery.

Time and again, the churches threw open their doors to abolitionists who were denied meeting places elsewhere. Generally, the churches charged no fees. In fact, they sometimes made donations to fund the meetings.

African American churches also provided safe places for runaways. More than one church acted as a station on the Underground Railroad. Richard Allen, for example, operated a station at Mother Bethel Church in Philadelphia until his death in 1831. The congregation continued the practice until the Civil War.

In another antislaver[...] American churches in [...] New York boycotted p[...] enslaved labor. They ca[...] ery supporters to buy o[...] by free labor. When [...] Angelina Grimké marr[...] baker to use "free suga[...] cake. In 1834, William Whipper opened a free-labor grocery store next to the Mother Bethel Church in Philadelphia. He stocked shelves with free-labor sugar, cloth made from free cotton, and a full supply of abolitionist pamphlets.

Taking Another Look

1. How and why did white Southerners restrict African American churches after 1830?

2. What methods did African American churches use to protest slavery and racial inequality in the North?

3. **Critical Thinking** If you were a free African American, would you have agreed with Richard Allen's or Frederick Douglass's view on separate churches for African Americans? Explain.

LOOKING AHEAD

The growth of separate African American churches went hand in hand with the growth of the antislavery movement in the North. Both developments stemmed from the same root—the desire for equality. By the 1850s, the activities of abolitionists further increased the division between North and South. Rumblings of war could be heard as Southerners threatened to leave the Union rather than give up slavery. But abolitionists showed no signs of backing down.

A Church Named Bethel

In 1794, Richard Allen hitched his horses up to a blacksmith shop and hauled it to a lot at Sixth and Lombard streets in Philadelphia. He dedicated the building as a church and named it Bethel—"the house of God to the gathering of thousands of souls." Four church buildings called Bethel have stood on this site. The fourth and present church is called Mother Bethel—for its historical leadership of the African Methodist Episcopal (AME) churches.

Today, AME churches span the globe. They can be found throughout the United States, and in Central and West Africa, the Caribbean, Bermuda, South America, and Europe. But the heart of the AME network still lies in Philadelphia. The present Mother Bethel Church, which is over a 100 years old, has been named a national landmark.

The congregation of Mother Bethel Church currently numbers about 700 and includes a direct descendant of Richard Allen. Over its long history, members of Mother Bethel Church have supported Allen's twin concepts of self-help and freedom for African Americans. For example, the church served as a station on the Underground Railroad in the mid-1800s. In the 1960s, church members marched in the Civil Rights Movement. Today, the church runs a summer day-care program, and church members are active in city affairs.

CLOSE UP: Chapter 15

The Who, What, Where of History

1. **Who** was Thomas James?
2. **Who** was Richard Allen?
3. **Who** was Absalom Jones?
4. **Where** was the African Methodist Episcopal Church established?
5. **What** does the term *denomination* mean?
6. **Who** was Samuel Ringgold Ward?

Making the Connection

What was the connection between African American churches and the antislavery movement?

Time Check

Use the time line on pages 144–145 to answer the following questions.

1. In what year did the African American church movement begin?
2. How many years after the beginning of the African American church movement was the first African American denomination in North America formed?
3. Approximately how many years after the foundation of the first African American denomination did white Southerners begin to suppress African American churches?

What Would You Have Done?

1. Imagine that you were attending church at the St. George Methodist Episcopal Church in Philadelphia on the day that ushers forcibly removed Absalom Jones from the gallery. You were a friend of Jones. What would you have done? Explain your actions.

2. Imagine that you have just read an editorial in which Frederick Douglass objects to the practice of forming separate African American congregations. He disapproves on the grounds that separate churches make racial equality hard to obtain. How would you have responded to his editorial in a letter to the editor?

3. Imagine that you are Samuel Ringgold Ward. An acquaintance of yours who is a Quaker heard you say that the Society of Friends carries on discriminatory practices against African Americans. Your friend says you are wrong because Quakers support freedom for African Americans. Write a dialogue in which you and your friend discuss your differences. Use your most convincing evidence to prove your position, and then suggest ways in which the Quakers can remedy the situation.

Thinking and Writing About History

1. Write a paragraph that describes the many roles the church played in the lives of African Americans.

2. Write the words for a plaque to be erected on the site of an African American church. The church was founded in 1820 and served as a station on the Underground Railroad. Many important abolitionists spoke at the church.

Building Skills: Making a Generalization

We make generalizations all the time. Suppose that you eat a pizza with anchovies—and you don't like it at all, although you usually love pizza. Then at a restaurant you try a dip that tastes terrible. When you ask what's in it, you find out it contains anchovies. You might generalize from those two experiences that you do not like anchovies and do not wish to eat any more of them.

Read each of the following two groups of related facts. For each group of facts, make a generalization, a broad conclusion, based on the facts.

1. a. Church officials of the St. George Methodist Episcopal Church in Philadelphia decided to forbid African Americans from sitting on the main floor of the church.

   b. Richard Allen and Absalom Jones were removed from the front of the gallery of St. George's because church officials did not wish African Americans to sit in that part of the church.

   c. In one church the minister refused to give communion to African Americans until all the white worshippers had received.

   d. Many churches maintained separate Sunday schools, separate pews, and separate communion services for African Americans.

2. a. Thomas James used his ministry in an African American church to speak out against slavery.

   b. Abolitionists were able to organize protests through African American churches.

   c. The African American churches provided training for African leaders of the abolitionist movement.

   d. African American churches gave money to antislavery causes.

UNIT 6

Dred Scott and Harriet Scott

HOPE FOR A NEW WAY OF LIFE

(1820–1880)

An African American cowboy

14th U.S. Colored Infantry
at Ship Island, Mississippi

Unit 6 traces the story of one of the most bitter periods in U.S. history. From 1819 on, the North and the South were on a collision course over slavery. The climax came in the 1860s with the **Civil War.** When the war ended in 1865, the government set about restoring the **Union** (the United States). This period, called **Reconstruction,** lasted until 1877. With the Civil War came the end of slavery, and with Reconstruction came the promise of a new life for freed African Americans—a promise that was not to be fully realized.

What was the purpose of the Missouri Compromise Line? Which new states did the Missouri Compromise create?

The Missouri Compromise.   As more Americans began moving to the new territories of the Louisiana Purchase, the debate over slavery went with them. Should slavery be allowed to expand into these new territories or should it be limited to the states where it was already established?

This issue was angrily debated in Congress when Missouri applied in 1819 for admission to the Union as a **slave-holding state.** Its resolution would have important political consequences. In 1819, there were 11 free states and 11 slave-holding states. The North opposed admitting Missouri as a slave-holding state because

---

An African American Speaks

A war undertaken and brazenly [shamelessly] carried on for the perpetual [everlasting] enslavement of colored men calls logically and loudly for colored men to help suppress [stop] it.

—Frederick Douglass

---

the South would then have more votes in the U.S. Senate than the North. This would tip the balance of power in the Senate in favor of the South.

After months of bitter debate, Northerners and Southerners in Congress finally reached a compromise in 1820. Known as the **Missouri Compromise,** it admitted Missouri as a slave-holding state, and Maine as a free state. At the same time, a line was drawn at latitude 36°30' N across the territory of the Louisiana Purchase. North of the line, except for Missouri, slavery would be barred "forever." South of the line, slavery would be allowed.

The issue of slavery in new territories flared up again 30 years later. This time the controversy centered on the huge area that Mexico had given up to the United States after the Mexican War (1846–1847). The new lands included California, New Mexico, and most of present-day Arizona, Nevada, Colorado, and Utah. What was to be done about slavery in these new territories?

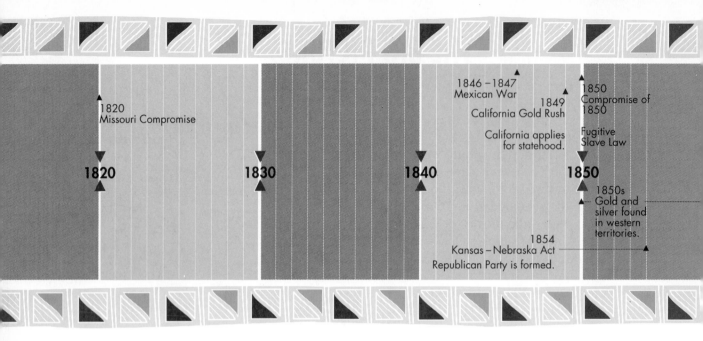

1820
Missouri Compromise

1846–1847
Mexican War

1849
California Gold Rush

California applies
for statehood.

1850
Compromise of
1850

Fugitive
Slave Law

1820

1830

1840

1850

1850s
Gold and
silver found
in western
territories.

1854
Kansas–Nebraska Act
Republican Party is formed.

The Compromise of 1850. When California applied for admission to the Union as a free state in 1849, Northerners and Southerners in Congress once again compromised. According to the **Compromise of 1850,** California was to enter the Union as a free state. In the other former Mexican lands, settlers would vote on whether or not to allow slavery. This voting plan was called **popular sovereignty.**

To gain Southern support, the compromise included a tough **Fugitive Slave Law** to help slave holders capture runaways. Not surprisingly, many Northerners, even those who were not abolitionists, bitterly objected to the law. One Northern member of Congress declared that returning a fugitive to slavery would be the same as murder.

The Kansas-Nebraska Act. An even more bitter clash over slavery occurred four years later. A bill to organize a Kansas Territory and a Nebraska Territory came before Congress. The Mis-

souri Compromise had barred slavery in that area. The new proposal, however, would repeal the Missouri Compromise, and the question of slavery would be decided by popular sovereignty. Although Northerners flooded Congress with protests, the **Kansas-Nebraska Act** became law in 1854. As a result, armed bands fought one another in Kansas over the issue of slavery. So much violence occurred in 1856 that the territory became known as **Bleeding Kansas.**

Lincoln. One effect of the Kansas-Nebraska Act was the formation of a new political party in 1854 by opponents of the extension of slavery. They called themselves the Republican party.

In 1860, the Republicans chose Abraham Lincoln of Illinois as their candidate for President. Although Lincoln strongly opposed slavery, he did not plan to end it in the South. His aim was to prevent its spread into the western territories. However, many Southerners thought that Lin-

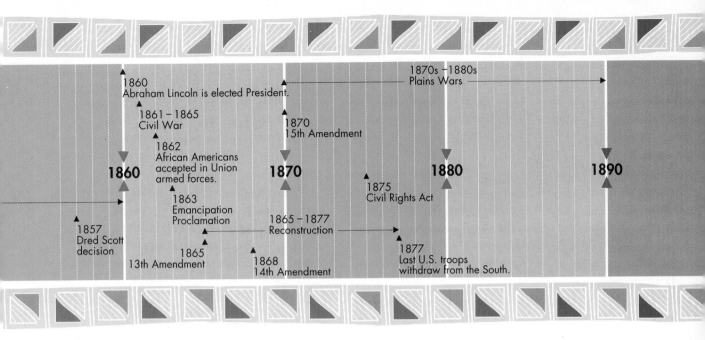

1860
Abraham Lincoln is elected President.

1861–1865
Civil War

1862
African Americans accepted in Union armed forces.

1870
15th Amendment

1870s–1880s
Plains Wars

1860

1870

1880

1890

1863
Emancipation Proclamation

1857
Dred Scott decision

1865–1877
Reconstruction

1875
Civil Rights Act

1865
13th Amendment

1868
14th Amendment

1877
Last U.S. troops withdraw from the South.

coln was an abolitionist. His main support came from the North and West, and he won the 1860 presidential election.

Secession. The news of Lincoln's victory outraged the South. Six weeks later, South Carolina **seceded,** or left the Union. It was soon joined by Mississippi, Florida, Alabama, Georgia, Louisiana, and Texas. In February 1861, delegates from these states met at Montgomery, Alabama, and formed the Confederate States of America.

On April 12, Confederate forces fired on Fort Sumter, in Charleston harbor. This fort was a **Union,** or Northern, stronghold. These shots were the first of the Civil War. Soon after, Virginia, North Carolina, Tennessee, and Arkansas joined the **Confederacy.** A total of 23 states, including the **border states** of Missouri, Kentucky, Maryland, and Delaware, remained in the Union.

The Civil War. The Civil War lasted from 1861 to 1865. It was the bloodiest war in U.S. history. About 620,000 people were wounded or killed, including 38,000 African Americans. In the beginning, the North appeared to have all the advantages over the South. The Union had over 22 million people. The South had 8 million, of whom 3.9 million were enslaved African Americans. The North had 92 percent of the nation's factories and almost all its iron, coal, and copper. Seventy percent of the country's railroads were in the North. Yet the South's armed forces were commanded by outstanding military leaders, and they fought with such determination that at times, especially in the early years of the war, the South appeared close to victory.

The Emancipation Proclamation. Early in the war, Lincoln was criticized by many for not freeing enslaved African Americans. In August 1862, he replied to his critics: "My paramount [main] object in this struggle is to save the Union, and is not either to save or destroy slavery."

Four years of a bloody Civil War were launched when the Confederates bombarded Fort Sumter on April 12, 1861.

However, as the war dragged on and Union forces suffered heavy losses, Lincoln reversed himself. On January 1, 1863, Lincoln signed the **Emancipation Proclamation,** which declared free all African Americans in those parts of the South that were still in rebellion. This move, he believed, would give the North a moral reason for continuing the terrible struggle. It would also lead enslaved African Americans to run away and further damage the economy, or system of producing goods and services, in the South.

The year 1863 was the turning point of the war. From then until April 1865, the Union armies scored one major victory after another. On April 9, 1865, General Robert E. Lee, the Confederate commander, surrendered to General Ulysses S. Grant, of the Union army, at Appomattox, Virginia. The Union had little time to celebrate, for less than a week later, President Lincoln was assassinated by a Southerner who blamed him for the South's defeat.

The Reconstruction Years. With the war at an end, the federal government had to decide what to do about the defeated South and how to rebuild, or reconstruct, the Union. Before the war had even ended, Congress had set up the **Freedmen's Bureau** to provide food and clothing to newly freed African Americans. The bureau also helped them find jobs and homes and negotiated labor contracts with landowners. Perhaps the bureau's most important work was building schools and providing teachers to give African Americans the education denied them under slavery.

After Lincoln's assassination, his successor, Vice President Andrew Johnson from Tennessee, ran into trouble with the plan for Reconstruction. Powerful Republicans in Congress attacked the plan as too generous to the South. The plan did, however, force the Southern states to ratify the 13th Amendment, banning slavery in the United States. This was the first of three Reconstruction Amendments. As a reaction against the 13th Amendment and the Freedmen's Bureau, many white Southerners passed **Black Codes** in their states. These laws severely limited the rights of African Americans.

Beginning in 1867, Radical Republicans pushed through their own tough plan to reorganize the South. The Radicals were bitter against the South and wanted to set much harsher terms than did President Johnson. They believed that the South should be treated as a conquered nation and that African Americans should have the same rights as white Americans.

The Radicals were joined by moderate Republicans who shared some of the same goals as well as the desire to keep Republicans in power in the South. Their plan divided the South into five military districts, each governed by a U.S. Army general with troops to back up his orders. Before any Southern state could be readmitted to the Union, it had to accept the 14th Amendment and to write a new constitution giving African American men the right to vote.

13th Amendment (1865)
Forbids slavery in any state of the Union.

14th Amendment (1868)
States that all persons born in the United States are U.S. citizens and cannot be deprived of "life, liberty, (or) property, without due process of law" nor be denied "equal protection of the laws."

15th Amendment (1870)
Forbids states to deny the right to vote to male citizens "on account of race, color, or previous condition of servitude."

Which Reconstruction amendment ended slavery? Which gave citizenship to African Americans?

White Southern Reaction. Many white Southerners bitterly resented the new state governments set up during Reconstruction. Some joined secret societies like the Ku Klux Klan, whose purpose was to terrorize African Americans and prevent them from voting. Many African Americans who tried to vote were beaten. Some were **lynched**—or murdered by mobs for supposed crimes. As Southern white men regained their right to vote, they replaced Reconstruction governments with ones made up of former supporters of the Confederacy.

The End of Reconstruction. By the mid-1870s, some of the leading Radical Republicans had died, and the nation was worried about economic problems. Many Northerners wanted to "leave the South alone," which meant abandoning its African Americans. By 1877, the last U.S. troops had been withdrawn from the South, and Reconstruction, a stormy period in U.S. history, was over.

Going West. Beginning in the late 1840s, the lands west of the Mississippi began to attract more and more people, African Americans among them. The Gold Rush of 1849 brought thousands to California seeking to strike it rich quick. Thousands more followed when gold and silver were discovered in the 1850s in what are today the states of Colorado, Nevada, Idaho, Montana, and South Dakota; and in the 1870s in the present-day states of Arizona, Wyoming, Utah, and New Mexico.

After the Civil War, these same territories attracted ranchers and farmers seeking new lives. Among them were some of the hundreds of thousands of European immigrants who had come to the United States. African Americans also joined the move westward to escape the growing oppression of the post–Civil War South.

These western lands, however, were not empty. Native Americans lived along the Pacific Coast, in the Rocky Mountains, and on the Great Plains—the land between the Mississippi River and the Rocky Mountains. In a series of plains wars, white and African American troops of the U.S. Army killed or sent to reservations thousands of Native Americans.

Taking Another Look

1. Describe the laws passed between 1820 and 1854 to try to settle the debate over slavery's expansion.

2. Explain the advantages the North had over the South in the Civil War.

3. How did the Emancipation Proclamation affect the war?

4. **Critical Thinking** If you had been a newly freed African American, would you have gone west? Explain.

A victim of the 1850 Fugitive Slave Law

The Road to the Civil War

(1820–1860)

THINKING ABOUT THE CHAPTER

What important events affecting African Americans occurred in the years immediately before the Civil War?

In 1854, cholera (KOL-uhr-uh), a dreaded disease, struck Pittsburgh. Dr. Martin Robison Delany, one of the few African American doctors in the city, drew praise from both African Americans and whites for the devotion and energy he showed in taking care of the sick.

When the scare was over, Delany returned to attacking another dread disease—slavery. For years, he had been a leader in rescuing African Americans from slavery through the Underground Railroad. Delany was also one of the African American abolitionists who never hesitated to emphasize his pride in his heritage. His friend Frederick Douglass once said of him, "I thank God for making me a man simply, but Delany always thanks him for making him a black man."

When the Fugitive Slave Law was passed in 1850, Delany's fury knew no bounds. Addressing a meeting in Pittsburgh, which included the city's mayor, he declared:

Sir, my house is my castle. . . . If any man approaches that house in search of a slave—I care not who he may be, whether constable or sheriff, magistrate or even judge of the Supreme Court—nay, let it be he who sanctioned [approved] this act to become a law [President Millard Fillmore], . . . and I do not lay him a lifeless corpse at my feet, I hope the grave may refuse my body a resting-place, and righteous Heaven my spirit a home.

Delany's strong words reflected the anger of many abolitionists at the new law. They were also typical of the debate over slavery that heated up in the 1850s.

1 CHALLENGES TO THE FUGITIVE SLAVE LAW
▼ What was the effect of the Fugitive Slave Law on African Americans?

Late in 1850, fear was spreading among free African Americans in the North because of the Fugitive Slave Law, passed by Congress in September. This law put the power of the federal government behind the efforts of slave holders to capture enslaved African Americans who had escaped to the North. It authorized federal marshals to hunt down runaways and return them to slavery. It provided stiff penalties for law officers and even ordinary people who did not provide help to slave catchers.

Law officers were paid a fee for capturing runaways. Professional slave catchers

frequently kidnapped free African Americans and took them South. The Fugitive Slave Law denied African Americans who were arrested as runaways a trial by jury or the right to testify in their own defense. Many free African Americans in the North no longer felt secure, and hundreds sought safety in Canada.

Many Northerners—white and African American—defied the law and stepped up their efforts to help enslaved African Americans to escape. Despite these efforts, over 330 fugitives were returned to slavery in the 1850s.

The Case of Anthony Burns. The recapture of one runaway African Ameri-

Angry Bostonians bought hundreds of copies of this pamphlet about the recapture of Anthony Burns.

SNAPSHOT OF THE TIMES

1833   Dred Scott is taken
to free territory.

1850   Fugitive Slave Law

1857   Supreme Court rules against
Dred Scott.

1858   John Brown's raid on Harpers
Ferry

can, Anthony Burns, attracted national attention in 1854. A Virginian, Burns had stowed away on a ship to Boston, where he found work as a tailor. But his former holder discovered where he was and tried to claim his "property."

Burns was arrested on May 24 and placed under guard in the federal courthouse. Soon after, a crowd of African American and white abolitionists held a protest meeting. Stirred by the speakers,

they resolved that "resistance to tyrants [unfair rulers] is obedience to God."

Led by a white minister, Thomas Wentworth Higginson, the abolitionists stormed the courthouse with axes, revolvers, and a battering ram. Higginson and an African American broke through the door but were driven back by marshals swinging clubs. A shot was fired and a deputy fell dead.

Although the attack failed, local authorities sent an appeal to President Franklin Pierce for help. He ordered federal soldiers to Boston to strengthen the guard around the courthouse. He also sent a telegram to the local district attorney: "Incur [undertake] any expense to insure the execution of the law."

Lawyers tried to win Burns's freedom in court, but failed. Other Bostonians raised money to buy Burns's freedom, but the district attorney would not allow it. A

In May 1854, thousands of Bostonians protested as federal troops escorted Anthony Burns to the ship that returned him to slavery after his trial.

federal commissioner had ruled that under the Fugitive Slave Law, Burns had to be returned to Virginia. A U.S. gunboat waited in the harbor to take him.

On June 2, about 1,500 troops began marching Burns to the ship. Some 50,000 angry Bostonians lined the streets crying "Shame!" Buildings were draped in black. Flags were hung upside down. Church bells rang mournfully as Burns was hustled aboard the ship.

Enslaved Again. The slave holder put Burns in jail. However, a group of Northerners convinced the slave holder to sell Burns to them. They freed Burns, who attended Oberlin College, became a minister, and moved to Canada. While in jail, Burns wrote down how he felt about his escape from bondage.

Look at my case. I was stolen and made a slave as soon as I was born. . . . God made me a *man*—not a slave; and gave me the same right to myself that he gave the man who stole me to himself. The great wrong he has done me . . . in compelling [forcing] me to work for him many years without wages, and holding me as merchandise—these wrongs could never put me under obligation to stay with him, or return voluntarily, when once escaped.

Freedom Laws. To prevent abuses in the recapture of enslaved African Americans, several Northern states, including Pennsylvania and Massachusetts, passed **personal liberty laws.** Some forbade state officials and anyone else from helping to enforce the Fugitive Slave Law. Some laws also tried to guarantee a fair trial for runaways who were caught.

Although these laws did not free a single captured African American, they were important. They showed a new willingness among Northerners to fight the Fugitive Slave Law. They also showed that people were ready to use state laws to try to overturn a federal law.

Taking Another Look

1. What effect did the Fugitive Slave Law have on runaway enslaved African Americans?

2. In what ways did abolitionists try to get around the Fugitive Slave Law to help runaways?

3. **Critical Thinking** Abolitionists who helped runaways were breaking the Fugitive Slave Law. Do you think they were justified? Explain.

2 ▼ THE DRED SCOTT CASE, A TEST OF SLAVERY

▼ Why was the Supreme Court decision in the Dred Scott case important in the fight to end slavery?

On March 6, 1857, anxious listeners on both sides of the slavery question packed the Supreme Court's chambers to hear the Court's decision in an important case. Only two days before, President James Buchanan had commented on the case in his inaugural address. He had also written to the Supreme Court justices, hoping that the Court would settle the slavery question once and for all by its decision. Buchanan and many others believed that since legislation had failed to settle the slavery issue, a decision by the Supreme Court was needed. The case was about the future of an African American named Dred Scott and his wife Harriet.

A PUBLIC MEETING

WILL BE HELD ON

THURSDAY EVENING, 2D INSTANT,

at 7½ o'clock, in ISRAEL CHURCH, to consider the atrocious decision of the Supreme Court in the

DRED SCOTT CASE,

and other outrages to which the colored people are subject under the Constitution of the United States.

C. L. REMOND,
ROBERT PURVIS,

and others will be speakers on the occasion. Mrs. MOTT. Mr. M'KIM and B. S. JONES of Ohio, have also accepted invitations to be present.
All persons are invited to attend. Admittance free.

Few Supreme Court decisions aroused as much furor as the one in the Dred Scott Case. Here, Philadelphians are invited to attend a meeting to protest the decision.

The Dred Scott Case. In 1833, a slave holder named Dr. John Emerson took Dred Scott from the slave–holding state of Missouri to the free state of Illinois and then to the Wisconsin Territory, where slavery was banned under the Missouri Compromise. In 1846, white friends of Scott advised him to sue for his freedom on the grounds he had lived in a free state and then a free territory, even though he had been taken back to a slave–holding state. Eventually, Scott's case reached the U.S. Supreme Court.

On that fateful March day, Chief Justice Roger B. Taney led the other eight justices into the courtroom. Five of them, including Taney, were from slave–holding states. A hush fell over the courtroom as Taney began to speak.

Issues of the Case. The justices had debated three issues in the case. Was Scott a citizen and therefore entitled to sue in a federal court? Did his residence on free soil entitle him to freedom in Missouri? Finally, was the Missouri Compromise, which had made the territories free, constitutional?

In a majority opinion written by Justice Taney, the Court denied African Americans citizenship. Scott and other African Americans, said Taney, "are not included, and were not intended to be included, under the word 'citizens' in the Constitution." Therefore, Scott did not have the right to sue in Court.

The Court might have stopped there. But it ruled on two other issues. First, the Court said that enslaved African Americans were a form of moveable property. As such, slave holders could take enslaved African Americans wherever they wanted. The fact that Scott had lived on free soil did not entitle him to freedom.

Second, the Court ruled the entire Missouri Compromise **unconstitutional,** or not permitted by the Constitution. The law, said the Court, violated the property rights of slave holders.

Only two of the nine justices, both from the North, upheld the basic human rights of African Americans. It would take a civil war and a constitutional amendment to undo this decision.

Reactions to the Decision. The Court's ruling was greeted with jubilation in the South. One newspaper wrote, "Southern opinion on the subject of Southern slavery . . . is now the supreme law of the land."

Once the meaning of the decision was realized—that all federal territories would now be open to slavery—Northerners were enraged. They held mass meetings to protest the decision. In Philadelphia, a convention of African Americans denounced the ruling. For African Americans, of course, the decision was particularly bitter. Not only did it permit slavery in the territories, but also it supported the idea that African American slaves were no more than property.

Frederick Douglass, however, believed that the Supreme Court's decision would actually hasten the end of slavery. He argued:

The Supreme Court is not the only power in this world. We, the abolitionists and colored people, should meet this decision, unlooked for and monstrous as it appears, in a cheerful spirit. This very attempt to blot out forever the hopes of an enslaved people may be one necessary link in the chain of events preparatory to the complete overthrow of the whole slave system.

The Supreme Court had not settled once and for all the question of slavery in the territories, as President Buchanan had hoped. Instead, it had, in the words of one historian, "exploded a bombshell."

Taking Another Look

1. On what grounds did Dred Scott claim that he should be a free person?

2. Why was the Supreme Court's decision such a tragedy to opponents of slavery?

3. **Critical Thinking** Which part of the Dred Scott decision do you think upset abolitionists the most? Explain.

3 JOHN BROWN'S RAID
▼ Why did John Brown's raid stir up such strong feelings?

Although most abolitionists at the time believed in ending slavery by trying to show how evil it was, the Fugitive Slave Law convinced some that direct action might be necessary. Frederick Douglass, for one, had never advocated violence as a way of ending slavery. Now, however, he took the position that "who would be free must himself strike the first blow." Others agreed with Douglass and went even further.

John Brown, a fiery abolitionist, said in disgust, "Talk! Talk! Talk! That will never free the slaves. What is needed is action—action!" Brown believed that victory over slavery could only be won by a violent uprising. Brown himself was no stranger to

"Bleeding Kansas" was a battleground of proslavery and antislavery forces. In May 1856, proslavery men attacked the antislavery town of Lawrence, Kansas, provoking John Brown to strike back.

violence. At Pottawatomie Creek, in Bleeding Kansas, he had led an attack against proslavery settlers, five of whom were killed.

John Brown's Plan.   Brown had long been planning an uprising by enslaved African Americans. In May 1858, he had met secretly with 34 former enslaved African Americans who now lived in Chatham, Canada. They drew up a constitution for a nation of liberated African Americans to be set up in the mountains of Virginia.

Brown also sought the help of Frederick Douglass. In August 1859, the two met in an old stone quarry near Chambersburg, Pennsylvania. "Come with me, Douglass," he said. "I want you for a special purpose. When I strike, the bees will swarm, and I shall want you to hive [orga-

nize] them." Douglass refused. He believed that Brown's mission was suicidal and "would array [set] the whole country against us." He warned Brown, "You will never get out alive."

The Raid on Harpers Ferry.   Brown was disappointed but went on with his plans. On the night of October 16, 1859, Brown and 18 men, including 5 African Americans, crossed a railroad bridge over the Potomac River from Maryland to Harpers Ferry, Virginia. There they seized the federal arsenal, capturing several million dollars worth of arms. Brown sent out patrols to rouse enslaved African Americans in the surrounding area. But the hoped–for uprising never occurred.

Soon a church bell rang out, warning farmers and neighboring militia that there was trouble. Local residents and troops rallied, and the shooting began. Trapped inside the arsenal, one after another of Brown's supporters fell. In the morning, marines stormed the arsenal and captured the remaining defenders. One of Brown's African American supporters, Osborne Perry Anderson, escaped and later wrote a book about the raid.

Reaction to Brown's Raid. The first reaction to the raid in both the North and the South was shock. In Virginia, angry mobs clamored for Brown's blood, and authorities feared a lynching. In the North, even some abolitionists saw Brown's raid as misguided and rash, the work of a "madman."

Brown, who was slightly wounded, was tried for treason to Virginia. His quiet and dignified behavior at his trial won over much public opinion in the North. More and more Northerners began to see Brown as a martyr. A group of African American women in Brooklyn, New York, expressed this view in a letter to Brown shortly before he was hanged:

We, a portion of the American people, . . . recognize in you a Saviour commissioned [sent] to redeem us, the American people, from the Great National Sin of Slavery; and though you have apparently failed in the object of your desires, yet the influence that we believe it [the raid] will eventually exert [have] will accomplish all your intentions.

Such expressions of sympathy enraged many in the South even more. A Baltimore newspaper asked if the South could afford any longer "to live under a government, the majority of whose subjects or citizens regard Brown as a martyr and a Christian hero?"

Taking Another Look

1. What was the purpose of Brown's raid on Harpers Ferry?

2. **a.** In what ways did Brown's raid fail? **b.** What, if anything, did it achieve?

3. **Critical Thinking** Should John Brown be considered a hero or an enemy of the state? Explain.

LOOKING AHEAD

Hopes for a peaceful settlement of the slavery issue faded rapidly in the 1850s. The Fugitive Slave Law of 1850 angered abolitionists and other Northerners. The U.S. Supreme Court's decision in the Dred Scott case further provoked abolitionists. An attempt by the abolitionist John Brown to stir up a revolt among enslaved African Americans failed but produced more angry voices—this time in the South. By now, many people in both the North and the South believed an armed conflict over slavery had become unavoidable.

How can you tell that the painter of this picture of John Brown's last moments was sympathetic to Brown?

CLOSE UP: Chapter 16

On April 6, 1846, Dred Scott and his wife Harriet climbed the stairs of the St. Louis Courthouse in St. Louis, Missouri. Thus began the Scott family's long journey through the legal system—from state courts to the federal court of appeals to the Supreme Court of the United States. Their walk up the steps that day made the Scotts and the Old Courthouse famous.

Lawyers battled out the first two trials in the Old Courthouse in 1847 and in 1850. The Scotts did not return to the building until 1858, a year after their Supreme Court loss. Climbing the stairs in 1858 were Dred Scott, Harriet, and their daughters Eliza and Lizzie. They had come to the Old Courthouse to apply for licenses to remain in Missouri as "free negroes."

In the 1930s, President Franklin D. Roosevelt declared the Old Courthouse an historic site. In 1977, a group of African Americans placed a plaque at the site of the actual courtroom of the Scott trials. It read: "Dred Scott: American Pioneer, participant in the legal struggle for citizenship that rocked America."

Today, the State Bar Association of Missouri holds mock trials in that courtroom to commemorate the case. Once again, the Scotts, portrayed by actors, stand in the Old Courthouse awaiting their freedom.

The Who, What, Where of History

1. **What** were the provisions of the Missouri Compromise?
2. **What** was the Compromise of 1850?
3. **What** was the Fugitive Slave Law?
4. **Who** was Anthony Burns?
5. **What** were personal liberty laws?
6. **What** was the Supreme Court's decision in the Dred Scott case?
7. **What** did John Brown do?

Making the Connection

1. What was the connection between the Fugitive Slave Law and personal liberty laws?
2. What was the connection between Dred Scott's claim to freedom and the Missouri Compromise?

Time Check

1. When was the Fugitive Slave Law passed?
2. Which of these events happened *first:* John Brown's raid, the Dred Scott decision, the capture of Anthony Burns in Boston?

What Would You Have Done?

1. If you had lived in Boston in 1854, would you have tried to help Anthony Burns? Explain.
2. If you had lived in the North when the Fugitive Slave Law was passed, would you have obeyed or disobeyed that law? Explain.

Thinking and Writing About History

1. Imagine that you are a former enslaved African American living in New York State in 1854. Write a letter to a friend explaining why you are moving to Canada.

2. Look at the picture of John Brown by Horace Pippin in "The Artist's View." Review the chapter for information about Brown, then write a brief newspaper article about the event in the painting.

Building Skills: Primary and Secondary Sources

If you ever watch mystery or detective shows on television, then you know something about how a detective solves a crime. First, the detective looks for clues.

When a historian tries to decide what really happened at a certain time in the past, he or she acts much like a detective. Some of the clues that historians use come from *primary sources*. A primary source is an original document that comes from the actual time period being studied. Letters, journals, legal records, autobiographies—all these are primary sources. A *secondary source* is an account written at a later time that describes or analyzes an event or person from the past. Usually, the writer of a secondary source, such as a textbook or a biography, has used primary sources to find the facts.

1. In this chapter, several primary sources are quoted. Scan the text to find three primary sources used in this chapter.

2. To be sure that you can tell the difference between primary and secondary sources, study the list of books and articles below. On a separate sheet of paper, write the letters of the primary sources and explain why each is a primary source.

a. "John Brown's Last Statement to the Court"

b. a book called *From Slavery to Freedom* by John Hope Franklin, first published in 1947

c. a book called *Narrative of the Life and Adventures of Henry Bibb, an American Slave, Written by Himself,* first published in 1850

d. a biography of Frederick Douglass called *Frederick Douglass,* by William McFeely, published in 1991

e. a book called *John Brown of Harpers Ferry,* by John Anthony Scott, published in 1988

f. *Army Life in a Black Regiment,* by Thomas Higginson, published in 1870

g. articles about the raid on Harpers Ferry from the October 18, 1859, New York *Herald*

h. *The Black Americans: A History in Their Own Words, 1619–1983* edited by Milton Meltzer, published in 1987 in paperback

i. "The Execution of John Brown," *The Anglo-African Magazine,* published in 1859

CHAPTER 17

54th Massachusetts Infantry at the Battle of Fort Wagner

The Civil War and the End of Slavery

(1861–1865)

THINKING ABOUT THE CHAPTER

What was the impact of the Civil War on African Americans?

It was not until 1862 that African Americans were officially allowed to enlist in the Union army. But once they joined, they fought with valor. Perhaps the most famous battle in which African Americans fought was the attack on Fort Wagner, which guarded the harbor of Charleston, South Carolina. The assault began at dusk on July 18, 1863, and was led by the 54th Massachusetts Infantry, an African American regiment. Its white commander, Colonel Robert Shaw, was eager to prove the ability, skill, and courage of his men.

At 7:45 P.M., 600 men of the 54th charged up an open beach toward the fort. Some 1,700 Confederate defenders raced to the walls of the fort and opened fire on them. Despite the heavy fire, African American soldiers reached the top wall of the fort and held it for an hour before being forced back. The 54th lost nearly half its men in the battle, including Colonel Shaw.

Although the attack failed, it proved the courage of African American soldiers. White Northerners who had believed African Americans would run in battle now saw them differently. The *Atlantic Monthly* declared, "Through the cannon fire of that dark night, the manhood of the colored race shines before many eyes that would not see."

The Civil War began as a war to save the Union, and African American troops made a significant contribution to reaching that goal. In 1863, a second and equally important goal of the war became the freeing of enslaved African Americans.

1 ON THE ROAD TO ENDING ▼ SLAVERY

▼ What did the Emancipation Proclamation do?

On a hot summer night in 1862, President Abraham Lincoln walked across the White House lawn to the nearby telegraph office. Borrowing some paper, he sat down at an old desk and began to write. Sometimes, he crossed out words, or chewed on his pencil as he thought. Finally, he put his notes in his pocket and walked back to the White House. What he had written was an early draft of the historic Emancipation Proclamation, a major step in ending the enslavement of African Americans in the United States.

Pressure to Free the Enslaved. Since the beginning of the Civil War, in 1861, Lincoln had been under increasing pressure from abolitionists to free enslaved African Americans. Free African Americans were particularly outspoken in

urging that the war be fought to end slavery. Frederick Douglass argued:

> The negro is the key of the situation— the pivot (hinge) upon which the whole rebellion turns. . . . Tell the rebels and traitors that the price they are to pay for the attempt to abolish this Government must be the abolition of slavery.

Lincoln resisted. He said that his main goal was to save the Union, not to destroy slavery. Lincoln personally opposed slavery, but he feared that outlawing it would drive the four border states—Missouri, Kentucky, Maryland, and Delaware—into the Confederacy. The border states were slave–holding states that had remained loyal to the Union. Lincoln was once told that freeing enslaved African Americans would put God on the Union side. He replied, "We would like to have God on our side, but we must have Kentucky."

Beginning in spring 1862, however, Lincoln took a series of steps that climaxed in the Emancipation Proclamation. In April 1862, he supported a bill that freed all enslaved African Americans in Washington, D.C. Slave holders were paid up to $300 for each individual. The same bill outlined a plan to pay for the passage of those African Americans who wished to move to Haiti in the Caribbean, or to Liberia in Africa. This was consistent with Lincoln's belief that African Americans and whites could not live together peacefully in the United States.

In June 1862, Lincoln signed a bill abolishing slavery in the territories. It was followed by a law setting free all enslaved African Americans who had escaped their Confederate slave holders and fled to Union–held territory. Lincoln also tried, unsuccessfully, to persuade the border states to end bondage.

1861–1865 Civil War

1862 Congress passes law freeing enslaved African Americans in District of Columbia.

Slavery is abolished in the territories.

Law passed freeing all enslaved African Americans who cross into Union-held territory.

Union army recruits African Americans.

1863 Emancipation Proclamation

54th Massachusetts Infantry distinguishes itself at Battle of Fort Wagner.

1865 Confederacy recruits African Americans.

African American units lead Union army into Richmond.

The Emancipation Proclamation.

Meanwhile, the war was going badly for the Union and Lincoln had to do something. In July 1862, he presented a plan to his cabinet for the emancipation of enslaved African Americans. To make emancipation an aim of the war would weaken the South by encouraging enslaved African Americans to desert slave holders. As a result, there would be no one to raise food or perform heavy labor and other noncombat jobs for the Confederate army.

Lincoln also believed that making emancipation a goal of the war would inspire abolitionists and other Northerners with a moral reason to fight, rather than merely a political one. It would be an "act of Justice," he declared in the Emancipation Proclamation. He waited for a Union victory before announcing the Emancipation Proclamation. Otherwise, it might appear that the Proclamation was a sign of weakness. The victory, a costly one, came at Antietam, Maryland, on September 17, 1862.

Five days later, Lincoln announced that on January 1, 1863, he would issue an Emancipation Proclamation. It would free all enslaved African Americans in areas that were in rebellion against the United States—in other words, those areas still held by the Confederate armies. It would not free the more than 800,000 enslaved African Americans in the border states or those in areas that were already in the hands of Union troops.

The Celebration of Emancipation.

Even though at the time it was issued, the Emancipation Proclamation freed only the enslaved people in the areas that were in open rebellion, African Americans greeted it with joy. Frederick Douglass spoke for most African Americans when he declared. "We shout for joy that we live to record this righteous decree."

When the Emancipation Proclamation went into effect, on January 1, 1863, celebrations were held in many Northern cities. African Americans were proud of the part they had played in bringing about this historic declaration and overjoyed at their victory—if still only a partial one. Henry M. Turner, an African American minister in Washington, D.C., described the scene in that city:

White and colored people shook hands, songs were sung, and by this time cannons began to fire at the navy-yard. . . . Great processions of colored and white men marched to

EFFECTS OF THE EMANCIPATION PROCLAMATION, 1863

Where the Emancipation Proclamation did not apply:

- Free states of the Union
- Border states loyal to the Union
- Confederate areas held by the Union

Where the Emancipation Proclamation applied:

- The Confederate States of America

In parts of which states were enslaved African Americans freed by the Emancipation Proclamation? Where in the South were they not freed by the Proclamation

and fro and passed in front of the White House and congratulated President Lincoln on his proclamation. The President came to the window and made responsive bows, and thousands told him, if he would come out of that palace, they would hug him to death. . . . It was indeed a time of times, and a halftime, nothing like it will ever be seen again in this life.

Taking Another Look

1. How did African Americans want the goal of the Civil War to change?

2. What did the Emancipation Proclamation provide?

3. **Critical Thinking** Why was the Emancipation Proclamation greeted so enthusiastically if it actually freed only a small portion of enslaved African Americans?

2 ON THE HOME FRONT

▼ How did the Civil War affect former enslaved African Americans and those still in bondage?

Fear of uprisings, always strong in the South, intensified after the Emancipation Proclamation. One Southern leader wrote: "Our Negro population are going to give us great trouble. . . . The necessary pains to keep them on our side and in order have been unwisely and sadly neglected." Some slave holders were so terrified that they even appealed for protection against uprisings from Union troops that had pushed into their area.

Resistance by Enslaved Africans. Actually, there was little violence by enslaved African Americans. They resisted slave holders in other ways. The most common method was by running away. As Northern troops pushed deeper into Southern territory, thousands fled—often

These enslaved African Americans are fleeing to Union territory across Virginia's Rappahannock River. What were such people called after they reached Union lines?

at great risk—to freedom behind Union lines.

One of those who escaped was Susie King Taylor, aged 14, of Savannah, Georgia. This was her recollection:

The whites would tell their colored people not to go to the Yankees, for they would harness them to carts . . . in place of horses. I asked grandmother one day if this was true. She replied, "Certainly not!", that the white people did not want slaves to go over to the Yankees, and told them things to frighten them. . . . I wanted to see those wonderful "Yankees" so much, as I heard my parents say the Yankee was going to set all the slaves free. Oh, how those people prayed for freedom!

Another form of resistance was refusing to work or to submit to punishment. One disgusted planter said, "*I wish every negro would leave the place* as they will do only what pleases them, go out in the morning when it suits them, come in when they please, etc." Some enslaved African Americans in Louisiana demanded wages for their work. Other forms of resistance included spying for Union troops and seizing a slave holder's property when Union troops arrived.

Forced Aid to the Confederates. By 1862, the Confederacy was faced with a severe labor shortage. At that time, it began forcing enslaved African Americans into service to build fortifications and repair destroyed railroads. They were also forced to work in factories that made weapons for the Confederate army. Large numbers of African Americans in bondage performed heavy labor for the army. They were also cooks, teamsters, mechanics, nurses in hospitals, orderlies and ambulance drivers.

Behind Union Lines. Over time, about half a million enslaved African Americans fled to the Union side during the war. These people were known as **contrabands.** Some 200,000 of them went to work for the army not as soldiers but as laborers, cooks, teamsters, carpenters, and

194

nurses. Some contrabands also provided the army with important information about Confederate supplies, troop movements, and morale in the ranks.

Life was hard for many African Americans who escaped to the Union lines. Often, they were regarded as burdens by the army. Many were put back to work on the land they had recently tended during bondage. Sometimes they had to work for former slave holders. Although free, they were often brutally treated and received only a fraction of the pay they were entitled to.

Taking Another Look

1. How did enslaved African Americans in the South resist slave holders during the Civil War?

2. What services did escaped African Americans perform for the Union army?

3. **Critical Thinking** Why do you think Union officers often considered former enslaved African Americans to be burdens?

3 ON THE WAR FRONT
▼ What was the contribution of African American soldiers to Union victory?

Why does the government reject the negro? Is he not a man? Can he not wield [handle] a sword, fire a gun, march and countermarch and obey orders like any other? . . . This is no time to fight with one hand when both are needed; this is no time to fight with only your white hand and allow your black hand to remain tied.

With these words, Frederick Douglass urged the U.S. government to change its policy and allow African Americans into the armed forces in the Civil War. When the war began, many African Americans volunteered to serve in the Union army, but they were turned down. In Cincinnati, whites shouted at them, "Keep out of this; this is a white man's war!" A great many whites at this time considered African Americans "inferior" and did not want them in the army.

President Lincoln opposed African American enlistment for political reasons.

These soldiers of the 4th U.S. Colored Infantry were part of the defense of the nation's capital.

Robert Smalls—Pilot in Charleston harbor; took control of Confederate ship and turned it over to Union

William Bronson—Member of first African American company to see action in the war

Nicholas Biddle—One of the first African American Union soldiers to be wounded in the war

Charles L. Mitchell—Captain in a Massachusetts regiment; captured two Confederate cannons and turned them on the enemy in battle at James Island, South Carolina

William H. Carney—Sergeant with 54th Massachusetts Infantry, received Medal of Honor for bravery in planting the flag under fire at the Battle of Fort Wagner

William H. Carney

Peter Vogelsang—Lieutenant with the 54th Massachusetts Infantry; one of three African Americans to be made officers in the regiment

Powhatan Beaty—Received Medal of Honor for assuming command of his company when all officers had been killed or wounded in 1864 battle

Decatur Dorsey—Received Medal of Honor for heroism in battle at Petersburg, Virginia, in 1864

Aaron Anderson—Served in Union navy, received Medal of Honor for courage in an 1865 naval battle

Milton M. Holland—Awarded Medal of Honor for taking command of his company after the officers had been killed or wounded

Harriet Tubman—Conducted raids on Confederate territory; spied for the Union

---

It was essential, he believed, to keep the slave-holding border states from leaving the Union and joining the Confederacy. "To arm the negroes," he said, "would turn 50,000 bayonets from the loyal Border States against us. . . ."

Change in Union Policy. Union defeats on the battlefield between 1861 and the first half of 1862 persuaded the government to change its policy about enlisting African Americans. In July 1862, Congress passed an act that permitted the President "to use as many persons of African descent" as he needed "for suppression of the Rebellion."

African Americans, free and enslaved, flocked to recruiting offices. Many runaways hoped that their joining the army would bring victory for the Union—and with it, freedom. Elijah Marrs, an African American who had escaped from bondage in Kentucky, recalled the moment when he joined the Union army: "I felt freedom in my bones," he said.

In time, some 186,000 African Americans saw combat in the Union army. About 29,000 African Americans served

In order to urge African Americans to volunteer in 1863, the Union army circulated advertisements showing this picture of African American troops in uniform.

in the Union navy. African Americans made up about 10 percent of the Union's armed forces, although they represented less than 1 percent of the population of the North. Between 75 and 100 became officers. Twenty African American soldiers were awarded the Medal of Honor, the Union's highest military honor.

About 38,000 African American troops died in the war, a much higher rate than for white soldiers. Often African American soldiers were inadequately trained and given inferior weapons. Many died because of poor medical care. The high death rate of African American troops was also a result of their frequent attacks on the strongest enemy positions.

African American women played a role in the war, too. Some served as nurses for the army. Harriet Tubman, the Underground Railroad conductor, led raids into Confederate territory and served as a Union spy. In some Southern cities captured by Union troops, African American women organized relief committees.

African Americans as Union Soldiers. Even though African Americans were recruited, they were generally not treated as the equal of white soldiers. For the most part they were used as laborers, rather than fighters. They were paid $10 a month minus clothing expenses, while white soldiers got $13 a month plus clothing expenses. African American soldiers objected strongly to this discrimination. Finally, in 1864, the War Department began paying them the same amount as whites. Throughout the war, African Americans served in separate units, almost always commanded by whites.

Many African Americans who enlisted complained that they were no better off than enslaved labor. African American units were employed mainly in the backbreaking work of building fortifications behind the lines. An African American soldier from Louisiana wrote a letter of protest to Lincoln. "Instead of the musket," he said, "it is the spade and the wheelbarrow and the axe."

Finally, an order was issued limiting the amount of heavy labor by African American troops to "their fair share . . . to prepare them for the higher duties of conflicts with the enemies." Eventually, African American soldiers saw action against Confederate forces in hundreds of engagements.

Southern White Reaction. The use of African American troops by the North enraged most Southerners. They regarded African American soldiers as traitors or rebels who should be treated as such. But when the tide of war had turned against the South, some Confederate leaders, commanding general Robert E. Lee and president of the Confederacy Jefferson Davis among them, agreed that African Americans should serve as Confederate soldiers. President Davis's decision in 1865 to recruit African Americans came too late to help the Confederacy. The South was already defeated and would surrender in two weeks.

Confederate Secretary of War James A. Seddon reacted to the news of African American Union troops by saying, "We ought never to be inconvenienced with such prisoners. . . . Summary [quick] execution must therefore be inflicted on those taken." Some Southern commanders carried out Seddon's directive. The worst example occurred at Fort Pillow, on the Mississippi River, on April 12, 1864. After its capture by Confederate forces under the command of General

What does this picture of an army cook show about how the Union army used many African Americans?

The aftermath of the battle of Fort Pillow was one of the worst examples of Southern revenge on African American troops. Why do you think Forrest ordered the massacre?

Nathan B. Forrest, all African Americans taken as prisoners were massacred.

Despite the fear of such acts, African Americans fought valiantly throughout the war. On the day Union troops finally marched into Richmond, Virginia, the Confederate capital, African American units were in the lead.

Taking Another Look

1. Why did President Lincoln at first oppose the enlistment of African Americans?

2. Why did the Union change its policy?

3. **Critical Thinking** About 125 years after the Battle of Fort Wagner, a major motion picture about the 54th Massachusetts Infantry was made. What qualities about the men of this regiment would you expect to see in this movie?

LOOKING AHEAD

The release of the Emancipation Proclamation changed the Civil War from a war to save the Union to a war that also sought to free enslaved African Americans. Hundreds of thousands of them escaped to Union lines, depriving the South of their invaluable labor. Others slowed down their work, reducing the production of food and other goods needed by the South.

Both free African Americans and contrabands entered the Union army in large numbers and played a substantial role in winning the war. The conduct of African American troops in battle won the admiration of many. Having played a major part in the war, African Americans now looked forward to living as free Americans.

FOCUS ON

THE MAKING OF GLORY

Union soldiers charge up the hill toward the fort. Confederate soldiers open fire. Many of the Yankees, including their commanding officer, fall, mortally wounded. "Cut!" yells the director.

This is not a real battle but the filming of a scene from the Civil War movie *Glory*. The movie tells the story of the 54th Massachusetts Volunteer Infantry—an African American regiment in the Union army.

Glory won three Academy Awards in 1989. Denzel Washington won the award for best supporting actor for his portrayal of Trip, an enslaved African American who enlists in the Union army. The movie also won for sound and cinematography.

Historian Shelby Foote helped the filmmakers make the movie realistic. For example, the film shows that the soldiers were not given a left shoe and a right shoe. Instead, both shoes were the same, becoming "left" and "right" after soldiers wore them. The film also paid attention to battle details, such as soldiers marching shoulder to shoulder. Historian Peter Burchard wrote: "It took great heart . . . to tell the story of the 54th as it is told in *Glory*—from the point of view of the regiment's rank and file [ordinary soldiers]."

The Who, What, Where of History

1. **What** was the 54th Massachusetts Infantry?
2. **Who** was President of the Union during the Civil War?
3. **What** does the word *secede* mean?
4. **What** does the word *emancipation* mean?
5. **What** were the four border states?
6. **What** did the Emancipation Proclamation do?
7. **What** did enslaved African Americans do to resist during the war?
8. **Who** were the contrabands?
9. **What** jobs were African Americans first given in the Union army?

Making the Connection

1. What was the connection between President Lincoln's refusal to free enslaved African Americans and the border states?
2. What was the connection between the battles fought between 1861 and the first half of 1862 and the decision to enlist African Americans in the Union army?

Time Check

By late 1865, all enslaved African Americans in the United States were free. Use the Snapshot on page 192 and the information in the chapter to answer this question: In which of the following places did slavery end last: Washington, D.C.; Kansas Territory; Richmond, Virginia?

What Would You Have Done?

1. If you had been a free African American man during the Civil War, would you have enlisted in the Union army? Explain.

2. If you had been an enslaved African American during the Civil War, would you have resisted slavery? Explain.

3. If you had been a free African American in the North on January 1, 1863, would you have celebrated the Emancipation Proclamation? Explain.

Thinking and Writing About History

1. Design a recruiting poster encouraging African Americans to enlist in the Union army. Give at least two reasons to join the army.

2. Choose one of the heroes listed in the Honor Roll of the Civil War. Write a letter to the state senators of the state where he or she lived explaining why you think that person should have a memorial in the state capitol. Write an inscription for the plaque that would be on the statue. See page 188 for a model.

Building Skills: Interpreting a Primary Source

Have you ever seen a mystery movie in which all the clues point to one suspect, but in the end you find out that someone else committed the crime? A good detective always interprets clues carefully. A good historian has to interpret carefully the sources he or she uses, as well.

Primary sources often express opinions. A historian must decide what value to place on the opinions he or she finds in a source. For example, sometimes the opinions are not based on facts; sometimes the opinions may be biased by a speaker's prejudices.

Imagine that you are a historian working on a book about the role of African American soldiers in the Civil War. You have found a letter dated 1864 about African American soldiers in the Union army. It says, in part:

At Milliken's Bend, at Port Hudson, Morris Island and other battlefields, they have proved themselves among the bravest of brave, performing deeds of daring and shedding their blood with a heroism unsurpassed by soldiers of any other race.

You are trying to interpret the letter and to decide how much value to place on it. Answer the following questions about the letter:

1. Does the letter express facts and/or the writer's opinion?

2. List the facts and/or opinion.

3. Is the opinion, if any, based on facts?

4. How could you find out?

5. Suppose the letter was written by one of two people: the editor of an abolitionist newspaper or Secretary of War Edwin Stanton writing to President Lincoln. Whose opinion would you value most in this case? Explain.

Sharecroppers during Reconstruction

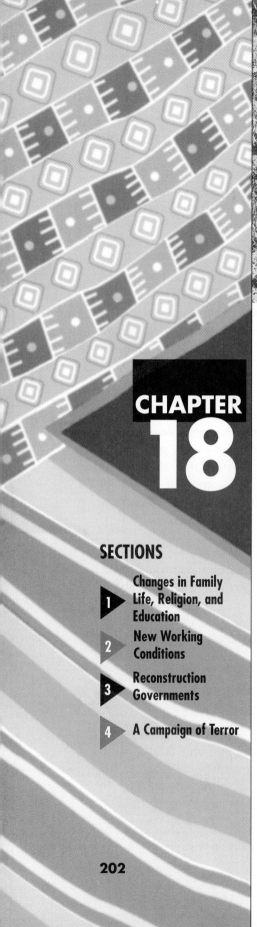
The Promise and Failure of Reconstruction

(1865–1877)

THINKING ABOUT THE CHAPTER

What were the benefits and disappointments of Reconstruction for African Americans?

Slavery was over at last, but what would freedom be like? How would the 4 million African Americans who had been held in bondage live? How would they find work? The account of a woman who had been enslaved in Mississippi typified the feelings of many newly freed African Americans as they faced the unknown world of freedom.

When freedom come, folks left home, out in the streets, crying, praying, singing, shouting, yelling, and knocking down everything. Some shot off guns. Then came the calm. It was sad then. So many folks dead, things tore up, and nowhere to go and nothing to eat, nothing to do.

In the 12 years of Reconstruction, from the end of the Civil War, in 1865, to 1877, enormous changes occurred in the lives of African Americans. As you will read in this chapter, Reconstruction was both a period of hope and achievement for African Americans and a time of great disappointment for them.

1 CHANGES IN FAMILY LIFE, ▼ RELIGION, AND EDUCATION

▼ What changes occurred in family life, religion, and education as a result of Reconstruction?

"Samuel Jefferson." "Charles Washington." These were the names two African Americans gave when they went to vote for the first time. Before emancipation, their white owners had called them by their first names only. But after the Civil War, many newly freed African Americans were able to use their **surnames,** or family names. Enslaved African Americans had chosen these names themselves, and they were often the names of early slave holders. These surnames helped to weave together a vast network of family—grandparents, great grandparents, aunts, uncles, and cousins—who lived on a particular farm or plantation. When a family was broken up through sale, its surname helped to preserve a sense of family among separated members.

At emancipation, those African Americans who did not already have surnames took them, but rarely chose the name of their recent owner. They often took the names of famous people like George Washington or Thomas Jefferson. Whatever their choices, newly freed African Americans were ready for a new life.

Reunited Families. During slavery, thousands of African American families had been broken up when husbands, wives, children, and other family members were sold to distant plantation owners. With freedom came the chance for separated families to reunite. Many African Americans appealed to the Freedmen's Bureau for help in finding long-gone relatives. Other African Americans took off on their own in search of their families. In September 1865, one freed African American walked more than 600 miles, from Georgia to North Carolina, looking for his wife and children.

New Patterns of Family Life. Now that they were free, African Americans wanted to establish a normal family life. Under slavery, many men and women lived together without having been formally married. Now, many insisted on being legally joined in marriage.

African American men now assumed the role of head of their family, a role often denied them under slavery. Many refused to allow their wives to work in the fields, as they had before the Civil War. Men also took over the disciplining of their children, a right their former slave holders had frequently exercised.

Churches of Their Own. Before emancipation, most enslaved African Americans did not have their own churches. They worshiped in separate sections of white churches. There were some African American churches in the South before the Civil War. However, after the Emancipation Proclamation, the numbers of such churches grew very rapidly.

Across the South, church members pooled their resources to buy land and erect houses of worship. There were many Baptist churches, but there were also African Methodist Episcopal and African Methodist Episcopal Zion congrega-

1865 Southern white secret societies begin campaign of terror.

1865–1877 Reconstruction

20 African Americans serve in U.S. House of Representatives, 2 in the Senate, 600 in Southern state legislatures.

1867 Freedmen's Bureau has set up almost 4,500 schools.

1867–1868 Southern states draw up new constitutions.

1870 Hiram Revels is sworn in as U.S. Senator from Mississippi.

1870s Public schools replace Freedmen's Bureau schools.

1874 Blanche K. Bruce is elected to U.S. Senate.

1877 White Democrats are in power in all former Confederate states.

tions. More than places of worship, they also housed schools, social gatherings, and political meetings.

African American ministers were often the most respected people in their communities, and they were expected to be leaders. Many of the African American men elected to political office were ministers. In the African American community today, ministers still hold a central position of power and esteem.

The Thirst for Education.

It is surprising to me to see the amount of suffering which many of the people endure for the sake of sending their children to school. . . . They are anxious to have the children 'get on' in their books and do not seem to feel impatient if they lack comforts themselves.

This is how a Northern white woman described the eagerness of former enslaved African Americans for the chance to educate their children and themselves. Before the war, some free African Americans in the South had gone to school. Some enslaved African Americans had learned to read and write on their own or with the help of sympathetic slave holders. However, their numbers were small.

After the war, groups of African Americans throughout the South raised money to buy land, build schools, and pay teachers' salaries. Also, by 1867, the Freedmen's Bureau had set up almost 4,500 schools. These schools were not free, and paying tuition was a considerable burden for families. Tuition often represented 10 percent or more of their monthly income. Yet the schools were full. By 1870, bureau schools enrolled 250,000 pupils.

Many of the teachers were African American women. A resident of Selma, Alabama, wrote, "I trust the fact will never be ignored that Miss Lucy Lee, one of the emancipated, was the pioneer teacher of the colored children."

In the 1870s, the bureau schools were replaced by public schools. During the short period when racially **integrated** governments ruled Southern states, the same schools were open to both African American and white children.

Taking Another Look

1. List two important changes that occurred in African American family life during Reconstruction.

2. What part did churches play in Southern African Americans' lives?

3. How did the Freedmen's Bureau help to provide education for Southern African Americans?

4. **Critical Thinking** Why do you think education for former enslaved African Americans has been described as the most revolutionary result of Reconstruction?

2 NEW WORKING CONDITIONS

▼ What changes occurred in how African Americans in the South earned their living?

Until Reconstruction, enslaved African Americans had worked for slave holders. Now, they had the chance to work for themselves. This was one of the most satisfying changes for African Americans that came from the Civil War. "I felt like the richest man in the world," said a former enslaved African American in Arkansas after receiving one dollar for work he had done for a railroad.

Why do you think most freed African Americans built their cabins away from the landlord's house?

▶▶ **DIAGRAM OF A SOUTHERN PLANTATION, 1880s**

What does this picture of a Freedmen's Bureau school tell you about the students' desire to learn?

New Freedoms. Not only could they work for wages, but African Americans in the South were free to work where they wanted. Although many worked for former slave holders at their old jobs, others did not. One African American woman who, when enslaved, had worked as a cook for a South Carolina family explained why she chose to leave: "I must go," she said. "If I stay here, I'll never know I'm free."

Those who did stay refused to live in their old quarters, which were generally near a slave holder's house. Instead, they insisted that their pay include money to build new cabins far from their old homes and far from the prying eyes of the plantation owner.

The Sharecropping System. Earning a living in the ruined South turned out to be very difficult. Few former enslaved African Americans could afford to buy land, and even if they could, whites would not sell it to them. Many states had laws that prohibited African Americans from owning land. How then were newly freed African Americans to survive?

At the end of the Civil War, newly freed African Americans were given the im-

Despite its drawbacks, why did sharecropping seem to African Americans to be an improvement over slavery?

pression that they would receive "40 acres and a mule" from the federal government. This would have enabled them to become independent farmers. Without land, they would be at the mercy of former slave holders. Some African Americans did become landowners, but hopes of government help never materialized. Gradually a system of farm labor known as **sharecropping** developed.

Under this system, a family farmed a small plot of land belonging to another, in return for a share of the crop. Having little means of support until the harvest, the family bought supplies and groceries on **credit,** the promise to pay in the future. After the harvest, the landowner or storekeeper (who was sometimes the same person), subtracted these growing debts from the money the family would receive from the sale of the crop. So little

money was left that the family needed more credit to start again.

As a result, sharecropping became a cycle of poverty and debt. As John Solomon Lewis, an African American sharecropper, put it, "I was in debt and the man I rented land from said every year I must rent again to pay the other year, so I rents and rents and each year I gets deeper and deeper in debt."

Taking Another Look

1. List three changes in African Americans' working conditions after the Civil War.

2. How did the sharecropping system work?

3. **Critical Thinking** Do you think an African American might have thought sharecropping was better than slavery? Explain.

3 ▼ RECONSTRUCTION GOVERNMENTS

▼ What part did African Americans play in Southern governments during Reconstruction?

During Reconstruction, African Americans in the South became politically active. Once given the right to vote, they used it to elect many African Americans to local, state, and federal offices. The high point of their political participation may have come on February 25, 1870. On that day, Hiram Revels, a Republican from Mississippi, was sworn in as senator, becoming the first African American ever to serve in the U.S. Senate. What made the event even more noteworthy was that Revels had been elected to fill the seat once held by Jefferson Davis, the former president of the Confederacy.

African Americans in State Conventions.

The Reconstruction plan enacted by Congress in 1867 called for conventions to be held in the former Confederate states to draw up new constitutions. All of the conventions had African American delegates, but they made up a majority only in South Carolina.

The state constitutions drawn up in 1867 and 1868 abolished property qualifications for voting and holding office. They granted the right to vote to adult males, except for some former Confederates.

African Americans in State Offices.

Backed by the presence of U.S. troops, African American men flocked to the polls. They represented about 80 percent of Republican voters, and they helped elect Republican legislatures that included African American members. Yet African Americans did not dominate any state government. In South Carolina, they had a large majority in the lower house of the legislature. However, whites controlled the upper house, and there was always a white governor.

In all, more than 600 African Americans served in Southern state legislatures during Reconstruction. Eighteen held

How did Hiram Revels make history when he was sworn in as a U.S. Senator from Mississippi?

A candidate for office campaigns. Why do you think the women were listening, even though they could not vote?

such major offices as lieutenant governor, treasurer, superintendent of education, and secretary of state. In Louisiana, Lieutenant-Governor P. B. S. Pinchback became governor for 43 days when the elected governor was impeached. Pinchback was the first African American governor in U.S. history.

Reconstruction governments, with considerable pressure from African Americans, greatly expanded services for both newly freed African Americans and poor whites. Public schools, hospitals, and institutions for the mentally ill were established for the first time in many areas. South Carolina pioneered medical care for needy citizens. Alabama was the first state to provide legal aid for poor defendants. State legislatures did away with earlier Black Codes, outlawed corporal punishment, and reduced both capital punishment and the penalties for theft.

African Americans in the Federal Government.

From 1869 to 1876, 20 African Americans were elected to the

U.S. House of Representatives, and 2 served in the U.S. Senate. As you have read, one of the senators was Hiram Revels. The other was Blanche K. Bruce, also from Mississippi.

Born into bondage in Virginia in 1841, **Blanche K. Bruce** (1841–1898) ran away to freedom when the Civil War began. He later attended Oberlin College in Ohio for two years, until his money ran out. In 1869, Bruce went to Mississippi, where he entered politics.

In 1871, he ran as a Republican candidate for sheriff of Bolivar County, Mississippi, against a white Democrat. In a debate, the Democrat accused Bruce of having been "a slave who did nothing but wait on his master." Bruce replied, "It is true that I was a house slave. But I freed myself, educated myself, and raised myself up in the world. If my opponent had started out where I did, he would still be there." Bruce won the election.

In 1874, Bruce was elected to the U.S. Senate. As a senator, he fought for the rights of African Americans. When he died, in March 1898, it was said that he was second in importance only to Frederick Douglass as a leader of his people.

A White Backlash. In taking back their state governments after 1877, many Southern whites accused Reconstruction governments of corruption. They ignored the fact that in the years after the Civil War, dishonesty in state and local governments was widespread—in North and South, among Democrats and Republicans, and whites and African Americans.

Another charge whites leveled against African Americans in government was that they were uneducated. In fact, almost all African American officeholders on the state and federal levels could read and write. Many were professionals with advanced degrees, or owned businesses and had at least high school educations.

Taking Another Look

1. In what ways did the new state constitutions benefit African Americans?

2. What did Reconstruction state governments accomplish?

3. **Critical Thinking** What qualities did Blanche K. Bruce have that would make all Americans proud of him?

4 A CAMPAIGN OF TERROR

▼ Why did Southern whites try to intimidate African Americans?

Many white Southerners were unable to accept the idea of African Americans' being free, attending school, being able to vote, and holding public office. Almost as soon as the Civil War was over, secret societies grew up in the South to terrorize African Americans. Groups such as the Ku Klux Klan and the White Camelia used violence, arson, and murder to keep African Americans "in their place." In time, the major aim became to destroy the Reconstruction governments.

Between 1865 and 1866, about 5,000 African Americans were murdered in the South in racial incidents. In a typical incident in 1866, a white mob in Memphis,

Tennessee, burned African American homes, churches, and schools, and killed 46 African Americans. Years later, an African American recalled Klan activity in North Carolina:

The government built schoolhouses, and the Ku Klux Klan went to work and burned 'em down. . . . The Ku Kluxes . . . wore long sheets and covered the horses with sheets so you couldn't recognize 'em. Men you thought was your friends was Ku Kluxes, and you'd deal with them in stores in the daytime, and at night they'd come out to your house and kill you.

For the most part, such activities went unpunished. Sometimes local white officials even participated. State and federal law enforcement officials did nothing to stop the murders and bring the murderers to justice.

Inevitably, the reign of terror against African Americans and their white allies had its effect. Although some African Americans voted in spite of threats, more and more African Americans stayed away

from the polls in fear. The result was that Republican candidates were defeated and were replaced by white Democrats. One by one, the Reconstruction governments fell. By 1877, when the last U.S. troops were withdrawn from the South, white Democrats were in power everywhere in the former Confederacy. The hopes of African Americans for their equal rights and economic independence were dead in the South.

Taking Another Look

1. Why did white Southerners conduct a campaign of terror against African Americans?

2. How successful were the Ku Klux Klan and similar organizations in their campaign against African Americans?

3. **Critical Thinking** Why do you think white state and local officials allowed the terror to continue without punishing the participants?

LOOKING AHEAD

Reconstruction has been called "America's unfinished revolution." African Americans took advantage of freedoms denied them under slavery. They formed their own churches, worked through political action to achieve full citizenship for males, and eagerly took advantage of the education available to men and women and children.

But generally African Americans remained poor and dependent on white landowners, after Congress failed to give them land of their own. Before long, whites were using terror and violence to destroy the Reconstruction governments. African Americans would have to fight long and hard for the promise of Reconstruction to become a reality.

Ku Klux Klan members disguised themselves before their raids. What was the purpose of the group?

FOCUS ON — MAKING A FEDERAL CASE

The slave went free; stood for a brief moment in the sun; then moved back again toward slavery.

So said W.E.B. Du Bois of Reconstruction. The laws passed during Reconstruction held out great hope for African Americans. Yet, for nearly a century after the end of Reconstruction, the federal government failed to enforce them.

The laws were passed to strike at terrorism by the Ku Klux Klan in 1870–1871. Local officials had refused to act against the Klan, so federal agents stepped in—as the new laws allowed. The laws enabled the government to enter into brutality cases in which a public official, such as a police officer, violated a person's civil rights.

The laws were not enforced again until the Civil Rights Movement of the 1960s. In a 1964 case, sheriff's deputies were charged with murdering three civil rights workers near Philadelphia, Mississippi. The federal government cited Reconstruction laws to justify its intervention into the local matter.

The laws passed during Reconstruction are still used and carry stiff penalties. If convicted, a person can receive up to ten years in prison for each civil rights violation, and a maximum life sentence for those violations that end in death.

The Who, What, Where of History

1. **What** was Reconstruction?
2. **What** is sharecropping?
3. **What** was the Freedmen's Bureau?
4. **Who** was Hiram Revels?
5. **When** were Freedmen's Bureau schools replaced by public schools?
6. **What** does the word *integrated* mean?
7. **What** were Black Codes?
8. **Who** was Blanche K. Bruce?

Making the Connection

1. What was the connection between the end of slavery and African Americans' going to school?
2. What was the connection between the end of slavery and the sharecropping system?

Time Check

1. When was Reconstruction?
2. **a.** Use the timeline on pages 176–177 to find out what amendments to the Constitution were passed during Reconstruction. **b.** Explain each one.

What Would You Have Done?

1. Imagine that you are a newly freed African American in the South during Reconstruction. Will you exercise your newly acquired right to vote? Explain.
2. Imagine that you are a newly freed African American. The plantation where you spent all your life was burned during the war. You have very little to eat. The planter asked you to

stay and work on the land. You have no money and no idea of where else to get a job. Will you stay on your old plantation? Explain.

Thinking and Writing About History

1. Imagine that you are a former enslaved African American woman, a wife and mother. Write a short autobiography. Describe at least two ways your life has changed with the end of slavery.

2. Imagine that you are a candidate for the Florida legislature in the first election after the Civil War. Write a campaign speech explaining what laws you will work to pass.

Building Skills: Classifying Information

Imagine trying to shop in a music store that didn't *classify* tapes and CDs by type of artist, music, and so on. You might have to dig through every item in the store to find what you wanted.

Classifying means grouping or arranging items into classes, or categories, based on similarities. We classify pieces of information for the same reasons we classify CDs and tapes—to keep them organized and to find what we want easily.

In this chapter, you have studied the many effects of Reconstruction. One way to keep these effects straight is to classify them into groups. Three categories into which you might classify the effects are *political, economic,* and *social.*

Review the chapter, looking for effects of Reconstruction that fall into these categories. On a separate piece of paper, organize them into a chart like the one below. Note that sample entries have been made in each category. Be sure to include at least three other effects in each category on your chart.

After you have completed the chart, review it. In which category do you think the effects of Reconstruction were most important? On a separate sheet of paper write a paragraph explaining your choice.

Effects of Reconstruction

Political Effects	Economic Effects	Social Effects
Passage of the 13th Amendment	Development of sharecropping	Reuniting of many African American families

African American settlers on the Great Plains

Miners, Farmers, and Cowhands

(1849–1880)

THINKING ABOUT THE CHAPTER
Why did African Americans leave the South and move west?

I one day said to the man I rented land from, "It's no use. I works hard and raises big crops and you sells it and keeps the money, and brings me more and more in debt. So I will go somewhere else and try to make headway like white workingmen."

These words were written in 1879 by an African American sharecropper who saw no hope for a decent life in the South. Out west, beyond the Mississippi, was a new chance. There African Americans might escape from the limited opportunities, violence, and racism of the South. In the years after the Civil War, thousands of African Americans went west, where they worked as miners, merchants, servants, farmers, and cowhands. Their lives were not easy, but they were better than they had been in the South.

1 THE GOLD RUSH AND AFTER

▼ What roles did African Americans play in the gold fields of California and Colorado?

In 1849, "gold fever" was sweeping the country. Tens of thousands of people were rushing to seek their fortunes in California, where gold had been discovered the year before. The human stampede resulted in an enormous increase in California's population, from 10,000 in 1848 to 100,000 by the end of 1849. Some

The California gold fields attracted many people in 1849. Did most African Americans in California earn their living mining?

came through Beckwourth Pass (see page 103) in the Sierra Nevada.

The California Gold Fields. Two thousand free African Americans were among those who arrived in California hoping to strike it rich. A number of enslaved African Americans also came with slaveholders who expected them to work in the gold fields. Some enslaved African Americans saw California as an opportunity to win their freedom.

Among them were people like Alvin Coffey, his wife, and their three children. With Coffey working on his own at night, he and his family saved more than $5,000 to buy their freedom. The slave holder took Coffey's money and then sold the family to another slave holder. The Coffeys again went to work and soon earned enough money to purchase freedom from their new owner. In time, the Coffeys became the wealthy owners of a laundry in northern California.

Like the Coffeys, few African American settlers in California spent their time searching for gold. Most of them made their living as merchants, barbers, and craftworkers. A few owned newspapers or restaurants.

William Alexander Leidesdorff, who arrived in California in 1841 as a ship captain, is an example of a successful African American settler. Born in the Virgin Islands, Leidesdorff soon established himself as a merchant in Yerba Buena, renamed San Francisco in 1847. He built a considerable business with the ships that came to the harbor and with nearby merchants and ranchers. In time, he owned a 35,000-acre (14,165-hectare) ranch and became an important civic and educational leader of the city.

SNAPSHOT OF THE TIMES

1849	African Americans join California Gold Rush.
1857	African Americans join Colorado Gold Rush.
1876	Deadwood Dick gets his nickname.
1870s	African Americans move west.
1879–1880	Exodusters migrate to Kansas.

The Colorado Gold Fields. In 1857, gold was discovered in Colorado, and once again, African Americans were among those who "rushed" there to make their fortunes.

One of them was **Clara Brown,** born into slavery in Virginia in 1803. At the first news of the gold strike, she bought her freedom with her savings and headed for Central City, Colorado. There, cooking and washing clothes for the miners, she saved enough money to bring many of her relatives to Colorado after the Civil War. She also invested in the mines and in time became one of Colorado's richest citizens. Clara Brown was equally well known for her contributions to charities that benefited both African Americans and whites.

Taking Another Look

1. Why did African Americans—free and enslaved—go to California?

2. How did most African Americans in California earn their living?

3. **Critical Thinking** What qualities do you think the Coffeys, William Leidesdorff, and Clara Brown had in common?

2 ▼ THE EXODUSTERS AND THE SODBUSTERS
▼ What was life like for African Americans on the Great Plains?

John Solomon Lewis, an African American sharecropper, lived in Tensas Parish, Louisiana. This was a heavily African American, Republican county that had been terrorized in the 1878 election by whites seeking to keep African Americans from voting. Lewis was angered not only by the violence but also by his family's poverty. He decided to move. Despite the landowner's threats to prevent them from leaving, Lewis, his wife, and their four children gathered up their belongings and headed west.

The Lewises were among the thousands of African Americans who fled the South in 1879 and 1880 and joined the exodus, or flight, westward. They called themselves **Exodusters** after the Book of Exodus in the Bible that described the Israelites' exodus from Egypt to the Promised Land. The Exodusters saw no other way to escape the poverty of sharecropping and the terror of the Ku Klux Klan than to leave the South.

Leaders of the Exodus. The exodus was organized by two African Americans, Henry Adams and Benjamin

214

"Pap" Singleton. Adams, a former enslaved African American who had served in the U.S. Army, organized a Committee of 500 to live among the newly freed African Americans and report on their condition. Adams recalled:

> We looked around. . . . We said that the whole South had got into the hands of the very men that had held us slaves. . . . Then we said there was no hope for us and we had better go.

Adams and Singleton believed that the way out of poverty and oppression for African Americans was to set up separate communities of African Americans. These communities, they believed, would provide the same economic opportunity for African Americans that the settlements established by white pioneers had done for white Americans.

Singleton, who had also been born in bondage, believed that he had a God–given mission to lead African Americans out of the South. To him, Kansas was the Promised Land, where African Americans would find their salvation.

As early as February 1879, groups of Exodusters, ranging in number from 50 to 600, began arriving in St. Louis for the trip west on the Missouri River to Kansas. Others traveled over land. In all, as many as 50,000 Exodusters went to Kansas and other western areas between 1879 and 1881. No one knows how many others tried to go but were turned back by armed bands of whites.

Settling the Great Plains. The Exodusters were not the only African Americans who left the South for territories beyond the Mississippi in the late 1870s and the 1880s. Hundreds of others also headed west and for many of the same reasons. They settled in Kansas,

Why did thousands of African Americans head west?

Oklahoma, and other areas farther west and north.

Some African American settlers set up their own towns. Most of them, however, moved to farm areas on the Great Plains. Life on the Great Plains was hard. With few trees for lumber, settlers built their houses of sod, the top layer of soil that is thick with grass. For this reason, the settlers were called **sodbusters.** Every season brought its hardships: in spring, swollen streams swept away homes; in summer, intense heat and frequent droughts withered crops and killed livestock; in fall, there were prairie fires; in winter, howling blizzards.

A New Life. Despite these hardships, African American sodbusters were better off than they had been as sharecroppers. Some even managed to buy large farms. Within a few years, African Americans had bought thousands of acres. The example of Henry Carter from Tennessee explains how some African Americans were able to start new lives.

Henry Carter and his wife were penniless in 1879 when they arrived in Topeka, Kansas. They trudged on foot to distant Dunbar with their only possessions—

some bedding and a few hand tools. By 1880, they had cleared 40 acres of land, built a small cottage, and owned a horse and two cows. Carter had earned the money by working on nearby ranches.

In the western states and territories, African Americans also found they were much freer than they had been in the white-controlled South. They could go where they pleased, when they pleased, and for as long as they pleased. There were no curfews. Racial prejudice existed, but it was not as severe as in the South. Although city schools separated whites and African Americans, rural schools, where most African Americans lived, did not.

Sympathetic whites in Kansas even helped some African American newcomers get settled. In May 1880, a newspaper in Topeka reported that about one third of the new settlers had received teams of horses and farm tools and should be self-supporting within a year. In general, the African Americans who fared best were those who had skills and some resources of their own. Only a few African Americans gave up and returned to the South.

Taking Another Look

1. Why did Henry Adams and Pap Singleton want to set up separate African American communities?

2. What was life like for African American settlers in the Plains?

3. Why did few settlers return to the South?

4. **Critical Thinking** Why do you think African American settlers faced less prejudice west of the Mississippi than they did in the South?

216

3 CATTLE DRIVES AND ▼ COWHANDS

What part did African Americans play in the cattle country?

After the Civil War, Texas ranchers found a way to make money from the millions of longhorn cattle that roamed wild on the plains. By 1865, railroads were pushing westward across Missouri and into Kansas. Enterprising Texans began driving herds of cattle 1,000 miles (1,600 kilometers) northward to Abilene and Dodge City, Kansas. There, the cattle were loaded onto railroad freight cars and shipped to market in the East, to be sold at $40 a head.

Countless movies and television programs have portrayed these cattle drives, but rarely, if ever, have African American cowhands been shown. Yet over 5,000 cowhands were African American. A typical trail crew of eight usually included two African Americans.

Some were brought west in bondage and were herding cattle before they were freed. Others came west after the Civil War. They were seeking a new life in a place where skill counted more than the color of a person's skin.

Life on a Cattle Drive.   As a rule, African American cowhands suffered less discrimination than African Americans in other occupations. Working and living conditions on the trail were always difficult, sometimes dangerous. All hands had to be prepared for stampedes, cyclones and tornadoes, rainstorms and snowstorms, and attacks by wild animals. Ranch owners, trail bosses, cowhands— all had to share the same rough living conditions. Even life back home on the ranch wasn't easy. But whereas African Americans were welcomed as cowhands and were paid the same wages as other cowhands—usually a dollar a day—they were rarely promoted to trail boss.

A Living Legend. The most famous African American cowhand was probably Nat Love, better known by his nickname, Deadwood Dick.

Nat Love was born into slavery in Davidson County, Tennessee, in 1854. Freed after the Civil War, he knew only poverty. At age 15, he decided to pull up stakes and head for Kansas.

Arriving in Dodge City, he landed a job as a cowhand at $30 a month plus room and board. For the next 20 years, he made the long drive that brought Texas cattle north to Kansas and beyond. On July 4, 1876, the trail took him to Deadwood, a mining town in the Dakota Territory. Love entered the rodeo held that day and won several roping and shooting contests. In his life story, *The Life and Adventures of Nat Love By Himself*, Love wrote, "Right there the assembled crowd named me 'Deadwood Dick' and proclaimed me champion roper of the Western cattle country." He proudly bore this nickname for the rest of his life.

Cowhands who wrote about themselves were usually boastful, and Love was no exception. But if much of what Love wrote seems unbelievable, his book does give a glimpse of the "Wild West" era and its code for cowhands.

In time, the railroads went south into Texas, making the long cattle drives unnecessary. But the legendary deeds of cowhands on the trail live on in countless stories, films, and TV shows. Contrary to history, however, these **folk heroes** are rarely shown as African Americans.

Taking Another Look

1. How do cattle drives shown in movies and TV programs differ from the way they really were?

2. **Critical Thinking** What did African American cowhands have in common with Exodusters and other settlers in the western states and territories?

LOOKING AHEAD

For thousands of African Americans, as for white Americans, the western states and territories seemed a promised land where it was possible to start life over. Some African Americans—free and slave—went as far as Colorado and California in the mining days. The largest single migration of African Americans took place in 1879 and 1880, when thousands fled the South and settled in Kansas and other parts of the Great Plains. The great majority of African Americans, however, remained in the South. There, in the last quarter of the 1800s, conditions worsened as white legislatures enacted laws to enforce separation from whites and to deprive African Americans of the right to vote.

FOCUS ON: THE BUFFALO SOLDIERS

They were the Buffalo Soldiers—African American soldiers sent west by the federal government during the Plains Wars. Native Americans gave the soldiers their nickname. Knowing the respect Native Americans had for the buffalo, the troops took the name as a compliment, and used it proudly for more than 80 years.

The Buffalo Soldiers came into being on July 28, 1866, when Congress created six African American regiments. Congress wanted some way to end fighting between Native Americans and new settlers on the Great Plains. The job fell to the 24th and 25th Infantries and the 9th and 10th Cavalries.

Some doubted that the newly formed African American units could fight. But 14 Buffalo Soldiers won the Congressional Medal of Honor for service on the Plains.

Buffalo Soldiers fought until 1952, when the federal government disbanded the units because it had ended segregation in the army. In recent years, African American sculptor Eddie Dixon created a monument honoring the accomplishments and courage of the Buffalo Soldiers. It stands in Fort Leavenworth, Kansas, the original home of the 9th and 10th Cavalries.

CLOSE UP: Chapter 19

The Who, What, Where of History

1. **Where** was gold discovered in 1849?
2. **What** did most African Americans do in the gold fields?
3. **Who** was Clara Brown?
4. **Who** were the Exodusters?
5. **Who** were the sodbusters?
6. **Where** are the Great Plains?
7. **Who** were Henry Adams and Benjamin "Pap" Singleton?
8. **What** are folk heroes?
9. **Who** was Nat Love?
10. **When** did the largest western migration of African Americans from the South take place?

Making the Connection

1. What was the connection between the end of Reconstruction and the exodus of African Americans to the Great Plains?
2. What was the connection between slavery and the number of African American cowhands?

Time Check

1. Did the gold rushes in California and Colorado happen before or after the Civil War?
2. Did the Exoduster movement happen before or after the end of Reconstruction?

What Would You Have Done?

1. If you had been an African American determined to leave the South in 1879, where would you have gone? Would you have chosen to be an

Exoduster, a sodbuster, or a cow-hand? Explain.

2. If you had been an Exoduster, would you have settled in one of Adams and Singleton's separate African American communities or in a racially mixed community? Explain.

Thinking and Writing About History

1. Imagine that you are an Exoduster. Write a letter to a friend urging him or her to join you on the trip to Kansas.

2. In the library, find stories and legends of cowhands. Then write your own story about an African American cowhand in which the hero defeats a dangerous opponent, either human or a force of nature.

Building Skills: Drawing Conclusions

A conclusion is a statement that is supported by facts. Every conclusion must have facts that support it. For example, the following sentence is a conclusion: "Despite hardships, African American sodbusters were better off than they had been as sharecroppers." What facts support this conclusion? Here is one supporting fact: "Some African Americans managed to buy large farms." Here is another: "Within a few years, African Americans had bought thousands of acres of land."

Each conclusion below has a set of facts that follow it. Some facts support the conclusion; others do not. For each conclusion, write the letters of the facts that support it.

1. Out west, beyond the Mississippi, African Americans had a new chance.
   a. African Americans might escape from the limited opportunities, violence, and racism of the South.
   b. In the years after the Civil War, thousands of African Americans went west, where they worked as miners, merchants, servants, farmers, and cowhands.
   c. Their lives were easier than in the South.

2. Life on the Great Plains was hard.
   a. In spring, swollen streams swept away homes.
   b. Some African American settlers set up their own towns.
   c. In summer, intense heat and frequent droughts withered crops and killed livestock.

3. In the western states and territories, African Americans found they were much freer than they had been in the South.
   a. City schools separated whites and African Americans.
   b. African Americans could go where they pleased, and for as long as they pleased.
   c. Racial prejudice existed, but it was not as severe as in the South.

4. African American cowhands were not usually victims of discrimination on their jobs.
   a. African Americans were welcomed as cowhands both on ranches and on trail drives.
   b. African American cowhands were paid the same wages as white cowhands, about a dollar a day.
   c. All cowhands, including African Americans, as well as ranch bosses shared the same living conditions on the job.

UNIT 7

MAPLE LEAF RAG.

The King of Ragtime writers
Scott Joplin.

From the cover of the sheet music

FREEDOM WITHOUT EQUALITY

(1877–1910)

Students at Tougaloo College, Tougaloo, Mississippi

Unit 7 traces the changes that took place in the lives of African Americans in the period from the end of Reconstruction, in 1877, to the early years of the 1900s. Growth is the key for this period.

During this time, the United States grew from a nation that was still basically agricultural into one of the world's great industrial powers. It was a time when "big business" expanded and took control of the nation's industry. Immigrants from Europe poured into the factories, mines, and farmlands of the nation. The population almost doubled, and cities mushroomed in the North and Midwest. Such rapid growth and change brought problems as well as benefits, and African Americans experienced more than their share of the problems.

The Growth of Industry. In the 1850s, an Englishman named Henry Bessemer and an American named William Kelly invented a way of making steel quickly and cheaply. When U.S. steel mills began using what was called the Bessemer process in 1867, the country was producing only small amounts of steel. Within 30 years, the United States was turning out 7 million tons (6.4 metric tons) a year, and by 1910, four times that amount. This strong, inexpensive metal was used to manufacture everything from farm equipment and girders for buildings to safety pins.

The greatest immediate use of steel was to enlarge the nation's railroad system. From 52,000 miles (83,700 kilometers) in 1870, it grew to over 166,700 miles (268,000 kilometers) by 1890. With the railroad, products—and people—crisscrossed the nation both quickly and inexpensively.

Two other developments played major roles in the **industrialization** of the United States. In 1879, Thomas Alva Edison, with coworkers such as Lewis H. Latimer, an African American, invented the incandescent light bulb. Later, they developed other applications of electricity. Industries replaced their steam-driven machinery with electrically run machinery. Electric trolleys replaced horse-drawn streetcars in the cities. The telephone, invented in 1876 by Alexander Graham Bell, became a necessity in every office and factory.

Industrial production soared. In the 33 years between 1879 and 1912, the **gross national product**, which is the total value of all goods and services produced in a country, soared from $11.2 billion to $39.4 billion. No other country in the world matched the United States in such growth or such wealth.

The Rise of Big Business. As industrial wealth grew, competitors used various ways to gain larger and larger shares

---

An African American Speaks

The first and dearest rights the Negro of the South wants are the right to pay for his labor, his right of trial by jury, his right to his home, his right to know that the man who lynches him . . . shall be convicted.

—Thomas E. Miller,
Member of Congress, 1891

1876
Alexander Graham Bell
invents telephone.

1880
South has one quarter
of nation's cotton mills.

1885
James B. Duke starts large-scale
cigarette manufacturing in the South.

1890
Sherman
Antitrust Act

1881
Tuskegee Institute
is founded.

1875

1880

1885

1886
Haymarket Riot

American Federation
of Labor (AFL) is organized.

1890

1883
Supreme Court
overturns 1875
Civil Rights Act.

1879
First practical electric
light is invented.

Jan Matzeliger invents
the shoe-lasting machine.

of business for greater and greater profits. Oilman John D. Rockefeller forced competing oil companies to sell out to him or be driven into bankruptcy.

Steel giant Andrew Carnegie chose another path to growth. He bought the mining companies that supplied him with iron ore, the shipping companies and rail lines that brought the ore to his factories, and the warehouses that stored his finished steel. By owning all steps of the steel business, Carnegie was able to outsell his competitors and force most of them out of business.

Through these and other means, more and more large companies secured **monopolies** in their industries. A monopoly is the complete, or nearly complete, control of an industry. As the next step, many large corporations joined together to form even larger corporations, called trusts. Their goal was to control entire industries. By 1888, trusts existed in a wide

range of industries—sugar, whiskey, steel, paper bags, plows, and glass.

Many Americans were worried about the power of these giant corporations. Demands for government regulation grew. In 1890, Congress passed the Sherman Antitrust Act in an attempt, largely unsuccessful, to ban the formation of trusts and monopolies.

Labor and Unions. While the owners of big business grew wealthy, the men and women who worked in their mills, mines, and factories received only a small share of this wealth. In 1900, the average income of a male factory worker was between $400 and $500 a year. The one fifth of U.S. women who worked in industry received even lower wages. The workweek was long—six days a week, ten hours a day. Children as young as ten worked alongside adults for the same long hours and low pay. Working conditions

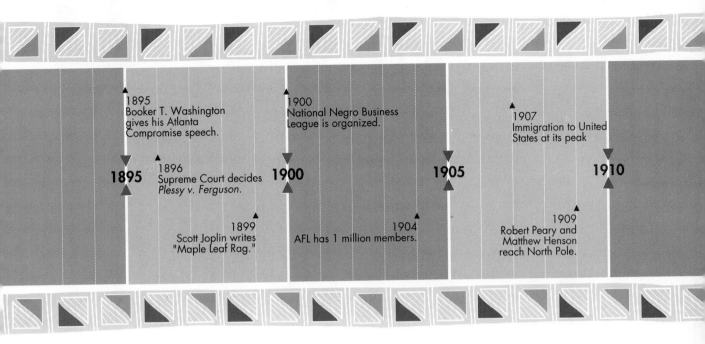

1895
Booker T. Washington gives his Atlanta Compromise speech.

1895

1896
Supreme Court decides *Plessy v. Ferguson.*

1899
Scott Joplin writes "Maple Leaf Rag."

1900
National Negro Business League is organized.

1900

1904
AFL has 1 million members.

1905

1907
Immigration to United States at its peak

1909
Robert Peary and Matthew Henson reach North Pole.

1910

were often unsafe. Injuries and even death from industrial accidents were common. In one year, 195 workers died in Pittsburgh steel plants alone.

Workers sought to improve their lives by forming **labor unions**. In 1869, workers organized the Knights of Labor. It was one of the few unions that accepted African American workers. Its goal was equal pay for men and women, an end to child labor, and a shorter workday.

In 1886, strikers against the McCormick Harvester Company held a meeting in Haymarket Square, Chicago, to protest the shooting of striking workers by the police. Someone threw a bomb into a group of policemen patrolling the meeting. Although the Knights of Labor condemned the attack, the union was accused of favoring violence. Its membership declined sharply.

The American Federation of Labor (AFL) organized the same year as the Haymarket attack and was more successful than the Knights of Labor. It won higher wages, shorter hours, and improved working conditions for its members. By 1904, the AFL was the most powerful union in the United States, with 1 million members. It did not, however, accept African Americans as members.

Immigration. The many new workers who were needed by the growing industries in the North and Midwest came from two sources. Some were U.S.-born farm workers, including African Americans, who left the land to work in the mines and factories. Others were immigrants, who came to the United States in great numbers in the late 1800s and early 1900s from eastern and southern Europe. In 1907, the peak year of immigration, 1,285,000 people entered the United States. Of these almost 70 percent were from Poland, Russia, Hungary, Bohemia,

223

These immigrants from southern Europe joined the millions of others who had fled persecution and poverty and found refuge in the United States.

Italy, and Greece. Most of them were unskilled and willing to take jobs at lower wages than native-born white workers and earlier immigrants. Not surprisingly, hard feelings developed against the newcomers, and they experienced prejudice for many years.

Growth of Cities. Almost all the new industries were located in cities in the Northeast and Midwest. As people streamed into the cities looking for jobs, the cities mushroomed in number and size. In 1870, there were only 14 cities in the United States with populations over 100,000. By 1910, that number had grown to 50. In 1870, fewer than 27 out of every 100 U.S. residents lived in cities. By 1910, that figure had almost doubled. In the same period, Chicago's population doubled, and New York's increased by more than 50 percent.

These large cities had separate Italian, Polish, Russian, Hungarian, and African American neighborhoods. Living conditions in these areas were harsh. Families often lived in one room. Sanitary conditions were lacking, and diseases such as typhoid flourished.

Yet, for many of the newcomers, the cities also served as steppingstones into American culture. Their children were educated in the public schools and, in the course of a generation or two, moved into the growing middle class. At the same time, the cities and the nation were enriched by the cultural traditions of each new ethnic group.

The New South. Beginning with Reconstruction, Southern merchants, bankers, and other businesspeople realized that the South could not continue with an economy based on agriculture if it was to prosper. Leading the call for change was Henry Grady, the white editor of the *Atlanta Constitution*. Grady proclaimed the opportunity for a "New South." He saw a South with a variety of farm crops, decent relations between African Americans and whites, and growing industry. Of these goals, only industrialization was to become a reality.

Attracted by the region's water power and rich coal, iron, and oil resources, Northerners invested in the South. They were also attracted by cheap, nonunion labor. Southern factory workers, almost all of them white, were paid about half the Northern wage scale. African Americans were given only the lowest factory jobs.

Across the South, new mills and factories went up. By 1880, the South had one quarter of the nation's cotton mills. Birmingham, Alabama, became a center of the iron and steel industry. Mining, smelting, and lumber industries developed. Between 1880 and 1890, railroads in the South doubled their track mileage in order to transport the new products.

Tobacco manufacturing, which had always been an important Southern industry, flourished after 1885. An aggressive Southern businessman, James B. Duke, bought the rights to a cigarette-making machine and gained almost a complete monopoly of the tobacco market.

Westward Expansion. While the cities of the Northeast and Midwest were expanding, so were the western borders of the United States. Thousands of farmers, cattle ranchers, and miners settled the lands west of the Mississippi. In the process of settlement, however, they destroyed the livelihood and culture of the many Native American peoples who had lived on the land for thousands of years.

Taking Another Look

1. In what ways did U.S. industry grow between 1877 and 1910?

2. How did cities change in this period?

3. **Critical Thinking** What groups did U.S. growth benefit at this time?

This steel mill in Birmingham, Alabama, employed hundreds of workers after the Civil War. As in most Southern industries, African Americans were allowed to work at only the lowest-paying jobs.

Sharecroppers' cabins

African Americans in the New South

(1877–1910)

THINKING ABOUT THE CHAPTER

Why were the closing decades of the 1800s and the first years of the 1900s a frightening time for African Americans in the South?

One day in 1832, a popular white entertainer named Thomas Rice stood in the alley outside a theater in Baltimore, Maryland. He was watching an African American street performer sing and dance. The song went:

> Wheel about, turn about,
> Do it jus' so,
> An' every time I wheel about
> I jump Jim Crow.

Rice was so impressed by the man's performance that he added it to his own act. Dressed in an exaggerated version of the street performer's clothes, he per-

Rice as Jim Crow

formed "Jim Crow" before laughing white audiences everywhere. Soon, the term *Jim Crow* began to be used by whites to apply to all African American people.

This is one of many versions of the origin of the term *Jim Crow*. Whatever its origin, however, *Jim Crow* at first was used to make fun of African Americans.

In the years after Reconstruction, the meaning of the term changed. Rather than being applied to African Americans, **Jim Crow** was used to refer to the laws being passed in the South to segregate African Americans in housing, transportation, and many other aspects of daily life. These laws were enacted at a time when African Americans were finding it difficult just to earn a living.

1883	Supreme Court overturns 1875 Civil Rights Act.
1890s	Southern states disfranchise African Americans.
1890s	States pass Jim Crow laws.
1891	Ida B. Wells begins antilynching crusade.
1896	Supreme Court decides *Plessy* v. *Ferguson*.
1901–1907	Streetcar boycotts occur in 20 Southern cities.

1 HARD WORK AND MORE POVERTY

▼ What was the economic condition of African Americans in the South in the late 1800s?

In 1884, T. Thomas Fortune, a leading African American journalist, wrote that African Americans in the South were "more absolutely under the control of the Southern whites; they are more poorly housed, clothed and fed, than under the slave regime [system]." He added, "The African American is an alien [stranger] in his native land."

Families in the Fields. No African Americans would have agreed more with Fortune than those who worked as sharecroppers on the farms and plantations of the South. When sharecropping began during Reconstruction (see page 205), African Americans saw it as a way to earn a living. But as the post–Reconstruction years rolled on, life under the sharecropping system turned more and more bitter. Not only was the work terribly hard, but sharecroppers were also constantly in debt to their landowners, who often cheated them.

Jobs in Industry. African Americans also provided needed labor in the industries of the New South. They filled low-level jobs in lumbering, mining, shipping, manufacturing, and some trades. African Americans also built the New South's roads, dug its sewers, and cleaned its streets. Although the pay was low, it was higher than what African Americans could earn from sharecropping, and they saw these jobs as a step up the economic ladder. The jobs were backbreaking, and some were dangerous as well. In the lumber industry, for example, forest workers could be killed by falling trees. African Americans were able to get these jobs because few white men wanted them.

Most African American women worked in laundries and in white people's homes, as cleaning women, cooks, or washerwomen. They earned the lowest pay of anyone in the United States, as little as $5.00 a month.

White and African American workers who did the same jobs did not always get

An African American officer of the Knights of Labor introduces union head Terence V. Powderly at a meeting.

the same pay. An African American fireman on the Southern Railway explained:

> If I take a train from here to Greenville, South Carolina, I get for that trip $2.60, the white engineer gets $6.00. But if that same train had the same engineer and a *white* fireman, the engineer would get his $6.00 just the same but the fireman would get $3.25. He gets 65 cents more for doing the same work I do.

A skilled African American woman working in Columbia, Georgia, earned between $5.00 and $6.00 a month. An unskilled white woman worker in the Co-lumbia cotton mill, where African Americans were not allowed to work, earned from $35.00 to $45.00 a month.

Labor Unions. Although labor unions were not strong in the post-Reconstruction South, when they did exist, they too discriminated against African Americans. White workers rarely allowed African Americans to join their unions. An exception was the Knights of Labor, which had 90,000 African American members in 1886.

When union members went on **strike,** or stopped work in an attempt to gain better pay and working conditions, employers sometimes offered their jobs to African Americans. In the 1870s, for example, mine owners brought African American workers to Ohio and Illinois to break strikes by white mine workers. Such incidents increased the ill will of the white workers toward African Americans. In other places, because African Americans would work for less, employers threatened to hire them and fire white workers.

On rare occasions, African Americans joined forces and went on strike also. This happened in the Southern sugar fields in 1880. African American workers struck to gain an increase in their pay from 75 cents a day to $1 a day. The strikers were arrested, and the strike was broken.

The Convict-Lease System. Imprisoned African Americans were organized, and literally chained together, in work gangs that were leased out to individuals or companies. Working under the most brutal conditions, these chain gangs built roads, and labored in lumber mills, quarries, factories, mines, and brickyards. The **convict-lease system** had the effect of decreasing the number of paying jobs available for others.

Taking Another Look

1. Describe some of the injustices suffered by African American workers in the South.

2. In what way did labor unions and the convict-lease system affect the job opportunities of African Americans in the South?

3. **Critical Thinking** What do you think T. Thomas Fortune meant when he said, "The African American is an alien in his native land"?

2 THE LAND OF JIM CROW

▼ What rights were denied African Americans by law?

Although white Southern political leaders returned to office in the years right after Reconstruction, many African Americans continued to vote. They sent African Americans both to state legislatures and to Congress. Between 1876 and 1895, for example, there were 57 African Americans in the North Carolina House of Representatives and 47 in the South Carolina General Assembly. There were three African Americans in Congress in 1890. That situation was soon to change.

Losing the Vote. In the 1890s, the Democrats, who by then controlled politics in the South, made an important decision. It was now clear that the federal government had lost interest in making sure that African Americans were not prevented from voting in Southern states. This left Southern states free to pass laws **disfranchising** African American men. Such laws denied them the rights of citizenship, especially the right to vote. The states developed a number of ways by which African American men could be

STATE BARRIERS TO VOTING BY AFRICAN AMERICANS

Poll Tax	A fee a voter must pay in order to vote; in effect, a voting tax that many African Americans were too poor to pay
Property Test	Requirement that a man must own a certain amount of property in order to vote; a test that few African Americans and poor whites could meet
Literacy Test	Requirement that to vote, a man must be able to read; white election registrars decided who passed the test
Grandfather Clause	Waived literacy and property tests for those men whose grandfathers had been eligible to vote before the Civil War, a test that few African Americans could meet
White Primary Elections	Primary, or nominating election, from which Southern Democrats could ban African American men because such elections were not covered by the 15th Amendment, which had given African Americans the vote

By 1910, seven Southern states had adopted some of these measures to disfranchise African Americans. Why did whites want to keep them from voting?

denied their voting rights. The table on this page lists the most widely used of these devices.

The measures described in the table above worked. In one Southern state after another, the number of African Americans who were able to vote dropped sharply. In Louisiana, for instance, 130,000 African Americans had voted in 1896. Two years later, after the grandfather clause had gone into effect there, the number dwindled to 5,000. By the end of the 1800s, African Americans had lost their power to elect officials.

The Rise of Jim Crow. Keeping African American men from voting was only one way the South attacked the rights of African Americans. The Southern states also saw to it that laws were passed establishing strict separation between African Americans and whites. Separation, or **segregation,** became the law. African Americans and whites could not ride in the same streetcars or railway cars or even sit in the same passenger stations. African Americans could not drink from the same public water fountains as whites. They had to sit in separate sections of theaters. African Americans and whites could not be treated in the same hospitals or buried in the same cemeteries. This was the system that became known as Jim Crow.

Plessy v. Ferguson. African Americans believed that Jim Crow laws violated the 14th Amendment, which guaranteed American citizens "the equal protection of the law" (see page 179). One African American who decided to test the legality of Jim Crow laws was Homer Plessy. While on a train trip in Louisiana, Plessy sat on a whites–only railroad car. When he refused to move to a car for African Americans, he was arrested.

Louisiana law required separate accommodations for African Americans and whites in public facilities. By riding in the whites-only car, Plessy had broken this law. He was found guilty by a Louisiana court, but he appealed his case to the U.S. Supreme Court.

In 1896, in the case known as *Plessy* v. *Ferguson,* the Supreme Court ruled against Plessy. As long as facilities for African Americans and whites were equal, keeping the races separate was constitutional. The Court reasoned that the 14th Amendment "could not have been intended to abolish distinctions based on color." This ruling established

Why do you think whites set up Jim Crow?

▶▶ SOME JIM CROW LAWS, 1870 – 1965

Date/Place		Intent of Law	Date/Place		Intent of Law
1870	Georgia	separate schools	1915	Oklahoma	separate phone booths
1891	Georgia	separate seating in railroad cars	1915	S. Carolina	unequal spending for education
1900	S. Carolina	separate railroad cars	1922	Mississippi	separate taxicabs
1905	Georgia	separate parks	1932	Atlanta	separate baseball fields
1906	Alabama	separate streetcars	1935	Oklahoma	no boating or fishing together
1910	Baltimore	separate residential blocks	1937	Arkansas	segregation at race tracks
1914	Louisiana	separate entrances and seating at circuses	1944	Virginia	separate airport waiting rooms
1915	S. Carolina	separate entrances and work areas in factories	1965	Louisiana	no state money for schools not segregated

These African American children are attending a segregated school in the nation's capital, which followed Southern segregationist policies.

what became known as the separate-but-equal principle.

The Spread of Jim Crow. Two years after the *Plessy* decision, a bill to make it illegal for African Americans and whites to ride in the same railroad cars was before the South Carolina legislature. The editor of a white newspaper wrote an editorial making fun of the proposal. "Why stop there?" he asked jokingly.

> If there must be Jim Crow cars on the railroads, there should be Jim Crow cars on the street railways. Also on all passenger boats. . . . There should be Jim Crow waiting saloons at all stations, and Jim Crow eating houses. . . . Jim Crow sections of the jury box, and a separate Jim Crow dock and witness stand in every court—and a Jim Crow Bible for colored witnesses to kiss. . . . Perhaps, the best plan would be, after all, to take the short cut . . . by establishing two or three Jim Crow counties at once, and turning them over to our colored citizens for their [use].

Except for the Jim Crow witness stand and the separate counties, everything the editor poked fun at eventually came true—even the Jim Crow Bible. The separate-but-equal doctrine of *Plessy* v. *Ferguson* became the South's justification for segregating all kinds of facilities, from schools, parks, and water fountains to cemeteries. It didn't matter that facilities for African Americans were rarely equal to those for whites. The separate-but-equal doctrine was to keep Jim Crow alive for more than 50 years.

Lynch Law. Added to the loss of African Americans' voting rights and the spread of Jim Crow was a campaign of terror against African Americans. For example, one day in March 1892, 12 armed white men attacked a grocery store owned by three African Americans in Memphis, Tennessee. The partners were armed and fought back. They were arrested and jailed on conspiracy charges. Some whites, outraged at the African Americans' actions, stormed the jail, dragged the partners out to the street, and shot them to death.

This was just one example of the wave of lynchings that swept the South at this time. Between 1882 and 1900, over 3,000 people—mostly in the south and nearly all African Americans—were lynched. This reign of terror continued well into the 1900s, as you will read in Chapter 23.

Taking Another Look

1. Describe three measures taken by Southern states to prevent African Americans from voting.

2. How did the *Plessy* v. *Ferguson* decision help the South justify its policy of segregation?

3. **Critical Thinking** As you will read later in this book, the separate-but-equal doctrine was eventually overturned by the Supreme Court. What wording in the *Plessy* decision might point to the outcome?

3 ▼ THE AFRICAN AMERICAN RESPONSE

▼ What did African Americans do to protect themselves?

"It is time to face the enemy and fight inch by inch for every right he denies us." This was the advice of journalist T. Thomas Fortune to his fellow African Americans living in the world of Jim Crow, lynchings, and absence of **civil rights.** Civil rights are those rights given to all citizens of the United States by the Constitution and its amendments.

Facing the Enemy. Many African American organizations took Fortune's advice and petitioned Congress for a new civil rights bill. In 1875, Congress had passed a civil rights law that outlawed racial discrimination in public places. The Supreme Court declared the law unconstitutional in 1883. African Americans then petitioned individual states. As a result, 15 Northern states passed or strengthened their civil rights laws.

Some African Americans took more direct action. In over 20 cities across the South from 1901 to 1907, African Americans boycotted streetcar companies that segregated their cars. In doing so, they were obeying the words of African American newspapers like the Savannah *Tribune*, which wrote, "Do not trample on our pride by being 'jim crowed.' Walk!" In some cities, the boycotts forced streetcar companies into bankruptcy. In some cases, African Americans then formed transit companies of their own.

Attack on Lynching. In the 1890s, one African American was lynched about every two days. One person who did more than anyone else to fight lynching was Ida B. Wells.

Ida B. Wells was born into bondage in 1862 in Holly Springs, Mississippi. At age 14 she became a teacher. She later continued her education by attending Fisk University in Nashville.

One day, when she was 22, Wells sat in the "white ladies only" car of a Memphis train. The conductor told her to move, and she refused. He grabbed her arm to pull her off, and she bit his hand. It took three men to force the embattled Wells from the coach. She sued the railroad for damages and won $500, although she later lost her case on appeal by the railroad.

In 1891, Wells became the editor and part owner of a Memphis weekly newspaper, *Free Speech,* in which she attacked lynching. A grocery-store owner who had been lynched in Memphis had been a close friend of Wells. After his murder, she wrote an editorial demanding the lynchers' arrest, but nothing was done. Wells advised her fellow African Americans to leave Memphis. "We are outnumbered and without arms," she wrote. "There is only one thing left we can do—leave a town which will neither protect our lives and property nor give us a fair trial, but takes us out and murders us in cold blood."

Some whites, angry at what Wells had written, destroyed her printing presses and threatened to hang her in front of the Memphis Courthouse. Wells had to flee the city for her own safety. She settled in Chicago, where she later married Ferdinand L. Barnett. After her marriage, she was known as Ida B. Wells-Barnett.

Wells dedicated herself to the anti-lynching crusade. She investigated lynchings and wrote about them for the African American press. In 1895, she compiled *The Red Record,* a study of lynchings that had occurred during the past three years. Within three years after she began her campaign, the number of lynchings dropped from 235 a year to 180. Until her death in 1939, Wells continued to fight for lynch laws. She also fought in other ways for the freedom and equality of African Americans, especially women, and was one of the founders of the NAACP.

Taking Another Look

1. Describe three ways African Americans fought racism in the South.

2. How did Ida B. Wells-Barnett fight against lynching?

3. **Critical Thinking** As you read in the story of Ida B. Wells-Barnett, fighting racial hatred could be dangerous. Why do you think many African Americans fought back despite the danger to them?

LOOKING AHEAD

Disfranchisement, Jim Crow laws, and lynching made life in the South unbearable for many African Americans. Unwilling to accept such conditions, African Americans fought back, none more actively than Ida B. Wells-Barnett. One man, however, Booker T. Washington, became the spokesman for a different path for African American advancement.

In 1892, African American and white farmers gathered in Texas to support the newly formed Populist party. "I am an emancipated slave of this state," declared one African American delegate, "[yet] my interest is yours and yours mine." To unseat the Republicans and Democrats, the Populists openly courted and won the backing of African American voters in the South.

In 1892, the Populists seated more than 90 African American delegates at their national convention. African Americans voted in large numbers and helped the Populists win many state and national offices throughout the South.

When the Populists declined in the late 1890s, many white Southerners vowed that never again would they allow African American votes to decide elections. In 1901, the last African American representative from the South, George H. White of North Carolina, left Congress. "This . . . is perhaps the Negro's temporary farewell to the American Congress," said White, "but . . . he will rise up some day and come again." That day came in 1972 when Georgia elected Andrew Young to the House of Representatives.

The Who, What, Where of History

1. **What** does the term *Jim Crow* mean?
2. **What** was the New South?
3. **What** are labor unions?
4. **What** was the convict-lease system?
5. **What** does the word *disfranchising* mean?
6. **Who** was Homer Plessy?
7. **What** was *Plessy* v. *Ferguson*?
8. **What** is a lynching?
9. **Who** was Ida B. Wells?

Making The Connection

1. What was the connection between strikes by labor unions in the South and increased anger of whites toward African Americans?
2. What was the connection between low employment rates in the South and the convict-lease system?

Time Check

1. When did the Supreme Court overturn the 1875 Civil Rights Act?
2. When did the Supreme Court decide *Plessy* v. *Ferguson*?

What Would You Have Done?

1. Imagine that you are an African American offered a job in a Southern textile mill during a strike. You are not allowed to join the union that is on strike. Would you become a strikebreaker? Explain.

2. Would you have taken Ida B. Wells's 1891 advice to leave Memphis? Explain in a letter to a friend.

Thinking and Writing About History

1. Write a paragraph that explains why sharecroppers could not get out of debt regardless of how hard they worked.

2. Write a journal entry describing a day in the life of an African American child living in a small Southern city in 1900. Include a description of the "separate but equal" facilities that the child must use.

Building Skills: Comparing Charts

Comparing charts that show differences over time can be a bit tricky. You need to be sure that you know what you are looking at before you start to make comparisons.

The two charts below, for example, show the requirements for voters in Southern states in 1860 and 1930. The chart for 1930, however, does not have the same categories as the chart for 1860. Look at the two charts and answer the following questions.

1. What category(ies) does the 1860 chart include that the 1930 chart does not have?

2. What category(ies) is a part of the 1930 chart but not of the 1860 one?

3. Which states had poll taxes in 1930?

4. Which states had an education requirement in 1930?

5. Using the information in the two charts, write a sentence explaining whether an African American had a better chance of voting in 1860 or 1930 and why.

▷ ▷ **Voter Qualifications in 1860**

State	Race	Residence	Citizenship
Alabama	White	1/2 year	U.S.
Arkansas	White	1/2 year	U.S.
Florida	White	1/2 year	U.S.
Georgia	White	1/2 year	U.S.
Kentucky	White	2 years	State
Louisiana	White	1 year	U.S.
Maryland	White	1 year	U.S.
Mississippi	White	1 year	U.S.
Missouri	White	1 year	U.S.
North Carolina	White	1 year	U.S.
South Carolina	White	2 years	U.S.
Tennessee	White	1/2 year	U.S.
Texas	White	1 year	U.S. or state
Virginia	White	2 years	State

▷ ▷ **Voter Qualifications in 1930**

State	Residence	Education	Property
Alabama	2 years	Read, write English	Poll tax, 40 acres
Arkansas	1 year	—	—
Florida	1 year	—	Poll tax
Georgia	1 year	Read, write English	Poll tax, 40 acres or $500
Kentucky	1 year	—	—
Louisiana	2 years	Read, write English	Poll tax, $300
Maryland	1 year	—	—
Mississippi	2 years	Read Constitution	Poll tax
Missouri	1 year	—	—
North Carolina	1 year	Read, write English	—
South Carolina	2 years	—	Poll tax
Tennessee	1 year	—	Poll tax
Texas	1 year	—	Poll tax
Virginia	2 years	Read Constitution	Poll tax, $300

George Washington Carver at Tuskegee Institute

Living in the Jim Crow World

(1877–1910)

THINKING ABOUT THE CHAPTER

What strategies were advanced in the late 1800s and early 1900s to improve the lives of African Americans?

Atlanta, Georgia, on September 18, 1895, was as hot as it usually is at that time of year. For the whites and African Americans crammed into the building where the Cotton States and International Exposition was to open, the heat was almost unbearable. Yet, when an African American whom the New York *World* described as "tall, bony," with a "high forehead . . . and strong, determined mouth" began to speak, the heat was forgotten. "Within ten minutes," continued the *World*, "the multitude [audience] was in an uproar of enthusiasm. . . . The fairest women of Georgia stood up and cheered."

The speaker who aroused such spirited response was Booker T. Washington. From that day on, he was thought by many to have succeeded Frederick Douglass as the leader of African Americans. At a time when African Americans such as Ida B. Wells-Barnett were vigorously protesting the wave of lynchings and the Jim Crow world in which African Americans lived, Washington had another answer. African Americans would succeed, he believed, not by protests but through industrial education, self-help, and business ownership. Washington devoted his life to making these goals a reality for African Americans.

1 A STRONG LEADER

▼ What were Booker T. Washington's accomplishments as educator and leader of African Americans?

Somehow 16-year-old Booker T. Washington heard of Hampton Institute in Hampton, Virginia, and was determined to attend the school. But it was 500 miles (800 kilometers) from his home in West Virginia, and he had no money to get there or to pay for classes. That did not stop Washington. If it meant walking the 500 miles, he would walk. If it meant getting up at four in the morning to work as a janitor to pay his expenses, that's what he would do. Booker T. Washington never regretted either decision. His education at Hampton became his steppingstone to leadership of Tuskegee Institute. Building Tuskegee into a first-class educational institution for African Americans was the proudest accomplishment of Washington's life.

Washington's Early Years. In many ways, Booker T. Washington's early years were typical of those of a Southern African American boy after Reconstruction.

Booker T. Washington was born into slavery on a small plantation in Virginia in 1856. He never met his father, who was said to be a white man living on a nearby plantation. After the Civil War, when he was nine years old, his family moved to West Virginia, where he worked first in a coal mine and then in a salt mine. He squeezed in a few hours at the local school whenever he could.

Washington was a bright student and learned enough to think seriously of attending Hampton Institute. Hampton had been founded in 1868 by General Samuel Chapman Armstrong as a college for African Americans. Armstrong believed that along with their basic academic studies, African Americans should learn practical skills that would help them get jobs and earn a living. Washington was especially attracted to this part of the Hampton program, and it influenced his later leadership at Tuskegee Institute.

Washington did well at Hampton, and in 1879, Armstrong offered him a job teaching there. After teaching for two years, he was given a chance to head Tuskegee, a new school in Alabama.

When Washington arrived at Tuskegee, he discovered that the school had no buildings and no land suitable for building. Undismayed, Washington and his small staff of teachers taught classes in a shanty lent him by the local African American church and had his students help clear the land for new buildings.

1881 Tuskegee Institute is founded.

1888 First African American insurance company is founded.

First African American bank is founded.

1895 Booker T. Washington delivers Atlanta Compromise speech.

1900 National Negro Business League is organized.

Washington's Goals for Tuskegee.

Washington's goals for what students should learn at Tuskegee were clear. As he wrote in his famous autobiography, *Up From Slavery:*

> We wanted to give them such a practical knowledge of some one industry, together with the spirit of industry, thrift, and economy, that they would be sure of knowing how to make a living after they had left us. We wanted to teach them to study actual things instead of mere books alone.

For the next 15 years, Washington worked to offer as fine an industrial education at Tuskegee as his students would have received at Hampton Institute. In addition to academic subjects, male students were taught farming, brick making,

Teaching African Americans to be skilled craftworkers was one of Booker T. Washington's goals for Tuskegee. Here students are assembling horse-drawn carriages.

Why did Booker T. Washington think an industrial education was important for African Americans?

carpentry, and other skills. Female students also learned cooking and sewing.

Under Washington's guidance, Tuskegee grew and prospered. By 1906, it had 1,500 students and a staff of 155. Among the staff was scientist George Washington Carver (see page 254), who came to Tuskegee at Washington's invitation in 1896. Many of Tuskegee's graduates became teachers, who carried the school's message into all the Southern states and to African nations.

Washington as Leader. As you read at the beginning of this chapter, Washington was invited to deliver an address at the Cotton States and International Exposition in Atlanta, Georgia, in 1895. That speech brought him national fame and guided his work as a national leader until his death in 1915.

In his Atlanta speech, which came to be called the **Atlanta Compromise**, Washington made public his belief that African Americans should advance not through political protest, but through education and job skills. According to Washington,

being able to earn a living and buy property was more important than being able to vote. Washington urged African Americans to take advantage of opportunities around them. This was his message:

> Cast down your bucket [seize the opportunity] where you are. . . . Cast it down in agriculture, in mechanics, in commerce, in domestic service, and in the professions. . . . No race can prosper till it learns that there is as much dignity in tilling a field as in writing a poem. It is at the bottom of life we must begin and not at the top.

Washington also urged whites to hire African Americans instead of looking to European immigrants as workers. As a reward, he promised, "you and your families will be surrounded by the most patient, faithful, law-abiding, and unresentful people that the world has seen."

Washington then addressed the question of whether African Americans and whites should mix together socially. He assured the white members of his audi-

239

ence that economic integration did not mean social integration. In what became the most remembered part of his speech, he said, "In all things that are purely social we can be as separate as the fingers, yet one as the hand in all things essential to mutual progress."

African Americans' Views of Washington. Washington seemed to be advising African Americans to ignore the evils of Jim Crow and discrimination. However, most ordinary African Americans supported him and viewed him as their leader.

However, the response of other African American leaders to Booker T. Washington was mixed. Some agreed that he was a great leader. Others were not so sure. They criticized his apparent acceptance of segregation and disfranchisement. They thought his system of industrial education kept African Americans in lower-paying jobs at a time when modern industry needed workers with more advanced skills. The table is a sampling of opinions about Washington by some of his African American contemporaries.

Washington's Influence Among Whites. Many prominent white leaders were pleased with Booker T. Washington's philosophy. He condemned slavery, but avoided open criticism of whites. Rather than calling for a reordering of U.S. society, he urged African Americans to learn economic skills that could support them in society as it existed. Wealthy industrialist Andrew Carnegie, impressed with Washington, called him "certainly one of the most wonderful men living or who has ever lived."

Political leaders also admired Washington. President Theodore Roosevelt invited him to dine at the White House in 1901, and he often consulted with him on racial policy. The President called Washington "a genius such as does not arise in a generation" and said he did not know "a white man of the South who is as good a man as Booker Washington today."

Even conservative Southern politicians liked Washington. His influence with them was so great that no African American could be appointed to an important politi-

Washington was very influential among politicians and businessmen. Here he is shown with President William Howard Taft (left) and Andrew Carnegie (right).

cal or educational position without his approval.

While Washington publicly advised African Americans to accommodate themselves to segregation and Jim Crow, in private, he opposed these policies. He secretly financed court cases that challenged voting laws, segregation, and discrimination. He also tried to get more African Americans to register and vote. He was careful to keep this work hidden, however, believing that public knowledge would hurt his ability to help African Americans.

Taking Another Look

1. What kind of education did Tuskegee Institute offer under Washington?

2. What was Booker T. Washington's stated policy on segregation?

3. **Critical Thinking** Why do you think Washington's speech in Atlanta came to be known as the Atlanta Compromise?

2 AFRICAN AMERICAN ▼ BUSINESSES

What did African Americans accomplish in the business world in the late 1800s and early 1900s?

Booker T. Washington did not believe that industrial education alone was the way for all African Americans to better themselves. According to him, business ownership was also a way for African Americans to succeed.

In 1900, five years after his Atlanta speech, Washington launched the National Negro Business League. Meeting for the first time, in Boston, 115 delegates from 20 states, mostly from the South, heard Washington declare that the purpose of the organization was to promote business.

By 1905, more than 300 local business leagues had been organized, and the number of businesses owned by African Americans had grown substantially. However, the total number of such businesses was still small and involved only a fraction of the African American population. Nevertheless, these businesses were the vehicle by which a significant number of African Americans were able to launch themselves into the middle class.

African American Businesses. Between the end of Reconstruction and 1910, African Americans set up a wide variety of small businesses in the South. They included food stores, restaurants, drugstores, cigar stores, dry-cleaning establishments, and shoe-repair shops. Other businesses provided personal services that whites refused to offer African Americans. Among these were beauty parlors, barbershops, and undertaking establishments. Almost all of these small businesses were located in the segregated African American neighborhoods of cities and towns.

More substantial than the retail businesses were the banks and insurance companies owned by African Americans. Since white insurance companies often refused to insure African Americans or charged them very high rates, many African American self-help societies set up their own insurance companies. The first of these was founded in Virginia by the Grand United Order of True Reformers in 1881. The North Carolina Mutual Life Insurance Company was founded in Durham. Under the leadership of C. C. Spaulding, it became the largest U.S. business owned and operated by African Americans.

Banks provided two services to the community. African American churches preached the virtues of thrift, and African Americans who took this advice needed a place to deposit their savings. At the same time, in order to grow, African American businesses needed credit, which white banks often denied them. Again, it was the Grand United Order of True Reformers that pioneered in the establishment of banks. It set up the True Reformers Bank in Richmond, Virginia, in 1888. By 1910, about 50 African American banks were operating throughout the South.

Problems of African American Businesses.
African American businesses did not have an easy time, and many failed. One reason was that African Americans did not have experience in business and often made poor business decisions. Some banks, for example, made loans that were out of proportion to the amount of money they had on deposit.

Since small businesses had little money, they frequently could afford to locate only in the least desirable, and therefore cheapest, areas of African American communities, where few customers were likely to come. Often, African American small businesses also had to compete with white-owned businesses located in African American neighborhoods. The white owners usually had more capital and could offer lower prices.

A Success Story. One of the great African American success stories was that of businesswoman Madame C. J. Walker. Her company was also unusual in that it was one of the few successful African American businesses that was not established in the South.

Madame C. J. Walker built a successful business and amassed a fortune from her beauty products. Born in Louisiana as Sarah Breedlove in 1867, she was raised in St. Louis, Missouri. While working as a laundress over a washtub she asked herself what she was going to do when she got old and her back got stiff. Her answer came, she said, in a dream in which an old man gave her a formula for a hair conditioner. She began to make the conditioner and sell it door to door. Encouraged by her success, she introduced a line of cosmetics and opened a chain of beauty parlors. By 1910, her company had sales of $1,000 a day and employed 5,000 saleswomen around the world. She died in New York City in 1919.

Importance of African American Businesses. Despite their problems, these early businesses were an important chapter in the story of African American economic progress. The people who owned these businesses and the many who worked in them demonstrated that they were capable of being more than the farm workers, laborers, and servants who made up most of the African American population of the period. People in business often had an economic stability that most African Americans had never experienced. The middle class of African American businesspeople of the time was small. However, it provided a base for the growing number of African Americans who would achieve greater economic success in the years ahead.

Taking Another Look

1. What kinds of businesses did African Americans establish in the late 1800s and early 1900s?

2. What difficulties did African American businesses face?

3. **Critical Thinking** Why do you think most African American businesses were established in the South rather than in the North?

LOOKING AHEAD

Although Booker T. Washington had his critics among prominent African Americans, most ordinary African Americans saw him as their spokesman. In fact, the years of his leadership are sometimes called the Age of Booker T. Washington. This was also the period when African Americans began to establish businesses in record numbers and enter the nation's growing middle class.

The African American middle class was increasing in numbers in the late 19th century. Here, a Washington, D.C., family poses for a family portrait.

At the same time, educators were establishing colleges for the growing number of African Americans who wanted to become professionals like doctors, teachers, and lawyers. African American artists, writers, and inventors were also breaking new ground.

The first funds for what is now Tuskegee University came at the urging of an unlikely pair—Lewis Adams, an African American who had been enslaved, and George W. Campbell, a former slave holder. At their request, the Alabama legislature approved $2,000 for African Americans in Tuskegee to start a school of higher learning. Adams and Campbell chose Booker T. Washington to work a miracle with the small amount of money.

On July 4, 1881, Washington met his first 30 students. Their campus consisted of a rundown church and a small building. In 1882, Washington borrowed $200 and bought 100 acres of abandoned farmland. He then asked his students to create a school—bricks for the walls, furniture for the classrooms, food for the dining hall—and they did.

Today, those early buildings are a National Historic Site and form the northern end of a 200-acre campus nicknamed Skegee. The school has grown from a technical-training center to an accredited university with more than 4,000 students. Nearly 90 percent of the students receive some financial aid, in keeping with Washington's aim: "quality education for those who are economically, educationally, or culturally disadvantaged."

CLOSE UP: Chapter 21

The Who, What, Where of History

1. **Who** was Booker T. Washington?
2. **Where** is Tuskegee Institute?
3. **What** was the Atlanta Compromise?
4. **What** was the National Negro Business League?
5. **Who** was Madame C. J. Walker?

Making the Connection

What was the connection between the African American self-help groups and the African American insurance companies and banks?

Time Check

When did Booker T. Washington deliver his Atlanta Compromise speech?

What Would You Have Done?

1. Would you have agreed with Booker T. Washington that earning a living and buying property were more important for African Americans than voting? Explain your reasons.

2. Imagine that you are an African American who wants more education in 1900. However, you do not agree with Booker T. Washington about the importance of practical education. You wish to study Latin, Greek, and literature. Your church has offered you a scholarship to Tuskegee. Do you go to Tuskegee? Explain.

Thinking and Writing About History

1. Imagine that you are a student at Tuskegee in 1902. Write a letter to a friend describing your studies and your plans for the future.

2. Write an off-the-record interview with Booker T. Washington in which you question him on his views on voting and the use of the courts to win civil rights for African Americans.

Building Skills: Drawing Conclusions

A conclusion is a reasoned judgment based on available facts. To reach a conclusion you must go through a series of steps. First, you identify the subject under study. Second, you study the facts related to this subject, looking for patterns among the data. Based on these patterns, you form conclusions about the subject. The conclusions are suggested, but not directly stated, by the data.

You can practice forming conclusions by using the table on this page. The following questions will help you to reach reasoned judgments based on information in the table. Write your answers on a separate sheet of paper.

1. What is the subject of this table?
2. What categories of information are provided on the table?
3. **(a)** How many of the top ten African American–owned insurance companies are located in the South? **(b)** How many are located outside the South?
4. **(a)** When was the oldest of these companies founded? **(b)** When was the youngest founded?
5. List evidence on the table that supports this conclusion: "Some insurance companies founded during the Jim Crow era have been highly successful."
6. Based on this table, what conclusions can you form about these insurance companies in the 1990s?

Top Ten African American-Owned Insurance Companies, 1996

Rank	Company	Location	Year Founded	Assets*
1	North Carolina Mutual Life Insurance Company	Durham, North Carolina	1898	$213,136
2	Atlanta Life Insurance Company	Atlanta, Georgia	1905	202,418
3	Golden State Mutual Life Insurance Company	Los Angeles, California	1925	102,952
4	Universal Life Insurance Company	Memphis, Tennessee	1923	62,347
5	Booker T. Washington Insurance Company	Birmingham, Alabama	1932	48,456
6	Protective Industrial Insurance Company	Birmingham, Alabama	1923	18,094
7	Winnfield Life Insurance Company	Natchitoches, Louisiana	1936	12,253
8	Williams-Progressive Insurance Company	Opelousas, Louisiana	1947	7,491
9	Golden Circle Life Insurance Company	Brownsville, Tennessee	1958	6,840
10	Reliable Life Insurance Company	Monroe, Louisiana	1940	6,034

*millions of dollars

Source: *Black Enterprise*, June 1997, p. 203

The Fisk Jubilee Singers

Advances in Education, the Arts, and Science

(1877–1910)

THINKING ABOUT THE CHAPTER

What were the educational, artistic, and scientific achievements of African Americans in the years after Reconstruction?

George White, the treasurer of newly founded Fisk University, was desperate. The school had run out of money, and bills were beginning to pile up. Fisk might have to shut its doors. Then, White had an idea. He loved listening to students sing the old spirituals from slavery days. Maybe other people would, too.

Soon afterwards, on a cold autumn day in 1871, nine young men and women set out on a series of concert tours to raise money for Fisk. For seven years, the Fisk Jubilee Singers toured the United States and Europe to wildly enthusiastic audiences.

The singers raised enough money to erect the buildings that form the core of Fisk today. The dedication of the

AFRICAN AMERICAN COLLEGES AND UNIVERSITIES, 1865–1915

Legend:
- College or university existing in 1865
- College or university founded 1865–1877
- College or university founded 1878–1915

In which states were the most African American colleges and universities founded after 1877? What does this tell you about where most African Americans lived?

young singers was only one of the many ways that African Americans showed how important education was to them.

1 EDUCATION

▼ What educational institutions were founded for African Americans?

As you read in Unit 6, the Freedmen's Bureau established thousands of schools for African Americans in the South after Reconstruction. It also founded colleges and universities, as did missionary societies and wealthy Northerners.

Public Education. After Reconstruction, public elementary and high schools in the South were segregated by race. Public schools for African Americans received much less financial support than schools for whites. Elsewhere in the United States, many African American children also had to attend segregated, underfinanced, poorly equipped schools.

Nevertheless, by 1910, over 70 percent of the African American population nationwide was literate. This was more than twice the number who could read in 1863. Over 1,700,000 African Americans were attending public schools, and 35,000 African Americans were teachers.

Higher Education. During and after Reconstruction, colleges for African Americans were built across the South. By 1900, more than 2,000 students had graduated from these institutions of higher learning.

The most prestigious was Howard University in Washington, D.C., which opened in 1867. Its goal was to train future African American leaders. Over the years, it graduated about half of the country's African American doctors and dentists, a fourth of its lawyers, and many of its engineers.

In their early years, schools like Hampton Insitutuţe and Tuskegee gave their

247

GALLERY OF AFRICAN AMERICAN MUSICIANS, WRITERS AND ARTISTS

▲▽▲▽▲▽▲▽▲▽▲▽▲▽▲▽▲▽▲▽▲▽▲▽▲▽▲▽▲▽▲▽▲▽▲▽

James A. Bland (1854–1911) Bland was a performer and composer, who wrote over 600 songs. These included the popular favorites "In the Evening by the Moonlight" and "Oh, Dem Golden Slippers." Virginia officially adopted Bland's "Carry Me Back to Old Virginny" as its state song. Bland lived and performed in England for almost 20 years.

Anna J. Cooper (1858–1964) Cooper, the daughter of an enslaved woman and a slave holder, wrote *A Voice from the South: By a Black Woman from the South.* In it, Cooper attacked prejudice against African American women, especially in education. She was the first African American woman to earn a Ph.D. from the Sorbonne in Paris and the fourth African American woman in the U.S. to hold a Ph.D.

Paul Laurence Dunbar (1872–1906) Dunbar was one of the first African American writers of poetry and fiction to be nationally known. He wrote many widely admired dialect poems, which he composed at the urging of white editors. Some of his best poems deal with the anger and hurt of the African American experience.

Sissieretta Jones (1869–1933) Jones's formerly enslaved parents struggled to send their 15-year-old daughter to Rhode Island's Providence Academy of Music, where she studied opera. She became one of the most celebrated African American vocalists of her time. Jones sang before four Presidents at the White House and worked with some of the world's leading composers, including Antonín Dvořak.

W. C. (William Christopher) Handy (1873–1958) Although Handy did not invent the blues, he became known as the Father of the Blues because he wrote two of the earliest blues songs to be published. These were "Memphis Blues," which appeared in 1912, and "St. Louis Blues," which he wrote in 1914. These songs introduced blues to the general public.

Scott Joplin (1868–1919) Composer and pianist, Joplin fought for the recognition of ragtime as a legitimate musical form. "Maple Leaf Rag," written in 1899, was the first of his many popular ragtime compositions. It was the first piece of sheet music to sell a million copies. Joplin also wrote ballet music and the folk opera *Treemonisha,* which was not produced in his lifetime.

Edmonia Lewis (1845–1890) Lewis was one of the few women sculptors of her time. She received her art training in Boston and in Rome. She specialized in portraits, producing highly admired busts of the abolitionists John Brown, Wendell Phillips, and Charles Sumner. Another famous work is *Forever Free,* which shows a newly freed African American mother and her child (see **The Artist's View**).

Carter G. Woodson (1875-1950) Born into poverty, Woodson received no formal schooling until he was 17. He taught himself on his own at night. Then, he went on to earn a Ph.D. in history from Harvard University. While teaching high school during the day, he wrote his first book *The Education of the Negro Prior to 1861.* In 1916, Woodson founded the *Journal of Negro History.* He began Negro History Week in 1926; it grew into today's African American History Month. Woodson inspired widespread interest in African American history.

George Washington Carver (1864–1943) Carver helped to revolutionize the agriculture of the South. He persuaded Southern farmers to raise less cotton, which wore out the soil, and raise other crops such as peanuts, sweet potatoes, and soybeans, which enriched the soil. To make these crops profitable, he invented over 300 uses of the peanut, over 100 for the sweet potato, and many for the soybean.

Matthew A. Henson (1866–1955) Henson was a member of Robert E. Peary's expedition to the North Pole in 1909. Henson claimed that he and the expedition's Eskimo guides reached the North Pole on April 4, 1909, an hour before Peary. They were the first people to stand on top of the world. Henson wrote about his feat in the book *A Negro Explorer at the North Pole*.

Lewis H. Latimer (1848–1928) Latimer was a draftsman and inventor whose father was an escaped slave. Latimer worked with inventor Thomas Edison, making improvements in the incandescent electric lamp. He supervised the installation of the electric lighting systems of New York City, Philadelphia, Montreal, and London.

Jan Matzeliger (1852–1889) In 1883, Matzeliger invented a machine that attached the upper part of a shoe to the lower part. This shoe-lasting machine cut the cost of making shoes in half and revolutionized the shoe industry. Matzeliger's invention was used to make almost all the shoes in the United States and was adopted by countries all over the world.

Bessie Coleman (1893–1926) Called "Brave Bessie," Coleman soared to new heights in aviation. Denied the right to earn a U.S. pilot's license, she traveled to Europe where she studied with leading French and German flyers. She returned home in 1922 with an international pilot's license. Coleman is a hero to modern pioneers in aviation, including Dr. Mae Jemison, the first African American astronaut.

Eslanda Goode Robeson (1896–1965) "Essie" Robeson, wife of actor Paul Robeson, earned a B.S. in chemistry from Columbia University. She then became the first African American to work at the Columbia Presbyterian Medical Center, where she was in charge of the laboratory. She later studied anthropology at London University and did her field work in Africa.

Daniel Hale Williams (1856–1931) In 1893, Dr. Williams performed the first successful heart operation in history. The operation was performed at Chicago's interracial Provident Hospital, which Williams founded in 1891 as a place where African American doctors and nurses could be trained and African American patients could be treated.

Granville T. Woods (1856–1910) Called the Black Edison, Woods is best known for his invention of the automatic air brake for railroad trains. He also developed a telegraph system for sending messages between moving trains, an invention that helped avoid train collisions.

The cakewalk, a high-stepping dance that developed among enslaved African Americans to poke fun at plantation owners, became a national dance in the 1890s.

students industrial-arts training. However, most African American colleges offered the same education as the leading white colleges of the time. Other important colleges were Spelman College in Atlanta; Wilberforce University in Wilberforce, Ohio; and Shaw University in Raleigh, North Carolina. Spelman admitted only women, and the emphasis at Wilberforce was training men for the ministry. Shaw had one of the first medical schools for African Americans. Most of the college-educated African Americans of the period were graduates of African American colleges and universities.

Taking Another Look

1. How did the literacy rate of African Americans change between 1863 and 1910?

2. List two African American institutions of higher learning and explain their importance.

3. **Critical Thinking** How did the establishment of African American colleges help African Americans?

2 THE ARTS

▼ What were some of the contributions of African Americans to the arts?

In 1890, many African Americans were making music their profession. Many military bands had only African American musicians. African American composers wrote classical music and Broadway shows, and African American stage performers sang and danced in shows that reached the general public.

By the turn of the century, two new kinds of music had been born—ragtime and blues. **Ragtime**, based on offbeat rhythms, became a national craze. By the 1870s, African American musicians—banjo players and piano players, on riverboats and in urban social clubs—were "ragging" their music.

No one knows when or how the **blues** began. The best guess is that the style grew out of the work songs sung by African Americans as they worked in the fields.

The blues used the call-and-response pattern of African music (see page 33). Blues songs became widely popular in the early 1900s with W.C. Handy's compositions such as "St. Louis Blues."

African American writers produced a variety of works in the last quarter of the 1800s and the early 1900s. Older writers such as abolitionists William Still Grout and William Wells Brown wrote about the years of slavery. Younger writers such as Charles W. Chesnutt and Paul Laurence Dunbar told about the experiences of African Americans in the freer, but still restricted, world of their own time.

In the late 1800s, prominent African American painters and sculptors faced bitter struggles for recognition in the United States. To escape racial prejudice at home, some artists moved to Europe to work.

Taking Another Look

1. What is ragtime?

2. Why did some African American artists leave the United States to work in Europe?

3. **Critical Thinking** The types of music described in this section were popular with both African Americans and whites. Why do you think this was so?

3 ▼ ACHIEVEMENTS IN SCIENCE AND INVENTION

What inventions were African Americans responsible for in this period?

In 1900, Henry E. Baker, of the U.S. Patent Office, published four thick volumes that described inventions made by African Americans. Many people were amazed that there were any African American inventors, let alone enough to fill four volumes with their work.

Inventions were the fuel that fired the industrialization of the United States in the late 1800s. African American Jan Matzeliger was among the inventors who worked on their own, while Lewis H. Latimer was one of those who worked in Thomas Edison's vast "invention factory." Along with white inventors, African Americans created new labor-saving devices, new uses for electricity, and new ways to increase the efficiency of industrial machines.

In the years after Reconstruction, African American colleges and universities were just beginning to turn out graduates with substantial training in the sciences. It is not surprising, then, that few African Americans made significant scientific contributions in this period. Therefore, the work of George Washington Carver and Dr. Daniel Hale Williams is especially noteworthy.

SNAPSHOT OF THE TIMES

1867	Howard University is founded.
1871	Fisk Jubilee Singers begin tours.
1872	Elijah McCoy invents device for oiling machines.
1883	Jan Matzeliger invents the shoe-lasting machine.
1893	Dr. Daniel Hale Williams performs first successful heart surgery.
1899	Scott Joplin composes "Maple Leaf Rag."
1909	Matthew Henson reaches North Pole.
1912	W. C. Handy writes "Memphis Blues."

Taking Another Look

1. What did Jan Matzeliger and Lewis H. Latimer have in common?

2. Why were there only a few African American scientists in the late 1800s and early 1900s?

3. **Critical Thinking** Explain the importance of African Americans' inventions to U.S. industries.

LOOKING AHEAD

The achievements of African Americans in education, the arts, and science in the years between 1877 and 1910 are impressive. This is all the more so since these were years when African Americans suffered from legal, political, and economic discrimination. But the times were changing, and new leaders would emerge to challenge Booker T. Washington's Atlanta Compromise.

THE WIZARD OF TUSKEGEE

"I cannot offer you money, position, or fame. I offer you in their place work—hard, hard work—the task of bringing a people from degradation, poverty and waste to full manhood!" With these inspiring words, Booker T. Washington convinced George Washington Carver to teach agricultural science at Tuskegee Institute.

In the fall of 1896, Carver stepped into his laboratory—an empty room. He gave students their first assignment: search for jars, bottles, pots, bits of rubber—anything that might be turned into lab equipment. Carver called his makeshift laboratory "God's little workshop."

Carver was born into slavery in 1864, the last year of the Civil War. He earned a masters degree in science when high school diplomas were rare. Carver's experiments earned him national fame and the nickname the Wizard of Tuskegee.

Carver's inventions touch our lives today. He developed over 300 uses for peanuts, including peanut butter. He proved the nutritional value of soybeans. Carver even made plastic out of soybeans! About himself, Carver remarked: "All I do is prepare what God has made, for uses to which man can put it. It is God's work—not mine."

CLOSE UP: Chapter 22

The Who, What, Where of History

1. **What** is Howard University?
2. **What** is ragtime?
3. **Who** was W.C. Handy?
4. **Who** was Charles W. Chesnutt?
5. **Who** was Paul Laurence Dunbar?
6. **Who** was Scott Joplin?
7. **Who** was Edmonia Lewis?
8. **What** were some of the achievements of George Washington Carver?

Making the Connection

1. What was the connection between colleges and universities such as Howard and Spelman and the growth of an African American middle class?
2. What was the connection between the patterns used in African music and the blues?

Time Check

1. When did Elijah McCoy invent a device for oiling machines?
2. When did Matthew Henson reach the North Pole?

What Would You Have Done?

Imagine that you are an African American opera singer in the early 1900s. Your career is at a standstill because discrimination will not allow you to sing on stage of the great opera houses of the country. You can see two choices: move to Paris or Rome and try to continue a career in opera, or switch to sing blues or show tunes. What would you choose? Give reasons to support your answer.

Thinking and Writing About History

1. Imagine that you are about to graduate from one of the African American colleges in 1912. Write a short speech that you will deliver at graduation. The topic of your speech is "The Value of College Education for African Americans."

2. Imagine that you are a newspaper reporter about to interview Granville T. Woods, Daniel Hale Williams, or Matthew A. Henson. Prepare at least three questions for the interview about your subject's inventions or discovery.

Building Skills: Identifying Point of View in Poetry

The poetry and fiction of a time period can tell you a great deal about the ideas, feelings, and life styles of the authors and their audiences. Reading fiction and poetry requires different skills than reading other kinds of writing.

Reading poetry is sometimes similar to reading a secret message. The poet leaves clues for you to unravel. You may unravel only a few clues and still get much meaning from the poem. Of course, if you unravel many clues, you will understand and enjoy the poem on a deeper number of levels.

A poem always has a *voice*, an attitude toward the reader. It may be friendly, cold, sarcastic, or joyous. We can figure out a poem's voice from the choice of words, from the use of details, and from the rhythm of the poem.

When you read the poem below by Paul Laurence Dunbar for the first time, read it through, experiencing it with no particular ideas in your mind. Then read it a second time, making sure you know the meanings of all the words Dunbar uses. Then read the poem a third time to answer the questions about the voice in the poem.

We Wear the Mask

We wear the mask that grins and lies,
It hides our cheeks and shades our
  eyes—
This debt we pay to human guile;
With torn and bleeding hearts we
  smile,
And mouth with myriad subtleties.

What should the world be otherwise,
In counting our tears and sighs?
Nay, let them only see us while
We wear the mask.

We smile, but O great Christ, our
  cries
To thee from tortured souls arise.
We sing, but oh the clay is vile
Beneath our feet, and long the mile,
But let the world dream otherwise,
We wear the mask.

1. What is "human guile"?

2. Give an example of how you might "mouth with myriad subtleties."

3. Who is the "we" of this poem? Who is "them"?

4. Why does the speaker say that "we" choose to wear a mask?

5. What does the poem tell you about how African Americans lived and acted in the early 20th century?

V UNIT 8

Flappers in Harlem

PROTEST AND HOPE IN A NEW CENTURY

(1900–1941)

Steel workers during World War I

Emergency unemployment relief line

An African American Speaks

We went in for agitation. We pushed our way into the courts. We demanded the right to vote. We urged and pushed our children into college. We encouraged Negro art and literature. We studied African history and in season and out of season we declared that the colored races were destined at least to share in the heritage of the earth.

—W.E.B. Du Bois,
Scholar and Writer

Unit 8 tells of the experiences of African Americans in the first 40 years of this century. This period opened with economic growth and a spirit of optimism. It ended with the nation trying to overcome the worst economic crisis in its history. As it did, growing conflicts in Europe and Asia threatened to pull the United States into global war for the second time in a little over 20 years. These events had a powerful impact on the lives of African Americans, leading to changes in where they lived, in the kinds of work they did, and in the political loyalties they held.

The Progressive Era. In 1900, the United States was in the midst of a period of remarkable economic growth. During the 35 years after the Civil War, the country had become a great industrial power.

Since its beginnings, the United States had been a rural nation, with most of its citizens living in small towns or on farms. With the growth of industry had come the growth of industrial cities, located mainly in the Northeast and the Midwest. This expansion would soon turn the United States into an urban nation.

Many of the new city dwellers had left farms and country towns seeking increased opportunities. They were joined by throngs of immigrants from Europe who also found jobs in the booming mills and factories.

A variety of problems accompanied the growth of this new, urban United States. Workers—male and female—toiled 10- and 12-hour days for low pay, often in unsafe factories. Child labor was common, as families scraped for every penny to make ends meet.

Off the job, conditions were not much better. Workers often lived in poor, overcrowded areas, or **slums**. Poor water supplies and sanitation facilities encouraged the spread of disease there. City governments were often more concerned with collecting bribes than with correcting problems.

Conditions like these encouraged the growth of reform movements. Individuals and organizations crusaded to improve unsafe working conditions and to fight corruption in city, state, and federal governments. Some tried to limit the influence of big business. Others aimed at bettering the lives of working people. Together, these reform movements were known as **Progressivism.**

Progressive Achievements. The Progressives had success in a number of areas. Jane Addams of Chicago founded Hull House in a poor immigrant neighborhood to help the people improve their lives. The National Consumers League pushed for new laws protecting custom-

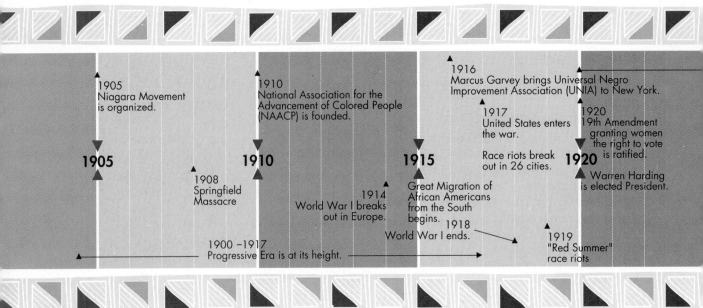

1905
Niagara Movement is organized.

1905

1908
Springfield Massacre

1910
National Association for the Advancement of Colored People (NAACP) is founded.

1910

1914
World War I breaks out in Europe.

1916
Marcus Garvey brings Universal Negro Improvement Association (UNIA) to New York.

1917
United States enters the war.

Race riots break out in 26 cities.

1915

Great Migration of African Americans from the South begins.

1918
World War I ends.

1920
19th Amendment granting women the right to vote is ratified.

1920

Warren Harding is elected President.

1919
"Red Summer" race riots

1900 –1917
Progressive Era is at its height.

ers from worthless or dangerous products. "Good government" organizations introduced new plans of government in many cities to improve efficiency and reduce corruption.

Progressives also brought change to the federal government. Their ideas led to constitutional amendments that permitted an income tax, gave women the right to vote, and banned the manufacture and sale of alcoholic drinks.

Most Progressives were white and middle class, and their efforts tended to focus on Northern and Midwestern cities. As a result, the Progressive movement had limited impact on the lives of African Americans, most of whom still lived in the rural South. One important exception, however, was the **NAACP** (National Association for the Advancement of Colored People). This organization, founded by African American and white Progressives in 1910, became a major force in attempts to win equal rights for African Americans.

World War I. The Progressives were chiefly concerned with conditions within the United States. In the summer of 1914, their concerns and those of many other citizens shifted abroad as war broke out in Europe. On one side, called the Central Powers, were Germany and Austria-Hungary. Great Britain, France, and Russia were the main countries on the other side, known as the Allies. Because the war eventually involved countries in all parts of the world, it became known as the World War.

When the war began, the United States declared its neutrality—that is, that it would not aid either side in the war. Gradually, however, it was drawn toward the Allied side, mainly because of actions of the German government. For example, German submarines sank ships in an effort to keep supplies from reaching Great Britain. Some of these ships were from the United States or carried U.S. passengers. In 1917, this nation entered the war on the Allied side.

U.S. troops, including many African Americans, reached Europe in large numbers the following year. The German army, on one side, and the British and

258

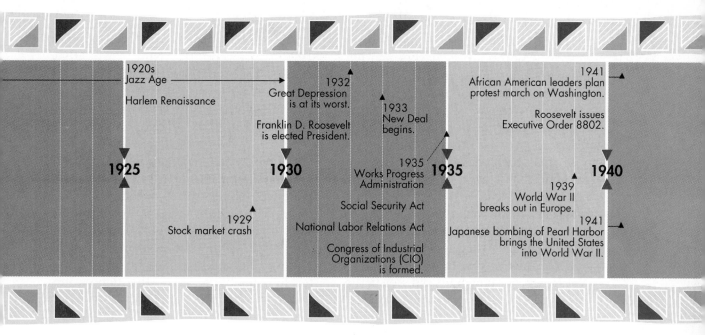

1920s
Jazz Age

Harlem Renaissance

1925

1929
Stock market crash

1932
Great Depression
is at its worst.

Franklin D. Roosevelt
is elected President.

1930

1933
New Deal
begins.

1935
Works Progress
Administration

Social Security Act

National Labor Relations Act

Congress of Industrial
Organizations (CIO)
is formed.

1935

1941
African American leaders plan
protest march on Washington.

Roosevelt issues
Executive Order 8802.

1939
World War II
breaks out in Europe.

1941
Japanese bombing of Pearl Harbor
brings the United States
into World War II.

1940

French armies, on the other, had fought to a standstill. The arrival of the U.S. soldiers finally turned the war in the Allies' favor, and in November 1918, Germany asked for peace.

The Home Front. The war brought changes into the lives of people at home. Factories had to increase their output to equip U.S. forces. But a military draft had taken many young men into the army, creating a shortage of workers. One result was the hiring of women to do what had been thought of as men's jobs.

Another result was the recruiting of African American agricultural workers from the South to do factory jobs in the North. By the end of the war, this **Great Migration** had brought more than 500,000 African Americans to industrial cities of the Northeast and Midwest.

The Aftermath of War. After the war, many people seemed more suspicious of immigrants and minorities. A revolution in Russia in 1917 had ended in a takeover of that country's government by Communists. As a wave of strikes swept the United States after the war, some people feared that Communists were trying to start a revolution here.

The "Red Scare" that followed resulted in the arrest and deportation of many immigrants. Reacting to such fears, Congress soon passed laws limiting immigration to the United States. Suspicion of minorities also led to a rebirth of the Ku Klux Klan and new tensions between whites and African Americans. Many African Americans lost their lives in riots and lynchings in the years after the war.

The Roaring Twenties. In 1920, Warren Harding, the Republican candidate—promising a "return to normalcy"— won election as President. "Normalcy" for many Americans seemed to mean making money and having a good time. They had little interest in working for Progressive reform.

For a large number of people, the decade of the 1920s was a time of prosperity. Industry was growing, and wages

259

were going up. Many people had enough money to play the stock market and get richer with no apparent effort.

Mass entertainment became a feature of what has been called the Roaring Twenties. Radio networks helped draw the nation closer together. Movie actors and sports stars became important national figures.

African American writers, artists, and entertainers made major contributions to popular culture during these years. This outpouring of creativity became known as the **Harlem Renaissance**.

Not everyone, however, did well in the 1920s. Farmers suffered from low prices, and so did agricultural workers, including most African Americans.

Pittsburgh steel workers greet Secretary of Labor Frances Perkins, first woman to serve in the Presidential Cabinet.

The Great Depression. In October 1929, prices on the New York stock market fell suddenly and deeply. This stock market crash led the United States into the greatest **depression**, or severe economic slump, it had ever known.

By 1932, one person in every four was out of work, and many others were working only part time or at reduced wages. Herbert Hoover, the Republican who had become President in 1929, could find no way to get a recovery started.

In 1932, Democrat Franklin D. Roosevelt was elected President on his promise to do something about the depression. His cheerful and optimistic personality helped restore the people's confidence. "The only thing we have to fear is fear itself," he announced, and he seemed to believe it.

The New Deal. In his election campaign, Roosevelt had promised "a new deal for the American people." Roosevelt quickly began to deliver on his promise. In his first 100 days in office alone, the President asked for, and Congress passed, 15 major bills.

This **New Deal** created dozens of new government agencies to deal with different apects of the nation's economic problems. The federal government provided money for food and clothing for the needy. It created jobs for the unemployed. Some policies aimed to raise farmers' incomes; others tried to regulate industrial production.

One important bill, the National Labor Relations Act, guaranteed workers the right to **collective bargaining** through unions. A later law for the first time set a national minimum wage and a national maximum workweek.

In 1935, Congress also passed the Social Security Act. Now, millions of citi-

During the Great Depression, thousands of homeless people built shacks like these in New York City. Why were such shanty towns called "Hoovervilles?"

zens were guaranteed old-age and unemployment insurance.

Not all New Deal laws proved successful, nor did all citizens benefit equally from them. Sharecroppers in the South, for example, many of whom were African Americans, were harmed by the New Deal's agricultural policies. But the New Deal gave people the feeling that something was being done.

As Roosevelt neared the end of his second term in 1940, unemployment was still high, but the worst of the Great Depression was over. More people were working, and farmers were better off.

In Europe, however, a new war had broken out, into which the United States would soon be drawn. That war and its aftermath would bring profound changes in the lives of all African Americans.

Taking Another Look

1. What were some successes of the Progressive movement?

2. How did the New Deal attempt to solve problems caused by what is now known as the Great Depression?

3. **Critical Thinking** If you had been an African American voter in the election of 1920, would you have voted for a candidate who promised a "return to normalcy"? Explain.

The NAACP-sponsored Silent March to protest lynching, 1917

The Civil Rights Struggle

(1900–1941)

SECTIONS

THINKING ABOUT THE CHAPTER

What gains in civil rights did African Americans make in the first half of the 1900s?

On the evening of July 30, 1903, Boston's African Methodist Episcopal Zion Church was packed with some 2,000 spectators and journalists. They had come to hear Booker T. Washington speak before the National Negro Business League. He would present his long-held view that African Americans should concentrate on trying to achieve economic success and temporarily accommodate themselves to segregation.

In the audience sat William Monroe Trotter, publisher of the African American newspaper the *Guardian*. Unlike Washington, Trotter wanted immediate equality for African Americans. Tonight he was going to raise a series of questions designed to embarrass Washington.

As Trotter started to ask his questions, Washington's supporters began to protest. Trotter had to shout his questions above the noise. Someone shouted, "Throw Trotter out the window!" Fistfights broke out around the room. Finally, the Boston police stepped in and arrested Trotter. He was later fined $50 and sentenced to 30 days in jail.

Newspapers across the country seized upon the incident, labeling it the "Boston Riot." The real news, though, was that some African Americans were openly questioning the views of Washington. This was the man who had long been regarded as the spokesman for African Americans (see page 237). In this chapter, you will read about how their rising voices led to new strategies in the fight for civil rights.

1 W.E.B. DU BOIS

▼ What were the basic differences between W.E.B. Du Bois's views and those of Booker T. Washington?

The events in Boston revealed divisions among African Americans. Certainly, by the early 1900s, many were beginning to turn away from Booker T. Washington and his ideas. But who would take Washington's place? What ideas would the new leader have?

A New Thinker. In 1903, a 35-year-old professor of history and economics at Atlanta University published a book called *The Souls of Black Folk*. It included a bitter attack on Booker T. Washington's strategy for African American advancement and proposed a new course of action. Its author, W.E.B. Du Bois (doo-BOYZ), was to become the most important leader of African American protest in the first half of the 1900s.

William Edward Burghardt Du Bois was born in 1868 in Great Barrington, Massachusetts, and was raised in a single-parent family. From an early age, Du Bois viewed education as the way to a better life. Supported by hard-earned scholarships, he graduated from Fisk University in Nashville, Tennessee. He later went on to become the first African American to receive a doctoral degree from Harvard University. For ten years, Du Bois was a professor at Atlanta University, doing research on slavery and the African American community.

Du Bois gradually came to realize that his work as a scholar would not end such evils as Jim Crow, lynching, unfair housing practices, and unequal treatment of African Americans in the courts. Not long after his 1903 book was published, he gave up his teaching career to apply himself full-time to the fight for civil rights. He devoted the rest of his life to this cause. In 1961, dissatisfied with the progress of African Americans, the 93-year-old Du Bois became a Communist and moved to Ghana. He died there two years later.

Du Bois, unlike Booker T. Washington, was not a great public speaker. Even his friends said he sometimes put them to sleep with his cold, intellectual speeches. His influence came through his writings, which were read by well-educated African Americans and by sharecroppers and factory workers.

Du Bois's Leadership. "The American Negro demands equality, and he is never going to rest satisfied with anything less." This was the core of Du Bois's ideas. It was founded on the belief that peaceful resistance would gain civil rights and economic progress for African Americans. Du Bois opposed Washington's belief that going along with segregation would win these goals.

Du Bois believed that "the Negro race, like all other races, is going to be saved by its exceptional men." By "exceptional men," Du Bois meant those men—and women—who made up the well-educated upper 10 percent of the African American population. He called this group the **Talented Tenth**. According to Du Bois, the most intelligent African Americans had a duty to become teachers, lawyers, doctors, politicians, artists, and other professionals and African American colleges had an obligation to educate them. Du Bois declared:

> The Talented Tenth of the Negro race, must be made leaders of thought and missionaries of culture among their people. No others can do this work, and Negro colleges must train men [and women] for it.

Du Bois also believed that African Americans should take pride in both their rich cultural heritage and their own abilities. He urged African Americans to look to Africa for their heritage and develop literature and art of their own. They had to see the beauty in their blackness.

Du Bois realized that more than words was going to be needed to make his program a reality. African Americans had to find ways or make ways to make their voices heard. "We must organize," Du Bois declared.

As you have read, the freedom that African Americans gained as a result of the Civil War left them with many problems. What could African Americans do to fight discrimination? No two African American leaders differed more sharply as to the best course for African Americans than Booker T. Washington and W.E.B. Du Bois.

Booker T. Washington's View

No race can prosper until it learns that there is as much dignity in tilling [plowing] a field as in writing a poem. It is at the bottom of life we must begin, and not at the top. . . .

The wisest among my race understand that the agitation [stirring up] of questions of social equality is the extremest folly [greatest mistake], and that progress in the enjoyment of all the privileges that will come to us must be the result of severe and constant struggle rather than of artificial forcing. No race that has anything to contribute to the markets of the world is long in any degree ostracized [shut out]. It is important and right that all privileges of the law be ours, but it is vastly more important that we be prepared for the exercises of these privileges. The opportunity to earn a dollar in a factory just now is worth infinitely more than the opportunity to spend a dollar in an opera house.

—*from the* Atlanta Compromise Speech, *1895*

V·I·E·W

W.E.B. Du Bois's View

[African Americans] do not expect that the free right to vote, to enjoy civic rights and to be educated, will come in a moment . . . but they are absolutely certain that the way for a people to gain their reasonable rights is not by voluntarily throwing them away and insisting that they do not want them; . . . on the contrary, Negroes must insist continually, in season and out of season, that voting is necessary to proper manhood, that color discrimination is barbarism, and that black boys need education as well as white boys. . . .

So far as Mr. Washington preaches Thrift, Patience, and Industrial Training for the masses, . . . we must strive with him. . . . But so far as Mr. Washington apologizes for injustice, North or South, does not rightly value the privilege and duty of voting, . . . and opposes the higher training and ambition of our brighter minds—
. . . we must unceasingly and firmly oppose [him].

—from The Souls of Black Folk, 1903

Taking Another Look

1. How does Washington think African Americans will gain full rights?

2. What is Du Bois's solution to African Americans' problems?

3. **Critical Thinking** Do you think that it is possible to agree with both Washington and Du Bois? Explain.

Taking Another Look

1. What was the basic difference between Du Bois's ideas and those of Booker T. Washington?

2. What part did education play in Du Bois's program for African Americans?

3. **Critical Thinking (a)** Why might some African Americans object to the idea of a Talented Tenth? **(b)** What do you think about Du Bois's idea?

2 ORGANIZING FOR JUSTICE
▼ What was the purpose in establishing the NAACP?

On a warm August day in 1906, W. E. B. Du Bois, William Monroe Trotter, and other members of the year-old **Niagara Movement** traveled to Harpers Ferry, West Virginia, for their annual meeting. There, 47 years before, the white abolitionist John Brown had tried to start a private war against slavery (see page 185). Now these African Americans were pledging to renew the struggle for their full civil rights.

We claim for ourselves every single right that belongs to a free born American. How shall we get them? By voting where we may, by persistent [determined], unceasing agitation, by hammering the truth, by sacrifice and work.

Earlier Pioneers. The Niagara Movement was not the first group to start a national civil rights organization. Sixteen years earlier, T. Thomas Fortune, a newspaper editor, had organized the Afro-American League of the United States in Chicago, Illinois. Its members worked in Northern cities to promote citi-

SNAPSHOT OF THE TIMES

1903 Du Bois writes *The Souls of Black Folk*.

1905 Niagara Movement is organized.

1908 Springfield Massacre

1909 First National Negro Conference

1910 NAACP is founded.

zenship rights and economic opportunity for African Americans. In 1896, the National Association of Colored Women elected Mary Church Terrell as its first president. Her goal was to organize women's clubs nationwide to work for voting rights and health and educational programs for African American women.

The Niagara Movement. What made the Niagara Movement different from these earlier groups was its sense of urgency. Its members demanded immediate action. They insisted on an immediate end to all racial discrimination, on equal justice and fair housing for all African Americans, and on full voting rights for African American men.

To symbolize its views, the group first met near Niagara Falls, Canada. This area had once been an important station on the Underground Railroad (see page 160). Also, the members wanted to use the mighty falls to symbolize the power of their beliefs.

Despite its ambitious goals, the Niagara Movement never attracted many followers. This was partly because many African Americans, including Booker T. Washington, opposed its program as too extreme. Failing to attract wide support, the Niagara Movement disbanded in

Why did African American leaders found the Niagara Movement? How successful was it?

1908. However, it had laid the groundwork for a more successful organization—the NAACP.

Gathering Momentum. In August 1908 in Springfield, Illinois, the home of Abraham Lincoln, white prejudice against African Americans erupted into two days of race rioting. Three African Americans and four whites died. Over 70 people were injured, and the entire African American community was terrorized.

The Springfield Massacre, as the riot came to be called, shocked the entire nation. A white journalist named William English Walling wrote a bitter newspaper article called "Race War in the North," in which he condemned the Springfield Massacre. He also pleaded for a "large and powerful body of citizens" to help African

Americans in their fight for political and social equality.

The response to his appeal was a meeting of nearly 300 African Americans and whites in New York City in May 1909 to discuss African American rights. Among the African Americans who attended this first National Negro Conference were W.E.B. Du Bois; Ida Wells-Barnett, the antilynching activist (see page 233); and the Reverend Francis Grimké, husband of the Reconstruction teacher Charlotte Forten. Booker T. Washington was not invited. Among the whites were Protestant and Jewish clergy; social workers such as Jane Addams; and Oswald Garrison Villard, grandson of abolitionist William Lloyd Garrison (see page 145). Grimké and Garrison were reminders that the struggle for African American freedom and equality went back many years and many battles.

Not all African Americans who attended the meeting were pleased that whites were involved. Du Bois later reported that at one point an African American woman cried out, "They are betraying us again—these white friends of ours." Nevertheless, the conference made progress. It condemned U.S. attitudes toward its African American citizens "as the greatest menace that threatens the country." It also set up a Committee of Forty to form a permanent organization.

Setting Up the NAACP. The Committee of Forty met in 1910 and founded a new organization called the National Association for the Advancement of Colored People (NAACP). Its objective was to secure "equal rights and opportunities for all." The NAACP was an interracial organization that brought together African Americans who had been involved in the Niagara Movement and white reformers. The NAACP soon became the most active and effective fighter for the rights of African Americans.

Taking Another Look

1. What were the goals of the Niagara Movement?

2. What led to the founding of the NAACP?

3. **Critical Thinking** Why do you think Booker T. Washington was not invited to the first National Negro Conference?

3 ▼ THE NAACP'S FIGHT FOR CIVIL RIGHTS

What tactics did the NAACP use to achieve its goals?

A blond, blue-eyed young man was being sworn in as a sheriff's deputy in a county in Oklahoma. After the ceremony, another deputy turned to him and told him he could now go out and kill any black he saw, "and the law'll be behind you."

The new deputy's name was Walter White. Despite the fact that he was usually taken to be white, he was an African American. He was also an undercover agent for the NAACP. For ten years, starting in 1920, he risked his life to gather evidence about race riots and lynchings. In 1930, White became executive secretary of the NAACP.

Organizing Nationwide. The NAACP had quickly built a strong national organization. The first local branch was established in Chicago, Illinois, in 1911. By the end of its first decade, the NAACP had over 400 local branches, with more

►► MAJOR NAACP VICTORIES, 1910-1940

1912 Desegregates New York City theaters	1930 Active in strong protests leading to U.S.Senate's rejection of appointment of John H. Parker, opponent of African Americans' voting rights, to Supreme Court
1913 Leads campaign against segregation in U.S. Post Office and Treasury departments	
1915 Supreme Court rules grandfather clause (see page 229) in Southern states unconstitutional.	1933 Helps organize committee to fight discrimination against African Americans in New Deal programs
1917 Organizes New York City parade protesting lynching Supreme Court bans legal African American ghettoes in Southern cities	1935 Forces University of Maryland through court action, to admit its first African American student
1923 Supreme Court rules African Americans must be permitted to serve on juries	1936 Files first suit in campaign to end differences in salaries between African American and white teachers
1925 In Detroit, Michigan, wins right of African Americans to use force in self defense	1940 Begins drive against segregation in the armed forces

What kinds of activities did the NAACP engage in to end discrimination?

than 91,000 members. The NAACP was committed to achieving its goals through legal, peaceful means.

Spreading the Word. The NAACP believed that public opinion was "the main force upon which [to rely] for victory of justice." The NAACP took out ads in newspapers to spread the word about lynchings and other acts of racial violence. Its own publications printed research studies about the living conditions of African Americans.

Soon after the NAACP was set up, W.E.B. Du Bois became director of publicity and research. His major role, however, was as editor of the NAACP's magazine, the *Crisis*. The *Crisis* reported on the organization's activities and the challenges that it faced. It published not only political articles, but also poetry and stories by African American writers. The

magazine was so successful that by 1912 it had a circulation of 16,000 copies an issue, when the NAACP had only 1,000 members. By 1919 the circulation had reached 100,000 copies.

Fighting Against Lynching. The articles and editorials in the *Crisis* urged the federal government to take action against lynching. From 1900 to the outbreak of World War I, more than 1,100 African Americans were lynched. To stop the killing, the NAACP in 1921 persuaded a member of Congress to introduce legislation making lynching a federal crime. Although the bill passed the House of Representatives, senators from the South prevented the law from being enacted. Later NAACP-sponsored bills met the same fate. Nevertheless, the NAACP's efforts kept the national spotlight on the problem of lynching.

Fighting in the Courts From the start, the NAACP fought some of its most important battles in the courts, as you can see from the table on page 268. Its long-term strategy was to attack laws that discriminated against African Americans. The NAACP, from the mid-1920s through the 1930s, won important court victories in the fields of housing, education, and voting rights. It also gave legal aid to African American victims of race riots. By 1935, the NAACP began to challenge segregation in the nation's schools, as you will read in Unit 9.

Taking Another Look

1. How did the NAACP attempt to use public opinion?

2. What action did the NAACP take in regard to the lynchings of African Americans?

3. **Critical Thinking** Do you think the *Crisis* was a good title for the NAACP magazine? Explain.

LOOKING AHEAD

In 1929, W.E.B. Du Bois summed up the accomplishments of the NAACP in these words:

> Twenty years ago . . . it was said . . . that the real effective organization for the attainment [winning] of the rights of black men in America was impossible. . . . But we went in for agitation. We demanded the right to vote. . . . We stand today at the threshold [edge] of a new generation.

Despite its record of achievements, the NAACP appealed largely to the middle and upper classes of African Americans. By focusing on political and social discrimination, it often ignored the bread-and-butter economic concerns of most African Americans. To them, the NAACP seemed an organization of well-off African Americans and whites who had little understanding of the day-to-day difficulties they faced.

W.E.B. DuBois (standing, right), was the editor of *Crisis*, the NAACP magazine, for many years.

THE NAACP TODAY

The NAACP began in 1910 in a small room of a New York City apartment. Its members included a handful of African Americans and whites. Among them were W.E.B. Du Bois, Mary Church Terrell, Mary White Ovington, Joel Elias Spingarn, and William English. Today, the national headquarters of the NAACP occupies a five-story building in Baltimore, Maryland. The staff coordinates activities of nearly 2,200 local chapters and hundreds of thousands of members.

Since 1914, the NAACP has awarded a gold medal annually for "the highest and noblest achievement by an American Negro." The first Spingarn medal was presented in 1915 to Ernest Everett Just, a scientist at Howard University, for his research in biology.

Today the Board of Directors for the NAACP appoints a nine-member committee to select the category and person to be honored in a given year. Traditionally, the prestigious award is announced at the NAACP's annual convention held each summer. Since 1915, some of the winners have included W.E.B. Du Bois; George Washington Carver; Marian Anderson; Martin Luther King, Jr.; Daisy Bates and the Little Rock Nine; Leontyne Price; Henry Aaron; Jesse Jackson; and Bill Cosby.

What category do you think should be honored at this year's convention? Whom would you nominate?

CLOSE UP: Chapter 23

The Who, What, Where of History

1. **What** was Progressivism?
2. **Who** was William Monroe Trotter?
3. **What** was the *Guardian*?
4. **Who** was W.E.B. Du Bois?
5. **What** was the Talented Tenth?
6. **Who** was T. Thomas Fortune?
7. **Who** was Mary Church Terrell?
8. **What** was the Niagara Movement?
9. **What** was the NAACP?
10. **What** was the *Crisis*?

Making the Connection

1. What was the connection between the Niagara Movement and the NAACP?
2. What was the connection between the Springfield Massacre and the organization of the first National Negro Conference?

Time Check

Use the timeline on pages 258-259 and the Snapshot on page 266 to answer these questions.

1. How many years separated the writing of *The Souls of Black Folk* and the formation of the NAACP?
2. How many years separated the formation of the Niagara Movement and the formation of the NAACP?

What Would You Have Done?

1. If you had been an African American living in the early 1900s, would you have joined the Niagara Movement? the NAACP? Explain the reasons for your decisions in a letter to a friend.

2. Imagine that you have attended a lecture at which Du Bois explains his idea that the Talented Tenth will "save" African Americans. After the lecture, you have the chance to talk with Du Bois. Explain why you either agree or disagree with his idea.

Thinking and Writing About History

1. Write a short newspaper article about the "Boston Riot" of 1903. Make sure you answer the questions *who, what, when, where,* and *why.*

2. Review what you read in Chapter 21 about Booker T. Washington. Then write two paragraphs comparing the ideas of Washington and of Du Bois on the subject of how African Americans should achieve civil rights and economic progress.

Building Skills: Interpreting a Primary Source

W.E.B. Du Bois criticized Booker T. Washington's strategy for African American advancement. Read the following selection from Du Bois's *The Souls of Black Folk.* Then answer the questions that follow.

Mr. Washington distinctly asks that black people . . . concentrate all their energies on industrial education, and accumulation of wealth, and the conciliation of the South. This policy . . . has been triumphant for perhaps ten years. . . . In these years there have occurred:

1. The disfranchisement of the Negro.

2. The legal creation of a distinct status of civil inferiority for the Negro.

3. The steady withdrawal of aid from institutions for the higher training of the Negro . . .

Mr. Washington . . . faces the triple paradox [contradiction] of his career:

1. He is striving to make the Negro artisans business people and property-owners; but it is utterly impossible . . . for workingmen and property-owners to defend their rights and exist without the right of suffrage.

2. He insists on thrift and self-respect, but at the same time counsels a . . . submission to civic inferiority such as is bound to sap . . . any race in the long run.

3. He . . . depreciates institutions of higher learning; but neither the Negro common-schools, nor Tuskegee itself, could remain open a day were it not for teachers trained in Negro colleges, or trained by their graduates.

1. On what has Washington asked African Americans to focus?

2. What have been the results of Washington's policies, according to Du Bois?

3. What do you think Du Bois means when he says that it is impossible "for workingmen and property-owners to defend their rights and exist without the right of suffrage"?

4. Do you agree or disagree with Du Bois's criticisms of Washington? Explain the reasons for your position.

Cotton on the way to market in 1910

The Great Migration
(1915–1930)

THINKING ABOUT THE CHAPTER

How did the thousands of African Americans who left the South for the cities of the North and Midwest adjust to their new lives?

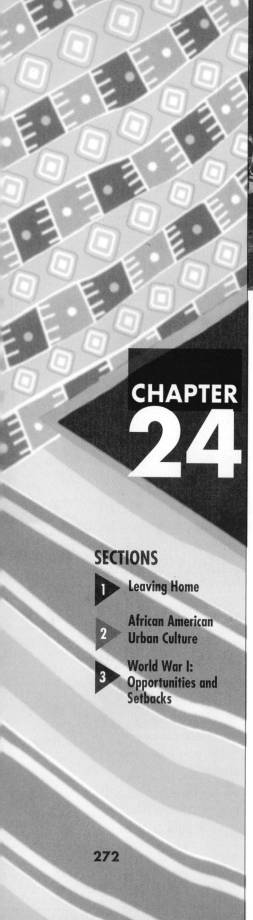
Bearing postmarks from distant worlds—Chicago, Milwaukee, New York, Philadelphia—letters and postcards poured into the South from 1910 through the 1920s. They were read aloud in rural African American churches and city markets and passed from hand to hand until they were too tattered to read.

Yet their message remained clear: There really were places in the United States where African Americans could live with dignity and a chance for financial security. A man from Hattiesburg, Mississippi, newly arrived in Philadelphia in 1917, proclaimed these wonders in a letter home:

Well, Dr . . . I am making very good. I make $75 per month. I can ride in the electric street and steam car anywhere I get a seat . . . and if you are first in a place here shopping you dont have to wait until the white folks get thro trading. . . . I am praying that God may give every well wisher a chance to be a man regardless of his color.

What began as a trickle of people swiftly became a river. Between 1915 and 1930, over a million African Americans abandoned the South. In this chapter, you will read why so many joined this Great Migration to the industrial cities of the North and Midwest and what their lives were like once they got there.

1 LEAVING HOME
▼ What conditions led many African Americans to leave the South?

On a cotton plantation in southern Georgia in 1910, 15 African American families—the Harrisons, the Battles, and 13 others—tried to scratch out a living as sharecroppers. By the end of 1917, not a single family remained. Like thousands of other African American families in the South, they had been the victims of a series of crushing blows.

Sharecroppers' Woes.   First had come the boll weevil. Starting east from Texas in the 1890s, these insects came in giant, hungry swarms, stripping fields bare of cotton. By 1922, they had ruined more than 85 percent of the South's cotton fields. Meanwhile, a series of fierce, driving rains brought deadly floods. Sharecroppers, many of whom were African Americans, were broke, tired, and close to starving.

Nature was not the only cause of their troubles. Sharecropping had not changed since Reconstruction. The plows that sharecroppers turned the soil with, the cotton seeds they planted, and the shacks they lived in belonged to the landowner.

Once the harvest was sold and their debts to the landowner were paid, the farm family had to make do on whatever was left until the next planting season. But by the fall of 1916, there was hardly any cotton left to harvest. Throughout Georgia, Alabama, Mississippi, Florida, and Louisiana, the boll weevil and the rains had done their work.

Trapped in the South.   There was not much hope of finding other jobs. Georgia state law, for example, forbade sharecroppers from leaving their fields until they had paid off their debts. If they tried to move to nearby towns or cities, local sheriffs had the legal right to hunt them down and bring them back. Southern law condemned the Harrisons, the Battles, and thousands of other families to a form of economic slavery.

SNAPSHOT OF THE TIMES

1890s	Boll weevils attack cotton fields.
1910	National Urban League founded.
1914–1918	World War I
1915	Great Migration of African Americans from the South begins.
1916	Cotton declines as important crop in the South.
1917	United States enters World War I.
	W.E.B. Du Bois urges African Americans to support the war.
	U.S. troops land in Europe.
	Race riots occur in 26 U.S. cities.
1919	U.S. troops are welcomed home.

In addition, white prejudice and the threat of brutality hung over African Americans. Many had seen friends and neighbors dragged off to jail for such "crimes" as being outside their homes past 10 P.M. The fear of lynching was very real. Few African Americans felt safe from local police, even inside their homes. For many, life seemed to lead to a dead end. "I am in the darkness of the South," a lonely voice cried, "and I am trying my best to get out."

Pulled to the North. Three thousand miles away, World War I was raging across Europe. Even before the United States entered the war in 1917, the nation was feeling the economic effects.

The war choked off the steady supply of cheap immigrant labor that Northern and Midwestern industries depended on. Then, in 1917, 4 million white workers were called into the U.S. armed forces. Factory owners had little choice but to recruit African Americans to work their steel furnaces, meat-packing plants, railroads, loading docks, and brickyards.

Company agents combed the South, armed with free railroad passes and promises of jobs that paid five dollars a day. Field hands who survived on less than a dollar a day and workers who sweated in Southern factories for 14 cents an hour leapt at the offer. They could make in a day what they earned in a week.

"Northern fever" was also intensified by headlines in African American newspapers. "Get out of the South," one paper shouted. Another, the *Chicago Defender,* urged, "For the hard-working . . . there is plenty of work."

The call was irresistible. One night in 1917, the 12 members of the Battle family slipped quietly away from their Georgia cotton plantation and boarded a train for Chicago. This scene was repeated thousands of times across the South.

Taking Another Look

1. What prompted many African Americans to leave the South between 1915 and 1930?

2. What attracted African Americans to Northern and Midwestern cities?

3. **Critical Thinking** Imagine yourself as a Southern sharecropper in 1917. Explain why you would or would not join the Great Migration.

2 ▼ AFRICAN AMERICAN URBAN CULTURE

How did African Americans respond to life in the cities?

The El rumbled to a halt above Chicago's South State Street. As the doors of the elevated train opened, a tide of weary women and men spilled onto the platform. They were mothers and wives, bone-tired from scrubbing fashionable homes on the shore of Lake Michigan. They were husbands and fathers back from the

What were some of the advantages that Southern arrivals found in Northern cities?

MIGRATION OF AFRICAN AMERICANS TO CITIES, 1910–1920

Legend:
- African American population in 1910 — Each box on bar = 10,000
- African American population in 1920 — Each box on bar = 10,000
- 1,777 — States with more than 400,000 African Americans in 1910 (Numbers in thousands on states)

State labels: MICH., WIS., IOWA, OHIO, IND., ILL., NEB., MO., KANSAS, OKLAHOMA, ARIZONA, NEW MEXICO, KY., W. VA., VA. 671, N.C. 687, TENN. 473, S.C. 836, ARK. 443, MISS. 1,009, ALA. 908, GA. 1,777, TEXAS 690, LA. 714, DEL., MD.

City labels: Cleveland, Detroit, Chicago, Indianapolis, Cincinnati, St. Louis, Kansas City, Pittsburgh, N.Y. New York, Philadelphia, Baltimore, Washington, D.C., Richmond, Norfolk, Charleston, Savannah, Jacksonville, Atlanta, Birmingham, Memphis, New Orleans, Houston

ATLANTIC OCEAN

0   250   500 Miles
0   250   500 Kilometers

110°W   100°W   90°W   80°W

What three cities gained the most African American population between 1910 and 1920?

grimy glass factories, stockyards, and blast furnaces that ringed the city. They were African Americans glad to be home from the white world.

It was payday for some, and they rushed to deposit their paychecks in African American banks. Some stopped to buy African American newspapers. Sports fans scanned the papers for the latest baseball scores from the professional Negro League.

As they fanned out to their homes, some passed a crowded record store where Jelly Roll Morton could be heard playing his "Smokehouse Blues" on the piano. From another store a record of Bessie Smith's "Nobody Knows You When You're Down and Out" was playing. This was a typical day in any city where African Americans had come to live.

City Living. In Chicago, it was called the South Side. In New York, Harlem. In Philadelphia, the Seventh Ward. In Washington, D.C., Northeast. These and similar neighborhoods in Northern and Midwestern cities were where African Americans lived—usually not by choice. In time, the African American sections of cities became known as **ghettoes.** A ghetto is a section of a city in which many members of one **ethnic group,** people who share a common culture, are forced to live, because of discrimination. Jews, Mexicans, and Asians were among other groups who lived in ghettoes.

Often because of lack of government interest, these neighborhoods were, or would soon become, the most rundown and neglected parts of cities. Nevertheless, rents were so high that several families of **migrants,** people who had moved looking for better economic opportunity, often had to share one apartment. In most cities, African American children attended neighborhood schools. Since their neighborhoods were almost all African American, so too were their schools.

City Churches. As in the South, African Americans looked to their churches for spiritual comfort, community support,

How would these children's lives be different if they were raised in the South?

and help in many parts of their lives. Older, established African American churches welcomed newcomers to the city. Sometimes a whole congregation moved North and rented a storefront for their church. New religious organizations such as the Church of God in Christ and the **Nation of Islam** (see page 350) also began to attract followers.

At a typical Sunday service, community concerns often took as much time as strictly religious matters. A sermon on the need for African Americans to vote might be followed by a report on the annual clothing drive to help the needy.

National Urban League. The goal of the **National Urban League**, founded in 1910, was also to help migrants. The League focused on helping them gain their economic and political rights. It aided new city dwellers in finding housing and work and made sure they were treated fairly on the job.

On crowded docks and in bustling train stations, Urban League workers searched out migrant families and directed them to apartments they had personally inspected. They demanded that union bosses and factory owners teach African American workers the skills that brought higher wages. If money was needed to build a playground or a health care center, for example, the Urban League helped raise the funds and often supervised the construction.

African American Newspapers. Newspapers helped strengthen ties in the African American communities. The *Washington Bee,* the *New York Age,* the *Cleveland Gazette,* the *Pittsburgh Courier,* and many others not only reported community news but also spoke out for the rights of African Americans. The most influential paper was the *Chicago Defender.* As you read earlier in this chapter, the *Defender* encouraged African Americans to leave the South. It also attacked discrimination, segregation, and lynching. The founder of the *Defender* was Robert S. Abbott.

Raised in Savannah, Georgia, **Robert S. Abbott** graduated from Kent Law School in Chicago. After being told that he was "too dark" to practice law in the United States, he decided to enter the newspaper business. In 1905, he brought out the first issue of the weekly *Defender,* which sold 300 copies. Abbott began to attract readers by using bold headlines and dramatic articles to announce both the ambitions and the accomplishments of African Americans. At its peak, Abbott's newspaper was distributed in cities from Chicago to New Orleans and had a circulation of over 300,000.

Taking Another Look

1. What living conditions did African American migrants face in the cities?

2. How did the African American community help migrants?

3. **Critical Thinking** Did the benefits of city life outweigh the social and economic hardships migrants found there? Explain.

3 WORLD WAR I: ▼ OPPORTUNITIES ▼ AND SETBACKS

How were African Americans involved in World War I?

According to President Woodrow Wilson, the goal of the United States in World War I was to make the world "safe for democracy." However, few African Americans saw democracy at work in the nation's armed forces. The Marine Corps barred them from service. The navy took them only as cooks, kitchen helpers, and boiler-room workers. Only the army reluctantly used them as fighting men.

Serving in the Armed Forces. When the nation began drafting men for the armed forces in July 1917, it also drafted Jim Crow. African American recruits were stationed throughout the country in segregated training camps. Many of these camps were in the South, where it seemed that whites disliked African American soldiers more than they did the German enemy.

A bitter racial incident took place in Houston, Texas, in August 1917. For several weeks, tensions had been building between soldiers and townspeople. One afternoon, several uniformed African American soldiers flagged down a public streetcar to board it. In an instant, they were surrounded by a gang of whites, who pulled them off, hurling racial insults at them. News of the incident quickly reached the training camp. Seizing their weapons, a band of angry African American soldiers raced to town. During the street fight that followed, 12 white civilians were killed.

After a brief trial, an army court-martial found 13 soldiers guilty of murder and ordered them hanged. Fourteen others were jailed for life. No whites were punished. The incident led to nationwide protests by African American organizations and white supporters. To prevent further violent flare-ups, the army began to ship some of its African American troops to Europe even before they had finished their training.

Serving Overseas. The U.S. Army trained over 370,000 African American

Known as the Harlem Hellfighters, the 369th Infantry returned in triumph to New York City in 1919. The unit also served in the Persian Gulf War in 1991.

soldiers for combat. Yet three out of four spent their time in the army in labor battalions. They hauled supplies, broke roads, or built fortifications. Although U.S. generals questioned the fighting fitness of African Americans, about 100,000 did see combat and most performed with distinction. They served in all-African American regiments, commanded for the most part by white officers. Only 1,400 African Americans became officers, none above the rank of colonel.

Despite the attitude of the American high command, their war-weary French allies gladly accepted African American units. Strapping on French backpacks and shouldering French rifles, African American soldiers fought under French officers in one vicious trench battle after another.

For their heroic efforts, African Americans were welcomed in French restaurants, hotels, and clubs. The French chose to ignore a secret memorandum

from the U.S. high command warning against treating African American soldiers too well.

Serving at Home. Most African Americans backed the war. W.E.B. Du Bois spoke for many when he declared, "If this is our country, then this is our war." He hoped that by supporting the war, African Americans would win the respect of the public and gain better treatment from whites.

African Americans stepped in to help fill the gap left by workers who had gone to war. They mined the coal that fueled the factories, and they labored to build badly needed tanks, trucks, and battleships. They bought Liberty Bonds to help finance the war and supported the Red Cross. African American women worked in army canteens.

However, events at home did not seem to reward their support. Race riots broke out in 26 major U.S. cities in 1917, including East St. Louis, Illinois, where 39 African Americans were killed. In protest, the NAACP organized a silent protest parade in New York City (see page 268). In the nation's capital, President Wilson, who had once promised "absolute fair dealing" for African Americans, ordered federal offices to be segregated.

Taking Another Look

1. What obstacles did African Americans face during World War I?

2. How did African Americans contribute to the war effort at home?

3. **Critical Thinking** Compare the reasons African Americans fought for the Union in the Civil War with their reasons for fighting in World War I.

LOOKING AHEAD

Huge parades in the nation's towns and cities greeted returning veterans of World War I. In New York City, nearly a million people lined Fifth Avenue to salute their heroes, among them Harlem's battle-hardened 369th Regiment. A grateful Chicago closed its schools and businesses to honor its triumphant warriors. For African Americans would this holiday from racism last?

From the NAACP magazine the *Crisis,* W.E.B. Du Bois issued a call to arms for African Americans. He proclaimed, "Make way for democracy! We saved it in France, and by the Great Jehovah, we will save it in the United States of America, or know the reason why."

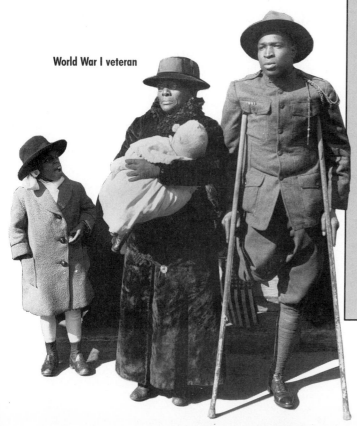

World War I veteran

World War I Honor Roll

Henry Johnson and Needham Roberts—First African Americans to receive the highest French award, the Croix de Guerre; awarded for fighting off attacking German soldiers while wounded

Sergeant Matthew Jenkins—Received the Distinguished Service Cross and the Croix de Guerre for holding a position against the enemy by himself for 36 hours

Corporal Isaac Valley—Awarded Distinguished Service Cross for covering a grenade with his foot to protect fellow soldiers

First Battalion of the 367th Infantry Regiment of the 92nd Division—Awarded the Croix de Guerre for bravery

369th Infantry Regiment of the 93rd Division—Cited 11 times for bravery; awarded the Croix de Guerre

CLOSE UP: Chapter 24

In 1919, the 369th U.S. Infantry marched triumphantly through New York, back from duty in Europe. When the African American regiment reached Harlem, its 60-piece band, led by Lieutenant James Europe, switched to **jazz**—the same music it had played to wildly enthusiastic crowds in France, Belgium, Britain, and Germany. European love of jazz began with James Europe's band.

Jazz is a unique musical form that developed in the United States at the turn of the century and then spread throughout the world. Blending a number of musical traditions, jazz combines West African rhythms, European harmonies, and African American spirituals and blues.

The popularity of jazz grew in Europe and the United States in the 1920s. However, many jazz musicians preferred playing in Europe, partly because Europeans were more appreciative of jazz than Americans were. African American musicians also found less racial discrimination in Europe, where talent was more important than skin color. But at home and abroad, African American musicians, including Billie Holiday and Jelly Roll Morton, drew large audiences. Their music later inspired present-day musicians like Wynton Marsalis, Hiram Bullock, and Grover Washington.

The Who, What, Where of History

1. **What** was the Great Migration?
2. **What** was the boll weevil?
3. **What** are migrants?
4. **What** are ghettoes?
5. **What** was the National Urban League?
6. **Who** was Robert S. Abbott?
7. **Where** was a silent protest parade held in 1917?

Making the Connection

1. What was the connection between the boll weevil and an increase in the African American population of cities of the North and Midwest?
2. What was the connection between state laws and the inability of African Americans to move from farms to cities in the South?
3. What was the connection between World War I and the increased employment of African Americans in manufacturing jobs?

Time Check

1. When did World War I begin?
2. When did the Great Migration of African Americans begin?
3. When did U.S. troops join the fighting in World War I?

What Would You Have Done?

1. Suppose you were starting a new weekly newspaper designed for African Americans. How would you attract readers?

2. If you had been an African American man in 1918, would you have chosen to try to get a factory job or to enlist in the army? Explain your choice.

Thinking and Writing About History

1. Imagine that you are an African American migrant who has come to Chicago in 1918. Write a letter to a friend in Mississippi explaining why you think the friend should or should not join you in the city.

2. Imagine that you are a member of the National Urban League in 1916. Write a letter to a friend explaining what sort of work you do for the league and why you enjoy it.

3. Write an editorial for the *Defender* about the court-martial of the soldiers following the racial incident in Houston in August 1917.

Building Skills: Making Generalizations Based on Statistics

Suppose your friend tells you that Willie Mays hit more home runs in his baseball career than Henry Aaron. You don't think he's right, and you consult an almanac and a baseball record book. You've just used some statistics—or as they call them in sports, stats. Statistics are numerical facts about a subject.

Historians often look at statistics to form ideas about trends and developments. They make generalizations from the information they find.

Following is a table that gives information about tenant farmers during the Great Depression. A tenant farmer is one who works land owned by another person. The tenant pays rent to the landowner. Study the table, then answer the questions that follow.

▷ ▷ Tenant Farmers in 1930

State	Percentage of farmers who were tenants	State	Percentage of farmers who were tenants
AL	64.7	NE	47.1
AZ	16.4	NV	12.9
AK	63.0	NH	5.3
CA	18.0	NJ	15.6
CO	34.5	NM	20.2
CT	6.2	NY	13.2
DE	33.8	NC	49.2
FL	28.4	ND	35.1
GA	68.1	OH	26.3
ID	25.3	OK	61.5
IL	43.1	OR	17.8
IN	30.1	PA	15.9
IA	47.3	RI	12.5
KS	42.3	SC	65.1
KY	35.9	SD	44.6
LA	66.6	TN	46.2
ME	4.5	TX	60.9
MD	26.5	UT	12.2
MA	5.6	VT	9.7
MI	15.5	VA	28.1
MN	31.1	WA	17.0
MS	72.2	WV	18.6
MO	34.8	WI	18.2
MT	24.5	WY	22.0

1. What do the numbers in the table represent?

2. a. Which are the five states with the highest percentage of tenants?
b. Which five have the lowest?

3. Write a generalization based on your answers to question 2.

4. Look at the percentages for Washington, Oregon, Utah, Arizona, California, Idaho, Nevada, Montana, Wyoming, Colorado, and New Mexico. Write a generalization about farm tenancy in the western states.

Marcus Garvey at right

1900-30

Black Nationalism

(1916–1929)

THINKING ABOUT THE CHAPTER

Why did African Americans become interested in black nationalism in this period?

On a steamy August day in 1920, some 50,000 African Americans set out on a march through the streets of Harlem, New York City's African American community. The march marked the opening of the first International Convention of the Negro Peoples of the World.

Thousands more African Americans lined the sidewalks, cheering the marchers. A sense of pride swept through the crowd. Many waved flags of black, red, and green—the black standing for their race, the red for their blood, and the green for their hopes.

The loudest cheers went up when a stocky Jamaican-born man in a gold-trimmed uniform rolled into view in an open car. This was Marcus Mosiah Garvey, the president-general of the convention.

That night, Garvey addressed 25,000 African Americans gathered at Madison Square Garden. "We are descendants of a people determined to suffer no longer," he proclaimed. "We shall now organize the 400 million Negroes of the world into a vast organization to plant the banner of freedom on the great continent of Africa." A participant in the meeting later recalled, "It was the greatest demonstration of colored solidarity [unity] in American history, before or since."

Garvey served as the inspiring leader of many African Americans for only a brief time. However, his ideas still move African Americans. He believed that they should take pride in their blackness and study and identify, or connect, with the history and culture of Africa. He also felt that, to get ahead, African Americans should rely on themselves rather than on white people. These ideas make up what has been called **black nationalism.**

1 THE APPEAL OF BLACK ▼ NATIONALISM

▼ Why were African Americans attracted to black nationalism?

A little over a year before Garvey addressed the convention in New York,

W.E.B. Du Bois had announced to African Americans that, "We are cowards . . . if now that the war is over we do not marshal every ounce of our brain and brawn [muscle] to fight a sterner, longer, more unbending battle against the forces of hell [discrimination] in our own land." Events in the coming months would demonstrate just how bitter that battle was to be.

Losing Ground. For many whites, the 1920s were good years. Spirits and fortunes soared as new jobs were created. The stock market and the nation's economy boomed.

Most African Americans, however, still faced discrimination, and many were jobless. African Americans who had found wartime jobs in the factories of the North and Midwest often lost them to returning white veterans. Barred from joining the powerful labor unions, African Americans could not protect themselves against such layoffs.

A revived Ku Klux Klan was again threatening African Americans and also Catholic, Jewish, and immigrant whites. By day, its members staged parades in Northern as well as Southern cities and put pressure on white politicians to support Klan policies. Under the cover of

This photo of Garvey's African Motor Corps was taken by Harlem photographer James Van Der Zee.

1916	Marcus Garvey brings Universal Negro Improvement Association to New York.
1919	"Red Summer" race riots
1920	First International Convention of the Negro Peoples of the World
1922	Garvey is charged with mail fraud.
1927	Garvey is deported.

darkness, its night riders assaulted African Americans in their homes. The number of lynchings, which had fallen during the war, began to rise again.

Race Riots. The Great Migration had steadily increased the African American populations of cities in the North and Midwest. Whites often resented these new neighbors, and tensions between the groups mounted steadily. Then, less than eight months after the end of World War I, tensions erupted in a series of race riots across the nation.

During the "Red Summer" of 1919, as this violent season was called, casualties mounted. Six died and 150 were injured in two days of fighting in Washington, D.C. The toll in Chicago stood at 38 dead and 537 injured. By year's end, race riots had ripped through 25 cities and towns, including Knoxville, Tennessee; Longview, Texas; and Tulsa, Oklahoma.

Fighting Back. This violence provoked a new spirit of defiance among African Americans. Tired of being the victims of discrimination and violence, many African Americans chose to fight back. "The time for cringing [shrinking away in fear] is over," announced the Kansas City *Call,* an African American newspaper. From New York City, the Jamaican-born poet Claude McKay agreed, writing in the poem "If We Must Die,"

> If we must die, let it not be like hogs
> Hunted and penned in an inglorious [undignified] spot.
> . . . .
> Like men we'll face the murderous, cowardly pack,
> Pressed to the wall, dying but fighting back!

Nevertheless, few believed that violence could permanently solve the problems that African Americans faced in the nation. Members of the NAACP and the National Urban League, who were mostly middle-class African Americans, still looked to legal and political strategies to bring about change.

Pan-Africanism. Some African Americans began to identify more closely with their African roots. Led by W.E.B. Du Bois, they championed the idea of **Pan-Africanism.** Pan-Africanists be-

Two million members of the revived Ku Klux Klan conducted a new reign of terror in the 1920s.

lieved that people of African descent had common interests and should join in a common struggle for freedom, at home and abroad (see page 288).

The roots of Pan-Africanism in the United States went back to the early 1800s. One of the earliest promoters was Paul Cuffe. He encouraged African Americans to leave the United States and make Africa their home (see page 139).

In the 1920s, there was renewed interest in Pan-Africanism. The ideas of black nationalism that Marcus Garvey developed, for example, stressed the importance of their African heritage to African Americans.

Taking Another Look

1. What does the term *black nationalism* mean?

2. List three responses of African Americans to conditions after World War I.

3. **Critical Thinking** Which of the responses you listed promised the strongest hope of success? Explain.

2 MARCUS GARVEY

▼ What message did Marcus Garvey bring to African Americans?

The violence of the Red Summer strengthened the resolve of many African Americans to make a new life for themselves. "Lynchings and race riots," said one leader, "all work to our advantage by teaching the Negro that he must build a civilization of his own or remain forever the white man's victim."

The speaker was Marcus Garvey, organizer of the International Convention of the Negro Peoples described at the beginning of the chapter. Garvey had a

vision of new strength for African peoples around the world. That vision and his plans for making it happen won him the title "Black Moses."

Marcus Mosiah Garvey was born in 1887 in Jamaica, in the British West Indies. He left school at the age of 14 to help support his family. In his early 20s, Garvey worked his way through Central and South America. As he traveled, Garvey was struck by the hardships black people everywhere faced.

At age 25, Garvey went to London to learn more about conditions for Africans in the British Empire. There he met African scholars, students, and workers. It was in London that supporters of Pan-Africanism opened his eyes to his rich African heritage.

Garvey believed that African peoples could win equality with whites only through economic, political, and cultural independence. He returned to his native Jamaica in 1914 and founded the Universal Negro Improvement Association (UNIA) to work toward this goal.

Beginnings of a Movement. Marcus Garvey stood at the center of a whirlwind of activity that swept out of Harlem from 1916 through the early 1920s. Garvey had brought the UNIA to New York from Jamaica in 1916. "Up, you mighty race!" he preached to African Americans. "You can accomplish what you will." Garvey thus started the first extensive black nationalist movement in

U.S. history that appealed to the great mass of the African American people.

Garvey set in motion a variety of UNIA programs aimed at fostering political, economic, and cultural independence. The UNIA's newspaper *Negro World* carried stories about African American leaders and heroes usually left out of white publications. Its meeting halls became the scene of rallies and of exhibitions highlighting the African American experience.

Garvey's Plans.

Garvey warned African Americans that "a race that is solely dependent upon others for its economic existence sooner or later dies." He felt that businesses owned and managed by African Americans offered a path to independence for them. With the UNIA as a base, Garvey began to develop such businesses.

In 1919, he founded the Black Star Line. He hoped this steamship company would develop commercial ties between African peoples the world over. Garvey also started the Negro Factories Corporation in 1919. Within a short time, the corporation operated grocery stores, a restaurant, a laundry, a publishing house, and several other businesses.

Yet, even if African Americans succeeded in owning businesses, Garvey believed that the "monster evil of prejudice" would deny them justice and equality in the United States. He therefore called upon black workers to join him in Africa and create a powerful nation there. "Let Africa be a bright star among the constellation of nations," he proclaimed. As part of a plan to develop the continent, the UNIA sent teams of surveyors and engineers to map potential settlement sites in Liberia (see page 144).

Garvey's Appeal.

Programs like these won Garvey a huge following. His approach differed from that of earlier African American leaders. Du Bois had focused on the Talented Tenth at the top of African American society. The NAACP's programs likewise attracted the upper and middle classes and professionals.

Garvey, however, tailored his appeal to ordinary African Americans. He offered pride, pageants, and uplifting messages. He was, according to one observer, "the first Negro to capture the imagination of the masses." The masses responded by flocking to join the UNIA. By 1920, Garvey claimed 4 million members for the organization. His critics protested that this figure was wildly exaggerated.

The masses also gave money—for contributions, membership fees, and pur-

Garveyite families valued their African heritage and belief in black nationalism.

chases of stock in Garvey's companies. Between 1919 and 1921, an estimated $10 million in nickels, dimes, and dollars poured in.

A Movement Collapses. As Garvey's popularity reached its peak, rumors began to spread that his Black Star Line was in danger of sinking. Garvey was a poor business manager, more comfortable speaking in a crowded lecture hall than running a company. As a result, he left many key decisions in the hands of associates who lacked practical business experience. They spent huge sums on leaky ships and ill-trained crews to run them.

The federal government began an investigation of the Black Star Line. In 1922, Garvey was arrested for mail fraud. The government charged that he had known the company was on the verge of ruin but had continued to urge people to invest in it.

Garvey was found guilty and sentenced to five years in prison. President Calvin Coolidge freed Garvey in 1927, after he had served two years. Upon his release from prison, Garvey was deported from the United States. Without its leader, Garvey's movement soon collapsed. His later efforts to restart the UNIA failed. Garvey died in London in 1940.

Garvey's Legacy. At the time of his death, Garvey was almost a forgotten figure. After his movement had collapsed in the 1920s, many African Americans had dismissed his programs as foolish schemes. Some leaders protested that the UNIA had taken attention away from better-planned efforts to gain equality.

However, as black nationalism resurfaced during the 1960s, people rediscovered Garvey. Publishers rushed his collected speeches and essays into print. In the 1970s, New York City named a housing project the Marcus Garvey Park Village. In 1987, an African American member of Congress presented a bill to reverse Garvey's 1925 conviction and clear his name.

African Americans had finally taken note of Garvey's major accomplishment. He had begun a movement to make African Americans a united people. He had also left them a lasting gift. "In a world where black is despised," said New York's *Amsterdam News,* "he taught them that black is beautiful."

Taking Another Look

1. How did Garvey attempt to build economic independence among African Americans?

2. How did Garvey's programs differ from those of earlier African American leaders?

3. **Critical Thinking** What benefits might the powerful African nation that Garvey wanted to build have offered for African Americans?

LOOKING AHEAD

When Marcus Garvey announced membership figures for the UNIA, critics attacked him. The real numbers were only a tenth of Garvey's figures, they said. But critics' charges did not bother him. "No one will ever know accurately the membership of the Universal Negro Improvement Association," he said, "because every second Negro you meet, if not an actual member, is one in spirit." Already, this spirit was flowering in a creative explosion of African American art and culture that would come to be known as the Harlem Renaissance.

FOCUS ON PAN-AFRICANISM

You have opened my eyes to liberty. I shall never rest until I have carried your message to Africa.

So wrote Kwame Nkrumah (KWAH-mee uhn-KROO-muh) as he left the United States at the end of World War II. The message that he carried back to his native Ghana and to all of Africa could be summed up in just two words—independence and unity.

Nkrumah and other young African thinkers at the time were caught up in the excitement of a movement known as Pan-Africanism. Inspired by W.E.B. Du Bois and Marcus Garvey, this movement stressed the shared interests and common struggle of all peoples of African descent.

The movement also emphasized Africa's historical importance. Du Bois promoted these ideas at a series of five international conferences that Nkrumah and other future African leaders, including Kenya's Jomo Kenyatta, attended. The objective was to help Africans shake off their colonial rulers.

In the 1950s and 1960s, the nations of Africa did win their freedom. Nkrumah, first president of Ghana, tried to forge a united Africa, but political turmoil prevented it. In spite of that, a desire still burns among Africans to chart their own independent course in world affairs.

The Who, What, Where of History

1. **Who** was Marcus Garvey?
2. **What** is black nationalism?
3. **What** is Pan-Africanism?
4. **What** was the Red Summer?
5. **What** was the UNIA?
6. **What** was the Black Star Line?

Making the Connection

What was the connection between the end of World War I and the increase in the unemployment rates among African Americans?

Time Check

1. When was the First International Convention of the Negro People of the World held?
2. How many years were there between Garvey's bringing the UNIA to the United States and his deportation?

What Would You Have Done?

1. Imagine that you are the editor of an African American newspaper in Chicago. It is September 1919. Write an editorial for your paper about the events of the Red Summer.
2. If Marcus Garvey had asked you which of his ideas you thought was most useful to African Americans, what would you have answered?

Thinking and Writing About History

1. Imagine that you are one of the founding members of the UNIA. Write a short paragraph explaining the goals and purposes of the organization.

2. Design a poster that advertises some UNIA-sponsored business or event.

3. Write an obituary for Marcus Garvey that might have appeared in a Harlem newspaper.

4. Shortly after Garvey's death, one scholar said:

> *That is the difference between success and failure. Had Garvey succeeded in his undertakings, he would have been uncontestably the greatest figure of the twentieth century. Having failed, he is considered a fool.*

Do you think this summary is still valid? Explain.

Building Skills: Recognizing Propaganda

When people hear the word *propaganda*, they often think of something sneaky or evil. However, propaganda is merely a method of using ideas and information to influence people's views. Some widely used propaganda techniques are listed below:

1. *Glittering generalities:* broad, sweeping statements that sound good but, in fact, mean little.

2. *Name calling:* trying to devalue something by attaching a bad label to it.

3. *Bandwagon:* trying to win support for something by conveying the idea that "everybody's doing it."

4. *Testimonial:* having a well-known person endorse an idea or product.

5. *Plain folks:* showing that something comes from ordinary, down-to-earth people, and is, therefore, good.

6. *Card stacking:* distorting facts and evidence to present only one side of an issue favorably.

7. *Transfer:* trying to shift the positive associations from a person or thing to something not directly related.

After studying the propaganda techniques above, see if you can recognize them at work. Read the list below. Write the type of propaganda each illustrates on a separate sheet of paper.

1. "Almost everyone on the block has joined the UNIA already. Why don't you sign up now?"

2. "To join an organization like the UNIA is un-American."

3. "The Black Star Line presents to every African American man, woman, and child the opportunity to climb the great ladder of industrial and commercial progress."

4. "Marcus Garvey has already bought a thousand shares of stock in this company. Why don't you buy some?"

5. "I'm a workingman just like you, so you know that if I'm willing to put my hard-earned money in this company, it must be a safe investment."

6. "Don't you want to invest in the Black Star Line? After all, its flagship is the S.S. *Frederick Douglass.*"

7. "Look, the stock is selling for $5.00 a share right now. That's a great buy! You don't need to know what it was selling for last month."

125th Street in New York City's Harlem

The Harlem Renaissance

(1920–1930)

THINKING ABOUT THE CHAPTER

How did conditions in New York City during the 1920s influence the work of African American writers, artists, and musicians?

New York City's African American community of Harlem lay to the north of fashionable white residential and business areas. Yet on Saturday nights in the 1920s, it seemed the world was traveling uptown to catch Harlem's fastest-rising stars. Along Lenox Avenue, caravans of taxicabs and limousines shuttled the well-to-do to New York City's hottest clubs and dance palaces.

The crowds might be bound for the Cotton Club, which billed itself as the "Aristocrat of Harlem" and limited its audience to whites only. There, high-stepping African American dancers in feathers and sequins pranced to the beat of an orchestra led by Duke Ellington.

The Artist's View

▲▽▲▽▲▽▲▽▲▽▲▽▲▽▲▽▲▽▲▽▲▽▲▽▲▽▲▽▲▽▲▽▲▽

Though less attention has been paid to African American artists than to writers and musicians, they have made a significant contribution to American culture. Some African American art draws on the West African artistic heritage. Other art has roots in more modern styles. Whatever the expression, African American art consistently portrays the inner strength and grace of African Americans and expresses pride in African American culture. This section, *The Artist's View*, presents striking examples of notable African and African American art. As you examine each work, ask yourself how the artist is expressing his or her notion of the African or African American experience.

Statue; Ife, Nigeria ▶

By A.D. 1000, the city-state of Ife, founded by the Yoruba, was the center of a powerful kingdom. Its artisans were famous for their wood, clay, and bronze figures.

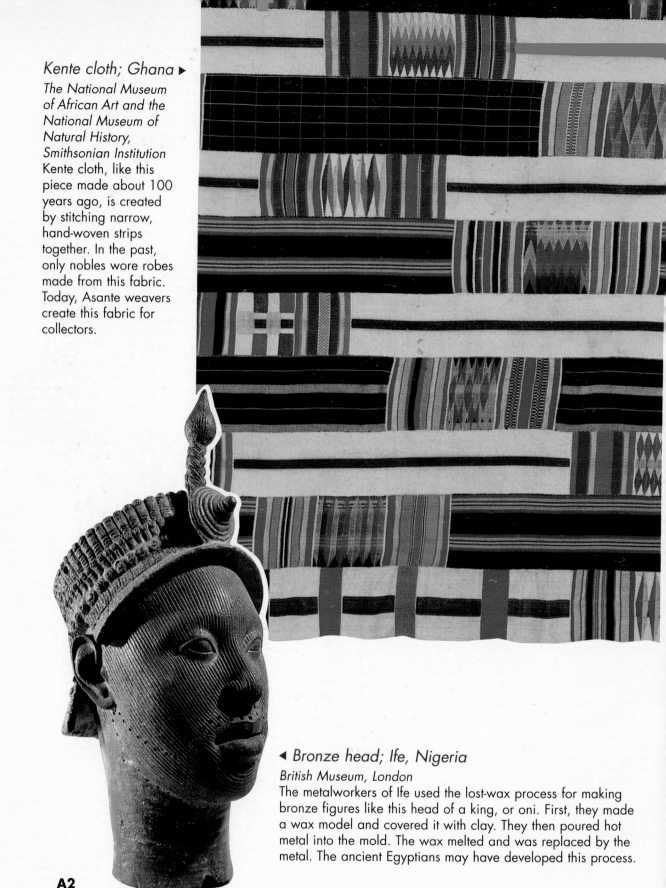

Kente cloth; Ghana ▶

The National Museum of African Art and the National Museum of Natural History, Smithsonian Institution Kente cloth, like this piece made about 100 years ago, is created by stitching narrow, hand-woven strips together. In the past, only nobles wore robes made from this fabric. Today, Asante weavers create this fabric for collectors.

◀ *Bronze head; Ife, Nigeria*

British Museum, London
The metalworkers of Ife used the lost-wax process for making bronze figures like this head of a king, or oni. First, they made a wax model and covered it with clay. They then poured hot metal into the mold. The wax melted and was replaced by the metal. The ancient Egyptians may have developed this process.

A2

▲ *Ceremonial mask; the Congo*
Africans used masks made of wood, ivory, and other materials in their religious ceremonies. Masks like this one inspired European artists such as Picasso and Derain to use elements of African art in their work.

▲ Ndebele home, northern South Africa

The brightly colored homes of the Ndbele (en–deh–BEL–eh) people provide a startling contrast with the brown grasslands of South Africa. The complex, exact geometric designs come in all the primary colors and take many months to complete.

▼ *Harriet Powers, pictorial quilt*

Museum of Fine Arts, Boston

Harriet Powers of Athens, Georgia, worked from 1895 to 1898 on this quilt depicting scenes from the Bible and from local history. To create the pictures, Powers sewed, or appliqued, pieces of fabric onto a backing.

Thomas Day, detail from a mantle ▶

Thomas Day's fine cabinetwork often had African-inspired designs. He worked as a cabinetmaker creating mahogany furniture and architectural pieces from 1818 to 1858.

▲ *Joshua Johnson, Portrait of a Cleric*

Bowdoin College Museum of Art, Brunswick, Maine
Painted in 1805, this is Joshua Johnson's only known portrait of an African American subject. Working from 1789 to 1825, Johnson, the most celebrated African American artist of his time, had to paint portraits of wealthy white people to make a living.

Henry O. Tanner, The Banjo Lesson ▶

Hampton Institute, Virginia
Painted in 1893, this is one of Henry O. Tanner's few works with an African American subject. After Reconstruction, the U.S. art world rejected African American art, so Tanner fled to Paris and focused his paintings on religious themes.

◀ N. Elizabeth Prophet, Congolais

The Whitney Museum of American Art New York
Nancy Elizabeth Prophet, one of the many African American artists who lived and worked abroad, sculpted this figure reminiscent of a Masai warrior in 1931.

Face vessel, South Carolina ▶

This porcelain face vessel was made in the 1800s. Called "monkey pots" by the enslaved African Americans who crafted them, the style of these water jugs has its roots in West Africa, where wooden sculptures have similar features.

A7

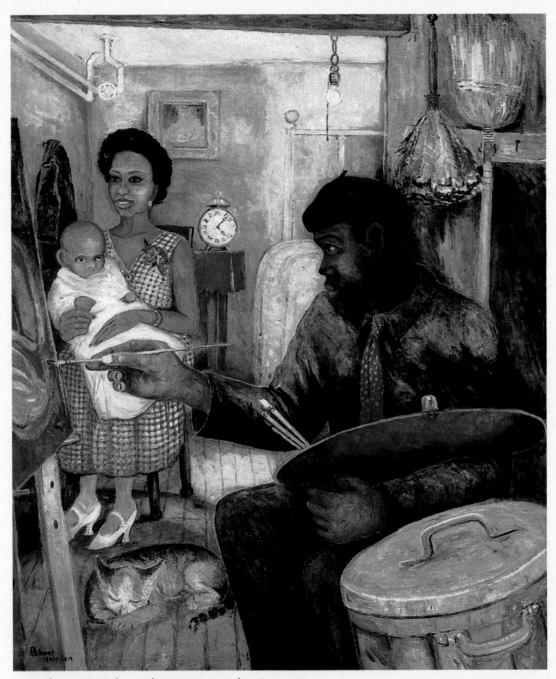

▲ *Palmer Hayden, The Janitor Who Paints*

National Museum of American Art, Smithsonian Institution, Washington, D.C.
Painted about 1937, this painting suggests the period when Hayden, like other
African American artists, was forced to take odd jobs to support himself. The
mask-like faces of the woman and children show Hayden's tie to African art.

▲ *Edmonia Lewis, Forever Free*
Howard University Art Gallery, Washington, D.C.
Sculpted of marble in 1867, Edmonia Lewis's
Forever Free celebrates the ratification of the
13th Amendment outlawing slavery. Her sculptures
often reflected her Chippewa and African American
heritage.

Aaron Douglas, "Song of the Tower," ▶
Aspects of Negro Life
Schomburg Center for Research in
Black Culture, New York
This work, from a four-panel series, illustrates
why African Americans migrated
to the industrialized North. In this 1930 series,
Aaron Douglas painted African American
history and experiences.

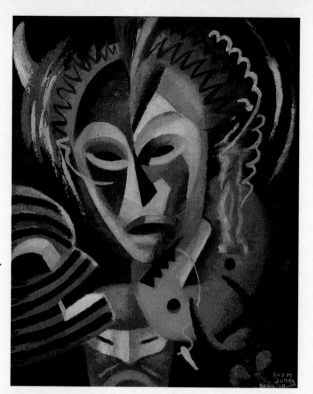

Lois Mailou Jones, Les Fetiches ▶

*National Museum of American Art,
Washington, D.C.*
The African mask in this work, painted
in 1938, reflects Louis Mailou Jones's
commitment to her African American
heritage. She often employed African
images in her work.

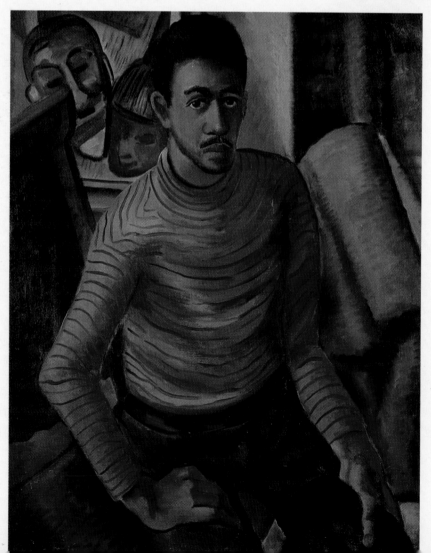

**◀ Malvin Gray Johnson,
Self–Portrait**

*National Museum of
American Art, Smithsonian
Institution, Washington,
D.C.*
This self-portrait was
painted in 1934, the year
Johnson died. Although he
lived only 38 years, Johnson
left a legacy of paintings of
African American life,
especially of the South.

▲ *Jacob Lawrence, from The Migration of the Negro*
Museum of Modern Art, New York
Jacob Lawrence painted his 60-panel series *The Migration of the Negro*
between 1940 and 1941. The series details the conditions that compelled many
African Americans to move to the North.

▲ *Horace Pippin, John Brown Going to His Hanging*
Pennsylvania Academy of Fine Arts, Philadelphia
Horace Pippin created a powerful effect using mainly gray, black, and white in this last in a series of paintings illustrating John Brown's life. When she was a young girl, Pippin's mother, an enslaved African American, had seen Brown's execution.

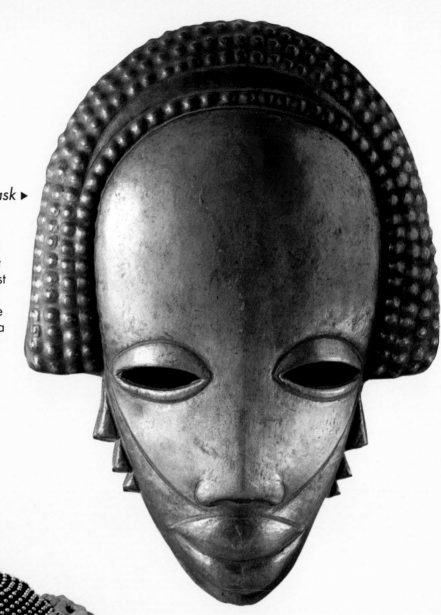

Sargent Johnson, Mask ▶

San Francisco Museum of Modern Art

This copper mask, made in 1933, reveals Sargent Johnson's effort to suggest but not copy forms from Africa. He interpreted the artistic traditions of Africa in contemporary African American art.

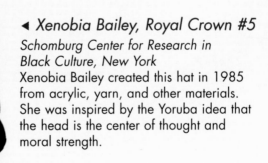

◄ Xenobia Bailey, Royal Crown #5

Schomburg Center for Research in Black Culture, New York

Xenobia Bailey created this hat in 1985 from acrylic, yarn, and other materials. She was inspired by the Yoruba idea that the head is the center of thought and moral strength.

◄ *Augusta Savage, Gamin*
*The Schomburg Center for Research
in Black Culture, New York*
Augusta Savage sculpted this piece
in 1930, using plaster as her medium.
She was the first African American
chosen for the National Association of
Women Painters and Sculptors.

▲ *John Biggers, Jubilee—Ghana Harvest Festival*
The Museum of Fine Arts, Houston
A painter, sculptor, and printmaker, John Biggers also painted
murals in the mid 1900s. His work shows aspects of African and
African American life.

▲ *Faith Ringgold, Bitternest Part II: Harlem Renaissance Party*

Bernice Steinbaum Gallery, New York

This 1988 mixed-media piece made of cloth and acrylic portrays Faith Ringgold's campaign for equality. It shows the artist at bottom right with leading figures from the Harlem Renaissance.

▲ *Romare Bearden, Trio*

The Estate of Romare Bearden
Working in 1964 on this collage, Romare Bearden combined
forms from African art with photographs, cloth, and painted
paper to represent various experiences of African Americans.

The more daring downtown whites might head for the clubs that accepted mixed audiences—places like Mexico's and the Catagonia Club—to hear jazz. Or they might join the crowds of African Americans that packed the glittering Savoy Ballroom. There they learned the Charleston or the Savoy Stomp on the Savoy's nearly block-long dance floor.

Uptown Saturday night entertainment was only the most visible part of the outpouring of African American artistic achievement in the 1920s. This burst of creativity by writers, musicians, and artists is known as the Harlem Renaissance.

The "New Negro." The Harlem Renaissance was another of the developments that affected the African American community after World War I. African American writers and thinkers proclaimed the appearance of a "New Negro." One African American newspaper announced, "The NEW NEGRO, unlike the old time negro, does not fear the face of the day."

For writers and artists this meant a new willingness to explore African American themes and topics. One poet stated,

We younger Negro artists now intend to express our individual dark-skinned selves without fear or shame. If white people are pleased, we are glad. If they are not, it doesn't matter.

Harlem. It seemed only natural that the New Negro Movement, as it is sometimes called, was centered in Harlem. The Great Migration had turned an almost all-white neighborhood into the nation's largest African American community. Here lived the most prominent African American leaders, such as W.E.B. Du

Bois and Marcus Garvey. The NAACP and the National Urban League had their headquarters in New York. The nation's largest collection of material on African American history and culture, which belonged to Arthur Schomburg, a Puerto Rican of African descent, could be found in Harlem as well. As African Americans poured into Harlem, once-spacious apartments were divided into smaller flats, and rents soared.

As buildings became overcrowded, landlords neglected them and decay set in. Yet the elegant houses of "Strivers' Row," the homes of doctors, dentists, and professionals, stood in the center of the community. They were symbols of the financial success that African Americans could achieve in New York. "Better to be a dishwasher in New York," commented one writer, "than to be head of a high school in Kansas City."

Near which streets did Langston Hughes live? Where was the Apollo Theater? the Savoy Ballroom?

HARLEM DURING THE HARLEM RENAISSANCE

145 St.

Abyssinian Baptist Church

Cotton Club

Strivers' Row

Savoy Ballroom

Mother A.M.E Zion Church

James Weldon Johnson home

Garvey's Liberty Hall

Sugar Cane Club

135 St.

Harlem Branch of N.Y. Public Library

Lafayette Theater

Apollo Theater

Langston Hughes's home

125 St.

St. Nicholas Ave.

Lenox Ave.

Fifth Ave.

Park Ave.

116 St.

Eighth Ave.

Seventh Ave.

Harlem River

CENTRAL PARK

N.J.

NEW YORK CITY

Countee Cullen (1903–1946) Cullen explored the African American experience in delicate poetry. One of his finest poems, "Heritage," deals with the importance of his African roots. Other poems describe emotional scars that prejudice caused. A popular Harlem high school teacher, Cullen also wrote a literary column that introduced new African American writers to a wide audience.

Jessie R. Fauset (1885–1961) Fauset was a novelist, editor, teacher, and poet. As literary editor of *Crisis*, the NAACP magazine, she tirelessly promoted the work of promising young African American writers. Both in her poetry and in her four successful novels, she gave readers the first real and compassionate picture of middle-class African American life.

Langston Hughes (1902–1967) Harlem's most famous poet captured the rhythms and spirit of African American music—especially jazz and the blues—in his work. Originally from Missouri, Hughes wrote poems, stories, plays, essays, autobiographies, and histories that helped define the African American urban experience.

Zora Neale Hurston (1901–1960) Hurston revealed the emotional intensity and genuine speech of southern African Americans in novels like *Jonah's Gourd Vine* (1934) and *Their Eyes Were Watching God* (1937). As an anthropologist, she pioneered the study of African American folktales and spirituals in her 1935 nonfiction book *Mules and Men*.

James Weldon Johnson (1871–1938)   Johnson began to write poetry late in his life, after a brilliant career as a lawyer, diplomat, and civil rights activist. During the Harlem Renaissance, he wrote and edited several major volumes of poetry and championed new writers. He wrote the lyrics to "Lift Ev'ry Voice and Sing," the unofficial African American national anthem.

Claude McKay (1890–1948)   This Jamaican writer's poetry helped define the spirit of the Harlem Renaissance. McKay first won critical acclaim in the United States for his widely published protest poem "If We Must Die." He set many of his short stories (*Gingertown,* 1932) and novels (*Home to Harlem,* 1928) in African American communities.

Alice Dunbar-Nelson (1875–1935)   Born Alice Moore, Dunbar-Nelson published her first book, *Violets and Other Tales,* in 1895. She collaborated on a second book, *The Goodness of St. Rocque,* with her first husband, poet Paul Dunbar. She later married journalist Robert J. Nelson and won acclaim during the Harlem Renaissance for her essays, poems, short stories, and hundreds of newspaper columns.

Jean Toomer (1894–1967)   Though he published only one novel, Toomer is considered one of the most original American writers of his time. In *Cane* (1923), he combined elements of poetry, drama, and fiction to depict African American life both in the rural South and in Northern cities.

GALLERY OF AFRICAN AMERICAN MUSICIANS AND PERFORMING ARTISTS

▲▽▲▽▲▽▲▽▲▽▲▽▲▽▲▽▲▽▲▽▲▽▲▽▲▽▲▽▲▽▲▽▲▽▲

Louis "Satchmo" Armstrong (1900–1971) Some people mark the beginning of the Jazz Age as 1922, when Louis Armstrong brought his golden cornet from New Orleans to Chicago. Armstrong's brilliant playing and remarkable musical invention forever changed the sound of U.S. music. Starting in 1932 with his first international tour, he served as the United States' global ambassador of music.

Duke Ellington (1899–1974) Beginning with a 1927 Cotton Club engagement, Ellington made his swinging orchestra a vital part of U.S. popular music. Radio broadcasts, annual concerts at Carnegie Hall, and sold-out tours made him a household name. Ellington wrote over 2,000 compositions, including the hits "Sophisticated Lady" and "Mood Indigo."

Rose McClendon (1884–1936) Recognized for her great dramatic range, McClendon became one of the finest American actresses of her day. First winning acclaim in the 1926 play *Deep River,* she later toured the United States and Europe in *Porgy,* a play about African American life in coastal South Carolina. McClendon was an original founder of the Negro People's Theater in Harlem.

Florence Mills (1895–1927) Mills was a celebrated singer and comedienne. A favorite of Harlem's cabarets and nightclubs, she won national attention in the 1921 Broadway show *Shuffle Along.* Later performances in *Dixie to Broadway* and *Blackbirds* added to her fame. When she died at 32, some 100,000 people lined the streets of Harlem to bid her goodbye.

Paul Robeson (1898–1976)   An athlete, scholar, lawyer, and actor, Robeson was also one of the most popular singers of his day. His career included performances in such plays as *The Emperor Jones* and *All God's Chillun Got Wings,* as well as recitals of African American spirituals in concert halls. Robeson was also a forceful activist for African American civil rights.

Bessie Smith (1894–1937)   Hailed by fans and fellow musicians as the Empress of the Blues, Bessie Smith sold more than 2 million copies of her 1923 recording of "Down Hearted Blues". In the 1920s and 1930s, her traveling blues show thrilled African American audiences across the nation. Through her records, Smith's musical style continues to influence popular vocalists to this day.

William Grant Still (1895–1978)   The "Dean of African American Composers" combined European classical music with American jazz and blues. His *Afro-American Symphony* was the first work by an African American to be performed by a major symphony orchestra. Still wrote operas and ballets, as well as sound tracks for television and movies.

Ethel Waters (1896–1977)   Known as Sweet Mama Stringbean, Waters was one of Harlem's leading entertainers. During the 1920s, her clear, seemingly effortless blues sound won her millions of fans. In 1927, she began a career on the Broadway stage. She achieved her greatest successes in the 1940 musical drama *Cabin in the Sky* and the 1950 drama *Member of the Wedding.*

GALLERY OF AFRICAN AMERICAN ARTISTS

Aaron Douglas (1899–1979)   Douglas was an artist who rejected stereotyped portraits of African Americans. During the Harlem Renaissance, his illustrations graced the books of such writers as Langston Hughes and Countee Cullen. Aaron used ideas drawn from African sculpture, most notably in his murals depicting African American history and life (see **The Artist's View**).

Richmond Barthé (1901–1989)   Though he began his artistic career as a portrait painter, Barthé made his reputation as a great sculptor. His small, realistic works reveal the inner grace, strength, and pride of African Americans. Among his best known sculptures are *The Singing Slave, The Blackberry Woman,* and *African Boy Dancing.*

Romare Bearden (1913–1988)   After experimenting with different art styles, Bearden achieved his greatest success with collage. In works using combinations of textured papers, vibrant colors, and delicate brush strokes, he explored the rituals and social customs of African American city dwellers (see **The Artist's View**).

Meta Vaux Warrick Fuller (1877–1967)   Fuller was one of the first African American artists to make black people the chief subject of her work. Her sculptures, such as the bronze *Water Boy,* are prized for their intimate appeal and human warmth. Her life-size sculpture *Awakening Ethiopia* symbolized the rebirth of African American culture for many Harlem artists.

Sargent Johnson (1888–1967) Like many African American visual artists of his time, Johnson looked to Africa for artistic inspiration. He once explained that the purpose of his art was to demonstrate "the natural beauty and dignity of the . . . American Negro." He sculpted in metal, wood, and ceramic. His finest works include *Sammy* and *Esther* (see **The Artist's View**).

Horace Pippin (1888–1946) A self-taught artist, Pippin overcame a severe World War I injury to his painting arm to emerge as one of the nation's leading artists. Using an original technique, he first burned the outlines of figures into wooden boards, then filled them in with brilliant colors. His paintings deal with the drama of African American history (see **The Artist's View**).

Augusta Savage (1900–1962) Working in marble, wood, and plaster, this sculptor and teacher used art to express her outrage at racial injustice. She won acclaim for her busts of W.E.B. Du Bois and Marcus Garvey and her antiwar sculpture *Glory*. Savage directed the Harlem Community Art Center, which provided many younger sculptors with steady work during the Depression (see **The Artist's View**).

Hale Woodruff (1900–1979) Woodruff was one of the nation's great mural painters. While at Atlanta University, he began to use painting as a tool for social change. His *Shantytown* and *Mudhill Row* shocked Atlanta citizens into building better urban housing. In 1948, he began a series of murals depicting the contributions of African Americans to California history.

Paul Robeson, shown here as Shakespeare's Othello, was a noted actor and singer of African American spirituals. He spent many years abroad because of discrimination.

The Arts. Visions of success lured promising African American artists to Harlem from other parts of the nation. In the 1920s the *Crisis* and *Opportunity,* the magazines of the NAACP and the Urban League, offered cash prizes for outstanding writing. The Harmon Foundation, a white charitable organization, likewise offered cash prizes for African American writers and artists. It also arranged important exhibitions of work by African American painters and sculptors.

In addition, Harlem lay just north of midtown Manhattan, center of the nation's commerce. The major book and magazine publishers were there. The Broadway theaters offered national recognition to performers and playwrights. Just around the corner, Tin Pan Alley, the hub of the music publishing business, attracted songwriters and musicians.

Perhaps most important, in Harlem aspiring artists could meet and exchange ideas. In this atmosphere of excitement and hope, many new talents blossomed. They included writers like Jean Toomer, Countee Cullen, Claude McKay, Zora Neale Hurston, and Langston Hughes. Such figures recognized that their history as African Americans had given them a unique perspective as writers. They probed many different aspects of the African American experience, dealing with the effects of racism and prejudice. They proudly used regional accents and dialects and sometimes worked the rhythms of the blues into their stories and poems. The works of such writers found an audience not only among African Americans, but among white readers as well.

Painters and sculptors, such as Aaron Douglas and Hale Woodruff, were an important part of the Harlem Renaissance. Many of them drew inspiration from African art or dealt with different aspects of African American history in their work. Traveling exhibitions sponsored by the Harmon Foundation brought the work of such artists to national attention.

African American musicians had an enormous impact on the nation and on the world, producing what has been called "an explosion of genius." The music played in the clubs, ballrooms, and theaters of Harlem by figures such as Fletcher Henderson, Fats Waller, and Duke Ellington was jazz. This musical form had grown out of the mixing of blues and ragtime (see page 280) in New Orleans early in the 1900. Jazz had moved north in the Great Migration, and was further developed by artists like King Oliver, Louis Armstrong, and Jelly Roll Morton.

Soon the appeal of jazz extended to white audiences. Jazz reached the Broadway stage in shows such as *Shuffle Along* and *Hot Chocolates*. Dances such as the Charleston, the Black Bottom, and the Lindy Hop became wildly popular. The rhythms of jazz captured the spirit of the times so well that the decade of the 1920s is often called the Jazz Age.

Taking Another Look

1. How did some organizations encourage the Harlem Renaissance?

2. What were the roots of jazz?

3. **Critical Thinking**   Do you think the "Jazz Age" was an appropriate name for the 1920s from the point of view of African Americans? Explain your answer. Suggest an alternative name for the period.

LOOKING AHEAD

African American artists continued creating new poems, books, plays, songs, musicals, and paintings after the 1920s. But the Harlem Renaissance did not survive the decade.

The nation had experienced an economic boom during much of the 1920s. Then in 1929 the stock market crashed. Banks failed, factories closed, and millions of people lost their jobs. African Americans for the most part had not shared in the boom. Now, they suffered greatly in the depression that followed.

A band leader, pianist, and composer, Duke Ellington, shown here at the piano, was one of the great jazz artists of all time. His career spanned almost 50 years.

FOCUS ON
ROCK 'N' ROLL

In the 1950s, African American artists such as Fats Domino, Little Richard, and Chuck Berry brought a new vitality to popular music. They wrote lyrics and music that excited teenagers, added a driving beat, and called the new sound rock 'n' roll. Its popularity spread so quickly that one music critic called it "the sound heard 'round the world."

Although rock burst on the scene in the 1950s, its roots lay in the distant musical past. Rock developed from many sources, including jazz, blues, and gospel—sources inspired by African rhythms. Rock grew most directly out of another African American music style, the rhythm and blues, or R & B, of the 1940s.

African American influence on rock did not end in the 1950s. Jimi Hendrix used distortion and feedback to produce hard rock in the 1960s. The Motown sound, written and performed by African Americans and produced by Motown Records, an African American company, appealed to teenagers of all ethnic groups. Today, artists and groups such as Salt N' Pepa, Wu-Tang Clan and Missy "Misdemeanor" Elliot are continuing the tradition of African Americans and rock 'n' roll.

The Who, What, Where of History

1. **Where** is Harlem?
2. **What** was the Harlem Renaissance?
3. **Who** was Aaron Douglas?
4. **Who** was Langston Hughes?
5. **Who** was Louis Armstrong?
6. **Who** was Zora Neale Hurston?
7. **Who** was Hale Woodruff?
8. **What** was the Harmon Foundation?

Making the Connection

1. What was the connection between New York City and the work of African American artists in the 1920s?
2. What was the connection between jazz music and the cities of New Orleans and New York?

Time Check

During what years did the Harlem Renaissance occur?

What Would You Have Done?

1. Imagine it is 1922, and you are a young African American who aspires to be a great writer or artist. Would you move to Harlem from Kansas? Assume that you have little money and no friends in Harlem.
2. Imagine that you work for an advertising agency in New York City in the 1920s. A group of Harlem business owners has hired your company to plan a campaign to attract more tourists to Harlem. Design a poster to use in the campaign.

Thinking and Writing About History

1. Write a travel article about Harlem for the Chicago *Defender*, an African American newspaper. The time is 1922.

2. Write one paragraph explaining why the Harlem Renaissance was important to U.S. cultural development.

3. Aaron Douglas was one of the leading artists of the Harlem Renaissance. Study the painting by Douglas in "The Artist's View." Write a paragraph explaining what you think Douglas's picture represents.

Building Skills: Understanding Points of View

Suppose that you are a teenager writing an essay about the Harlem Renaissance in the present day. How likely is it that what you have to say will be similar to an essay about the development in Harlem by a French scholar living there in the early 1920s? If you said "Not very likely," you are probably correct. You have one point of view, and the French professor had his.

Any author, whether a writer of fiction, history, poetry, or biography, has a *point of view*—a particular way of looking at things. A person's point of view is shaped by his or her experiences, family, education, reading, and friends. A person's point of view is also shaped, at least to some extent, by the times in which he or she lives.

Read the following poem by Langston Hughes and see what you can learn about his point of view.

The Negro Speaks of Rivers

I've known rivers:
I've known rivers ancient as the world
and older than the flow of human blood
in human veins.

My soul has grown deep like the rivers.

I bathed in the Euphrates when dawns
were young.
I built my hut near the Congo and
it lulled me to sleep.
I looked upon the Nile and raised the
pyramids above it.
I heard the singing of the Mississippi
when Abe Lincoln went down to New
Orleans, and I've seen its muddy
bosom turn all golden in the sunset.

I've known rivers:
Ancient, dusky rivers.

My soul has grown deep like the rivers.

1. What rivers does Hughes use? Where are they located?

2. Based on this poem, do you think that Langston Hughes was sympathetic to the ideas of Pan-Africanism? Explain your answer.

3. Who do you think is "the Negro" who is speaking in the poem?

4. Why do you think the poem emphasizes the great age of the rivers?

5. Explain what you think Hughes means by the line "My soul is deep like the rivers."

6. Do you think Hughes was proud of his African American background? Explain your answer.

New Deal work project

The Great Depression and the New Deal

(1929–1941)

THINKING ABOUT THE CHAPTER

How did the Great Depression affect the lives of African Americans?

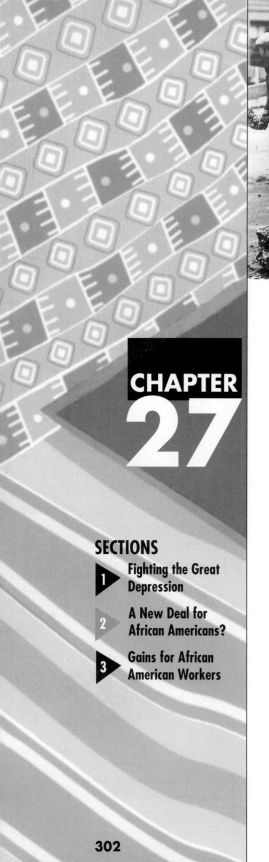

On the sidewalk in front of a Chicago apartment building one day in the early 1930s, an African American family stood surrounded by their furniture and belongings. Unable to pay their rent, they had been evicted from their home. A crowd of neighbors gathered, determined to help them regain their apartment.

Police cars screeched up. Officers sprang out and ordered the people to move on. The angry crowd refused, and one man stepped forward to say, "All we want is to see that these people, our people, get back into their home. We have no money, no jobs, and sometimes no food. We've got to live someplace. We are just acting the way you or anyone else would act."

Scenes like this were common in the 1930s all across the United States. The stock market crash of 1929 had set off a depression that almost paralyzed the nation's economy. The Great Depression affected all parts of U.S. society, but African Americans bore some of the greatest hardships. As writer Langston Hughes put it, "[T]he Depression had brought everyone down a peg or two. And the Negroes had but a few pegs to fall."

SNAPSHOT OF THE TIMES

1929	Stock market crash sets off Great Depression.
1932	Franklin D. Roosevelt is elected President.
1933	New Deal begins.
1935	Social Security Act is passed. CIO is organized.
1941	A. Philip Randolph calls for march on Washington.

1 ▼ FIGHTING THE GREAT DEPRESSION

▼ How did the Great Depression affect the lives of African Americans?

The effects of the stock market crash quickly spread out through the economy. Banks failed, factories closed down, and stores shut their doors. Often, people lost their savings as well as their jobs.

Hard Times. Even during good times, African Americans received lower wages and had higher unemployment rates than whites. As the economy slumped, these conditions grew worse. One member of the Urban League stated, "At no time in the history of the Negro since slavery has his economic and social outlook seemed so discouraging."

At the beginning of the 1930s, most African Americans still lived in the rural South. As cotton prices plunged from 18 cents a pound to 6 cents, sharecroppers, who had always had a difficult time, could no longer make a living on the land. Thousands gave up and moved out of the South seeking jobs in the cities.

They found little hope there. African Americans had usually held the lowest paying, least desirable jobs. Jobs such as janitor, porter, and street sweeper were "Negro work."

But as jobs became scarce for everyone, whites increasingly took on "Negro work." Unemployment among African Americans soared. In Chicago, the unemployment rate for African American men reached 40 percent, in Pittsburgh it was 48 percent, and in Detroit it rose to 60 percent. The rates of unemployment among African American women were even higher.

Seeking Relief. Without regular paychecks coming in, people could not afford to pay their rents or mortgages or even to buy food and clothing. Many families quickly spent what little savings they had. Often they had to pawn clothes or furniture to buy food or keep a roof over their heads.

Private organizations and charities tried to help the needy. Such groups, however, often practiced discrimination. Soup kitchens sometimes turned away African Americans seeking food. Clothing meant for the poor often was not distributed to African Americans.

Needy people looked to government to help them. President Herbert Hoover, however, did not believe relief for the needy was the federal government's concern. Instead he tried to help big businesses and farms with loans, hoping this aid would "trickle down" to the rest of U.S. society.

In the bleakest days of the Great Depression, New York City officials provided food for hundreds of Harlem's unemployed African Americans.

States and cities had programs that provided food or small sums of money to the needy. But so many people now needed help that state and local governments could not help them all. In addition, relief programs often discriminated against African Americans. At times, they received smaller payments than whites, or they had to meet stricter standards to qualify for relief.

Self Help. The economic outlook continued to worsen through 1931 and 1932. As it did, African Americans began to work together to do what the federal government refused to: defeat unemployment and hunger.

For the first time, many African American churches became involved in welfare work, starting soup kitchens and distributing clothing to the needy. The National Urban League organized emergency relief committees. Their members set up survival shelters where the needy could get food, clothing, medical care, and help in finding the few jobs available.

The Fight for Jobs. The fight for jobs during the depression led to scenes like one in a Northwest Washington, D.C., neighborhood. There, a line of African American picketers marched in a circle in front of the Hamburger Grill, a popular restaurant. Many carried signs reading "Buy Where You Work—Buy Where You Clerk."

After weeks of being picketed, the white restaurant manager admitted his defeat. He agreed to rehire those African American workers he had replaced with whites. Inspired by this success, community leaders expanded their campaign to other stores. Soon what was called the New Negro Alliance was winning jobs for African Americans in white-owned department and grocery stores.

"Don't Buy Where You Can't Work" campaigns spread to Chicago, New York, and 23 other cities. Although they had some success in gaining jobs for African Americans, such campaigns could not hope to solve all the problems that the Great Depression created for African Americans.

The Election of 1932. By 1932, many Americans had become convinced that strong federal action offered the only hope of curing the nation's economic ills. In the presidential election of that year, Republican Herbert Hoover stood by his belief that the federal government should play only a limited part in solving the crisis. Democrat Franklin D. Roosevelt, whose cheerful manner inspired confidence, promised a "new deal for the American people."

For African American voters, the election presented a difficult choice. The Republican party had been Lincoln's party— the party that had passed the civil rights laws of Reconstruction. The Democratic party was the party of white Southern governments—the party that helped pass Jim Crow laws.

Could African Americans now "turn Lincoln's picture to the wall" and vote for a Democrat as President, as African American newspaper publisher Robert Vann urged? In 1932, the answer was no. Over two thirds of African American voters backed Hoover that year, but Hoover was soundly defeated by Roosevelt nevertheless. In the years that followed, Roosevelt's policies won the back-

ing of African American voters. In huge numbers, they shifted their loyalty to the Democratic party beginning with the election of 1936.

Taking Another Look

1. What limited the amount of government aid that reached African Americans at the beginning of the Great Depression?

2. How did African Americans help themselves during the depression?

3. **Critical Thinking** If you had been an African American voter during the election of 1932, would you have voted for Roosevelt or Hoover? Explain your answer.

2 ▼ A NEW DEAL FOR AFRICAN AMERICANS?

How did President Franklin D. Roosevelt's recovery programs affect African Americans?

In the late 1960s, a man who had lived through the Great Depression was asked to comment on African Americans' feelings about Roosevelt in those years. He answered:

Oh yeah, that was something. He broke the tradition. My father told me: "The Republicans are the ship. All else is the sea." Frederick Douglass said that. They didn't go for Roosevelt much in '32. But the WPA came along and Roosevelt came to be a god.

The WPA, or Works Progress Administration, established in 1935, was one of the dozens of Roosevelt's New Deal programs. The hope these programs held out to African Americans had a great impact on their lives. By the 1936 election, 75 percent of African Americans supported Roosevelt. But in its beginnings, the New Deal seemed to offer little to African Americans.

New Deal Programs. "Our greatest primary task is to put people to work," Roosevelt announced on taking office in 1933. In the next 100 days, Congress passed a variety of New Deal measures aimed at restoring the nation's economy.

However, these programs did not aid African Americans and whites equally. "They don't give us any work and don't give relief to colored people," one African American woman complained to the NAACP about a work-relief program. "Kindly get in tutch with Washington. See why they don't."

The reason "why" was politics. To get his New Deal programs through Congress, Roosevelt needed the support of white Southern politicians. "First things come first," Roosevelt said, "and I can't alienate [lose] certain votes I need . . . by pushing any measures that would entail [involve] a fight."

This meant that Roosevelt at first did little to see that the benefits of New Deal programs were designed to reach African Americans on an equal basis with whites. Some New Deal measures called for lower pay for African American workers than for whites doing the same job. In other government work projects, African Americans had to live in segregated housing. Often, they were kept from skilled jobs on federally sponsored dam and electric-power projects. One NAACP member soon concluded, "The New Deal [is] the same raw deal."

Even the Social Security Act of 1935, widely hailed as the New Deal's greatest accomplishment, proved indirectly unfair

The Daughters of the American Revolution banned Marian Anderson from singing in Constitution Hall in 1939 because she was African American. Eleanor Roosevelt won permission for her to sing at the Lincoln Memorial in Washington, D.C.

to African Americans. The act provided millions of citizens with unemployment and old-age insurance. Yet, because it excluded farmers and domestic workers like house cleaners and cooks, the act kept nearly two thirds of African American workers from receiving benefits.

A Changing Deal.   From the beginning, African Americans pressed for changes in these practices. They found that they had, as one African American newspaper reported, "a staunch [loyal] ally in the First Lady of the Land"— Eleanor Roosevelt.

Eleanor Roosevelt became a prominent worker for African American rights. She invited African American leaders to the White House. She defied Jim Crow laws by refusing to sit in a "whites only" section while attending a meeting in the South. She wrote newspaper columns that called for "fair play and equal opportunity for Negro citizens."

Most important, she pushed Franklin Roosevelt and other government officials to take action. Roosevelt began to name African Americans as advisers in different departments of the federal government. The leading figures made up what was called the **Black Cabinet,** an informal group of advisers to Roosevelt.

This group pushed for economic and political equality for African Americans. One of its members was Robert C. Weaver, who held several different posts in government and went on to become the first African American in President Lyndon Johnson's Cabinet in 1966. Another was William H. Hastie, dean of the Howard University Law School, who worked in the Department of the Interior. Perhaps the best-known was Mary McLeod Bethune.

Many considered that **Mary McLeod Bethune** was the glue that held the Black Cabinet together. A well-known educator, Bethune had founded and supervised Bethune-Cookman College, in Daytona Beach, Florida. Her work for the National Council of Negro Women focused new attention on the long-ignored subject of the rights of African American women.

As the director of the Division of Negro Affairs of the National Youth Administration (NYA), she traveled thousands of miles each month. Bethune's goal was to ensure that the funds that were targeted for African American high school and college students actually reached them. "I cannot rest," she told her friends, "while there is a single Negro boy or girl lacking a chance to prove his worth."

Some New Government Policies. Bethune's NYA was one of the New Deal agencies that actively sought to improve conditions for African Americans. It gave direct aid to over 300,000 African American young people seeking education.

The Public Works Administration (PWA) pressed contractors working on its projects to use African Americans for both skilled and unskilled labor. About a third of the space in PWA housing projects went to African Americans.

The Farm Security Administration (FSA) offered loans to poor farmers and sharecroppers. It saw that this money was distributed fairly among whites and African Americans.

307

Many unemployed young African Americans volunteered for the Civilian Conservation Corps (CCC). They served in segregated units to improve roads, plant forests, and create parks.

The Works Progress Administration (WPA) became one of the largest employers of African Americans. They made up 15 to 20 percent of the workers on its construction projects.

More and more bills passed by Congress to authorize New Deal programs included this statement: "There shall be no discrimination on account of race, creed, or color."

This order was not always obeyed, but the New Deal aided African Americans far more than any earlier administration had, and in many different ways. African American employees in the federal government jumped from 50,000 in 1933 to over 150,000 in 1941. A million African Americans took part in federally funded literacy programs. Relief funds and im-proved health care meant that the life expectancy of African Americans increased during the 1930s.

The New Deal did not end discrimination toward African Americans. Nor did it eliminate the huge economic inequalities that separated whites and African Americans. But it did begin to move toward these goals. As actor Paul Robeson remarked in 1939, "Conditions were far from ideal. . . . But change was in the air, and this was the best sign of all."

Taking Another Look

1. What was the Black Cabinet?

2. How did the New Deal improve job opportunities for African Americans?

3. **Critical Thinking**   Reread Franklin Roosevelt's statement on page 306 about why he would not push for equal aid to African Americans. Then write your reaction to it.

3 ▼ GAINS FOR AFRICAN AMERICAN WORKERS

How did African Americans force a change in government policies on discrimination?

"A way must be found of gradually raising the living standards of the colored laborers. . . . " So said Secretary of Labor Frances Perkins in 1934. But African American workers were already taking steps to help themselves.

New Union Policies.   One way African American workers helped themselves was by joining unions. In the past, many major U.S. unions had excluded African Americans. Some unions admitted African Americans but had rules that kept them out of skilled jobs, like pipe fitter or machinist, and in lower-paying jobs, like janitor or messenger, with little chance of advancement. The nation's largest labor organization, the American Federation of Labor (AFL) refused even to meet with African American leaders to discuss problems of discrimination. By 1930, African Americans made up only 1 percent of union membership. Half of those, some 50,000 workers, belonged to one segregated union.

The depression helped unions realize they needed to enlist African Americans to increase their membership rolls, in order to apply more pressure on employers. As one African American union organizer said, "We colored folks can't organize without you and you white folks can't organize without us."

New Deal laws like the National Labor Relations Act had guaranteed the right of workers to form unions. Labor leaders now aimed to organize workers in large industries—steel, textiles, and car manufacturing—that employed unskilled African American workers.

This history of African Americans was one of many valuable literary works created by WPA writers. (See the "Focus On. . .", page 312.

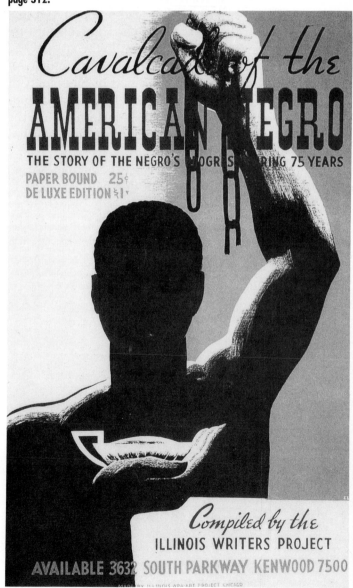

A new labor group, the Congress of Industrial Organizations (CIO), formed in 1935. It opened its membership to African American workers. Thurgood Marshall, a noted NAACP lawyer, declared the CIO's charter of job equality for all workers, "a Bill of Rights for Negro labor." By 1940, the CIO had some 210,000 African American members.

A March on Washington. One African American labor leader hoped to translate this new union participation into increased political power. In the late 1930s, A. Philip Randolph, the founder and president of the Brotherhood of Sleeping Car Porters, had noted the outbreaks of fighting in Asia and Europe. He felt that the United States was heading into another world war.

U.S. factories were beginning to get rich on government defense contracts to manufacture guns, ammunition, airplanes and other war goods. Yet, many still refused to hire African American workers. When Randolph's pleas to end this discrimination went unanswered by President Roosevelt, Randolph launched a civil rights crusade.

In 1941, Randolph called on African Americans to join him in a "nonviolent demonstration of Negro mass power" in Washington, D.C., on July 1. Leading African American newspapers backed Randolph's call. March committees were organized, and press releases announced that 100,000 marchers were expected.

President Roosevelt feared that such a march might hurt him politically. He tried to get Randolph and the organizers to call it off. They refused unless the government took steps to end discrimination.

Finally, four days before the march was scheduled, Roosevelt gave in. He issued

African Americans joined white members of CIO unions to show their strength in a New York City protest march. Thousands of African American workers benefited from union membership.

Labor leader A. Philip Randolph, shown seated at the microphone, led the fight to pressure the New Deal administration to end job discrimination in defense industries.

Executive Order 8802, which barred discrimination in defense industries, government agencies, and work-training programs. To enforce the order, he set up the Committee on Fair Employment Practices (FEPC). For the first time since the Civil War, a U.S. President had issued an order guaranteeing the rights of African Americans.

Taking Another Look

1. Why did many African American workers join the CIO?

2. What was the purpose of Executive Order 8802?

3. **Critical Thinking** Why do you think President Roosevelt was so eager to stop Randolph's march on Washington?

LOOKING AHEAD

Organizers of the march on Washington in 1941 had also demanded an end to segregation in the nation's armed forces. Roosevelt, however, refused to take any action on that issue. Thus, when the Japanese bombing of Pearl Harbor brought the United States into World War II, African Americans were still serving for the most part in segregated units. Meanwhile on the home front, discrimination in the workplace still affected African Americans in spite of union gains, Executive Order 8802, and the FEPC.

Discrimination toward African Americans continued after World War II. Twenty-two years after A. Philip Randolph announced plans for a march on Washington, civil rights leaders again called on African Americans to come to the nation's capital and march for their rights. This time the march took place.

311

During the Great Depression, the federal government hired writers and artists to create "American stuff." American stuff included anything from folktales and dramas to histories.

With government grants, African American scholars were able to research the history of their people. In one project, African Americans ranging in age from 70 to over 100 vividly described their experiences during enslavement. The researchers published these interviews.

The Theater Project created 16 "Negro Units" to tour the country. These troupes staged impressive productions of Shakespeare with an African twist. These theatrical units added African drummers and other touches of African culture. The plays were hits.

These and other projects grew out of the Works Progress Administration—a program that paid artists, writers, musicians, and actors to create works of art for the nation. Such projects nurtured the careers of talented African Americans such as Ralph Ellison, Richard Wright, and Jacob Lawrence. As African American artist Ernest Critchlow observed, "Without that [WPA] aid, many of today's important artists might never have made their contributions to the nation's art."

CLOSE UP: Chapter 27

The Who, What, Where of History

1. **What** is an economic depression?
2. **Who** was Herbert Hoover?
3. **Who** was Franklin Roosevelt?
4. **Who** was Eleanor Roosevelt?
5. **What** was the Black Cabinet?
6. **Who** was Mary McLeod Bethune?
7. **What** was the PWA?
8. **What** was the WPA?
9. **Who** was A. Philip Randolph?
10. **Where** did Randolph plan to hold a great protest march of African Americans?

Making the Connection

1. What was the connection between the Great Depression and fewer jobs for African Americans?
2. Explain the connection that many African Americans saw between Lincoln and Hoover.
3. What was the connection between the Great Depression and increased African American membership in labor unions?

Time Check

1. When did the Depression begin?
2. When was Franklin Roosevelt first elected President?

What Would You Have Done?

1. Would you have participated in a "Don't Buy Where You Can't Work" picket line? Explain.
2. Would you have voted for Franklin Roosevelt in 1936? Explain.

Thinking and Writing About History

1. Write a paragraph comparing Hoover's beliefs about the role of the federal government during the Great Depression and Roosevelt's beliefs about what the government should do to end the depression.

2. Imagine that you are a reporter listening to President Roosevelt and A. Philip Randolph discuss the march on Washington. Write a newspaper article that includes "quotations" from their conversation.

Building Skills: Generalizing From a Primary Source

The following chart comes from the *Statistical Abstract of the United States, 1932*. The Department of Commerce puts together the *Statistical Abstract* every year, collecting information from many federal departments and agencies. Look at the chart and then answer the questions.

1. Look at the percentages of illiterate persons for the United States in 1920 and then for the United States in 1930. Now make a generalization based on the chart about whether illiteracy was increasing or decreasing in the United States as a whole in 1930.

2. Using the regional divisions, make a generalization about where schools were the poorest for African Americans and for all residents.

3. Make a generalization based on the information in the chart about illiteracy in rural areas.

Division and Age	Native White, Native White Parentage	Native White, Foreign or Mixed Parentage	Foreign-born, White White	African American
Percentage of Illiterate Persons 10 Years of Age and Over: Continental United States, 1920 and 1930, and by Geographic Divisions, 1930.				
United States 1920	2.5	.8	13.1	22.9
10–20 years	1.3	.6	5.7	13.0
21 years and over	3.0	.9	13.7	27.4
Urban, total	.8	.5	13.0	13.4
Rural, total	3.8	1.4	13.3	28.5
United States 1930	1.8	.6	9.9	16.3
10–20 years	.8	.3	1.3	7.5
21 years and over	2.2	.7	10.3	20.0
Urban, total	.6	.4	10.0	9.2
Rural, total	3.0	1.0	9.4	22.4
New England	.6	.7	11.6	5.5
Middle Atlantic	.6	.5	12.2	3.7
East North Central	.7	.6	8.8	4.7
West North Central	.8	.5	4.9	4.7
South Atlantic	3.9	.8	10.4	19.7
East South Central	5.1	1.2	7.4	22.0
West South Central	2.7	2.0	9.4	17.0
Mountain	1.5	.4	5.6	4.1
Pacific	.3	.3	4.9	3.1

UNIT 9

Civil rights march, Selma, Alabama, 1965

THE CIVIL RIGHTS REVOLUTION
(1941–1973)

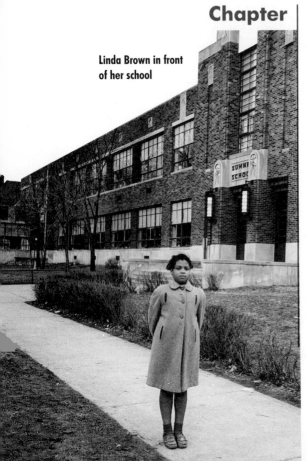

Linda Brown in front of her school

World War II troops heading home

In 1941, the United States entered World War II. Four years of warfare led to a victory that left the nation one of the strongest in the world—a superpower. Spared the destruction of war at home, the United States was now the world's mightiest economic power.

Over the next 25 years, the United States reached a new height of prosperity. The nation also played a larger part in world affairs than it ever had before. The United States presented itself as a model of democracy that nations around the world could follow.

At the same time, African Americans complained that the democracy the nation's leaders were praising still did not apply to them. They renewed their efforts to secure their civil rights. In doing so, they brought about the greatest changes in U.S. society since the days of the Civil War and Reconstruction.

World War II. In 1939, war broke out in Europe, with Germany and Italy opposing Great Britain, France, and, after 1941, the Soviet Union. By 1941, Germany, under its Nazi dictator, Adolf Hitler, had conquered much of Europe. In Asia, war had been going on since 1937, when Japan invaded China.

The United States managed to keep out of the fighting until December 7, 1941. On that date, the Japanese attacked Pearl Harbor, a U.S. naval base in Hawaii, destroying many ships and killing more than 2,000. Four days later, Germany and Italy, who had an alliance with Japan, also declared war on the United States.

As in World War I, the United States quickly prepared to fight the war. The Great Depression came to a swift end as industrial production soared to meet the demands of war. African Americans benefited not only because there were more jobs, but also because A. Philip Randolph's efforts had made the jobs more available to them (see page 310). As in the earlier war, many African Americans moved from the rural South to the industrial cities of the Northeast and Midwest, seeking jobs.

The armed forces grew until, by 1945, there were more than 12 million men and women in uniform. Of these, about 1 million were African Americans. Most of them served in segregated army units.

The Truman Years, 1945–1953. In 1945, shortly before the end of World War II, President Roosevelt died. His successor was Vice-President Harry S Truman. During Truman's first years in office, the United States found itself caught up in the **Cold War**. The Cold War was a conflict with the Soviet Union that stopped short of actual warfare between the two nations. For almost half a century, it would shape U.S. attitudes and policies toward the rest of the world.

In 1950, the Cold War turned hot when Soviet-backed North Korea invaded

---

An African American Speaks

I have a dream that one day this nation will rise up and live out the meaning of its creed: "We hold these truths to be self-evident—that all men are created equal."

—Martin Luther King, Jr.
Civil Rights Movement leader

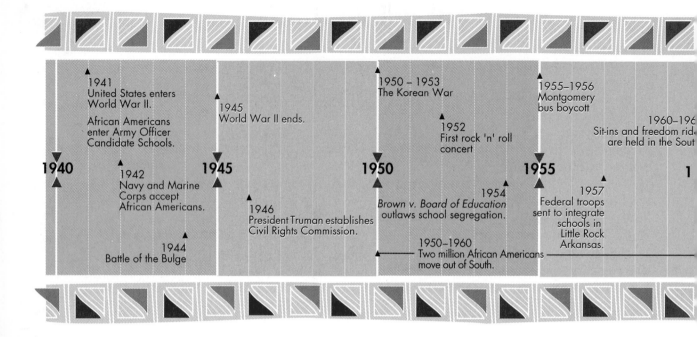

1941
United States enters
World War II.

African Americans
enter Army Officer
Candidate Schools.

1942
Navy and Marine
Corps accept
African Americans.

1944
Battle of the Bulge

1940

1945
World War II ends.

1946
President Truman establishes
Civil Rights Commission.

1945

1950 – 1953
The Korean War

1952
First rock 'n' roll
concert

Brown v. Board of Education
outlaws school segregation.
1954

1950–1960
Two million African Americans
move out of South.

1950

1955–1956
Montgomery
bus boycott

1957
Federal troops
sent to integrate
schools in
Little Rock
Arkansas.

1955

1960–196
Sit-ins and freedom rid
are held in the Sout

1

U.S.-backed South Korea. The United States joined the war on South Korea's side. China, which, like the Soviet Union, had a Communist government, entered the war on North Korea's side. The Korean War ended in a stalemate in 1953.

At home, Truman proposed many New Deal-style programs. In addition, he pressed hard for civil rights legislation. In 1946, he established a Civil Rights Commission. Its report, which Truman supported, called for a complete end to segregation in U.S. life.

In 1947, Truman issued an order integrating African Americans into all army units. Later orders by Truman and his successor, Dwight Eisenhower, completed the integration of the military. Truman's actions meant that during the Korean War, African American and white soldiers were fighting side by side in the same units for the first time since the early days of the Republic.

In 1948, Truman's loyalty to civil rights threatened his reelection. At the Democratic convention that year, Northern Democrats managed to have a strong pro-civil rights statement written into the party's platform. Many Southerners, called Dixiecrats, left the Democratic party to support a Southern candidate, but Truman won anyway.

In his second term Truman proposed laws to make lynching a federal crime, to protect African American voters, to abolish poll taxes, and to set up a federal commission to prevent discrimination in hiring. Because of Southern opposition, none of these laws was passed.

The Eisenhower Years, 1953–1961. In 1953, Truman was succeeded by Republican Dwight D. Eisenhower. Eisenhower, or "Ike," was a hero of World War II. He remained a popular President throughout his two terms in office.

In foreign affairs, Eisenhower continued to oppose the Soviet Union. At home, the country enjoyed growth and prosperity. For many white citizens, times were good. They could not see much that needed reform, and neither could Ike.

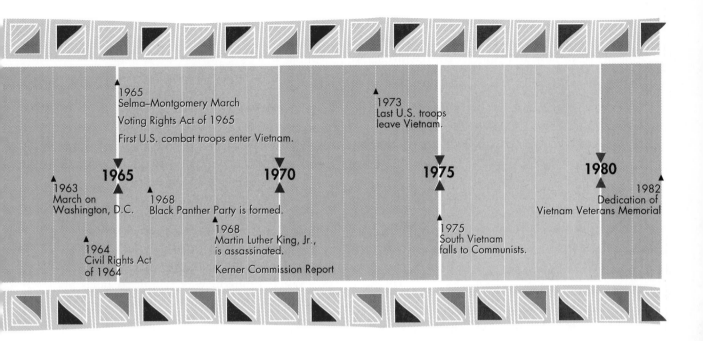

1965
Selma–Montgomery March
Voting Rights Act of 1965
First U.S. combat troops enter Vietnam.

1973
Last U.S. troops
leave Vietnam.

1965

1970

1975

1980

1963
March on
Washington, D.C.

1968
Black Panther Party is formed.

1982
Dedication of
Vietnam Veterans Memorial

1964
Civil Rights Act
of 1964

1968
Martin Luther King, Jr.,
is assassinated.

Kerner Commission Report

1975
South Vietnam
falls to Communists.

For African Americans, this meant that the President took little interest in civil rights legislation. Eisenhower did, however, complete the integration of the military that Truman had begun, and he took steps to desegregate other branches of the federal government. In 1957, Congress passed the first civil rights law since Reconstruction. The law offered some protection to African Americans who had been denied the vote. It was weak, but it showed the federal government was willing to take some action on civil rights.

Challenging Segregation. By the time the civil rights bill passed, there had been important developments in other areas. In 1954, the Supreme Court overturned *Plessy* v. *Ferguson,* the 1896 case establishing the principle of "separate but equal." Now, in *Brown* v. *Board of Education,* the court unanimously ruled that segregation of public schools was illegal.

Actual desegregation was slow in coming. White Southern officials often tried to prevent African American chil-dren from entering all-white schools. In many cases, integration came only after it was ordered by a federal court and overseen by federal marshals or troops.

The successful challenge to segregated education led to similar challenges in other areas. A young Baptist preacher, the Reverend Martin Luther King, Jr., soon emerged as the best-known leader of the growing **Civil Rights Movement** with his calls for nonviolent protest.

The Kennedy Years, 1961–1963. In 1960, King was arrested and jailed after a civil rights demonstration. John F. Kennedy, the Democratic candidate for President that year, helped King win release from jail. Kennedy's action gained him the support of African American voters, and he won a narrow victory.

Kennedy was sympathetic to African Americans. However, he hesitated to propose new civil rights laws because, like earlier Presidents, he wanted the support of white Southern politicians for other programs.

Meanwhile, King and other civil rights leaders organized protests that often met with violent resistance from whites. At times, the violence grew so great that Kennedy was forced to send federal troops and officials to help protect the rights of African Americans.

In June 1963, Kennedy made a televised speech strongly supporting many civil rights goals, and he sent proposals for several new laws to Congress. But Kennedy did not have the chance to see his proposals through Congress. He was assassinated in Dallas, Texas, in November 1963.

The Johnson Years, 1963–1969. Kennedy's Vice-President, Lyndon B. Johnson, a Texan who had spent many years in Congress, became the new President. As the nation mourned Kennedy, Johnson promised that he would work to have the civil rights bill passed as a memorial to the fallen leader. By applying enormous pressure in the Senate, he succeeded, and the Civil Rights Act of 1964

President Lyndon B. Johnson gives Dr. Martin Luther King, Jr., a ceremonial pen after signing the 1964 Civil Rights Act.

became law. The main provisions of the law dealt with outlawing segregation in public places. "Jim Crow" was dead.

In 1964, Johnson won reelection by a landslide, and the Democrats won large majorities in Congress. Johnson was in a strong position for enacting new legislation. In 1965, he proposed a civil rights bill guaranteeing that African Americans' right to vote would be enforced by the federal government. Johnson called his legislative program the **Great Society.** It included many laws to help poor or disadvantaged people in various ways. Many who benefited were African Americans.

While Johnson was trying to build his Great Society, he also continued the Cold War against communism. He sent large numbers of U.S. troops to Vietnam in Southeast Asia. In 1954, Vietnam was split by an international agreement. North Vietnam had a Communist government, while the U.S.-backed South Vietnam claimed to have a democratic one.

Soon after the division, North Vietnamese–backed guerrillas, seeking to reunite the country, began fighting against the government in the south. The South Vietnamese government kept telling U.S. Presidents that with a little more help, it could defeat the guerrillas. But the guerrillas apparently could not be defeated. By 1968, some 540,000 U.S. combat troops were in South Vietnam.

As the war dragged on, it became very unpopular in the United States. Antiwar demonstrations were held in many cities and on college campuses. Antiwar candidates challenged Johnson in the 1968 election. In early 1968, Johnson announced that he would not seek reelection.

During these same years, the Civil Rights Movement changed direction. The Civil Rights Act of 1964 and the Voting Rights Act of 1965 had ended legal segregation of African Americans. Yet many

▶▶ GREAT SOCIETY LEGISLATION, 1965

Elementary and Secondary School Act
  programs to improve schools and libraries

Medicare
  provides medical care for those over 65

Voting Rights Act of 1965
  ensures the right to register to vote

Omnibus Housing Act
  rent supplements and other housing funds
  for low-income persons

Economic Opportunity Act of 1964
  programs to help the poor, leading to Job
  Corps training and Head Start preschools

*Department of Housing and Urban
Development (HUD)*
  aid to cities through urban planning and
  housing

Higher Education Act
  federal scholarships to college students

How might each of these pieces of legislation have helped African Americans?

problems remained, often related to poor conditions in the cities where most African Americans now lived. Rioting broke out in many of these cities during the mid-1960s as African American rage exploded.

Violence seemed to overwhelm American society in the late 1960s. War raged abroad. Antiwar demonstrations often turned violent. Riots ripped major cities. Assassins killed Martin Luther King and Robert Kennedy, the brother of the slain President. Kennedy had been running for President as an antiwar and civil rights candidate at the time of his death.

People were dismayed and disheartened by these events. Not surprisingly, in the November 1968 election, many of them wanted a change in leadership. Voters elected the Republican candidate, Richard M. Nixon.

The First Nixon Term, 1969–1973. Nixon had aimed his campaign at what he called the Silent Majority, people upset and angered by the turmoil of the 1960s. Although he did not try to change the civil rights laws of Johnson's administration, he was less enthusiastic about enforcing them. He also tried to cut back on some Great Society programs.

Nixon continued the Vietnam War, under a new policy of gradually replacing American troops with South Vietnamese. Antiwar protests continued. At Kent State University in Ohio, National Guard troops fired into a group of college students, killing four and wounding several others. Two African American students were killed by police at Jackson State University in Mississippi during another antiwar protest.

Early in 1973, representatives of the two Vietnams and the United States signed a cease-fire agreement, and the last U.S. forces pulled out. Two years later, the South Vietnamese government collapsed, and the North Vietnamese government took over. More than 58,000 U.S. citizens had died there, a high percentage of them African Americans.

Peace had come. But the changes that shook the United States in the 1960s would affect the nation and the lives of its African American citizens for years.

Taking Another Look

1. Where did the United States become involved in armed conflicts in its efforts to halt communism?

2. How did Presidents Johnson and Nixon differ on civil rights?

3. **Critical Thinking** How might the denial of civil rights to its African American citizens have affected the U.S. role as a world leader?

Dorie Miller receiving the Navy Cross

World War II and African Americans

(1941–1945)

THINKING ABOUT THE CHAPTER

How was this war different from World War I for African Americans?

When December 7, 1941, dawned over the U.S. naval base in Hawaii's Pearl Harbor, Dorie Miller was below decks of the battleship *West Virginia*. He was sorting laundry, part of his job as a mess attendant, a worker in the ship's kitchen. Suddenly, he heard bombs exploding above his head. He rushed up on deck, where he saw Japanese aircraft attacking the ship. Amid the noise and confusion of the attack, he spotted his captain lying wounded on the deck. Quickly, Miller dragged him to safety.

Then, although he'd never handled a machine gun before, Miller seized a gun and began firing at the planes zooming in for attack. He shot down four. Although the ship began to sink, he continued firing until an officer ordered him to leave the ship.

Five months later, Dorie Miller, the first hero of World War II, was awarded the Navy Cross for his bravery. However, Miller's job in the navy did not change. He was still only a mess attendant—just like most other African Americans in the navy at that time.

A million African Americans—men and women—took part in World War II. About 6,000 were officers. But African Americans fought a "Double-V" campaign—for victory over discrimination in the military and at home, and for victory over the enemy overseas.

1 IN THE ARMED FORCES
▼ What progress was made in desegregating the armed services?

In 1991, playwright Leslie Lee was talking about his new play, *Black Eagles*. "I want to rectify [make right] a wrong, and the wrong is that nobody knows about the Tuskegee airmen." In 1941, Tuskegee Institute had become a training base for African American fliers. The 99th Pursuit Squadron, which was attached to the 332nd Fighter Group, earned the name "Black Eagles" because of the success it had in escorting all-white bomber crews over Europe during the war.

By the end of the war, the Eagles had destroyed or damaged about 400 enemy aircraft yet never lost a bomber. In 1945, the 332nd Fighter Group was awarded a Distinguished Unit Citation. Together, the 99th Pursuit Squadron and the 332nd Fighter Group won 800 air medals and clusters. However, throughout their military service, like almost all other African Americans in the war, they were victims of segregation.

Protest by Black Leaders. At the beginning of World War II, fewer than 5,000 African Americans were in the armed forces. Not more than a dozen were officers. African Americans served in segregated units in the army and were barred from serving in the Army Air Corps and the marines. Of the 4,000 African Americans in the navy in 1940, most were mess attendants. This was the situation in a country that claimed to be opposed to the racism of the Nazis. Such discrimination was unacceptable to African Americans and many whites.

In September 1940, when the United States began to increase the size of its armed forces, three African American leaders visited President Roosevelt. Walter White of the NAACP, union leader A. Philip Randolph, and T. Arnold Hill of the National Urban League urged Roosevelt to end the segregationist policies of the military.

Many in the military opposed ending segregation, but eventually the services were forced to change their policies. In 1942, the navy and the Marine Corps began accepting African Americans to serve in many positions. The army's women's division, the Women's Army Corps (WAC), and the women's branch of the Navy, the WAVES, welcomed over 4,000 African American women during

Part of the 99th Pursuit Squadron, these pilots were trained at Tuskegee. How did armed forces policy toward African Americans differ in World War I and World War II?

SNAPSHOT OF THE TIMES

1941 U.S. enters World War II. Dorie Miller is hero of Pearl Harbor.

African Americans admitted to army Officer Candidate School.

1942 The Navy and the Marine Corps accept African Americans.

Army Air Corps trains African American pilots at Tuskegee.

African American women join WAC and WAVES.

1943 Detroit race riot

1945 World War II ends.

the war. As you have read, the Army Air Corps opened a post at Tuskegee to train African American pilots.

Continuing Segregation and Discrimination. Segregation was still the rule, however. African Americans and whites did not serve in the same units, nor did African American officers command white troops.

In addition, African American troops frequently faced discrimination and hostility in the small towns and cities around the military bases where they were stationed. One soldier recalled the time he and some other GIs entered a lunchroom in segregated Salina, Kansas:

> The owner said, "You boys know we don't serve colored here." . . . We . . . just stood there inside the door, staring at what we had come to see—the German prisoners of war who were having lunch at the counter. . . . The people of Salina would serve these enemy soldiers and turn away black American G.I.'s.

African American Officers. African Americans also wanted to be able to become officers. The military agreed because it needed officers to command the growing number of African Americans entering the armed forces. In summer 1941, African Americans began to enter army Officer Candidate School on an equal basis with whites. Two years later, the navy opened its officer ranks to African Americans.

During the war, one of the highest ranking African American officers was Colonel Benjamin O. Davis, Jr.

Benjamin O. Davis, Jr., was the son of the man who became the first African American general, in 1940. The younger Davis graduated from West Point in 1936, the first African American to do so in almost 50 years. He commanded the 99th Pursuit Squadron, which fought in North Africa and Italy, and later he became commander of the 332nd Fighter Group. After the war, the younger Davis was made a major general, the first African American to hold such a high rank. In 1952, he was appointed commander of the 51st Fighter Interceptor Wing in Korea. He retired in 1970 with the rank of lieutenant general. In 1991, Davis wrote about the exploits of the Black Eagles in his autobiography.

African Americans Overseas. Of the 1 million African American men and women who were in the armed forces during World War II, half served overseas. They carried out essential, often dangerous, assignments on many fronts.

Twenty-two African American combat units—field artillery, antiaircraft artillery, tank battalions, and air combat units—took part in the invasion of Sicily, off the coast of Italy, in 1943, and the invasion of Normandy, in France, in 1944. In France, 1,500 African American truck drivers barreled down what was called the Red Ball Highway to supply General George S. Patton's Third Army. On Pacific islands, African Americans slashed through rain forests to build airplane landing strips as Allied forces pressed on to Japan.

African Americans in the navy were radiomen, gunner's mates, and supply officers on ships that escorted destroyers and tracked enemy submarines. They built naval bases in the Pacific. African American marines defended captured enemy outposts in the Pacific. On the supply ships of the merchant marine, African Americans and whites worked together as seamen, radio operators, and engineers.

The Battle of the Bulge. The officers commanding the army were slower to see how well integrated forces could work. Not until the closing days of the war did they move toward integrating combat troops. In late 1944, in the Ardennes Forest of Belgium and Luxembourg, the Germans launched a surprise counterattack. Short of soldiers to repel the attack, the army asked for volunteers. About 2,500 African Americans came forward. Fighting side by side, white and African American soldiers turned back a fierce Nazi attack, in what became known as the Battle of the Bulge. But once the Germans surrendered, the troops returned to their separate white and African American units.

Despite discrimination and segregation, African Americans in World War II had had more opportunity to serve their country than in any previous war. They had served well.

Taking Another Look

1. Why did the armed forces accept African Americans into Officer Candidate School?

2. What was the significance of the Battle of the Bulge for African Americans in the armed forces?

3. **Critical Thinking** How do you think African Americans who served in the war felt when they returned to a still-segregated nation?

2 ON THE HOME FRONT
▼ How did the war affect African Americans at home?

Sybil Lewis, a young African American, was trained to work in a defense plant and got a job riveting airplane parts. Lewis later told what happened on the job:

The women worked in pairs. I was the riveter, and this big strong white girl from a cotton farm in Arkansas worked as the bucker. . . . Bucking was harder than shooting rivets; it required more muscle. Riveting required more skill . . . . The boss came around one day and . . . assigned [the white woman] to do the riveting and me to do the bucking. . . . I was never given the riveting job back. That was the first encounter I had with discrimination in California, and it didn't sit too well with me.

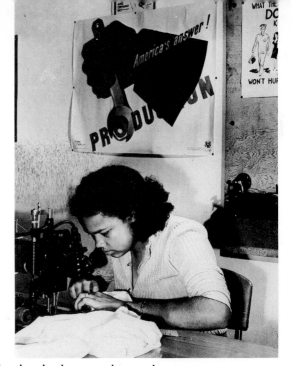

In the nation's factories, African American men and women helped produce the planes, parachutes, and other war equipment used by its armed forces.

World War II opened many jobs for African Americans in the nation's defense factories. However, discrimination and segregation were still the rule.

Employment. Defense industries—aircraft, shipbuilding, iron and steel, and others—needed workers. As you read in Chapter 27, to make sure that African Americans would get their fair share of the new jobs, union leader A. Philip Randolph threatened to organize a massive march on Washington in May 1941. Only then did the government act. The following month, President Roosevelt set up the Fair Employment Practices Committee (FEPC) to end discrimination in defense industries.

With the FEPC to back them up, large numbers of African Americans got high-paying, skilled jobs in defense plants. They joined labor unions, too, even in the South.

Like Sybil Lewis, thousands of African American women worked alongside white women in the war plants. Women war workers, who were given the title "Rosie the Riveter," were praised for their patriotism. Most of the African American women workers earned higher wages than they ever had before.

Migration North. Defense work lured many African Americans to abandon Southern farms for the cities of the North, Midwest, and West. Once again, as in the early years of the 20th century, the cities swelled with thousands of newcomers (see page 274). They were not always received warmly. In a number of cities, friction between African Americans and whites erupted into riots.

The most serious riot took place in Detroit. Fifty thousand African Americans had come to work in the many defense plants of the city. One day in spring 1943, a fistfight between an African American man and a white man stirred up smoldering tensions. Within a few hours, a race riot blazed across the city. Whites roamed the streets beating African Americans and burning their cars. It took 30 hours and 34 deaths before 6,000 soldiers, called in by President Roosevelt, ended the riot.

Taking Another Look

1. How did World War II improve employment opportunities for African Americans?

2. Why did many African Americans leave the South during the war?

3. **Critical Thinking** What do you think were the causes behind race riots like the one in Detroit?

LOOKING AHEAD

World War II ended on September 2, 1945. Whether in the armed forces or at home, the lives of African Americans had been changed by the war. Many African Americans had worked at new jobs, gone to new places, and seen new things. For the first time, many had earned a decent living. After the war, some took advantage of the GI Bill, which gave them a chance for a college education. African Americans faced the future with more hope and greater expectations than ever.

WORLD WAR II HONOR ROLL

24th Infantry—Routed Japanese from New Georgia Islands

92nd Division—As part of the Fifth Army, pushed northward in Italy to the Arno River; lost over 3,000 men; won 65 Silver Stars, 65 Bronze Medals, 1,300 Purple Hearts

93rd Division—Fought in the Pacific: Treasury Islands, the Philippines, Dutch East Indies, and Bougainville

99th Pursuit Squadron—Downed eight Nazi planes in one of the fiercest fights of the Italian campaign

450th Anti-Aircraft Artillery Battalion—First African American unit in invasions of Africa and in Europe; cited by General Mark Clark for "outstanding performance of duty."

614th Tank Destroyer Battalion—Fought several important actions; one of its officers, Captain Charles L. Thomas, received Distinguished Service Cross for heroism in action

761st Tank Battalion—Won 391 awards for 183 days of combat; knocked out 331 machine-gun nests and captured a German radio station

969th Field Artillery—Won a Distinguished Unit Citation for "outstanding courage and resourcefulness and undaunted determination"

World War II soldiers

CLOSE UP: Chapter 28

It was during World War II that the United States discovered a new type of soldier—women—and formed women's military branches. In World War I, women had been limited to working in the Red Cross as ambulance drivers and nurses. During World War II, women joined the military, where they served as clerks, typists, drivers, and nurses—but not fighters. Although this was a step forward for women, their units were not on an equal footing with the regular military.

In the service, African American women faced double discrimination—against skin color as well as gender. African American women were housed, fed, and trained in separate facilities from white women. At first, there were no African American women officers. Mary McLeod Bethune changed that. Bethune ensured that African American women were a part of the first women's Officers Training School. By 1946, there were 115 African American officers in the WACs. Among the outstanding African American officers were Major Charity B. Adams and Captain Abbie N. Campbell.

Today, women are integrated into all branches of the military. In 1991, Congress authorized women to fly combat missions.

The Who, What, Where of History

1. **Who** was Dorie Miller?
2. **Where** is Pearl Harbor?
3. **Who** is Leslie Lee?
4. **Who** were the Black Eagles?
5. **Who** is Benjamin O. Davis, Jr.?
6. **What** was the WAC?
7. **What** was the FEPC?

Making the Connection

1. What was the connection between World War II and the migration of African Americans to cities of the North and Midwest?
2. What was the connection between the Fair Employment Practices Committee and increased employment of African Americans in high-paying, skilled jobs?

Time Check

1. When did the bombing of Pearl Harbor occur?
2. In what year did the U.S. armed services' policies regarding segregation begin to change?
3. In what year did World War II end?

What Would You Have Done?

1. Reread the incident about the segregated lunchroom in Salina, Kansas, on page 322. If you had been one of the African American soldiers who was refused service, how would you have responded to the lunchroom owner's statement?

2. If you had been an African American woman during World War II, would you have chosen to join the military, or would you have taken a job in the defense industry? Explain.

Thinking and Writing About History

Imagine that you are one of the African American truck drivers who helped supply the Third Army during the Battle of the Bulge. Write a letter home explaining what you think about the work you are doing and how you think it might affect your life after the war.

Building Skills: Comparing Points of View

Friday night, Frank missed a party because he had to go to a family birthday celebration. The next morning, Frank asked his friend Sam about the party, and Sam said it was the worst party he had ever been to. Later Frank's friend Alexis told him that he'd missed a fantastic party.

Who was telling the truth? Both Sam and Alexis were, but they were giving their opinions, or points of view.

People writing about the same historical event can also have different points of view. A point of view represents someone's opinion or judgment. For the opinion to be valid, it should be supported by facts. It is important to figure out writers' points of view as you read, so that you can decide whether the evidence supports their views. Then you can logically agree or disagree with their judgments.

The two quotations below were both written by well-known, well-respected writers. Read the quotations and answer the questions that follow.

No one had expected it, . . . but the war had been the watershed of the postemancipation struggle for equality. These were the years when American Negroes began for the first time to fight for their rights effectively and independently. Their relationship to white America had undergone a fundamental change. Here was where the modern civil rights movement began; here was where it scored its first important victories.

—Geoffrey Perrett, *Days of Sadness, Years of Triumph*

The treatment accorded the Negro during the Second World War marks, for me, a turning point in the Negro's relation to America. To put it briefly, and somewhat too simply, a certain hope died, a certain respect for white Americans faded.

—James Baldwin, quoted in J. Milton Yinger, *A Minority Group in American Society*

1. Both writers believe that World War II marked a major change in the history of African Americans. Write the key words from each quotation that describe the change.

2. a. Would you say that Baldwin's view of the results of the war years is positive or negative?
   b. Do you think Perrett is positive or negative in his description?

3. Summarize in your own words the views of both writers.

4. With which point of view do you agree? Explain why.

5. Explain how both Perrett and Baldwin could be correct.

Mechanical cotton pickers

CHAPTER
29

Gains and Losses in the Postwar Years

(1945–1960s)

THINKING ABOUT THE CHAPTER

What important changes took place in African Americans' lives in the decades after World War II?

On October 2, 1944, a crowd of people gathered at a cotton plantation in Mississippi. At the edge of a 42-acre (17-hectare) cotton field stood eight new bright red machines. At a signal, the operators of the machines began to drive along the rows of cotton, stripping the plants of their fuzzy white bolls. By the end of the day, not a single open boll of cotton was left in the field.

That day, the mechanical cotton picker foreshadowed the end of the centuries-old practice of picking cotton by hand. The bale of cotton that each machine picked cost the plantation owner a little over five dollars to harvest. If it had been picked by sharecroppers, it would have cost almost eight times more.

By 1960, mechanical cotton pickers had replaced almost all the sharecroppers who labored in the cotton fields. Just as the cotton gin had led to a massive increase in slavery in the 1800s, the mechanical cotton picker led to a massive migration of African Americans out of the South from the 1940s to the 1960s. This migration to the cities of the Northeast and the Midwest transformed the African American way of life.

1 A NEW WAVE OF MIGRATION

▼ Why did millions of African Americans leave the South in the years after World War II?

On a gray day in November 1951, a long-distance bus from Memphis, Tennessee, pulled into the Chicago bus terminal. Down the bus steps trudged 35 tired African Americans—men, women, and children—with battered suitcases, parcels of pots and pans, and children's toys. Relatives rushed up to greet some of the newcomers and take them home to their apartments. The others, bewildered by the noise and bustle, found their own way out of the bus terminal and to the African American neighborhoods.

To the Cities. In the ten years between 1950 and 1960, almost two million African Americans moved from the South to the nation's 12 largest non-Southern cities. With work on the cotton plantations shrinking every year and the discrimination and segregation of the South becoming more unbearable, migration North seemed the only answer.

Because the years after the war were times of general prosperity for the nation, jobs were not hard to find. However, most of the migrants had few skills that could be used in the industrial economy of the North. In addition, discrimination by whites often confined African Americans to low-paying "Negro work"—unskilled jobs, such as janitor or maid. Compared with those who remained in the South, though, their incomes were high.

Housing. Housing was expensive and in short supply. In segregated neighborhoods, African Americans had to live in older buildings. Low incomes for African Americans often meant more tenants had to share an apartment to meet the rent. Overcrowded buildings became run-down more quickly, and white owners often neglected repairs on buildings in

Many African American migrants from the south moved into housing projects like Chicago's Robert Taylor Homes. Built in the late 1950s and early 1960s, it is the largest housing project in the world.

1944 Development of mechanical cotton picker

1950–1960 2 million African Americans move to cities in Northeast and Midwest.

1950s Bebop, cool jazz, free-form jazz, rock 'n' roll develop.

1953 Race riot in Chicago public housing

1954 Three African Americans elected to House of Representatives.

1952 Ralph Ellison publishes *Invisible Man.*

1959 *A Raisin in the Sun* opens on Broadway.

African American neighborhoods. When public housing projects began to be built in the 1950s, they seemed to offer a way out for African Americans.

However, bitter disputes broke out when African Americans tried to move into the new buildings. In 1953, violence erupted when several African American families moved into a Chicago housing project occupied by whites. For four years, police were assigned to maintain order there.

Eventually, whites moved away from many of the public housing projects in the cities, and African Americans became the large majority of tenants. Although this eased the housing shortage for them, before long the cities neglected the buildings. They became rundown and crime-ridden. African Americans in the cities thus became segregated in fact, rather than by laws as in the South. This **de facto segregation** applied not only to housing, but to schools as well.

Education. Schools in the African American neighborhoods had difficulty accommodating the rapid increase in students. After the 1954 *Brown* decision ending legally segregated schools (see page 337), more African American students shared classrooms with white students. However, city school budgets did not increase enough to solve the new problems of large classes, overcrowded school buildings, and low teachers' salaries. As neighborhoods became segregated, so did schools.

Political Power. The concentration of large numbers of African Americans in the big cities gave them greater political power. In 1954, for example, for the first time in this century, three African Americans—William Dawson of Chicago, the Rev. Adam Clayton Powell of New York City, and Charles C. Diggs of Detroit—were elected to seats in the House of Representatives.

In local politics, too, African Americans began to have political power. White politicians sought African Americans' votes in return for promises—not always kept—to improve African American neighborhoods. At the same time, the growing numbers of African Americans who were elected to city posts tried to make the local governments more responsive to the needs of the African American community, such as better schools.

Taking Another Look

1. What was the main reason for the migration of millions of African Americans from the South to the North in the 1940s through the 1960s?

2. How did the growing political power of African Americans in the cities show itself?

3. **Critical Thinking** Refer to Chapter 24 and compare the African American migration from 1915 to 1930 with that from the 1940s through the 1960s.

2 THE ARTS

▼ What contributions did African Americans make to the nation's cultural life after World War II?

Charlie Parker, a Kansas City high school student, knew that Count Basie, whose band was playing at a local nightclub, allowed amateurs to play with the band after hours. One evening, the intense, self-confident Parker, who was just 15, walked into the club with his saxophone, stepped up to the bandstand, and began playing. Before long, the players were jeering at Parker's poor performance, and one of them sounded the gong to get him off the stage. But Parker continued to play. Nothing stopped him until a cymbal crashed next to his ears. Reluctantly, Parker left the bandstand, more determined than ever to become the

Saxophonist Charlie "Bird" Parker, with Dizzy Gillespie, introduced bebop.

greatest saxophone player in the world.

For the next few years, Parker spent 11 hours a day practicing saxophone exercises from music books and playing along with jazz records. Eventually, Charlie "Bird" Parker became ranked with Louis Armstrong as one of the jazz greats.

When Parker came to fame in the mid-1940s, white Americans were gradually coming to appreciate African Americans in all the arts, not only music. However, segregation of African Americans and discrimination against them continued and as a result, social contacts between African Americans and whites were limited.

Writers. In 1940, the African American author Richard Wright wrote a novel called *Native Son,* about a 19-year-old African American in Chicago who kills a white woman. In it, Wright condemns the pressures of white society that lead the young man to commit the crime. The book quickly became a bestseller, the first by an African American writer. *Native Son* was important because it departed from earlier books by African Americans, which tended to avoid dealing with tensions between African Americans and whites. It was also important because it was so outspoken in its attack on the world in which African Americans were forced to live.

Wright led the way for books of protest by other writers. In 1952, Ralph Ellison wrote a novel, *Invisible Man,* that shows how African Americans are "invisible" to whites, who do not accept them as part of U.S. society. In his essays, poetry, and novels, James Baldwin also expressed the anger felt by African Americans. Imamu Amiri Baraka (LeRoi Jones) wrote works, including his play *Dutchman,* that deal with confrontations between African Americans and whites.

Lorraine Hansberry won the Drama Critics Circle Award for Best American Play for the 1958–1959 Broadway season for *A Raisin in the Sun*. Sidney Poitier, right, starred in the movie version.

Women writers also explored the conditions African Americans faced in their daily lives. The poet Gwendolyn Brooks celebrated the life of African Americans in the ghetto. When Lorraine Hansberry's play *A Raisin in the Sun* opened on Broadway in 1959, audiences, mostly white, were astonished and delighted at the humor and warmth of the urban family in the play.

The works of the writers mentioned were huge successes with white readers and theatergoers as well as with African Americans. Rather than resenting the attacks of even the bitterest of the works, thoughtful whites welcomed them as unique contributions that enriched U.S. literature.

Music. "I'm playing the same notes, but it comes out different. You can't teach the soul. You got to bring out your *soul* on those valves." This was how African American trumpeter Dizzy Gillespie spoke about the new kind of jazz music he was playing. In the 1940s, Gillespie, Charlie Parker, and pianist Thelonious

Monk developed what came to be called bebop, a form of jazz that soon rivaled the more rhythmic and more hard-driving traditional jazz.

In other developments, trumpeter Miles Davis later popularized a variation of bebop called cool jazz. Saxophonist Ornette Coleman moved modern jazz closer to contemporary classical music in what was called free-form jazz.

Gospel music made its way from the African American church to the popular stage. In her rich contralto voice, Mahalia Jackson sang gospel music throughout the United States and the world to enthusiastic African American and white audiences.

The 1950s saw the birth of rock 'n' roll. Small African American record companies first produced the strong, rhythmic music of African American performers such as Chuck Berry, Ruth Brown, Little Richard, and Fats Domino. Soon rock 'n' roll swept the country. In 1952, some 18,000 people attended the first rock 'n' roll concert, held in an auditorium in Cleveland, Ohio, that seated 10,000. All the performers were African American, but half

332

the audience was white. Within a short time, rock became the most popular musical form among teenagers and spread to all corners of the world.

In its many forms, the music of African Americans in the 1940s, 1950s, and 1960s had an enormous impact. In earlier times, this music had been set apart as "race music" and sold mostly to African Americans. Now all Americans were beginning to appreciate and buy the music of African American musicians.

Artists. Although there were many African American visual artists in the 1950s and 1960s, few made the impact on U.S. culture that writers and musicians did. The best-known of the group was Jacob Lawrence. He represented the first generation of artists who were born in the African American community, had African American teachers, and devoted themselves to portraying the African American experience. Lawrence painted scenes of African American history and city life. Most noted are his 40 panels on the life of Frederick Douglass, a similar work on Harriet Tubman, and a longer series on the migrations of the African American people (see "The Artist's View").

Actors. For many years, African Americans were seen in movies mostly as servants or as objects of ridicule. That

Mahalia Jackson helped bring African American gospel music to the general public.

began to change in the 1950s and 1960s. Sidney Poitier won an Oscar as best actor of 1963 in a dramatic role. Harry Belafonte also had serious roles in pictures. In general, more films with African Americans as central characters were shown on the nation's screens.

Television programs also began to include African Americans as major figures. Bill Cosby became a nationwide favorite in his "I Spy" series, for which he won an Emmy in 1966.

Taking Another Look

1. Why was Richard Wright's *Native Son* an important book?

2. What new forms of jazz were introduced in the postwar years?

3. **Critical Thinking** Review the painting on page A–11 of "The Artist's View." What point do you think the painter is trying to make in this painting?

LOOKING AHEAD

Despite rundown, overcrowded housing and segregated neighborhoods, the migration to the Northeast and Midwest benefited many African Americans. From the 1940s through the 1960s, jobs were plentiful. Although discrimination imposed limits on both wages and the types of job available to African Americans, even unskilled workers had more opportunities than they had had in the South. In the arts, especially in writing and music, the period was as rich in achievement as the Harlem Renaissance (see page 290).

While these economic and artistic developments were taking place, the fires of a new protest movement were being fanned as African Americans, joined by whites, sought to secure full civil rights for all Americans.

FOCUS ON

CELEBRATING EXCELLENCE

In a world of despair, we wanted to give hope. In a world of negative Black images, we wanted to provide positive Black images. In a world that said Blacks could do few things, we wanted to say they could do everything.

This is how African American publisher John H. Johnson described his reasons for founding *Ebony* in 1945. When *Ebony* first hit the newsstands on November 1, 1945, segregation and discrimination were facts of life for African Americans. Johnson struck back by publishing a glossy national magazine celebrating African American triumphs.

When it first came off the presses, *Ebony*'s total circulation was 25,000 copies. Since then, its readership has grown to more than 9.5 million. It is the world's best-selling African American publication.

Johnson's success did not stop with *Ebony*. In 1951, he introduced *Jet*, a weekly news magazine. By 1962, Johnson Publishing Company was producing books. In 1996, President Bill Clinton honored Johnson by awarding him the Medal of Freedom, the nation's highest civilian honor. He shared the stage with another civil rights great—Rosa Parks, who fought segregation in Alabama.

The Who, What, Where of History

1. **What** was responsible for the end of the Southern sharecropping system?
2. **Who** was Adam Clayton Powell?
3. **Who** was Charlie Parker?
4. **Who** was Richard Wright?
5. **What** is *Invisible Man*?
6. **Who** was Lorraine Hansberry?
7. **What** is bebop?
8. **Where** was the first rock 'n' roll concert held?
9. **Who** was Jacob Lawrence?

Making the Connection

1. What was the connection between the mechanical cotton picker and the migration of African Americans to the North from the 1940s through the 1960s?
2. What was the connection between the migration of African Americans to the North and the election of increased numbers of African Americans to Congress?
3. What was the connection between *Native Son* and the writing of *Invisible Man* and of *Dutchman*?

Time Check

1. In what year was the mechanical cotton picker first used?
2. During which decade did 2 million African Americans move to cities in the North and Midwest?

What Would You Have Done?

If you had been an African American living in the South, would you have chosen to move to the North during the 1950s? Explain.

Thinking and Writing About History

Imagine that you are an 85-year-old African American living in a Northern city in 1968. Write a letter to a young relative explaining the differences you see between the lives and work of African Americans in 1968 and in the days when you were young.

Building Skills: Analyzing Fiction

A well-written fictional description of a time period can give the details and the feeling of being there that most historical works do not. Of course, when you are reading a work of fiction, you must remember that it *is* fiction. You may come away with the flavor and atmosphere of a time period, but you must remember that a writer of fiction doesn't have to list his or her sources as a historian does. Don't take everything in a piece of historical fiction as fact. Also, be very alert to the author's point of view.

Following is a brief excerpt from "Flying Home" by Ralph Ellison. Todd, an African American pilot in training during World War II, has been injured in a crash on a Southern farm. Read it, and on a separate sheet of paper, answer the questions that follow the reading.

"We kin ride him into town on old Ned," the boy said.

Ned? He turned, seeing the boy point toward an ox team browsing where the buried blade of a plow marked the end of a furrow. Thoughts of himself riding an ox through the town, past streets full of white faces, down the concrete runways of the airfield made swift images of humiliation in his mind. With a pang he remembered his girl's last letter. "Todd," she had written, ". . . And I have always known you to be as brave as anyone else. The papers annoy me. Don't you be contented to prove over and over again that you're brave or skillful just because you're black, Todd. . . . [T]hey don't want to say why you boys are not yet fighting. . . . Anyone with brains can learn to fly, but then what? What about using it, and who will you use it for? . . . I sometimes think they're playing a trick on us. It's very humiliating. . . ." He wiped cold sweat from his face, thinking, What does she know of humiliation? She's never been down South. Now the humiliation would come. When you must have them judge you, knowing that they never accept your mistakes as your own, but hold it against your whole race—that was humiliation.

1. What do you learn about African American pilots at the beginning of World War II?

2. What is the pilot's greatest fear?

3. What does the pilot indicate about the different attitudes toward African Americans in the North and South during World War II?

Jackie Robinson scoring a run

The Battle for Civil Rights

(1954–1963)

THINKING ABOUT THE CHAPTER

What tactics did civil rights workers use to win equality for African Americans?

On April 18, 1946, people packed the stands of the Jersey City, New Jersey, ballpark. They had come to see the first game played by the New York Giants since the end of World War II. In the exhibition game, the Giants faced the Montreal Royals—the top farm team for the Brooklyn Dodgers.

The excited crowd was waiting for Jackie Robinson to take his first turn at bat. Just six months before, Dodgers president Branch Rickey had made headlines by signing Robinson with the Royals. Now an African American was about to shatter the color barrier in baseball. Never before had an African American played outside the Negro National League.

His first time up, Robinson grounded out. The second time, he sent the baseball over the left-field fence.

336

Thus started a career that brought Robinson into major league baseball with the Dodgers in 1947 and into baseball's Hall of Fame in 1962. Robinson opened the way for other African American baseball greats—Roy Campanella, Willie Mays, and Hank Aaron, to name a few. Still, Robinson knew that winning equality for African Americans took more than hitting home runs. Like other African Americans, he soon became caught up in the Civil Rights Movement—the movement to extend the Constitution's promise of equality to all citizens.

1 ▼ EXPELLING JIM CROW FROM SCHOOL

Why was the decision in *Brown* v. *Board of Education* a turning point in U.S. history?

About the same time that Jackie Robinson played his first game for the Dodgers, the University of Oklahoma admitted George McLaurin to its all-white law school. In 1938, the Supreme Court had ruled that states had to provide separate-but-equal graduate facilities for African Americans. Because Oklahoma did not have a separate law school for African Americans, the all-white law school had to admit McLaurin.

In 1948, the university accepted McLaurin on "a segregated basis." McLaurin studied at a segregated desk in the library. He sat in a roped-off area of classrooms or attended class alone. He ate in a separate part of the school cafeteria. Was he being offered an equal education with white students? Lawyers for the NAACP thought not.

Challenging Segregation Policies. The NAACP had set up the Legal Defense and Education Fund to tackle cases

just like this. Thurgood Marshall, director of the fund, decided to take *McLaurin* v. *Oklahoma State Regents* all the way to the Supreme Court.

No one doubted that **Thurgood Marshall** had courage. He had a reputation as the African American "lawyer who stood up in white men's courts." Born in 1908 in Baltimore, Maryland, Marshall earned his law degree from Howard University. He then practiced under Charles

337

Hamilton Houston, a brilliant Harvard law graduate and legal director for the NAACP who inspired Marshall to use the courts to fight segregation. From the 1930s on, Marshall used the law to battle segregation and racism. In 1967, he became the first African American appointed to the Supreme Court. He served there until his retirement in 1991.

On June 5, 1950, Marshall faced the Court. He argued that the university had pinned "a badge of inferiority" on McLaurin by setting him apart from his fellow students. The Court agreed with Marshall and ordered an end to segregation at the law school. But the McLaurin decision affected only those schools that admitted African Americans in the first place. Many all-white schools denied African Americans entry because supposed "separate but equal" facilities existed.

That same year, Marshall won another important victory in the case of *Sweatt* v. *Painter*. In it, he argued successfully that a separate law school established by the state of Texas for African Americans was anything but equal to the whites-only University of Texas Law School.

A Landmark Victory. The cases that the NAACP had won so far all involved colleges and universities. The Supreme Court's 1896 decision in *Plessy* v. *Ferguson* remained firmly in place in regard to public elementary and high schools. With the victory in *Sweatt* v. *Painter,* Marshall now felt he had the grounds on which to overturn *Plessy*.

Many African American lawyers, out of fear of the consequences, held back their

Which Supreme Court ruling do you think has had the greatest effect on African Americans?

▶▶ SELECTED SUPREME COURT DECISIONS AND AFRICAN AMERICANS

Case (year)	Decision Summary	Case (year)	Decision Summary
Dred Scott v. *Sandford* (1857)	African Americans are not U.S. citizens; Congress has no power to forbid slavery in U.S. territories.	*Swan* v. *Charlotte-Mecklenburg* (1971)	Busing can be used to integrate urban schools.
Plessy v. *Ferguson* (1896)	Segregation can be legal as long as the separate facilities are equal.	*Bakke* v. *University of California* (1978)	Race may be used as one factor—but not the only factor—in making affirmative action decisions.
Nixon v. *Herndon* (1927)	States cannot prohibit African Americans' voting in primary elections.	*Batson* v. *Kentucky* (1986)	Prosecutors in criminal cases cannot exclude jurors on the basis of race.
Brown v. *Board of Education* (1954)	Racial segregation in public schools is unconstitutional.	*Edmonson* v. *Leesville Concrete Co.* (1991)	Prosecutors and defendants in civil cases cannot exclude jurors on the basis of race.
Heart of Atlanta Motel v. *U.S.* (1964)	A motel may not refuse to rent rooms to African Americans.		

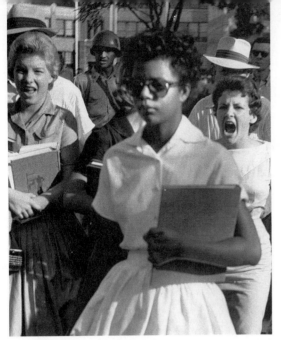

Elizabeth Eckford braves the hatred of whites to enter her high school in Little Rock, Arkansas, in 1957.

support. The risks were high. What if they lost? Segregation might then be more solidly in place than ever.

In the end, Marshall won enough support to continue the campaign against segregated schools. He convinced the NAACP to back parents suing to integrate school systems in four states and the District of Columbia. The Supreme Court lumped the cases together under *Brown* v. *Board of Education of Topeka, Kansas.* The decision in *Brown* would apply to all cases and to the nation as a whole.

Marshall's argument rested upon the psychological effects of segregation. He produced expert testimony demonstrating that segregation lowered the self-esteem of African American children. Thus, segregation violated the equal protection clause of the 14th Amendment.

In a unanimous 1954 decision, the Court declared segregation unconstitutional. Chief Justice Earl Warren read the majority opinion, which said in part:

To separate [those children] from others of similar age and qualifica-

tions solely because of their race generates a feeling of inferiority as to their status in the community that may affect their hearts and minds in a way unlikely ever to be undone. . . . Separate educational facilities are inherently unequal. . . . Any language in *Plessy* v. *Ferguson* contrary to these findings is rejected.

Resisting Desegregation. The Court ordered school districts to desegregate "with all deliberate speed." Many did. But resistance developed in the Deep South. A key test came in Little Rock, Arkansas, in 1957. There, Governor Orval Faubus called in the state's National Guard to prevent nine African American students from entering the city's public high school. When 15-year-old Elizabeth Eckford tried to walk into the school, soldiers with bayonets on their rifles turned her back. An angry mob of whites jeered "Lynch her!" She managed to escape with the help of a white bystander.

The crisis at Little Rock forced President Eisenhower to act. He took command of the Arkansas National Guard and sent the 101st Airborne Division to enforce the *Brown* decision.

The following year Faubus shut down Little Rock's high schools. The state set up "private" academies and blocked African Americans from entering them.

Desegregation did come—slowly. In 1957, Congress passed a new Civil Rights Act, increasing the power of the Attorney General to protect African Americans' rights. The Supreme Court also heard a new round of desegregation cases in the 1950s and 1960s. But it became clear that more than court decisions would be needed to end segregation. A new plan of action soon emerged in Montgomery, Alabama, the first capital of the Confederacy.

339

How did Rosa Parks make U.S. history in Montgomery, Alabama, in 1955?

Taking Another Look

1. What court decisions paved the way for the decision in *Brown*?

2. What arguments did Thurgood Marshall use to win the *Brown* case?

3. **Critical Thinking** Why do you think the NAACP made ending segregation in education a top priority?

2 RESISTING WITHOUT ▼ BITTERNESS

What tactics did Martin Luther King, Jr., use to oppose segregation?

On December 1, 1955, Rosa Parks boarded a bus in Montgomery, Alabama. The 42-year-old African American seamstress took a seat in the first row of the "colored" section of the bus. An active church member and secretary of the local chapter of the NAACP, the soft-spoken Parks had no intention of violating the law that day. But by the time she left the bus, she had started a movement that would shake the nation.

As the white section of the bus filled up, the bus driver ordered Parks and three other people to stand. Parks stayed put.

"Well, if you don't stand up," said the bus driver, "I'm going to call the police and have you arrested." "You may do that," answered Parks. The police arrested Parks and booked her for violating Montgomery's Jim Crow laws. News of Parks's arrest quickly spread through the African American community.

Taking to the Streets. E. D. Nixon, who had been a leader in the local chapter of the NAACP for years, posted bail for Parks. Nixon and Jo Ann Robinson, president of an African American organization, the Women's Political Council, came up with a plan to boycott segregated buses in Montgomery. Nixon marshaled the support of African American churches in the community, including the Dexter Avenue Baptist Church. Its pastor was 26-year-old Dr. Martin Luther King, Jr. King was elected head of the Montgomery Improvement Association, the organizing force behind the boycott.

African American volunteers mimeographed thousands of leaflets urging people to join the boycott. "Don't ride the bus to work, to town, to school, or any place on Monday," declared the leaflets.

African Americans made up nearly 75 percent of the city's bus riders. Most could not afford cars, but that Monday they stayed off the Montgomery buses.

The day of protest proved so successful that the boycott was extended to the next day and the next and the next. African Americans willingly endured the hardship of walking nearly every place they went. One older African American woman turned down the offer of a ride saying, "I'm not walking for myself, I'm walking for my children and my grandchildren."

The boycott lasted 381 days, nearly crippling Montgomery bus companies. In late 1956, the Supreme Court found that segregation on Alabama buses was unconstitutional. On December 21, King and other African Americans climbed aboard integrated Montgomery buses for the first time.

King's Beliefs. The success of the Montgomery bus boycott strengthened Martin Luther King, Jr.'s belief that nonviolent protest was the most effective tool for gaining civil rights. King had studied the ideas of India's Mohandas Gandhi, who earlier in the century had waged a struggle to free India from British rule. Gandhi had preached **nonviolence,** the peaceful refusal to obey unjust laws. King's study of history had convinced him that it would be suicidal to protest segregation with violence. He decided to draw upon the tactics that had helped Gandhi in India. He also drew upon a tradition of protest within his own family.

Martin Luther King, Jr., was born in Atlanta, Georgia, in 1929. He grew up in a devout Baptist family. Both his grandfather and father were ministers. King's grandfather led a protest to force Atlanta to build its first high school for African Americans. King's father continued speaking out for African American rights as pastor of Ebenezer Baptist Church. By age five, King could recite Bible passages from memory. By age 15, he had entered Morehouse College. By age 26, he had earned a Ph.D. in theology from Boston College. He soon moved to Alabama with his wife, concert singer Coretta Scott.

King quickly became the most visible and eloquent spokesperson of the Civil Rights Movement. In 1957, he joined with nearly 100 other church leaders in founding the Southern Christian Leadership Conference (SCLC). The SCLC reflected King's philosophy for change: "To resist without bitterness; to be cursed and not reply; to be beaten and not hit back."

In 1960, King moved the SCLC headquarters to Atlanta. There he served as SCLC president and as a part-time pastor in his father's church.

That same year, another civil rights group, the Student Nonviolent Coordinating Committee (SNCC), was formed. It was based in part on King's ideas of nonviolence. The young people who made up this organization had been teenagers when the Supreme Court handed down the *Brown* decision. Now, as college students, they stood ready to reshape the Civil Rights Movement.

Taking Another Look

1. What were the events leading up to the Montgomery bus boycott?

2. What was King's philosophy of protest and social change?

3. **Critical Thinking** How do you think King would have defined *courage?*

These civil rights demonstrators are determined to desegregate a lunch counter in Jackson, Mississippi.

3 A NEW GENERATION

▼ How did African American youth step up resistance to segregation?

On January 31, 1960, Ezell Blair, Jr., went to see his parents. Ezell, a freshman at North Carolina's Agricultural and Technical College in Greensboro, asked his parents a strange question. Would they be upset if he stirred up trouble in town. "Why?" they replied. "Because," explained Ezell, "tomorrow we're going to do something that will shake up this town."

Sit-Ins. On February 1, four students from the college walked into Woolworth's variety store in Greensboro. They bought a few items, then sat down at a "whites only" lunch counter. When a waitress asked what they were doing, one of them replied, "We believe since we buy books and papers in the other part of the store we should get served in this part."

The store manager refused them service. The four, including Blair, continued to sit. They were not served that day. But 20 students returned to sit at the counter the next day. More arrived the next day as news spread of the **sit-in,** as this form of protest came to be called.

Television cameras and radio and newspaper reporters poured into Greensboro. Within months, thousands of students—African Americans and a few whites—were staging sit-ins across the state. Whites beat them, jeered at them, and dumped food on them. The protesters refused to strike back.

Martin Luther King, Ralph Abernathy, and other leaders of the SCLC gave students their support. King called being arrested for taking part in sit-ins "a badge of honor." Over the next year, an estimated 70,000 students took part in sit-ins. Some 3,600 received their "badge of honor" by serving time in jail.

Freedom Rides. While sit-ins shook the South, the Congress of Racial Equality (CORE) organized another form of protest. James Farmer had struggled to keep CORE alive since its founding in Chicago in 1942. He worked without pay and recruited other dedicated volunteers to do the same.

The new burst of civil rights activity helped Farmer revitalize CORE into a national organization. Like the SCLC and SNCC, CORE followed a program of nonviolence. But the course of action chosen by CORE met with brutal backlash.

In May 1961, a group of 13 African American and white volunteers set out from Washington, D.C., for a **freedom ride** through the South. Six boarded a Greyhound bus; seven got on a Trailways bus. The freedom riders were testing the effectiveness of court orders barring segregation on interstate buses and in bus terminals. At first, the riders had few problems. But when they hit the Deep South, angry mobs of whites gathered. Both African American and white protesters received savage beatings. One bus was firebombed.

Farmer considered calling the freedom ride off. But now student leaders of SNCC wanted to carry them on. Diane Nash begged Farmer to let them continue the rides. "You know that may be suicide," warned Farmer. Responded Nash:

We know that, but if we let them stop us with violence, the movement is dead! . . . Your troops have been badly battered. Let us pick up the baton and run with it.

Farmer agreed. The SNCC freedom riders rolled into Birmingham, Alabama. Sheriff Eugene "Bull" Connor's police beat the riders, took them into custody, and drove them into Tennessee. But the students came back and boarded a bus for Montgomery. Again they met with violence. Mobs cracked open heads and left students bleeding or unconscious.

The violence forced the Kennedy administration to act. Attorney General Robert Kennedy ordered federal marshals to protect the freedom riders as they headed farther south, chanting, "Freedom! Freedom!" In Mississippi, entire groups of freedom riders were arrested. Carried off to jail, they sang,

I'm taking a ride on the Greyhound bus line
I'm riding the front seat to Jackson this time.

As the freedom rides continued, the federal government issued tougher regulations barring segregation in interstate travel. It also put more pressure on local communities to obey the regulations.

Despite these measures, the turmoil over desegregation increased throughout the South. In 1961 and 1962, the Ku Klux Klan claimed credit for bombing four African American churches. In 1962, riots broke out in Oxford, Mississippi, when James Meredith tried to integrate the University of Mississippi. Federal troops had to escort him to and from classes.

Pressure mounted on the federal government to take stronger action for civil rights. On television, President Kennedy promised to send a new civil rights bill to Congress. It was 1963, the centennial of the Emancipation Proclamation.

Freedom riders in Anniston, Alabama, in May 1961 watch their burning bus, bombed by angry whites.

Taking Another Look

1. What was the purpose of the sit-ins and freedom rides?

2. What dangers did civil rights workers face in the Deep South?

3. **Critical Thinking** Why might it have seemed in 1963 as though the Civil War had never ended in the South?

4 MARCHING FOR FREEDOM

▼ How did the freedom marches of 1963 mark a turning point in the civil rights struggle?

On April 3, 1963, Martin Luther King, Jr., stepped off an airplane in Birmingham, Alabama. He had come at the invitation of Fred Shuttlesworth and other African American community leaders to start a new round of civil rights protests. King planned to celebrate the 100th anniversary of the Emancipation Proclamation by marching through one of the most stubbornly segregated cities in the South. King faced Bull Connor—the sheriff committed to crushing civil rights protests.

When reporters asked King how long he planned to stay in Birmingham, he replied, "[Until] Pharaoh lets God's people go." Bull Connor responded, "I got plenty of room in the jail." He also had club-wielding troopers, K-9 dogs, and fire hoses that could blast bark off a tree.

Freedom Now! Bull Connor had obtained a court order banning demonstrations until a full court hearing could be held. King and the other march leaders decided to go on with the protests anyway. Connor then set about arresting the demonstrators. At first, the protests were peaceful, and relatively few African Americans were jailed.

Then, on Good Friday, April 12, King stepped into the streets. Connor threw him into jail. Some whites believed King was openly courting crisis. King answered them in his "Letter from a Birmingham Jail."

For years now I have heard the word "Wait!" . . . when you have seen hate-filled policemen curse, kick and even kill your black brothers and sisters; when you see the vast majority of your twenty million Negro brothers in an airtight cage of poverty . . .; when you have to concoct an answer for a five-year-old son who is asking: "Daddy, why do white people treat colored people so mean?" . . . —then you will understand why we find it difficult to wait.

On April 20, King posted bail, but he did not leave Birmingham. Day after day, he and other civil rights workers marched. Then, on May 2, King decided to allow children in the marches.

Thousands of school-age students poured out of the public schools and into the street. Over 900 children went to jail that day. Helmeted police swept marchers off their feet with high-pressure hoses. Police dogs tore at marchers' arms and legs. As protesters lay helpless on the ground, police beat them with clubs and dragged them into waiting wagons.

Television cameras brought these scenes to a national audience. More rage and violence against the protesters followed. Bombs tore apart King's motel room and his brother's home.

Amid this crisis, Kennedy posted federal troops around Birmingham. An uneasy calm settled over the city as protesters agreed to halt demonstrations in exchange for an agreement that businesses would desegregate and also hire African Americans.

Events in Birmingham convinced President Kennedy to face the issue of civil rights. On June 10, the President addressed the nation: "Now the time has come for this nation to fulfill its promises." He demanded that Congress pass a new civil rights bill.

Within 24 hours of Kennedy's speech, an assassin crept up behind Medgar Evers, a leading Mississippi civil rights worker, and fired a bullet into his head. Evers fell dead.

The death brought African Americans together. They shot their fists into the air and shouted "Freedom Now!" Soon, a quarter of a million people would carry that cry to the nation's capital.

March on Washington. A. Philip Randolph and Bayard Rustin were among the African American leaders who organized a protest march on the nation's capital. On August 28, 1963, more than 250,000 people poured into Washington, D.C., from around the country. They had come to pressure Congress into passing the civil rights bill.

Amid memories of the recent violence, Martin Luther King spoke to the marchers about unity and racial harmony. "I have a dream," said King repeatedly. Each time he spoke these words, the crowd erupted in cheers. He then described his vision for the nation:

> When we let freedom ring, when we let it ring from every village and hamlet, . . . we will be able to speed up that day when all of God's children . . . will be able to join hands and sing in the words of that old Negro spiritual: "Free at last! Free at last! Thank God Almighty, we are free at last!"

"I have a dream," Dr. Martin Luther King, Jr., told the thousands at the March on Washington, D.C., in August 1963.

Taking Another Look

1. Why did King go to Birmingham?

2. What was King's dream for the United States?

3. **Critical Thinking** What role did television have in advancing the Civil Rights Movement?

LOOKING AHEAD

A few days after King's Washington speech, a bomb tore through an African American Bible school in Birmingham, killing four young girls. Two other African Americans were killed in the unrest that followed. On November 22, 1963, an assassin killed President Kennedy. His successor, Lyndon Johnson, pushed through Kennedy's civil rights bill in July 1964. But racial violence still ripped the nation. People prayed for the nightmare to end and King's dream to begin.

On March 2, 1955, police dragged 15–year-old Claudette Colvin from a bus in Montgomery, Alabama, and jailed her for refusing to give up her seat to a white passenger. In October 1955, another teenager, 18-year-old Mary Louise Smith, was arrested on the same charge.

Relatives for the two teens appealed to officials of the Montgomery NAACP to fight the charges, but the organization turned them down. The timing was not yet right, says African American scholar Lamont Yeakey. "Blacks weren't ready to give up their reliance on their buses for a teenager's troubles," he explains. "Not just yet."

Leaders at the time worried whether either teenager could inspire African Americans in Montgomery to challenge segregation. Later that year, they rallied behind Rosa Parks, a known civil rights activist and an inspiring person. Both Colvin and Smith soon became lost to history.

It was not until the 1990s that these two unsung teenage heroes received credit for their bravery. "They primed the pump," says Taylor Branch, author of a Pulitzer Prize-winning history of the civil rights era. "They were the first to stand up," agrees Rosa Parks. If you could write a tribute to these teenagers from the 1950s, what would you say?

CLOSE UP: Chapter 30

The Who, What, Where of History

1. **Who** was Jackie Robinson?
2. **Who** was George McLaurin?
3. **What** arguments did Thurgood Marshall use to show that segregation was harmful to African Americans?
4. **What** was the significance of *Brown v. Board of Education*?
5. **Where** were federal troops sent in 1957 to enforce school integration?
6. **What** did Rosa Parks do to help end segregation?
7. **What** is the SCLC?
8. **Who** was Martin Luther King, Jr.?
9. **What** was SNCC?
10. **What** was a freedom ride?

Making the Connection

1. What was the connection between the decisions in *Sweatt* v. *Painter* and *Brown* v. *Board of Education*?
2. What was the connection between Rosa Parks's arrest and the Montgomery bus boycott?
3. What was the connection between Bull Connor's actions and the growth of public support for the Civil Rights Movement?
4. What was the connection between Martin Luther King and Mohandas Gandhi?

Time Check

1. When was the *Brown* decision handed down?
2. When did the Montgomery bus boycott take place?

What Would You Have Done?

1. If you had been a student in Greensboro, North Carolina, during the time of the sit-ins, would you have participated in them? Explain.

2. Imagine that it is 1963 and you are a student in Birmingham. How would you explain to your parents your decision to join the demonstrations?

Thinking and Writing About History

1. Write a letter to the editor of a Little Rock, Arkansas, paper giving your reaction to the governor's use of National Guard troops to prevent school desegregation.

2. Write a brief paragraph explaining why you agree or disagree with King's idea of nonviolent resistance.

Building Skills: Sequencing

It would make studying history easier if no two events happened at the same time. Then, you could read about how one event or movement began and ended, and how another event or movement began. It doesn't work like that, of course. Just as you often are involved in more than one thing at a time, events, and movements overlap in all sorts of ways.

The time lines at the beginning of each unit and chapter of your textbook give you a very clear, visual picture of the dates of the main events you are studying. A writer gives you such a picture, too, with words such as *before, after, during, while, meanwhile, at the same time, then, the next year, first, soon, next,* and *later.* These can help you to keep straight the flow of events. These and other transition words and phrases help place events in chronological, or time, order.

Read the following sentences from your textbook. Then answer the questions that follow.

On June 5, 1950, Marshall faced the Court. . . . That same year, Marshall won another important victory in the case of Sweatt *v.* Painter. . . . *A key test came in Little Rock, Arkansas, in 1957. There, Governor Orval Faubus called in the state's national guard to prevent nine African American students from entering the city's public high school. . . . The following year, Faubus shut down Little Rock's high schools. . . . Congress passed the 1957 Civil Rights Act. . . . The Supreme Court also heard a new round of desegregation cases in the 1950s and 1960s. . . . On December 1, 1955, Rosa Parks boarded a bus in Montgomery, Alabama. . . . In late 1956, the Supreme Court found that segregation on Alabama buses was illegal. . . . In 1957, [Martin Luther King, Jr.] joined with nearly 100 other church leaders in founding the Southern Christian Leadership Conference. . . . In 1960, King moved the SCLC headquarters to Atlanta.*

1. List two transition words and phrases used in the reading above.

2. List three events mentioned in the extract that happened in 1957.

3. List in order three things that happened between 1949 and 1957.

4. Did the Supreme Court rule against segregation on Alabama buses before or after Faubus shut down Little Rock High School?

Florida students being bused to school

New Directions in the Civil Rights Movement

(1964–1975)

THINKING ABOUT THE CHAPTER

What changes took place in the Civil Rights Movement after 1963?

On December 10, 1964, Dr. Martin Luther King, Jr., stepped forward to receive the Nobel Peace Prize in Oslo, Norway. Only two other blacks had ever claimed the award. In 1950, Ralph Bunche, the U.S. representative to the United Nations, had accepted the prize for negotiating an Arab–Israeli armistice after the creation of Israel in 1948. In 1960, Albert Luthuli won the award for his nonviolent drive for racial equality in South Africa. The 35-year-old King was the 14th American and the youngest person ever to receive the prize.

King won the award for his use of nonviolent resistance in the struggle for racial equality. Yet, equality still eluded African Americans. King stressed this fact in his acceptance speech:

I accept the Nobel Prize for peace at a moment when 22 million Negroes of the United States are engaged in a creative battle to end the long night of racial injustice. I accept this award in behalf of a civil rights movement which is moving with determination and a majestic scorn for risk and danger to establish a reign of freedom and a rule of justice.

This chapter tells the story of the Civil Rights Movement and the risks and dangers it faced during the late 1960s and early 1970s.

1 A LONG, HOT SUMMER

▼ Why did members of SNCC develop more militant attitudes during the mid-1960s?

A new resolve among African Americans filled the air as the election of 1964 neared. Republican candidate Barry Goldwater had voted against the Civil Rights Act of 1964. In response, civil rights workers vowed to campaign for the election of Democrat Lyndon Johnson.

Members of the NAACP, CORE, SNCC, and the SCLC formed the Council of Federated Organizations (COFO) to lead a voter registration drive in the South. They called the campaign Freedom Summer.

COFO sent some 1,000 African American and white volunteers into Mississippi alone. The state beefed up its police force to greet the "invaders." The Ku Klux Klan held white-sheeted rallies to intimidate activists who dared to cross state lines. But the young people came anyway.

On August 4, 1964, FBI agents found the bodies of three volunteers, an African American and two white students, in a Mississippi swamp. Missing since June,

the three had been brutally murdered. The FBI charged 20 men with conspiracy, including 7 Klan members who were charged with the killings. After three years of trials and appeals, convictions were upheld and the accused went to jail.

A New Mood. The murders were only part of a summer of violence. COFO officials in Mississippi reported 65 fire-bombings, 3 shootings, and 80 mob attacks. To make the nation aware of the violence, SNCC sent members of the Mississippi Freedom Democratic Party (MFDP) to attend the Democratic National convention. They came prepared to argue that the MFDP, rather than white politicians who supported segregation, truly represented the Democratic party in Mississippi. Fannie Lou Hamer spoke for the MFDP in a televised speech before the convention.

▶▶ **AFRICAN AMERICAN VOTER REGISTRATION BEFORE AND AFTER THE VOTING RIGHTS ACT OF 1965**

State	Years		Percent Increase
	1960	1966	
Alabama	66,000	250,000	278.8
Arkansas	73,000	115,000	57.5
Florida	183,000	303,000	65.6
Georgia	180,000	300,000	66.7
Louisiana	159,000	243,000	52.8
Mississippi	22,000	175,000	695.4
N. Carolina	210,000	282,000	34.3
S. Carolina	58,000	191,000	229.3
Tennessee	185,000	225,000	21.6
Texas	227,000	400,000	76.2
Virginia	100,000	205,000	105.0

Source: U.S. Department of Commerce, Bureau of the Census, *Statistical Abstract of the United States: 1982-83,* 103rd Edition

What did the Voting Rights Act provide? Which two states showed the greatest increase in voter registration?

1964	Civil Rights Act of 1964
	Martin Luther King, Jr., wins Nobel Peace Prize.
	Freedom Summer
	Riots break out in Harlem.
1965	Malcolm X is assassinated.
	Selma–Montgomery March
	Voting Rights Act of 1965
	Riots break out in Watts.
1966	Meredith March Against Fear
	Black Panther Party is formed.
1967	King begins Poor People's Campaign.
1968	King's assassination is followed by riots in 125 cities.
	Kerner Commission report

Fannie Lou Hamer was the youngest of 20 children in a Mississippi sharecropping family. Hamer lost her job as a timekeeper on a Mississippi cotton plantation for registering to vote in 1962. The plantation owner had warned her: "Fannie Lou, . . . we are not ready for this in Mississippi." Replied Hamer: "I didn't register for you, I tried to register for myself." Mrs. Hamer left the plantation to join SNCC. She soon became involved in the voter registration drives of Freedom Summer.

In that June 1964 speech, Hamer told the nation what it was like to register African Americans in Mississippi. "I was beaten until I was exhausted," said Hamer of her treatment on one voter drive.

I began to scream, and one white man got up and began to beat me on the head and tell me to "hush." . . . All of this on account we wanted to register, to become first class citizens. [If] the Freedom Democratic Party is not seated now, I question America.

Support poured into the Democratic Convention for the MFDP. But Lyndon Johnson refused to allow the seating of MFDP delegates. He feared such a move would anger white Southern voters.

The MFDP and their young supporters in SNCC felt betrayed. In fall 1964, the leaders of SNCC, including Hamer, met in New York City to rethink their tactics. Here they met Malcolm X.

The Revival of Black Nationalism. The followers of Martin Luther King and the SCLC wanted an integrated society. The followers of Malcolm X preached black nationalism. They revived the spirit of African nationalism inspired by earlier leaders like Marcus Garvey (see Chapter 25). They sought unity among people of African descent throughout the world. They also looked to Africa for cultural models, including the practice of Islam.

In the 1950s and early 1960s, Malcolm X was a follower of Elijah Muhammad, head of a religious group known as the **Nation of Islam.** Muhammad had led the Black Muslims, as members were known, since the 1930s. He preached African American solidarity and said that advancement would come through self-help. Whites were "blue-eyed devils" to be avoided. Malcolm X became the most forceful spokesman of the Black Muslims. He saw in Muhammad's teaching a way to help African Americans gain control of their own destinies.

Born Malcolm Little in Omaha, Nebraska, about 1925, **Malcolm X** was one of 11 children. His father, an outspoken Baptist minister and a follower of Pan-Africanist Marcus Garvey, was harassed by the Ku Klux Klan. The family moved to Lansing, Michigan. Shortly afterward, Malcolm's father died in an accident in which Malcolm believed whites had played a part. The troubled youth moved to Boston and later to Harlem, where an attempted burglary led to a seven-year prison term. In jail, Malcolm converted to Islam.

After his release in 1952, Malcolm devoted all his energies to the Nation of Islam. In 1964, after a trip to Africa and Mecca, he split with Elijah Muhammad to build his own movement. Malcolm changed his name to Al Hajj Malik al-Shabazz. His experiences abroad also convinced him to drop his hatred of whites and focus instead on building Pan-African American pride.

Malcolm X urged young people to think of themselves as part of an African majority, not an African American minority. "There can be no black–white unity unless there is first black unity," explained Malcolm. "We cannot think of unity with others until after we have first united among ourselves." He left the door open to cooperation with whites. But he stressed self-determination and self-defense by African Americans. "We won't get our problems solved depending on the white man," he declared.

Malcolm X attracted a large following, including many members of SNCC. A good number of these followers, however, focused on Malcolm's earlier message of anger toward whites.

Explosion in the Cities. In the sweltering heat of July 1964, the anger that many African Americans felt about living conditions in the decaying inner cities erupted. The first major riot in the central section of a U.S. city began in Harlem on July 18. There, an incident between white police and African American teenagers left a 15-year-old student dead. Before the rioting ended, casualties had risen into

What were the goals of the Nation of Islam under Elijah Muhammad?

the hundreds. Riots soon followed in Brooklyn and Rochester, New York; in Chicago; in Philadelphia; and in several New Jersey cities.

President Johnson tried to stop future rioting by announcing a "War on Poverty" with increased federal spending on programs to aid the nation's neediest citizens. But his efforts seemed too little, too late. More trouble lay ahead in 1965.

Taking Another Look

1. What events led SNCC to seek representation for the MFDP at the Democratic Convention?

2. What was the Nation of Islam?

3. **Critical Thinking** How did the programs of Marcus Garvey influence Malcolm X?

2 YEAR OF RAGE: 1965
▼ What troubles faced the Civil Rights Movement in 1965?

Malcolm X began 1965 with a new slogan: "Ballots or bullets." He focused on winning political power for African Americans, and he warned whites of a revolution if African Americans did not win such power. Malcolm X also let it be known that he would cooperate with other civil rights groups—and even whites—to achieve his goal. But he stuck fast to the need for a revolution in U.S. society. Peaceful or violent—the method of change was up to whites, said Malcolm X.

In following this broader course of action, Malcolm X turned his back on the separatism of the Nation of Islam. Because of this, he believed loyal followers of Elijah Muhammad might soon kill him for what they saw as his treason.

On February 21, Malcolm X addressed a crowd of about 400 followers in the Audubon Ballroom in Harlem. Three men in the audience, who may have been Black Muslims, suddenly pulled out guns and opened fire. At 39, Malcolm X, with his new vision of African nationalism, died. His death dramatized the conflict that increasingly tore at both the Civil Rights Movement and U.S. society.

Selma. In one of his last speeches, Malcolm X had said, "If white people realize what the alternative is, perhaps they would be more willing to listen to Dr. King." But in the South, white officials were trying everything possible to crush the Civil Rights Movement. SNCC decided to focus its voter registration drives on one stronghold of white power— Selma, Alabama.

At the beginning of 1965, some 15,000 African Americans lived in Selma. Only 65 dared register to vote. After SNCC volunteers—African American and white— poured into town, there were soon more African Americans in Selma jails than on its voting rolls.

King and the SCLC decided to join the SNCC campaign in Selma. They believed violent white resistance to voter registration would win them nationwide sympathy. Such sympathy could translate into support for a federal voting rights bill.

King announced a 50-mile march from Selma to Montgomery to ask the Alabama governor to protect African American voters. The march began on Sunday, March 7. News reports that night interrupted television programs to show what looked like a war. Claiming the marchers were breaking the law, the police tore into the demonstrators. Tear gas swirled around marchers. Police mounted on horseback charged into the crowd swing-

Civil rights marchers assemble in front of the state capitol in Montgomery, Alabama. What was the purpose of the five-day march from Selma to Montgomery in 1965?

ing billy clubs. The sight moved thousands to fly to Selma and join the march.

On March 15, President Johnson appeared on nationwide television to announce his support of a voting rights bill. The bill would allow federal examiners to register African American voters wherever discrimination was practiced.

Two days later, a federal judge gave the SCLC and SNCC a permit to complete their march. Johnson ordered federal troops to protect them. On March 25, some 25,000 marchers strode into Montgomery in triumph, with Nobel Prize winners Martin Luther King and Ralph Bunche in the lead.

Watts. The Selma march had helped win a civil rights victory for African Americans. Yet just four days after the federal Voting Rights Act of 1965 took effect came a reminder of the economic ills that African Americans faced. The reminder came from the nation's cities, where poverty-stricken families in ghettoes struggled not so much to win civil rights but simply to survive.

On August 11, 1965, police in a Los Angeles ghetto known as Watts pulled over 21-year-old Marquette Frye for drunken driving. When African Ameri-

cans saw one of the police pull a gun, tempers boiled over. Charges of police brutality flew. By evening, thousands of people had filled the streets.

For six days, violence ripped through Watts. Cars and stores were burned. Snipers shot at police and firefighters. Roving bands of looters stripped pawnshops and gunshops of weapons and ammunition. Nearly $45 million in property was destroyed.

The nation had seen riots before, but the violence in Watts was shocking. The rioters' rage about their treatment in U.S. society had fueled the destruction in Watts. It also fueled a new movement that had begun in the voter registration drives in the South: Black Power.

Taking Another Look

1. How did Malcolm X's approach to achieving his goals change in 1965?

2. What was the purpose of the SNCC and SCLC campaign in Selma?

3. **Critical Thinking** One commentator called the Watts riot "a purposeful symbolic protest." Explain why you agree or disagree.

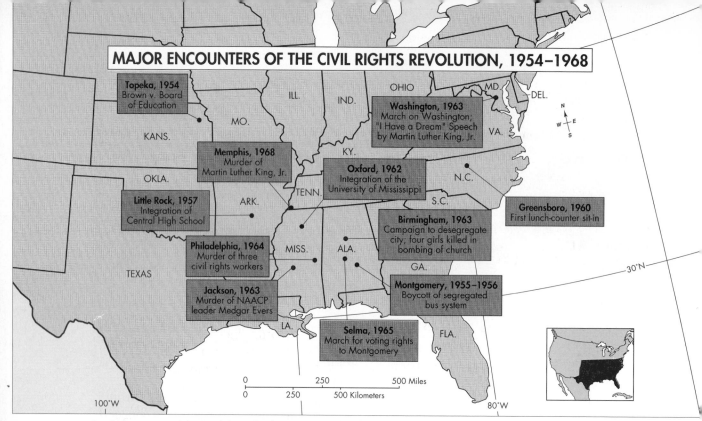

MAJOR ENCOUNTERS OF THE CIVIL RIGHTS REVOLUTION, 1954–1968

Topeka, 1954
Brown v. Board of Education

Washington, 1963
March on Washington; "I Have a Dream" Speech by Martin Luther King, Jr.

Memphis, 1968
Murder of Martin Luther King, Jr.

Oxford, 1962
Integration of the University of Mississippi

Little Rock, 1957
Integration of Central High School

Greensboro, 1960
First lunch-counter sit-in

Philadelphia, 1964
Murder of three civil rights workers

Birmingham, 1963
Campaign to desegregate city; four girls killed in bombing of church

Jackson, 1963
Murder of NAACP leader Medgar Evers

Montgomery, 1955–1956
Boycott of segregated bus system

Selma, 1965
March for voting rights to Montgomery

ILL. IND. OHIO MD. DEL. MO. KANS. KY. VA. OKLA. TENN. N.C. ARK. S.C. MISS. ALA. GA. TEXAS LA. FLA.

N W E S

30°N
100°W 80°W

0 250 500 Miles
0 250 500 Kilometers

In which two states did most of the civil rights encounters take place?

3 BLACK POWER

▼ How did the goals of the Black Power movement differ from those of Martin Luther King?

On June 5, 1966, James Meredith decided to march from Tennessee through his native Mississippi to encourage the state's nearly 450,000 African Americans to vote. He planned to walk 220 miles from Memphis to Jackson. That Sunday, a handful of people started the walk.

On the second day of the march, a white man armed with a 16-gauge shotgun fired a round of birdshot into Meredith. Other marchers hit the ground. As Meredith lay bleeding, he cried out: "Oh, my God, is anyone going to help me?"

March Against Fear. Help arrived in the form of Martin Luther King. Joining him were Stokely Carmichael, the newly elected leader of SNCC, and Floyd Mc-

Kissick of CORE. The three leaders decided to finish Meredith's march.

The new "Meredith March Against Fear" set out June 7. King tried to rally crowds with the traditional cry of "Freedom Now." Carmichael, however, used a new language of protest. "We've been saying freedom for six years," he told one crowd in Canton, "and we ain't got nothin'." He then used a new phrase: "What we're gonna start saying now is Black Power!" At this point, SNCC worker Willie Ricks jumped up on the stage next to Carmichael. He yelled out to the crowd: "What do you want?" The crowd yelled back: "Black Power!" "What you want?" he called out again. The crowd exploded. "Black Power! Black Power! Black Power!"

Carmichael defined **Black Power** as:

a call for black people . . . to unite, to recognize their heritage, to build a sense of community. It is a call for black people to begin to define their own goals, to lead their own organizations and to support these organizations.

Some African American leaders urged Carmichael to stop using the phrase. They felt it would frighten whites whose support they needed to get civil rights measures through Congress. Carmichael refused, and the split between SNCC and more conservative organizations, such as the NAACP, widened.

"Black Is Beautiful." Carmichael urged SNCC to stop recruiting whites into its ranks. He argued that African Americans did not want to be assimilated, or merged, into white society. They wanted to stand apart as their own people. A slogan took hold, "Black is beautiful," that went back to Marcus Garvey.

Carmichael's tough talk found an audience among many of the nation's African Americans. Frustrated by poverty and police brutality, these people embraced Carmichael's outspoken racial pride.

In October 1966, in Los Angeles, Bobby Seale and Huey Newton, founded a new militant political party—the **Black Panthers.** The Panthers demanded the right of African Americans to control their own communities. They asked the federal government to rebuild the ghettoes in repayment for the years African Americans had spent in slavery. They wanted African Americans freed from jail and re-tried by African American juries.

Not everyone knew about the Panthers' political platform. But nearly all recognized their dress: black trousers, black leather jackets, blue shirts, and black berets.

Groups of Panthers soon formed in other cities around the country. A white

backlash set in against all civil-rights groups, including the moderate SCLC.

King's Death. By 1967, Martin Luther King had come to believe that the nation's main enemy was economic injustice. Poverty, he said, bred violence. To end the violence, the nation needed to wipe out poverty. King therefore began building what he called the Poor People's Campaign.

King planned to start his campaign in April 1968 with a huge march on Washington. That spring, he traveled about the nation drumming up support. He visited Memphis, Tennessee, to lend support to a strike by the city's garbage workers.

On April 3, King addressed a Memphis crowd. "I've been to the mountaintop," said King, "[and] I've seen the glory." He then described his vision of a world free of poverty. "I may not get there with you," he continued, "but I want you to know that we as a people will get to the promised land."

The next afternoon, King stood on the balcony of his motel room, joking with members of his staff. Suddenly, a shot

Black Panther leader Huey Newton brings his militant message to thousands of young people in Philadelphia.

Two African American winners at the 1968 Olympic games give the black power salute in a gesture of protest.

rang out from a high-powered rifle. King fell, a bullet through his jaw. An hour later, the leader who dared dream of interracial peace lay dead.

King's assassin, James Earl Ray, was a white man. That fact alone set off a burst of fury among African Americans. President Johnson tried to calm passions. He addressed the nation, saying: "I ask every American citizen to reject the blind violence that has struck down Dr. King, who lived by nonviolence." Despite his plea, African American rage led to riots in 125 cities, leaving 45 people dead.

King was buried in an African American cemetery in Atlanta. His tombstone read: "Free at last, free at last, thank God almighty I'm free at last." The world that King left behind, however, was anything but free.

Taking Another Look

1. How did the Meredith March Against Fear reveal splits in the Civil Rights Movement?

2. How did the aims of the Black Power movement differ from King's?

3. **Critical Thinking** Imagine it is April 1968. You work on a major city newspaper. How would you word the obituary for Martin Luther King, Jr.?

4 NO TURNING BACK
▼ What did the Civil Rights Movement accomplish?

"Our nation is moving toward two societies, one black, one white—separate and unequal." That was the conclusion drawn by the Kerner Commission in 1968. At the request of President Johnson, the 11-member panel spent seven months looking into the causes of the riots of the 1960s. In a 200,000-word document, the commission pinned the riots on one main cause—prejudice.

Painful Legacies. The Kerner Commission report described a society with deep-rooted social and economic differences between African Americans and whites. These differences fueled the anger of the Black Power movement, which continued into the 1970s.

As the 1970s unfolded, the average income for African American families still lagged more than 50 percent behind that of white families. In 1975, unemployment among African Americans was 13.7 percent, while unemployment among whites stood at 7.6 percent.

African American activists in the late 1960s increasingly focused on improving conditions for what they called the nation's **underclass**—the group of people with incomes below subsistence level. This class included a large number of African Americans—particularly rural sharecroppers and urban ghetto dwellers. In 1970, only about 13 percent of all African

Americans belonged to the nation's middle class.

The Promise of Change. Although inequities existed in the 1970s, the Civil Rights Movement had achieved lasting advances. Supreme Court decisions had ended legal segregation and thrown open educational and public facilities to all. The Civil Rights Act of 1964 was the most sweeping civil rights legislation since Reconstruction. The Voting Rights Act of 1965 and the registration drives gave African Americans the political power to take part in shaping their futures.

Most important, the Civil Rights Movement exposed flaws within U.S. society. No longer could people pretend that the blessings of liberty fell equally on all citizens. Because of the Civil Rights Movement, people learned how to force political and social change. So successful was the movement that other groups adopted its tactics—women, the aged, the handicapped, and other ethnic groups.

As African Americans took greater control over their affairs, the number of African American elected officials increased. Between 1970 and 1975 alone, their numbers grew by 88 percent. For the first time, African American mayors took office in large cities, such as Atlanta, Detroit, Los Angeles, and Newark, New Jersey.

Building on these gains, African Americans broke new cultural ground in the United States. Students demanded—and won—courses in African American studies. African Americans adopted styles of dress or took names that expressed pride in their heritage. In the 1920s, Marcus Garvey had preached of the beauty of blackness. In the 1960s and 1970s, many African Americans came to share his idea, proudly proclaiming "Black is beautiful."

Taking Another Look

1. What obstacles faced African Americans as the 1970s began?

2. What did the Civil Rights Movement achieve?

3. **Critical Thinking** What do you consider the greatest achievement of the Civil Rights Movement?

LOOKING AHEAD

Toward the end of the 1960s, turmoil surrounding the Vietnam War increased in U.S. society. Stories of the war and the protests against it often pushed news of the Civil Rights Movement off the front pages. Yet, the importance of that movement to U.S. society cannot be overstated. In the words of African American politician Barbara Jordan:

> The civil rights movement called America to look at itself in a giant mirror. . . . Do the black people who were born on this soil, who are American citizens, do they really feel this is the land of opportunity, the land of the free. . . . America had to say no.

The demand for African American studies in schools and colleges spread during the Civil Rights Movement.

FOCUS ON

SINGING FOR FREEDOM

During the Civil Rights movement of the 1960s, African American and white demonstrators sang songs to inspire and unite them. One freedom song summed up the hopes of demonstrators — "We Shall Overcome." The promise of the title was repeated in the final stanza:

We shall overcome
We shall overcome
We shall overcome someday.
If in our hearts we do believe
We shall overcome someday.

Freedom songs grew out of the African American musical heritage. The songs echoed the spirituals sung by enslaved African Americans, the gospels and hymns of African American churches, and even a little Motown—the sound of African American pop singers of the 1960s. The melody of "We Shall Overcome" is based on the spiritual "I'll Be Alright." The words are based on a hymn, "I'll Overcome Someday." "We Shall Overcome" became the theme song of the Civil Rights Movement.

Both enslaved African Americans and the demonstrators of the 1960s sang about emancipation. Spirituals promised freedom from slavery, and freedom songs demanded an end to racial inequality.

The Who, What, Where of History

1. **What** was COFO?
2. **What** was the MFDP?
3. **Who** was Fannie Lou Hamer?
4. **Who** was Malcolm X?
5. **What** is the Nation of Islam?
6. **Who** was Stokely Carmichael?
7. **Where** did SNCC want to focus its voter registration drives in 1965?
8. **Who** founded the Black Panthers?
9. **What** is the underclass?
10. **What** was the Kerner Commission?

Making the Connection

1. What was the connection between the riots in Harlem in 1964 and Lyndon Johnson's War on Poverty?
2. What was the connection between the events in Selma, Alabama, in 1965 and the Voting Rights Act?
3. What was the connection between African American activists and the underclass?

Time Check

1. In what year was Martin Luther King assassinated?
2. In what year did the Kerner Commission report come out?
3. In what year was the Black Panther party formed?

What Would You Have Done?

Imagine that you are living in Los Angeles in fall 1966. A good friend announces he is thinking of joining the Black Panthers. He asks your opinion. How do you respond?

Thinking and Writing About History

Write a paragraph explaining which African American leader discussed in this chapter you think was the most effective spokesperson for the African American community.

Building Skills: Analyzing Oral History

Which would you rather do? Read a history book or a scholarly article about Malcolm X or talk to someone who knew him personally and heard him speak? By reading or listening to oral history, you can actually capture the experiences of people who lived through a historical period.

Oral history gives the atmosphere and mood of an event in much the same way that fiction does. Oral history is immediate and down-to-earth.

When you read or listen to oral history, however, you must remember that you are hearing one person's version of an event, sometimes years after it occurred. Look for generalizations and opinions. Take the point of view into consideration as you decide whether you accept everything or not.

Below are two quotations from a book of oral history called *Voices of Freedom*, edited by Henry Hampton and Steve Fayer. The quotations are both about Malcolm X. Read the quotations and on a separate sheet of paper, answer the questions that follow.

When [Malcolm X] talked that night . . . he was absolutely mesmerizing. He was brilliant. He was funny. He expressed the rage that all of us continued to feel at the slow pace of change in the country, but he did it in just the cleverest and funniest way you could imagine. I just remember laughing uncontrollably at some of the ways in which Malcolm would answer questions and put down whites who were trying to trick him at that point. So, he was a new outlet for the anger and the frustration. But he sure was smart.

—Marian Wright Edelman

Nowadays you might hear a lot of people talking about how they followed [Malcolm X] and so forth, but my perception at the time was that the large majority were frightened by the things Malcolm said. They were so extreme, it seemed, and so radical by comparison with what others were saying. But there were those who were . . . feeling that Malcolm was having the courage to say aloud, publicly, things which they had felt or which they wished somebody would say.

—Alex Haley

1. Does the quotation from Edelman give facts or opinions?

2. What quality of Malcolm X did Edelman find most appealing?

3. Does the quote from Haley give facts or opinions about the response to Malcolm X?

4. Write the phrase from Edelman's quotation and the one from Haley's quotation that express the same thought about Malcolm X.

5. Do you think that Edelman and Haley share the same opinion of Malcolm X? Explain.

John Wilkins (at right) and buddies in Vietnam

Marching Off to Vietnam

(1963–1982)

THINKING ABOUT THE CHAPTER

How did the Civil Rights Movement affect African Americans serving in Vietnam?

On the night of April 4, 1968, John Wilkins climbed into an army truck at Fort Sill, Oklahoma. Fresh out of basic training, the young African American from Beacon, New York, had expected to be shipped off to Vietnam. Instead, it looked as if his first tour of duty might be on U.S. soil. Wilkins and other members of the 82nd Airborne stood on alert, waiting for orders to put down the riots that broke out after the assassination of Martin Luther King. But the orders never came.

Later that April, Wilkins flew off to Fort Lewis, Washington. There, Wilkins and a couple of his buddies decided to see *The Green Berets,* a movie about the Vietnam War starring John Wayne. The film showed lots of heroics. But what Wilkins and his friends saw were the casualties. The teenagers knew that they would soon be facing real battles in a real war.

Still shaken by the movie, Wilkins left for Vietnam. He wore a heavy field jacket against the chilly Washington weather. Hours later, he stepped off the plane into the hot, humid air of Vietnam. Soon another flight carried him to a base deep in the country.

The next time Wilkins touched down, a wave of rocket fire greeted him. Someone barked out for the recruits to take cover. When the attack ended, Wilkins stared back at the plane. He saw troops loading the cargo bay with aluminum coffins. Battle-tested soldiers shouted out to the still-green troops, "Mr. Charlie's waiting for you." Mr. Charlie was the nickname for the Vietcong—the enemy Wilkins had come to fight. This chapter tells the story of what it was like for African Americans, such as Wilkins, to fight in Vietnam.

1 UNDER FIRE
▼ What role did African Americans play in Vietnam?

The war that Wilkins and other African Americans found themselves fighting in Vietnam demonstrated some of the changes the United States had undergone since World War II. Through the end of World War II, the vast majority of African Americans who fought in the nation's wars did so in segregated units. Toward the end of World War II, the number of integrated units slowly increased.

Korea. In 1948, President Truman issued an executive order to integrate the armed services. A commission that he had appointed recommended increased integration in all the armed forces. By 1949, the various branches of the service had begun to take action toward implementing that goal.

The move toward an integrated military got another boost in 1950. In that year, Communist North Korea invaded neighboring South Korea. The United States quickly entered the conflict on the side of South Korea. When the first U.S. combat troops arrived, fewer than 9 percent of the units were integrated. U.S. troops and their allies won early success, but late in 1950, the Communists launched a major attack.

Army commanders, desperate for men to hold back the enemy, began to integrate their fighting units rapidly. By August 1951, 30 percent of the fighting units in Korea were integrated. The enemy advance was stopped, and a later report concluded that the integration of African Americans into units had greatly aided U.S. efforts.

The Korean War ended in 1953. By the following year, the process of integration in the armed forces was complete. How this fully integrated military force would perform in combat would not be known until ten years later in another war in Asia, this time in Vietnam.

African Americans in Vietnam. Vietnam had been divided after World War II. By the early 1960s, rebels supported by the Communist government in North Vietnam were seeking to overthrow the U.S.-backed government of South Vietnam. The United States began to send military advisers to aid South Vietnam. By 1965, it was sending combat troops, large numbers of which were African Americans.

One U.S. magazine reporter studied the involvement of African Americans in

1965	First U.S. combat troops arrive in Vietnam.
1967	Muhammad Ali resists draft on religious grounds.
	Martin Luther King speaks out against Vietnam War.
1969	Vietnam Moratorium day
1973	Last U.S. troops leave Vietnam.
1975	Vietnam falls to Communists.
1982	Vietnam Veterans Memorial is dedicated.

the war. The reporter offered the following evaluation:

> For the first time in the nation's military history, its Negro fighting men are fully integrated in combat. . . . In the unpredictable search-and-destroy missions, . . . on the carrier decks and in the gun mounts of the Seventh Fleet offshore, in the cockpits of helicopters and fighter-bombers, . . . the American Negro is winning—indeed has won—a black badge of courage that his nation must forever honor.

The acts of many individual African Americans helped the reporter reach this conclusion. Army nurse 1st Lieutenant Dorothy Johnson cared for the wounded while pinned down under mortar fire. Air Force Major James T. Boddie, Jr., flew more than 153 missions over North and South Vietnam in seven months. Milton Olive threw his body over a live grenade to save his squad-mates.

Back in the United States, dissent over the Vietnam War was tearing the nation apart. But in Vietnam, many African Americans supported the war. In 1967, African Americans reenlisted at three times the rate of whites. Some reenlisted to avoid high unemployment back home, but others saw Vietnam as a chance to build a career in the integrated military. Still others viewed military service as a patriotic duty.

Such soldiers looked down on African Americans and whites who resisted the draft for whatever reason. The most controversial **conscientious objector** case involved boxer Muhammad Ali.

> **Muhammad Ali** was born Cassius Marcellus Clay in 1942 in Louisville, Kentucky. As a teenager, Clay won the light heavyweight boxing title at the 1960 Olympics. He turned professional and took the world heavyweight championship from Sonny Liston in 1964. That same year, Clay converted to Islam, joined the Nation of Islam, and changed his name to Muhammad Ali.
>
> In 1967, Ali was drafted, but he refused to serve. The war, said Ali, violated his Muslim faith. He said that the real enemy was in U.S. society. Ali's decision cost him a $10,000 fine, a five-year jail sentence, and his boxing title. In 1971, the Supreme Court overturned the conviction, and Ali went on to win the heavyweight title two more times.

In Vietnam, some soldiers criticized Ali's decision. "He gave up being a man when he decided against getting inducted," said one. However, many African Americans applauded Ali's courage. The debate over Ali revealed a widening split among African Americans, and the nation in general, over the war.

Taking Another Look

1. How did African American involvement in Vietnam differ from that in earlier wars?

2. Why did Muhammad Ali refuse to fight in Vietnam?

3. **Critical Thinking** One African American veteran said of his experience in Vietnam, "Why should I come over here when some of the South Vietnamese live better than my people in the world?" Explain.

2 WAR AND PROTEST

▼ Why did many African Americans oppose the Vietnam War in the late 1960s?

In 1967, Martin Luther King, Jr., spoke out to protest the Vietnam War. "The Great Society has been shot down on the battlefields of Vietnam," exclaimed King. "It would be very inconsistent for me to teach and preach nonviolence in this situation [the Civil Rights Movement] and then applaud violence . . . in this war."

Growing Opposition. Leaders of CORE and SNCC joined King in opposing the war. They pointed out that although African Americans made up only about 10 percent of the nation's population, they accounted for 20 percent of the draftees fighting in Vietnam. African Americans there represented only 5 percent of the commanding officers. Moreover, in the first 11 months of 1966 alone, African Americans accounted for nearly 22.4 percent of combat deaths.

Some African Americans used these figures to argue against the war. "I don't trust a black dude who stays in the Army," said one supporter of Black Power. "I don't see why a brother would live with this prejudice for more than two or three years."

The war had other costs for African Americans as well. By 1967, the federal government was spending $24 billion a year on the war. Many African Americans believed that such sums would be better

An integrated artillery unit in Vietnam bombards the enemy. Why did many African Americans turn against the Vietnam War?

spent on improving conditions in the cities. King complained:

> I watched the [Great Society] poverty program broken . . . and I knew that America would never invest the necessary funds or energies in rehabilitation of its poor. So long as adventures like Vietnam continued to draw men and skills and money.

Racial Turmoil Overseas.
A Gallup Poll taken in late 1968 reported that some 70 percent of African Americans on the home front opposed the war. A growing number of African Americans drafted after the 1968 demonstrations opposed it, as well. Many of these draftees carried the Black Power movement with them to Vietnam. Local draft boards sometimes unintentionally aided the growth of the Black power movement among troops in Vietnam. They often drafted African Americans who were active in the Civil Rights Movement as a way of removing them from their communities.

Stirrings of racial discontent soon appeared in Vietnam. Many African Americans wore their hair Afro-style and greeted each other with the Black Power handshake or a closed-fist salute. The gestures silently sent a message of unity.

By late 1968, many African American soldiers preferred to spend their free time apart from white enlistees. They took their passes in the area called Soulsville—the self-segregated section of Saigon, capital of South Vietnam. In "soul kitchens" there, soldiers ate turnip greens, barbecued ribs, chitlins, or other food that reminded them of home, while jukeboxes played Motown songs.

Racial tensions grew. In spring 1968, Staff Sergeant Clide Brown woke up one night to find Confederate flags and burning crosses outside his tent. By 1969, hate-filled racial graffiti written by both African Americans and whites became a common sight. Fights broke out at military bases throughout Vietnam.

Holding Ranks.
The Vietcong tried to take advantage of the racial tensions. Leaflets pinned to bodies read: "Black GIs in the U.S. Army. Twenty million of your fellow countrymen in the U.S.A. are being abused, oppressed, exploited, manhandled, murdered by racist authorities." Radio stations in Hanoi, capital of North Vietnam, boomed out a similar message: Defect to our side.

But the Vietcong plan didn't work. African American GIs refused to buy into the propaganda. "I've seen enough of their brutality," explained one medic, "to know that the V.C. [Vietcong] draws no color line in their killing . . . of American soldiers—black or white." By the end of the 1960s, not a single African American had crossed over to the enemy.

Taking Another Look

1. Why did some civil rights leaders feel African Americans carried an unfair burden in the Vietnam War?

2. What effect did the war have on African Americans at home?

3. **Critical Thinking** Study the table on page 367. What generalizations can you form about African American involvement in the nation's wars?

3 COMING HOME
▼ What difficulties faced African American veterans after Vietnam?

In late summer 1969, John Wilkins was going home. He walked straight off his base and onto a plane, still wearing his raggedy infantry fatigues. Wilkins flew to New Jersey, where he and other returning veterans got new uniforms and any medals they had earned.

Wilkins then took a 30-day leave and headed home to his native Beacon, New York. Everything seemed different now. Wilkins felt out of touch with his once-familiar world.

Moratorium Day. When his leave ended, the Army assigned Wilkins to Fort Meade, Maryland, with the 6th Armored Cavalry. That October, Wilkins pulled riot duty in Washington, D.C. Armed with gas masks, rifles, and bayonets, his unit headed into the nation's capital to stand guard over a peace demonstration. One of the leaders of the march, Coretta Scott King, demanded that President Johnson "bring the boys home and bring them home now."

The march formed part of a nationwide Vietnam Moratorium—a day of reflection and protest over the war. Some protesters spat on the soldiers. Others shook their hands and gave them peace medals. Home little more than a month, Wilkins felt conflicting emotions about the demonstration:

> There I was in Vietnam with weapons turned against one people. Then I come home, and I watch weapons turned against my own people. It was all so confusing. I was angry because I couldn't figure it all out.

The Vietnam Syndrome. A lot of returning veterans felt as Wilkins did. With civil rights leaders and students loudly protesting the war, they grew silent. Yet, privately, they supported the troops still in Vietnam. "I knew what those guys were going through," said Wilkins. "Like me, most didn't care about politics. Their thing was getting home—getting home alive."

The silence, the anger, the confusion—some people called this widespread reac-

There were many African Americans among those Americans who wanted the United States to pull out of the Vietnam War. Here they take part in a Moratorium Day protest in 1969 in Washington, D.C.

tion among veterans the Vietnam Syndrome. Many had marched off to war expecting to fight clear-cut battles. Instead, they slogged through steamy jungles and flooded rice paddies searching for an enemy that could easily fade into the general population.

Relatively few GIs fought in hand-to-hand combat with the Vietcong. But some 76 percent came under enemy rocket fire, and about 56 percent were wounded.

Many soldiers expected to return home heroes. They had honored their country's call to duty and had fought to stop the spread of communism. But the country was not yet prepared to honor their sacrifices. Debate raged over the war even after the last United States troops left Vietnam on March 29, 1973.

The Long Process of Healing.
South Vietnam fell to the Communists in 1975. According to a 1980 poll by the Veterans Administration, more than 71 percent of all veterans—African American and white—still expressed pride over their service. But some 82 percent felt their government had let them down by not fighting an all-out war. They also felt let down by the lack of recognition by their country. It took until November 11, 1982, and the dedication of the Vietnam Veterans Memorial in Washington, D.C., for the nation to honor its Vietnam veterans formally.

Public recognition of their service did not solve the problems Vietnam vets faced. Many suffered from depression. Some battled with drug and alcohol abuse. One of the Vietcong's not-so-secret weapons had been a ready supply of cheap drugs to undermine GIs' fighting ability. Unlike the soldiers who fought in World War II, Vietnam vets had a hard time find-

The names of over 58,000 Americans who died in the war are carved on the granite walls of the Vietnam Veterans Memorial in Washington, D.C.

AFRICAN AMERICANS IN U.S. WARS

War (years)	Numbers Who Served	Other Information
American Revolution (1775-1781)	5,000 in the Continental Army	fought in integrated units
Civil War (1861-1865)	386,000 (Union Army)	38,000 died
World War I (1917-1918)	367,000	100,000 served in France
World War II (1941-1945)	1,000,000	6,000 officers; 4,000 women
Vietnam War (1965-1974)	274,937	5,681 killed in combat
Gulf War (1990-1991)	132,300	24.5% of total troops

Source: Figures for the Gulf War from the Directorate of Defense Information, U.S. Secretary of Defense; for other wars, *World Almanac*, 1991

What percentage of those who fought in the Gulf War were African American?

ing their own way back into school or the job market.

A Changed Military. Despite the problems many African American veterans faced after the war, their service during the war brought far-reaching changes to the U.S. military. African American enrollment at all the service academies increased. In 1973, 79 African Americans entered West Point, up from the 9 who attended in 1968. In 1973, 46 African American cadets joined the first-year class at the Air Force Academy, compared with none in 1963. Also in 1973, the Naval Academy counted 150 African Americans among its students.

African Americans broke into the top ranks of the military in significant num-

bers, too. In 1969, the army promoted 27 African Americans to colonel. By 1971, the army claimed 12 African American generals. In 1971, the navy made Samuel L. Gravely, Jr., the first African American admiral in U.S. naval history.

The scope of these changes became clear when the nation entered its next major war, against Iraq in 1991. At that time, the highest position in the nation's armed forces, Chairman of the Joint Chiefs of Staff, was held by General Colin Powell, an African American.

Taking Another Look

1. What difficulties did African American veterans face when they came home?

2. How did African American service in Vietnam reshape the United States military?

3. **Critical Thinking** Some African Americans have said Vietnam was the second front of the war for civil rights. Do you agree? Explain.

LOOKING AHEAD

African Americans have performed military service for their nation since the American Revolution. But the African Americans who came home from Vietnam arrived in the midst of a civil rights revolution. "I don't know whether I would march if I became a civilian again," one soldier said in 1967. "But nobody is going to shove me around." This was the attitude that many African American veterans brought home with them. Together with the civil rights leaders of the 1960s, they helped produce a new United States— one that would never again be the same for African Americans or whites.

FOCUS ON REMEMBERING VIETNAM

When we got to the memorial, I grabbed his hand. Like brothers do. . . . We looked for one name on the memorial. Louis. We found it, and I called his mother. I told her it was nice, and she said she might be able to come see it one day.

This is how one African American ex-soldier described his reaction to visiting "the Wall"—the Vietnam Veterans Memorial in Washington, D.C.

Like the war itself, the Vietnam Veterans Memorial generated controversy. First, people argued over its funding, and then they argued over its design. In the end, some 650,000 people contributed to the cost of creating the Wall, which was designed by Asian American Maya Ying Lin.

Lin's design was selected from among many submitted in a contest. Some thought her plan for a black granite wall was too stark, too cold. However, the memorial committee foresaw that the Wall—with the names of the more than 58,000 who died in Vietnam inscribed on it—would be a powerful monument.

Over 5,600 African Americans were killed in Vietnam. Their names are among those inscribed on the Wall. Many who visit the Wall find a chance to remember and to heal.

The Who, What, Where of History

1. **Who** were the Vietcong?
2. **Where** was Soulsville?
3. **Where** is Hanoi?
4. **Who** is Muhammad Ali?
5. **Who** is Samuel L. Gravely, Jr.?
6. **Who** is Colin Powell?

Making the Connection

1. What was the connection between government spending on the Vietnam War and Great Society programs?
2. What was the connection between public protests over the Vietnam War and problems that many Vietnam veterans experienced after the war?

Time Check

1. In what years did the Korean War take place?
2. When did the first U.S. combat troops arrive in Vietnam?
3. In what year did South Vietnam fall to the Communists?
4. When was the Vietnam Veterans Memorial dedicated?

What Would You Have Done?

1. If you had been alive during the Vietnam years, would you have supported the U.S. government's actions in Vietnam, or would you have joined the protesters against the war? Explain.
2. If you had been a 19-year-old African American in 1967, would you have enlisted in the army? Explain.

Thinking and Writing About History

Imagine it is the year 1967. Write a newspaper editorial either supporting or criticizing Muhammad Ali's refusal to fight in the Vietnam War.

Building Skills: Interpreting a Newspaper Article

On a day-to-day basis, newspaper articles and radio and television newscasts and news bulletins provide most of us with all we know about current events. Newspaper articles provide a great supply of primary source material for the historian. However, there are a few things to keep in mind when you refer to newspaper material. Most newspaper reporters write to a strict style. They stick to the basic facts of the story without analyzing them, comparing the story to events of the past, interpreting the story, or stating an opinion about it.

Read the following article that appeared on the front page of the *New York Times* on April 6, 1968. Then answer the questions that follow.

Khesanh, South Vietnam—The 76-day North Vietnamese siege of the Marine base at Khesanh was officially declared lifted today.

United States marines and helicopter-borne Army troops today pushed toward what was described as North Vietnamese regimental headquarters south of the base.

The 20,000-man relief column reached the base and then fanned out on three sides in search of the vanishing enemy soldiers. Army helicopter units entered the base.

The sweep could take the Americans all the way to the Laotian border, less than 10 miles away, in the effort to root out the 7,000 men said to remain in the enemy force once estimated at 20,000. North Vietnam uses Laos as a staging area for attacks along South Vietnam's borders.

The United States command said that helicopter gunships of the First Cavalry Division (Airmobile), crisscrossing the skies ahead of the ground troops, killed 50 North Vietnamese late yesterday near the town of Khesanh, which is two miles south of the base.

Earlier, United States troops fought about 150 enemy soldiers four miles east of the town. Nine enemy soldiers and one American were reported killed.

1. Write one sentence explaining what the article says happened at Khesanh on April 6, 1968.

2. What does the reporter presume the reader already knows about the conflict in Vietnam?

3. Does the article tell you anything about the opinions of the journalist who wrote it? Explain.

4. **a.** What is one source for some of the information contained in the article?
   b. Might that source be biased in any way? Explain.

5. What would you like to know about the siege at Khesanh that is not in the article?

UNIT 10

African American youth moving forward

BUILDING A NEW AMERICA

(1965–Present)

Wall mural showing community spirit

Volunteers painting a neighbor's house

▲ ▲ ▲ ▲

THE BIG PICTURE

▼ ▼ ▼ ▼

An African American Speaks

We have a wonderful history behind us. . . . It reads like the history of a people in a heroic age. . . . We're going back to that beautiful history and it is going to inspire us to great achievements.

—Carter G. Woodson, Historian

The Civil Rights Movement of the 1950s and 1960s changed the United States forever. No longer would African Americans be forced by law to sit in separate sections of trains and buses. No longer would they be required to eat in separate restaurants or sleep in separate hotels. No longer would "Whites Only" signs bar them from the mainstream of American life.

Armed with new laws and rights, African Americans set out in the late 1900s to realize the promise of equality. After 1968, they entered the U.S. Congress and other political offices in record numbers. In the 1970s and 1980s, two African Americans, Shirley Chisholm and Jesse Jackson, made bids for the presidency. In 1996, Americans across the nation tried to convince retired General Colin L. Powell to step forward as a presidential candidate.

Politics was not the only area of progress for African Americans. They graduated from high schools, colleges, and professional schools in record numbers. After graduation, they increasingly took jobs that once routinely went to white people.

A new generation of pioneers proved once more the courage and diverse talents of the African American people. In 1983,

Guion S. Bluford, Jr., became the first African American in space. In 1988 and 1992, Jackie Joyner-Kersee became the first woman to win back-to-back Olympic gold medals in the heptathalon. In 1993, Toni Morrison became the first African American to win the Nobel Prize in Literature. In 1997, Kenneth I. Chenault became president of American Express— the highest-ranking African American executive in a major U.S. corporation.

The list of achievements by African Americans in areas once dominated by whites fills the pages of recent U.S. history. The new power of these movers and shakers has helped African Americans to tackle the tough issues that still trouble them and the nation.

One of the most serious challenges for African Americans has been a change in attitudes toward "big government." In many cases, this has meant a reaction against the policies and programs of the federal government.

Changing Attitudes on Government. The federal government had grown greatly since the 1930s. Efforts to overcome the Great Depression, fighting in World War II and the Korean War, and the struggle against communism known as the Cold War contributed to this growth. By the 1960s, there were more federal programs, with more federal employees, costing more in taxpayer dollars, and touching more parts of average citizens' lives.

A reaction against the size and activity of government grew, in large part, out of the

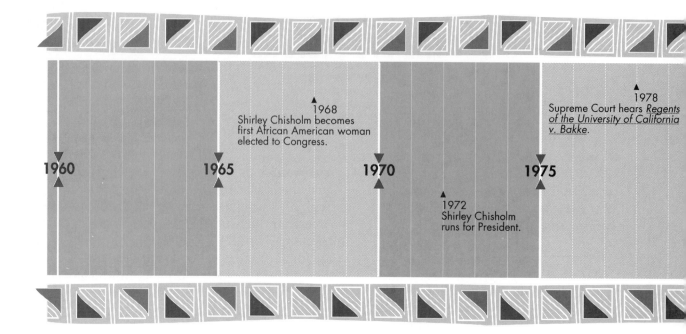

1960

1965

1968
Shirley Chisholm becomes
first African American woman
elected to Congress.

1970

1972
Shirley Chisholm
runs for President.

1975

1978
Supreme Court hears *Regents
of the University of California
v. Bakke*.

turmoil of the 1960s. The Vietnam War, the demonstrations against it, and the disturbances in the cities combined in many people's minds to form a picture of a society coming apart.

In 1968, Republican candidate Richard M. Nixon campaigned on a platform of "law and order." He appealed to Americans who felt left out of the social movements of the 1960s, such as Vietnam protests and the Civil Rights Movement.

Nixon won the presidency in 1968 in a closely contested election. Some of the steps that he then took as President slowed down progress on civil rights. For example, he kept government officials from taking action against school districts that had not desegregated. He also cut back on the money for some of Lyndon Johnson's Great Society programs. He turned other programs over to the states, which were allowed to continue them—or not.

Despite Nixon's intentions, the power of the federal government grew while he was President. Nixon especially increased the power of the presidency. For example, he did not get Congress's approval when he widened the Vietnam War by ordering the secret bombing of Cambodia. He also used the powers of federal agencies to gather information on his political "enemies."

In 1973 and 1974, a series of investigations by Congress revealed that many of Nixon's associates had been involved in planning and then in covering up a break-in at the offices of the Democratic National Committee. Nixon had been involved in the cover-up, which took place during and after the 1972 election campaign. As a result of this so-called "Watergate scandal," named after the building where the break-in had occurred, Richard Nixon resigned from the presidency in 1974.

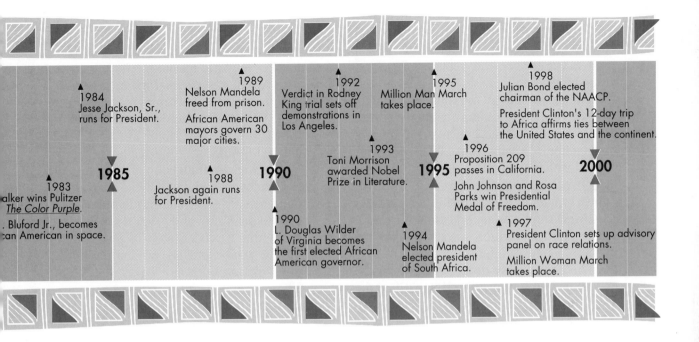

1983
alker wins Pulitzer
The Color Purple.

. Bluford Jr., becomes
:an American in space.

1984
Jesse Jackson, Sr.,
runs for President.

1985

1989
Nelson Mandela
freed from prison.

African American
mayors govern 30
major cities.

1988
Jackson again runs
for President.

1990

1990
L. Douglas Wilder
of Virginia becomes
the first elected African
American governor.

1992
Verdict in Rodney
King trial sets off
demonstrations in
Los Angeles.

1993
Toni Morrison
awarded Nobel
Prize in Literature.

1994
Nelson Mandela
elected president
of South Africa.

1995
Million Man March
takes place.

1995

1996
Proposition 209
passes in California.

John Johnson and Rosa
Parks win Presidential
Medal of Freedom.

1997
President Clinton sets up advisory
panel on race relations.

Million Woman March
takes place.

1998
Julian Bond elected
chairman of the NAACP.

President Clinton's 12-day trip
to Africa affirms ties between
the United States and the continent.

2000

Restoring Confidence. The four presidents who followed Nixon—Gerald Ford, Jimmy Carter, Ronald Reagan, and George Bush—faced a nation that distrusted government. With the exception of Reagan, Americans did not reelect these leaders to office. Even Reagan failed to restore confidence. His failed promise to deliver a balanced budget and his support for right-wing governments left many Americans uneasy.

When George Bush entered office, he inherited the Reagan legacy—a huge national debt and slashed social welfare programs. Despite the collapse of the Soviet Union in 1990 and the U.S. triumph in the Persian Gulf War in 1991, voters failed to return Bush to office.

In 1992 and again in 1996, voters elected Bill Clinton to office. Clinton was the first President born in the post-World War II era. He looked for inspiration to the reform movements of the 1960s. After an initial burst of optimism, however, Clinton faced the same challenges as other Presidents who followed John F. Kennedy—measuring up to the nation's sense of idealism and convincing voters that he could heal the nation's divisions.

New Voices on the Supreme Court. For large numbers of African Americans, changes in the Supreme Court in the late 1900s became a major concern. One of Nixon's campaign promises had been to fill vacancies on the Court with conservative justices who would counter activists such as the former civil rights lawyer Thurgood Marshall. By the time Nixon left office, he had appointed four of the nine members of the Court.

Presidents Reagan and Bush filled other slots with conservative justices. Reagan added Sandra Day O'Connor, the first woman member of the Court, and two

373

other conservative members. Bush made two more conservative appointments. One included Clarence Thomas, the African American justice who replaced Thurgood Marshall.

The appointment of Thomas caused a great outcry among many African Americans. Thomas had made public his opposition to many affirmative action and social welfare programs. He felt these policies went beyond the powers given to the government by the Constitution. He also believed they stamped African Americans and other minorities with what Thomas called "a label of inferiority."

The controversy over Thomas exploded when law professor Anita Hill testified during Senate confirmation hearings for Thomas that he had sexually harassed her when she worked for him. Thomas strongly denied the charges. Thomas eventually won approval by a final vote of 52 to 48.

Republican appointments ended the era of judicial activism that had begun during the presidencies of Franklin Roosevelt and the Democrats who followed him. The appointments became significant, as you will see in Chapters 33 and 34, when the Court ruled on cases that grew out of the application of the Civil Rights Act of 1964 and the Voting Rights Act of 1965.

Seeking Economic Stability. Attacks on social welfare programs came at a time of increased economic turmoil within the United States. The costs of the Vietnam War and new social welfare programs drove up federal spending as well as the federal debt.

Then in 1973 and again in 1979, developments in the Middle East caused sharp rises in the cost of oil. The resulting increased costs of gasoline, diesel fuel, and heating oil spurred **inflation.** Inflation is a general increase in prices over a period of time. At the same time, foreign industries, particularly in Germany and Japan, were becoming strong competitors with U.S. industries in world markets.

The result was **recession,** or a decline in production and employment. Plants closed, people lost their jobs, and greater competition existed for the jobs that remained. African Americans of both sexes, as well as white women, now sought jobs that once had been held mainly by white males. Meanwhile, immigrants from Spanish-speaking and Asian countries entered the United States in large numbers. These new arrivals swelled the ranks of job seekers.

The increase in job seekers came at a time when technological advances were causing huge upheavals in the U.S. Fewer unskilled workers were needed than in the past. Many skilled workers also found that their jobs were becoming outdated by the rapid changes in technology.

By the 1990s, the cost of industrial development rose as U.S. companies sought to modernize and compete with foreign companies. To cut expenses, they **downsized,** or reduced the number of employees on their payrolls. Unskilled workers, workers with outdated skills, and even high-salaried executives lost their jobs.

As Americans of all backgrounds felt economically squeezed, a backlash grew against programs funded by tax dollars. This led to the welfare-to-work reform of 1996. This program, a compromise between a conservative Congress and Bill Clinton, a President, linked time and work requirements to welfare.

Many Americans feared that these changes in government policy would increase poverty. They pointed out that the burdens of the reduced job market and government cutbacks fell most heavily on nonwhites and the disadvantaged.

Robots are used in automobile and truck assembly plants like this one in Tennessee. What effects do you think the use of robots has on the employment of factory workers?

Reviving the Dream. African Americans have a long history of surviving adversity. The Civil Rights Movement has taught African Americans important lessons. They know how to organize to bring about change. They have the votes and the economic clout to make government listen to them. African Americans, for example, helped force the government to take a stand against the racial polices of South Africa.

African Americans also know how to work outside of government to promote change. As Shirley Chisholm once told a crowd of her supporters, "The law cannot do it for us. *We must do it for ourselves!*"

In the 1990s, African Americans did not wait for the government to solve pressing problems. A wide and varied number of African American organizations have sought ways to relieve the grinding poverty in the inner cities and the under-education of African American youth. Unit 10 traces efforts to bring about change and to celebrate the living heritage that has shaped and continues to shape the African American people.

Taking Another Look

1. How did some of Richard Nixon's policies affect the nation's progress on civil rights?

2. What economic problems have worsened the impact of cutbacks in social welfare programs?

3. **Critical Thinking** List two policies important to African Americans that you think should be part of a presidential platform in the next election. Explain.

Chuck Burris, mayor of the city of Stone Mountain, Georgia

A Greater Voice in Politics

(1965–Present)

THINKING ABOUT THE CHAPTER

How have African Americans increased their influence on U.S. politics?

"There's a new Klan in Stone Mountain," declared Chuck E. Burris in November 1997, "only it's spelled with a C: c-l-a-n, citizens living as neighbors." The 46-year-old computer consultant had just claimed victory as the first African American mayor of Stone Mountain, Georgia, a city about 16 miles east of Atlanta. The 20th-century version of the Ku Klux Klan was born in Stone Mountain. The Klan, driven underground in the 1870s by federal laws, resurfaced in 1915 when Klan members held a meeting in Stone Mountain. Through much of the 1900s, Klan members used rallies there to make poisonous racial speeches aimed at African Americans and their supporters. At night, they stood around the Klan's blazing symbol of hatred—a huge burning cross.

Dr. Martin Luther King, Jr., included Stone Mountain in his 1963 "I Have a Dream" speech. "Let freedom ring from Stone Mountain of Georgia," cried King. More than 30 years later, Burris fulfilled this part of King's dream.

As a 3-year-old child, Burris had watched a cross burn in his family's front yard. Then on January 6, 1998, Burris stepped forward to take the oath of office as mayor of a town that once lit these crosses. Thurbert Baker, the first African American attorney general of Georgia, read the oath. The election, said one citizen of Stone Mountain, left the Klan "all dressed up with nowhere to go." Chapter 34 evaluates the many other political gains that African Americans have achieved since the late 1960s.

1 INTO THE HALLS OF POWER

▼ How have gains in African American voting rights changed government in the United States?

When Jesse Jackson, Jr., was born in 1965, his father was dodging billy clubs and tear gas canisters in the 50-mile (80-kilometer) march from Selma to Montgomery, the capital of Alabama. In 1995, at age 30, Jackson, Jr., won election to the House of Representatives from Chicago's 2nd District. After his victory, he repeated advice given to him by his father, Jesse Jackson, Sr.

> Both tears and sweat are wet and salty, but they win with different results. Tears get you sympathy; sweat will bring you change.

The sweat of the civil rights leaders of the 1950s and 1960s helped lead to a record number of African Americans in government during the closing years of the 20th century. The movement into government had begun, in large part, with the passage of the Voting Rights Act of 1965. This act increased African American voter registration dramatically.

A Time of Mixed Gains. The 1968 elections marked a turning point in U.S. history. That year, African Americans won ten seats in Congress—the highest number since Reconstruction. In 1972, Shirley Chisholm, one of the new faces in Congress, announced that she would be a candidate for President. She won enough delegates in state primaries to put her name on the first ballot at the Democratic National Convention. Chisholm's campaign raised new questions in the minds of many: Why not an African American or a woman for President?

By 1973, African Americans had increased their presence in government sharply. That year, African American mayors controlled governments in a number of Southern towns and cities and in major cities across the nation, such as New Orleans, Detroit, Los Angeles, Cleveland, and Newark. More than 200 African

African Americans campaigned vigorously for a national holiday in honor of Martin Luther King, Jr.

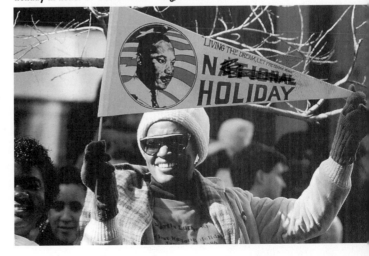

Americans sat in 37 state assemblies. Sixteen held seats in Congress—nearly double the 1968 number. In 1971, African Americans in the House formed the **Congressional Black Caucus** to address African American concerns and to work for legislation that would benefit African Americans and other minorities.

Despite such gains, African Americans still faced an uphill battle to win their fair share of government posts. By mid-1975, they held only 3,503 of the more than 500,000 elective offices in the nation.

The Rainbow Coalition. Armed with the vote, African Americans flexed their political muscle in the 1980s. The decade opened with a stepped-up campaign to make the birthday of Martin Luther King, Jr., a national holiday. President Ronald Reagan offered little support for the idea, but he finally bowed to pressure and approved the holiday in 1983 (see Focus On, page 390).

Reagan's act came too late to win many African Americans over to his side. He had favored sharp cutbacks in too many social welfare programs that benefited minorities to win their support. African Americans searched for a candidate more to their liking. In 1983, they found their candidate in the Reverend Jesse Jackson.

Jesse Jackson was born in Greenville, South Carolina, in 1941. He studied at North Carolina Agricultural and Technical University and later attended the Chicago Theological Seminary. In the 1960s, Jackson became a Baptist minister and a close aide to Dr. Martin Luther King, Jr., in the Southern Christian Leadership Conference (SCLC). Under King's direction, Jackson organized Operation Bread Basket in 1966, a program in Chicago to help expand educational and job opportunities for African Americans. In 1971, Jackson left SCLC and founded People United to Save Humanity (PUSH). He served as its president until 1983. Operation PUSH soon claimed 80,000 members. This thrust Jackson into the national spotlight. By the 1980s, Jackson had pressured a number of major businesses to open their doors to African Americans.

Jackson used his great popularity among African Americans to make a run for the presidency. He told African Americans that they had the political power to make a difference in the United States. "Hands that picked cotton in 1884," said Jackson, "will pick the President in 1984."

Jackson's political appeal was not limited to African Americans. He called his followers the Rainbow Coalition. In a speech at the Democratic National Convention, Jackson explained what this meant:

> Our flag is red, white, and blue, but our nation is a rainbow—red, yellow, brown, black, and white. . . . America is not like a blanket—one piece of unbroken cloth, the same color, the same texture, the same size. America is more like a quilt—many patches, many pieces, many colors, many sizes, all woven and held together by a common thread.

Jackson's speech rocked the convention. One governor said, "If you are a human being and weren't affected by what you just heard, you may be beyond redemption." Still, Jackson had entered the Democratic

►► AFRICAN AMERICAN MEMBERS OF THE HOUSE, 1977–1997

Number of representatives vs. Year (1975–1995)

Source: *Statistical Abstract of the United States, 1997*

Which election created the largest increase in African American members of the House?

National Convention in 1984 with only 300 delegates. Like Shirley Chisholm, he lacked the votes to gain the nomination.

In 1988, Jackson went to the convention again. This time, he had organized a more extensive voter registration campaign among African Americans. As a result, he entered the convention with more than 1,200 delegates that he had captured in 13 state primaries. Although this number was not enough to win him the nomination, Jackson's strong showing in 1988 electrified African Americans. They turned out to vote in record numbers that year.

A Growing Presence. For most of the 1980s, African Americans battled against huge cuts in social welfare programs proposed by Presidents Reagan and Bush. As you will see, they also faced a political climate that threatened to undo some of the gains made during the Civil Rights Era.

In 1990, African Americans used ballots to register their discontent. That year, they elected 16 new African Americans to Congress. When the next session of Congress resumed in 1991, it included a total of 25 African Americans—the largest group of African American members of Congress in U.S. history.

African Americans also made gains at the state and local levels. In 1990, L. Douglas Wilder became the nation's first elected African American governor. He won his victory in Virginia, a state with a white population of 81.2 percent. At the local level, African American mayors oversaw the governments of 30 major cities, 16 of which had white majorities. One of these African American mayors was David N. Dinkins, whose election in New York City in 1989 made him the head of the nation's largest city.

In 1992, African American voters helped Bill Clinton win the presidency. Upon entering the White House, Clinton kept his pledge to bring more African Americans into government. He appointed a record number of African Americans to Cabinet-level posts. Appointments included Commerce Secretary Ron Brown, Energy Secretary Hazel O'Leary, Agricultural Secretary Mike Espy, Transportation Secretary Rodney Slater, and Veterans Affairs Secretary Jesse Brown.

A New Generation of Leaders. By late 1995, African Americans held 8,015 of the elective offices in the United States—a gain of 4,512 since mid-1975. However, this number still represented little more than 1.5 percent of all elected officials in the United States

In the mid-1990s, the struggle to win greater representation in government fell to a new generation of African American

379

African American Women, a new legislative force

politicians. In 1994, two new mayors—Dennis Archer of Detroit and Bill Campbell of Atlanta—replaced two legends of the Civil Rights Movement—Detroit's Coleman Young (see Gallery, page 399) and Atlanta's Maynard Jackson. In 1996, Jesse Jackson, Jr., entered Congress. He joined 38 other African Americans, including 13 women. One of these women was Carol Moseley-Braun of Illinois, the first African American woman elected to the U.S. Senate.

In 1997, Representative Maxine Waters of California assumed leadership of the Congressional Black Caucus—a measure of the progress of African American women since the election of Shirley Chisholm. Waters, a 20-year veteran of politics, said:

I'm always pleasantly surprised and humbled by the outpouring of young women who identify with the work that I and other women legislators do. They tell me, "You're my role model. You're my mentor. You inspire me." And I think it's important for us . . . to help show them what women, particularly African American women, can do.

In the late 1990s, Waters and other members of the new generation of African American leaders joined with veterans of the Civil Rights Movement to ensure continued progress in the 2000s. One of their biggest challenges would be the continuing issue of racial prejudice.

Taking Another Look

1. What part did Reverend Jesse Jackson play in national politics during the 1980s?

2. What political gains did African Americans make in the 1980s and 1990s?

3. **Critical Thinking** What was the effect of the Voting Rights Act of 1965 on politics within the United States?

2 CHALLENGES AND CHANGES
▼ Why have many African Americans pledged to continue the battle for civil rights into the 2000s?

"The problem of the Twentieth Century," declared W.E.B. Du Bois in 1900, "is the problem of the color line." Du Bois was talking about the laws, practices, and prejudices that separated African Americans and whites. For much of the 20th century, Du Bois and other civil rights workers tried to erase racial prejudice from U.S. law books and to win passage of new laws that would advance equality.

Progress was made. Even so, as the nation prepared to head into the 21st century, troubling and divisive racial issues remained unsettled.

Redrawing Voting Districts. "At night, the enemies of civil rights strike in white sheets," said Jesse Jackson, Sr., in June 1996. "By day, they strike in black robes." With these heated words, Jackson compared the black-robed justices of the Supreme Court with the white-sheeted members of the Ku Klux Klan.

What had provoked this angry outburst? The answer lay in two separate Supreme Court decisions in the cases of *Bush* v. *Vera* and *Shaw* v. *Hunt.* Each case involved gerrymandering on the basis of race. **Gerrymandering** is the redrawing of voting districts to win an election advantage.

Five of nine justices ruled against redistricting plans in Texas and North Carolina. The plans were intended to strengthen non-white voting power through the creation of new districts. In the past, states had used redistricting to enforce the Voting Rights Act of 1965. For example, a state might have had three election districts. One district had a majority of African American voters and usually elected an African American representative. The other two districts had substantial numbers of African American voters, but not majorities. Under redistricting, state legislatures might redraw the boundaries of those districts so that at least two districts now had majorities of African American voters. This would greatly increase the chance of adding an additional African American representative.

The Court decisions provoked swift and bitter debate. Clarence Thomas, the only African American member of the Court, defended the decisions. "Government cannot make us equal," said Thomas, "it can only recognize, respect, and protect us as equal before the law." Cynthia A. McKinney, an African American representative from Georgia, felt differently. She argued that redistricting gave minority candidates a chance "to develop a track record, name recognition, and the local and national contacts . . . to win [future elections]."

In the November 1996 elections, African Americans lost only one seat in Congress. However, most members of the Congressional Black Caucus worried about the long-range effects of the Court decisions. Could African Americans hold on to, or

The Congressional Black Caucus, shown at the beginning of the 1998 session, has been bolstered by the increasing voter strength of African Americans.

Surveying the ruins of a burned-out church

increase, their representation in Congress if minority districts were dismantled?

The Ugly Face of Racism. The Supreme Court decisions on redistricting came at a time when racism had once again shown its face. From 1993 to 1996, arsonists set dozens of African American churches on fire throughout the South. Civil rights organizations and members of the Congressional Black Caucus pressured the government to take action to stem the attacks. A federal investigation failed to turn up evidence of an organized conspiracy, or plot. But arrests of individual suspects proved a pattern of racial hatred.

The church burnings brought back memories of the civil rights era. African American churches had formed the backbone of the Civil Rights Movement. As such, they had been singled out for attack. The arson attacks brought back memories of incidents like the 1963 bombing of a church in Birmingham, Alabama, in which four young girls died.

Bitter memories were triggered by other events. In 1996, corporate executives at Texaco publicly apologized for racial slurs against African American employees. In September 1997, a sea of Confederate flags marred televised coverage of a football game at the University of Mississippi, where African Americans account for about 12 percent of the enrollment.

Incidents such as these angered African Americans and other minority groups who had benefited from laws passed during the civil rights era. Joseph Lowery, leader of SCLC in 1996, said:

> We've marched too far, prayed too long, wept too bitterly, bled too much, and died too young to let anybody turn back the clock.

Fighting Back. "It's never a waste of time to correct a wrong," said Hillman Frazier in March 1995. Frazier, a member of the Mississippi state senate and the great-grandson of enslaved Africans, was celebrating ratification of the 13th Amendment. "Wait a minute, wasn't the 13th Amendment ratified in 1865?" you might ask. It was, but Mississippi never adopted it—never, that is, until Frazier decided it was time for his state to abolish slavery officially.

The following year, African American legislators in Tennessee called upon the state government to ratify the 15th Amendment. Because Tennessee was the first state to rejoin the Union after the Civil War, it had not been required to ratify the 13th, 14th, and 15th Amendments as other Southern states had to do. Although Tennessee ratified the 13th and 14th Amendments, passage of the 15th Amendment did not come until April 1997.

African Americans also took steps to correct wrongs committed in the modern era. The Congress of National Black Churches (CNBC) organized "challenge deposits," a

Kweisi Mfume, center, is sworn in as president of the NAACP as U.S. President Bill Clinton, left, watches.

fund-raising program to raise some $12 million to rebuild African American and multi-racial churches destroyed by arson. Some of the funds were devoted to educational programs to foster racial understanding in neighborhoods where churches had been burned. "We hope we can begin the new millennium [1000-year period] without this issue being a threat to persons or property," explained John Hurst Adams, Bishop of the African Methodist Episcopal Church and founder of the CNBC.

In early 1996, Kweisi Mfume (KWAY-see em-FOO-may) of Maryland gave up his seat in Congress to become president of the NAACP. Mfume promised to lead the NAACP out of debt and to set the organization on a course of leadership for the 2000s. By year's end, Mfume announced that the NAACP had climbed out of its more than $3.2-million debt. He then committed the organization to a five-point program that included civil rights enforcement, voter empowerment, educational excellence, economic empowerment, and youth recruitment.

Involving Young People. Youth recruitment took on great importance for the NAACP in the late 1990s. Said Mfume in an interview with *Ebony*:

> If we do not usher in a whole new generation of young people to take over the reins of the organization, to join us in a shared vision and to help us do the work, we will be an asterisk [a footnote] in someone's history book.

In 1997 and 1998, more than 2,200 local chapters of the NAACP launched a campaign to rekindle the interest of young people in the organization. "It's a monumental job," said a New York regional director of the NAACP. "There is, in [young people's] minds, no active civil rights movement." One indication of how hard a task that rekindling would be came from a reporter

GALLERY OF AFRICAN AMERICAN ARTISTS, FILMMAKERS, WRITERS, AND EDUCATORS

Maya Angelou (1928–) Angelou—writer, actress, singer, dancer, and writer—first won literary fame for *I Know Why the Caged Bird Sings*, one of several autobiographical novels. In 1993, President Bill Clinton asked her to write a poem for his inaugural. Angelou, the first African American and the first woman to receive such an honor, presented "On the Pulse of the Morning," a stirring recollection of Martin Luther King Jr.'s dream.

John Henrik Clarke (1915–1998) Born the son of Alabama sharecroppers, Clarke eventually hopped a freight train and headed for Harlem, New York. In Harlem, he discovered a love for African history and became one of the leaders in promoting African American studies and African-centered education in the United States. In 1997, acclaimed actor Wesley Snipes produced a film called *A Great and Mighty Walk*, a documentary about Clarke's life.

Henry Louis Gates, Jr. (1950–) Gates, one of the nation's leading African American literary scholars, heads Harvard's African American Studies program and the Du Bois Institute. His works include several anthologies of African American writers, numerous articles, and an award-winning book on his West Virginia childhood called *Colored People*. In 1997, TIME Magazine named Gates one of the "25 Most Influential Americans."

Lani Guinier (1950–) "I have always wanted to be a civil rights lawyer," Guinier once said. Conservative criticism of Guinier's views on voting rights cost her the nomination for Assistant Attorney General for Civil Rights in 1993. Guinier, a former lawyer for the NAACP and U.S. Justice Department, continued to teach, write, and speak about her vision of civil rights. In January 1998, she became the first African American woman appointed to the Harvard Law School. She was the first African American woman to become a tenured professor at Harvard.

Spike Lee (1957–) "Making films has got to be one of the hardest endeavors known to humankind," Lee once remarked. As actor, screenwriter, producer, and director, Lee has created media projects including commercials, music videos, blockbuster movies such as *Jungle Fever, Malcolm X, When We Were Kings,* and *He Got Game.* Lee calls his production company "40 Acres and a Mule Filmworks," after the hope of many African Americans for land during Reconstruction.

Toni Morrison (1931–) While working as a textbook editor and a professor of literature, Morrison came to believe that too few writers were telling the stories of African Americans. Morrison changed that with a string of novels—*Sula, Song of Solomon, Tar Baby, Beloved,* and *Jazz*—that led her to fame and the Nobel Prize in Literature (see p. 408).

Faith Ringgold (1934–) Ringgold broke into the art world during the 1960s with highly political paintings that captured the struggles of the civil rights movement. Since then, she has experimented with a variety of topics and styles, including award-winning "story quilts" such as "Bitternest Part II: Harlem Renaissance Party," on p. A15 of **The Artist's View**.

Cornel West (1953–) Influenced by traditions as diverse as the Baptist Church and the Black Panthers, West built a reputation in the 1990s for publicly exploring the threats to democracy posed by racism. His publication of *Race Matters*, a look at racial division in America, led West to Harvard in 1994. He joined Henry Louis Gates, Jr., in building one of the nation's most respected African American Studies programs.

1968	Shirley Chisholm is first African American woman elected to Congress.
1971	Congressional Black Caucus is formed.
1983	Martin Luther King, Jr.'s birthday becomes a national holiday.
1984	Jesse Jackson makes first run for President.
1991	First African–African American Summit.
1994	Nelson Mandela elected president of South Africa.
1996	Record number of African American women elected to Congress.
1998	President Clinton makes 12-day trip to Africa.

Voting in the state of Mississippi

in Poughkeepsie, New York, who was doing a story on the NAACP. He found that only 1 in 8 young people between the ages of 15 and 25 were able to identify the NAACP and its goals.

To overcome the "generation gap," the different interests and concerns of people from different generations, the NAACP focused on two issues: education and crime. The fight for equality in the classroom and the courtroom would become focal points for change in the 1990s.

Taking Another Look

1. What events in the 1990s seemed to threaten the gains of the Civil Rights Movement?

2. What past and present injustices did African Americans work to correct in the 1990s?

3. **Critical Thinking** What issues do you think the NAACP and other civil rights organizations should emphasize in their efforts to recruit young people? Explain.

3 BRIDGING THE CONTINENTS

▼ How have African Americans helped shape U.S. foreign policy toward Africa?

In October 1997, President Bill Clinton and Secretary of State Madeleine Albright selected Jesse Jackson, Sr., as the U.S. special envoy to Africa. His assignment, said Albright, was to promote progress toward democracy.

Jackson, who had visited many African nations unofficially in the past, welcomed the appointment. In an interview, he expressed a sentiment shared by many African Americans.

Africa and our destiny are amazingly intertwined. We need each other. And if we work together with a commitment to shared democratic values, we can be a force for good.

By the time of Jackson's appointment, African Americans had already helped promote democracy in Africa through their opposition to **apartheid**—the legalized segregation of races practiced in South Africa. The role of African Americans in ending this policy showed their growing influence on federal policy in the late 1900s.

Battling Apartheid. Whites made up only 17 percent of South Africa's population. To ensure their continued control over the nation, white leaders established apartheid as the official policy of government in 1948. Under apartheid, black South Africans were denied any voice in the country's political affairs.

Opponents of the unjust treatment of black South Africans had formed the **African National Congress (ANC)** in 1912. After apartheid became law in 1948, the ANC stepped up its opposition to the white South African government. Nelson Mandela, who had joined the ANC in 1944, quickly rose to a position of leadership.

Nelson Mandela was born in 1918, the son of a chief of the Thembu people. He was educated at a Methodist boarding school, then at a black African college in South Africa. Mandela then moved to Johannesburg and became a lawyer. It was there that Mandela joined the ANC and dedicated himself to ending apartheid.

As part of a crackdown against the ANC, the South African government arrested him in 1962. In a speech at the end of his trial, Mandela summed up his political beliefs. "During my lifetime," declared Mandela,

I have fought against white domination. I have fought against black domination. I have cherished the ideal of a democratic and free society in which all persons live together in harmony with equal opportunities. It is an ideal which I hope to live for and to see realized. But . . . if needs be, it is an ideal for which I am prepared to die.

Mandela would spend more than 27 years of his life in prison. During these years, he remained a powerful symbol of the movement to end apartheid.

Freedom in South Africa. The world did not forget Mandela while he was imprisoned. As more and more African nations won independence in the post-World War II era, they pressured South Africa to end its racial policies. Some nations imposed **economic sanctions,** or put limits on trade with South Africa.

In the United States, civil rights groups became active in pushing for an end to apartheid. They urged corporations to end business dealings with South Africa. They also pushed the U.S. government to impose economic sanctions. In 1987, Congress finally barred the importation of foods and consumer products from South Africa.

The combination of international pressure and continuing protests from black African groups within South Africa finally succeeded. In 1989, the South African government resumed talks with the ANC and soon freed Mandela.

In 1990, Mandela paid a visit to the United States to thank Americans for their help in ending apartheid. The years spent behind bars had not cooled Mandela's fiery spirit. In a speech delivered in Harlem, Mandela stilled an audience of more than 100,000 people with a wave of his hand. He declared:

> I have come here to claim you because . . . you have claimed our struggle. Harlem signifies the glory of resistance. We are on the verge of victory. . . . Death to racism!

Four years later, in 1994, Mandela was elected president of South Africa. He vowed to oversee the creation of an "all-race" government—one that promoted the ideals of equality and justice.

Forging Closer Economic Ties. The long years of apartheid had left most black South Africans in poverty. To build black-owned businesses in South Africa, Mandela looked to the United States for help. Here he found a strong ally in Ron Brown, the first African American Secretary of Commerce.

Brown became an ambassador of U.S. industry. He organized trade missions to nearly every region of the world, visiting nations on five continents. He personally led dozens of top executives to South Africa. He made similar trips to Ghana, Kenya, Uganda, and Botswana. On every mission, Brown included minority business leaders. Brown's efforts to forge new markets in Africa and other developing nations were cut short when his plane crashed while he was on a trade mission to war-torn Bosnia in 1996.

African American business interest in Africa did not end with Ron Brown's death.

African Americans protesting against South African apartheid

Independent African American **entrepreneurs,** people who risk money in business in hope of earning a profit, still looked to Africa as a place for investment. To help find investment opportunities, delegates from around the world met in a series of African–African American summits organized by U.S. civil rights leader Reverend Leon H. Sullivan.

At the first summit, Sullivan set out a lofty goal: "Let us build a bridge together that will help move Africa forward as it has never moved before." To achieve this goal, delegates hammered out programs to expand cooperation between the United States and Africa. Ideas included fairer prices for African exports, cancellation of debts owed by African nations to the United States, and sponsorship of U.S. teachers to work in Africa.

Linking Past and Present. After he was named special envoy to Africa, one of Jesse Jackson's assignments was to make contact with leaders on that continent in preparation for a visit by President Clinton. In March 1998, President Clinton set out on his African trip.

During his visit, President Clinton spoke constantly of the need for the United States and African nations to form a "partnership" that would build "a bright common destiny" with those nations. Clinton visited small villages and met with heads of state.

Perhaps the most moving stop on Clinton's journey was Gorée Island in Senegal. From this island, millions of Africans were taken in chains to begin their voyages to the Americas.

President Clinton acknowledged the terrible toll slavery had taken on Africa:

Going back to the time before we were even a nation, European-Americans received the fruits of the slave trade. We were wrong in that . . . although . . . if you look at the remarkable delegation we have here from Congress, from our Cabinet, and from the citizens of America, you can see there are many distinguished African Americans who . . . are making America a better place today.

Taking Another Look

1. How did African Americans try to force an end to South Africa's policy of apartheid?

2. How have African Americans worked to build stronger economic ties with Africa?

3. **Critical Thinking** Which of the ideas for expanding cooperation between the United States and Africa that were set out at the first African–African American summit do you think would effectively achieve that goal? Explain your answer.

LOOKING AHEAD

African Americans used their increased influence on government to help shape economic and educational policies within the United States. They concentrated on programs that would benefit their children–the generation who would carry the struggle for equal opportunity into the 2000s.

Can a song and a songwriter help promote such a cause? At least one could. Stevie Wonder wrote and recorded a song entitled "Happy Birthday." The song was about the debate over a national holiday in honor of Martin Luther King, Jr. Wonder, who helped to propel soul into the music mainstream, had decided to use his talent to influence people's opinion on the issue. He added "Happy Birthday" to a 1980 album called *Hotter Than July*.

"Happy Birthday" intensified the debate for politicians who opposed a holiday for King. The song shot to the top of the charts. "I just never understood," sang Stevie, "how a man who died for good could not have a day . . . set aside."

The support generated by "Happy Birthday" helped Wonder to build a national campaign in favor of honoring King's birthday of January 15 as a holiday. On November 2, 1983, President Ronald Reagan signed the King holiday bill. In 1994, President Bill Clinton declared a federal holiday in honor of King's birthday. This holiday falls on the third Monday of each January. As Wonder might say, "Happy Birthday, Martin Luther King."

The start of a long legislative campaign to declare Martin Luther King's birthday a holiday began in 1968.

CLOSE UP: CHAPTER 3

The Who, What, Where of History

1. **Who** is Shirley Chisholm?
2. **What** was the Rainbow Coalition?
3. **What** is the Congressional Black Caucus?
4. **Who** is Maxine Waters?
5. **What** is gerrymandering?
6. **Who** is Hillman Frazier?
7. **What** was the "challenge deposits" program?
8. **Who** is Kweisi Mfume?
9. **What** was apartheid?
10. **Who** is Nelson Mandela?
11. **Who** was Ron Brown?
12. **Where** was the first African–African American Summit held?
13. **Who** is the Reverend Leon Sullivan?

Making the Connection

1. Explain the connection between the Civil Rights Movement of the 1960s and the record number of African Americans in Congress in the 1990s.
2. Explain the connection between African American opposition to apartheid and U.S. economic sanctions against South Africa.

Time Check

1. In what year did each of these political "firsts" take place: election of first African American woman to Congress, election of first African American governor, appointment of first African American Secretary of Commerce?

2. Explain the importance of each of these dates in the history of South Africa and the life of Nelson Mandela: 1962, 1990, 1994.

What Would You Have Done?

1. Imagine that Hillman Frazier asked you to support his campaign to have the Mississippi legislature ratify the 13th Amendment. As you know, that amendment had already been ratified by other states and had become a part of the Constitution in 1865. Would you offer your support to Hillman? Explain why or why not.

2. Suppose you were a member of the ANC with Nelson Mandela in the 1960s. You have a difficult choice to make. If you stay in South Africa, you are certain to go to jail, probably for many years. If you leave the country, you will be free to do what you believe in, but you will be far away from the political action. Would you stay or leave? Explain.

Thinking and Writing About History

1. Write a one-minute radio commercial supporting the presidential campaign of either Shirley Chisholm or Jesse Jackson.

2. Suppose you were one of the African American students at the University of Mississippi. Write a speech that you will present before the student government in which you argue in favor of a ban against displaying Confederate flags at football games.

3. Write a series of questions that you would ask Nelson Mandela if you could have a half-hour interview with him. Then answer each question as you think Mandela would answer it.

Building Skills: Summarizing

Imagine that a friend calls you, excited about a new movie. "It's all about these two cowhands," your friend begins. "One is African American and one is white. When the movie opens, they're riding together behind a herd of cattle. The African American is on one of those tan horses with a white tail. What do you call those horses? They have a special name. But the color of the horse is going to be important later on, because, see. . . ."

"Hold on, a minute," you interrupt. "Can't you just give me a summary?"

"A what?"

"A *summary*," you answer. "You know. Just the main points. The main ideas."

Here is a summary of the opening story on pages 376–377 of the chapter:

In 1997, Chuck E. Burris won election as mayor of Stone Mountain, Georgia. He was the first African American to hold this job. In the past, Stone Mountain had hosted meetings of the Ku Klux Klan, a group that spread racial hatred against African Americans. With Burris in charge, some citizens believed these meetings would now end.

Notice that the summary gives only the main points of the section. It leaves out all the details, even though the details may be very interesting.

On a separate sheet of paper, write a summary of one of the numbered sections in this chapter. Write the main ideas of the sections without any details. *Hint:* Look for main ideas in the first sentence of the paragraphs.

392

Doctors from different cultures staff a Chattanooga hospital.

CHAPTER 34

Seeking Equal Opportunity
(1972–Present)

THINKING ABOUT THE CHAPTER

What economic and educational advances have African Americans made since the civil rights era?

"To pretend that we're in a world in which there is equal opportunity is just nonsense to me," declared Bob Lanier, the mayor of Houston, in 1996. In that year, Lanier and other officials in Houston worked to expand those opportunities for many groups of people—African Americans, Latinos, Asian Americans, Native Americans, and women.

In the past, when the city had contracted for goods and services, businesses owned and run by white men received the greatest number of those contracts. Lanier had campaigned and won office in part on his pledge to change these old ways of doing business.

After Lanier took office, he set about trying to follow through on his promise. He got support for his plans for change from African American state representative Ron

Wilson. Wilson threatened to hold up funding of Houston's programs unless imbalances in the awarding of its contracts were corrected.

Lanier worked out a deal with Wilson that changed how the city handled its contracts. Under the new program, Houston accepted a greater number of bids from African American and other minority business owners.

The program that Lanier helped put in place in Houston was an example of **affirmative action.** That was the name given to measures employers and other institutions were legally required to take to remedy past discrimination.

In a 1996 interview with *Black Enterprise,* Lanier expressed hope that Houston might serve as a model for the rest of the country.

> When we get to the point that the problem of discrimination is solved, I would agree that we won't need . . . programs [like this one]. But I don't think we're there yet.

As you'll see, however, Lanier's actions and statement came at a time when there was a growing trend to cut back on affirmative action programs.

1 ▼ OVERCOMING ECONOMIC BARRIERS

▼ What were some of the economic issues that concerned African Americans in the post-civil rights era?

"A lot of people like to talk about 'post civil rights,' " commented the Reverend Joseph Lowery at a 1991 reunion of freedom riders. "We won some important battles," Lowery conceded, "but the war never did end, particularly in the economic area. We won the right to check into the Hyatts

An African American business success

and the Hiltons [hotels]. But too few of us have the means [money] for checking out."

Economic Gaps. The Civil Rights Movement had been responsible for many changes in the economic conditions of African Americans. Some of these changes were due to affirmative action programs that grew out of the Civil Rights Act of 1964.

By the 1990s, for example, more African American high school and college graduates were entering the work force than ever before. Some of these individuals started their own businesses, building upon a strong tradition of African American private enterprise (see table page 394). Others filled top slots in the nation's major corporations.

A growing number of African Americans in the 1980s and 1990s moved into the middle and upper classes. By the mid-1990s,

State	African American Firms	Revenues (in millions)
California	68,968	$5,478
New York	51,312	$2,268
Texas	50,008	$2,339
Florida	40,371	$2,265
Georgia	38,264	$1,677
Maryland	35,758	$1,242
North Carolina	29,221	$ 893
Illinois	28,433	$1,773
Virginia	26,100	$1,211
Ohio	22,690	$1,096

Source: *U.S. Department of Commerce, Bureau of Census,* 1992

How many of the top ten states for African American business ownership are in the West?

for example, 28 percent of African American families earned between $25,000 and $50,000 a year. About 11 percent earned between $50,000 and $75,000, while more than 6 percent earned more than $75,000.

Despite such gains, salary gaps still existed between African Americans and whites. In 1994, for example, a white high school graduate earned $1.22 for every dollar earned by an African American high school graduate. On average, white college graduates earned $8,045 more per year than African American college graduates. When overall income levels were considered for 1995, African American families earned $22,393 a year compared to the $35,766 earned by white families.

A large gap also existed in unemployment rates for African Americans and whites. Although unemployment has dropped overall since 1980, African Americans still experienced an unemployment rate more than double that of whites. In 1996, for example, the unemployment rate for African Americans was 10.5 percent, compared to 4.7 percent for whites. Of all the groups studied by the government in 1996, African Americans aged 16 to 19 had the highest unemployment rate in the nation—33.6 percent.

Poverty in America. In the 1960s, President Lyndon Johnson bowed to civil rights activists and launched a "War on Poverty." Despite programs started at that time, a large number of Americans, particularly African Americans, still live below the poverty level today. The **poverty level** is a level of income below which a family cannot meet its basic needs.

In 1995, census data showed that 29.3 percent of African American families fell below the poverty level. Among white families, only 11.2 percent were below that level. The data also showed that African American children were almost three times as likely to live in poverty as white children. Most of these children lived in households headed by a single parent, usually a mother.

Economic recessions and federal budget cuts accounted for some of the economic hardship. Another reason for the hardship lay in the movement of middle-class families—both African American and white—into the suburbs during the last half of the 20th century. As they moved out, cities lost jobs, business income, and taxes. That led to further decay in some sections of major cities such as New York's South Bronx and East Harlem and Chicago's Southside.

Fewer jobs were thus available to African Americans who remained in the inner cities, as disadvantaged neighborhoods are often called. As federal funds were cut, there were fewer or more limited programs to aid these people. Sociologist Douglas

Glasgow called this group "the Black underclass" in a 1981 book. He described its members as "unemployed, welfare dependent, and without sufficient income to secure a decent quality of life."

Challenges to Affirmative Action.

To reduce economic gaps and poverty, supporters of affirmative action like Bob Lanier have fought to continue this policy into the 21st century. However, they have met with increasing opposition. Much of this opposition comes from people who feel government has gone beyond its constitutional powers in advancing the interests of the poor, the nonwhite, and the disadvantaged. These feelings helped drive the backlash against big government that took shape in the 1960s and 1970s.

In 1978, opponents of affirmative action won a victory in the Supreme Court case of *Regents of the University of California v. Bakke.* In that case, Allan Bakke, a white man, sued the University of California because of reverse discrimination. He claimed that he had been kept out of medical school in order to admit a less qualified African American man. In its decision, the Court upheld the principle of affirmative action. At the same time, though, it issued new and tighter guidelines that would limit how to apply the principle in the future.

Nearly 20 years later, California became the scene of another challenge to affirmative action. In 1996, opponents of affirmative action there put Proposition 209 on the ballot. Prop 209, as it was known, allowed the state's voters to decide on whether to end state-government-sponsored affirmative action programs.

One of the leading authors of Prop 209 was an African American businessperson named Ward Connerly. Connerly had tasted racism. As a youth, landlords and restaurants turned him away because of race. Yet Connerly spearheaded the effort to end affirmative action. When asked why he opposed affirmative action, Connerly responded, "It is a fundamentally different view than the one I grew up with, of individuals working hard to succeed and . . . to move up the ladder on the basis of individual effort."

Other African Americans disagreed strongly with Connerly. Rosa Parks; Jesse Jackson, Sr.; Martin Luther King III; and Colin Powell all worked to defeat Prop 209. So did representatives from a wide range of groups, including spokespersons for Asian Americans, Latinos, and California senior citizens. In the end, however, their effort failed. California voters approved Prop 209 by a vote of 54 percent to 46 percent.

In which year did income for African Americans rise above $400 billion?

▶▶ AVERAGE INCOME BY GROUP (in billions of dollars)				
Group	1995	1996	1997	1998
All Households	$ 4,477.80	$ 4,760.30	$ 5,030.70	$ 5,727.20
White	$ 3,949.10	$ 4,167.40	$ 4,381.70	$ 4,572.60
African American	$ 351.90	$ 393.10	$ 425.10	$ 454.40
Other Groups	$ 176.00	$ 199.80	$ 223.90	$ 245.60

Source: *Black Enterprise*, January 1998

1978	Supreme Court issues *Regents of University of California* v. *Bakke* decision.
1992	Verdict in Rodney King trial sets off disturbances in Los Angeles.
1994	Byron De La Beckwith convicted of 1963 murder of Medgar Evers.
1995	Myrlie Evers-Williams elected first woman chairperson of the NAACP.
1996	Bob Lanier strengthens affirmative action programs in Houston. Proposition 209 passed in California.
1997	President Clinton announces his "racial initiative."
	Houston voters turn down an initiative curbing affirmative action.

Turning Back the Tide. Just hours after voters approved Prop 209, a coalition of 12 labor and civil rights groups challenged the law as unconstitutional. They charged that it violated the equal protection clause of the U.S. Constitution as well as provisions of the Civil Rights Act of 1964, which empowered the government to help women and minorities overcome past discrimination.

In November 1997, the case made its way to the Supreme Court, which refused to hear it. The Court's action was not a decision for or against the proposition. By not taking any action, however, the Court left Prop 209 in place.

One of the justices who refused to hear the case was Clarence Thomas. Thomas, like Connerly, opposed affirmative action. In a 1995 case called *Adarand Constructors, Inc.* v. *Pena,* the Court handed down a ruling that limited federal affirmative action programs. In support of that ruling Thomas wrote, "These programs stamp minorities with a badge of inferiority and may cause them to . . . adopt an attitude that they are entitled to preferences."

In the 1990s, civil rights groups fought to stop attacks against affirmative action. When Representative Charles Canaday of Florida and Senator Mitch McConnell of Kentucky introduced their own version of Prop 209 in Congress in June 1997, civil rights groups organized a national campaign to defeat the bill. Canaday and McConnell named their bill the "Civil Rights Act of 1997."

The name of the bill infuriated African Americans such as Jesse Jackson, Sr. Jackson and his supporters appeared before the Senate Judiciary Committee along with witnesses and civil rights experts who opposed the bill. In November of that year, the bill was removed from discussion for the rest of the Congressional session.

Other support for affirmative action came out of Houston, Texas. In late 1997, supporters of affirmative action defeated a move to cut back the city's affirmative action programs like the one Bob Lanier helped put in place.

Civil rights groups also worked to defeat moves against affirmative action programs in several other states and cities. They alerted voters through letter-writing campaigns and through postings on the Internet about elected officials who opposed affirmative action.

In California, civil rights activists used tried-and-tested weapons to battle Prop 209. Building on the example of the 1955–1956 Montgomery Bus Boycott, African American groups such as the NAACP and National Urban League called for a boycott of all conventions and meetings within California, which drew millions of dollars annually from such business. Meanwhile, NAACP lawyers began filing discrimination suits against the state.

In assessing the attack on affirmative action, Earl Graves, the editor and publisher of *Black Enterprise,* wrote in early 1998:

> Our resolve to better ourselves and to create a better future for ourselves and our children is being challenged as never before. The good news: we have never been better equipped to meet this challenge.

Taking Another Look

1. What was the goal of affirmative action programs?

2. In what ways do economic gaps still separate African Americans and whites?

3. What arguments did opponents make against affirmative action?

4. **Critical Thinking** Do you favor or oppose affirmative action programs? Explain.

Students protest the ending of affirmative action

2 THE PURSUIT OF JUSTICE

▼ What are some of the reasons many African Americans distrust the judicial system?

Most Americans like to think that justice is handed out fairly. But many African Americans believe otherwise. Incidents like the following, reported in a 1996 story in *Ebony,* underscore the fact that racism can cause people to see crime or the possibility of crime where there is none.

Former Virginia governor Douglas A. Wilder finds himself pushed down and choked by a white airport security guard when his suspenders set off a metal detector. A white woman grabs her purse more tightly when Georgia Congressman John Lewis gets on an elevator. Michael McCary of Boyz II Men is stopped routinely by police who ask him to prove ownership of an expensive four-wheel-drive vehicle.

If well-known public figures have problems like these, many people asked, how can average African American citizens hope to be treated in the nation's justice system?

Crime in America. That question is a critical one because crime touches such large numbers of Americans today. Many consider crime one of the top problems the nation faces. Even though the crime rate has declined in recent years, public concern remains high. Some experts feel this is because of press coverage of violent crimes such as murder.

Although crime rates vary widely from neighborhood to neighborhood, African Americans as a group fall victim to crime more often than whites. Part of the reason lies with the concentration of poverty in inner cities, where unemployment among youth can reach 50 percent. Some

▲▼

Mary McLeod Bethune (1875–1955)   In 1904, Bethune opened the first school beyond the elementary level for African Americans in Florida. In 1935, she founded the National Council of Negro Women. That same year, she became director of the Division of Negro Affairs—the first African American woman to receive a major U.S. government appointment.

Julian Bond (1940–)   In the 1960s, Bond helped organize the Student Nonviolent Coordinating Committee. At age 25, he won election to the Georgia legislature, a seat he held for 21 years. At age 28, he was nominated for U.S. Vice President, but was too young to accept. In 1998, the NAACP tapped Bond to serve as chairperson to guide the organization into the 2000s.

Marian Wright Edelman (1939–)   As a college student, Edelman was arrested in a civil rights sit-in in Atlanta, Georgia. The experience convinced her to become a civil rights lawyer. Her defense of the disadvantaged led her to focus on the poverty and abuse of youth. In 1973, she founded the Children's Defense Fund, which has become a powerful defender of the rights of children.

Jesse Jackson (1941–)   Jackson proved that an African American could make a serious bid for the presidency. In 1984, he won Democratic primaries in five southern states—Alabama, Georgia, Louisiana, Mississippi, and Virginia—as well as Michigan. In 1988, he won primaries in seven states. When President Clinton tried to build stronger ties with Africa in the 1990s, he turned to Jackson for support and assistance.

Barbara Jordan (1936–1996)   Jordan—lawyer, judge, politician—became the first African American woman to represent Texas in state and federal governments. She was state senator from 1966 to 1972 and U.S. Representative from 1972 to 1978. During impeachment hearings of Richard Nixon, Jordan delivered a ringing defense of the Constitution and the inclusion of African Americans in the phrase "We the People."

Adam Clayton Powell, Jr. (1908-1972)   In 1944, Powell became the first U.S. Representative from Harlem. He held his seat for 24 years and used it to battle for civil rights. In 1960, he became Education and Labor Committee chairman. Charges of misuse of funds led to Powell's expulsion from the House. However, the Supreme Court ruled his expulsion improper, and voters reelected him. He remained in Congress until 1970.

Maxine Waters (1938–)   Waters's outspoken support of women, children, people of color, and the poor won her election to the California legislature from 1976 to 1990 and to the U.S. Congress in the 1990s. Waters seconded the nominations for president of Jesse Jackson in 1984 and 1988 and Bill Clinton in 1992. In 1996, her colleagues elected Waters chair of the Congressional Black Caucus.

Coleman Young (1918–1997)   Young became a union organizer in the 1930s. During World War II, he joined the Tuskegee Airmen, flying dangerous combat missions. In the 1960s, he won election to the Ohio state senate, where he fought for open housing and school busing. In 1972, he moved into Detroit politics and became the city's first African American mayor, a post he held for 20 years.

teenagers deal drugs to earn fast cash. Others use drugs in an effort to escape misery. But a drug habit often leads to crime and more misery.

The consequences of crime affect African Americans severely. For example, a 1996 report by the National Urban League revealed that the proportion of African Americans entering state and federal prisons rose from 21 percent of the prison population in 1926 to more than 55 percent in 1996.

This comes at a time when crime committed by African Americans has actually dropped. Research by New York's Criminal Justice Services showed similar evidence of bias. It proved that African Americans often receive harsher penalties than whites convicted of the same crime and with similar criminal records.

Bias can creep into the law in many ways, but it usually starts at the local level. This is where people interact with one another and with law officials. Each year, the police arrest millions of people—more than 11 million in 1995—and question millions of others.

During the mid-1990s, a series of celebrated cases forced the nation to look at the effects of prejudice and racism on the practice of law. Media coverage showed that the nation had not yet reached one of its most cherished ideals: equal justice for all.

Explosion in Los Angeles. On April 29, 1992, central Los Angeles erupted in flames. Scenes of looting blazed across television screens all over America. On May 1, nearly 4,500 U.S. troops moved into Los Angeles to restore order. The incident looked like a horrible flashback to the urban disturbances of the late 1960s.

At the heart of the violence was Rodney King, who was charged with fleeing police in a high-speed chase. After police caught up with King, they used an electric stun gun on him and beat him with nightsticks, fists, and feet. A person living nearby videotaped the incident. When the tape was shown on television, people across the nation were outraged. Some 14 months after King's beating, however, a mostly white jury found the officers not guilty. When it did, the anger of some African Americans in Los Angeles exploded into violence.

On May 1, Rodney King faced television cameras for the first time since the verdict. In a halting voice, he said:

> People, I just want to say, can't we all get along? We'll get our justice. They have won the battle, but they haven't won the war. We'll have our day in court, and that's all we want.

Civil rights leaders met with President George Bush to ensure that King's words would be proven true. They acknowledged the lawlessness of rioting. However, they

Rodney King talks to the press after disturbances in Los Angeles. What caused the disturbances?

also emphasized to the President the deep mistrust that many African Americans held toward the nation's judicial system.

In a televised speech, President Bush vowed that the "verdict . . . was not the end of the process." He ordered the Justice Department to start an independent investigation of the case. In 1993, three of the four officers were convicted on federal charges.

Televised Justice. A year after the King trials ended, the trial of former football star O.J. Simpson for a double murder grabbed the nation's attention. Apart from the legal issues in the case, months of televised deliberations proved once again that a wide gulf existed between African Americans and whites in their confidence in the law. The trial was marred by, among other things, taped-recorded racial slurs by one of the arresting officers.

A Past Wrong Righted. Can the justice system be made to work evenhandedly? Evidence that it could came in 1994 when civil rights activists won a resounding victory in a case first tried 30 years earlier. The case involved the assassination of civil rights activist Medgar Evers outside his home in Jackson, Mississippi, in 1963. The alleged assassin, Byron De La Beckwith, had been tried twice for the crime. In both trials, the all-white juries deadlocked, or failed to reach a verdict. As a result, Beckwith went free, even though strong evidence linked him to the murder.

Though the case faded from the newspapers, Myrlie Evers refused to let her husband's death go unpunished. She spent the next three decades of her life seeking to reopen the case.

▶ **Myrlie Beasky** had dropped out of college at age 18 to marry Medgar Edgars. At that time, Medgar Evers was dedicated to registering African American voters in Mississippi, one of the most segregated states in the Union. "You don't challenge a system like that without knowing the price to be paid," recalled Myrlie Evers. "We lived with threats on a daily basis."

After her husband's assassination, Myrlie Evers moved with her children to California. There she earned a college degree and held a series of positions as a business executive. Myrlie later married a union and civil rights activist named Walter Williams. However, she continued to visit Mississippi in search of new leads on Beckwith. In the early 1990s, witnesses reported hearing Beckwith boast of the murder. Their testimony helped reopen the case.

In 1994, a jury of eight African Americans and four whites delivered a unanimous verdict of guilty. Outside the courtroom, Myrlie Evers-Williams raised a clenched fist to the sky in triumph. She later commented, "People long for justice, you know."

In February 1995, Evers-Williams won another victory. She was elected chairperson of the NAACP. She was the first woman to hold this position in the organization's history. At the NAACP's 88th national convention in 1997 Evers-Williams declared: "We must send a clear message to all Americans that we are prepared to . . . crack the neck of prejudice and racism in America."

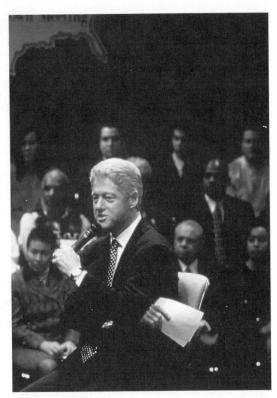

President Bill Clinton supports his "racial initiative" at an Akron, Ohio, meeting.

Talking About Racism. President Bill Clinton used the 1997 NAACP convention to push what he called a "racial initiative." The events of the mid-1990s had shown the depth of racial division in the United States. Clinton promised to promote "racial healing" though a "nationwide dialogue on race." The dialogue was directed by a panel chaired by African American historian John Hope Franklin. It consisted of town meetings all over the United States. At the core was the education of the nation's youth, especially African Americans.

How did young people see the nation? In February 1998, *The Detroit News* released the results of a national survey called "Generation 2001." The survey polled 2,001 college freshmen scheduled to graduate in 2001. Although most students took a dim view of race relations now, almost 50 per-

cent expected race relations to improve in the future. Nearly 75 percent expected a person of color to be elected President in their lifetime.

Such hope has continued to fuel the movement for equal rights. As Martin Luther King, Jr., said, "We must accept finite disappointment, but we must never lose infinite hope."

Taking Another Look

1. What was the cause of disturbances in Los Angeles during the spring of 1992?

2. How was justice finally achieved in the assassination of Medgar Evers?

3. **Critical Thinking** What topics relating to crime and justice would you want to have discussed at a town meeting on race relations in your community?

3 EDUCATION FOR THE FUTURE
▼ Why is desegregation still an issue today?

Elizabeth Eckford—one of the Little Rock Nine—turns down most interviews. Memories of the court-ordered integration of Central High School in Little Rock, Arkansas, are painful for her. But she could not turn down an urgent request for an interview in 1996 from three white students —Heather Jurgensen, Jeremy Johnston, and David Foster—from a small high school in Uniontown, Kansas. They wanted to make her story the subject of a project for National History Day.

Research by the students turned up Ken Reinhardt, one of the few white students who had befriended Eckford in 1957. The three classmates prepared two projects, one on Eckford and one on Reinhardt. The projects carried them to the finals of the

Elizabeth Eckford, Ken Reinhardt, and Kansas students

History Day competition at the University of Maryland, College Park. The event brought Eckford and Reinhardt together for the first time in almost 40 years. The two former classmates watched the reenactments of their lives with tear-filled eyes.

Because of Eckford's presence, the students' history projects earned them a place at ceremonies marking the 40th anniversary of the integration of Little Rock's Central High.

A Civil Rights Anniversary. In September 1997, the Little Rock Nine stood again at the doors of Central High—the brown brick building that once symbolized the racial conflicts of the era of desegregation. At Central High in 1957, nine African American teenagers endured racial taunts in an effort to win a better education for all students.

Today the doors of Central High open easily to African Americans. In 1997, the school had an African American principal. Because of busing, Central High today is a largely integrated school. Its students win their share of academic prizes and admission to top colleges.

However, problems remain. African American and white students stay apart from one another. They eat lunch and attend pep rallies and other events in separate groups. As in many public schools elsewhere in the nation, African Americans are twice as likely to drop out of school as white students.

Members of the Little Rock Nine expressed disappointment that full racial equality is not yet a reality. But they urged young people to work toward this goal—not to give up. Said Jean Brown Trickey, one of the Little Rock Nine, "I would like young people to know about . . . [us], to know that everyone can be heroic. We were just teenagers and friends."

A Mixed Record. What have been the overall gains and losses in the education of African Americans since the beginning of the Civil Rights Movement? Consider these facts. In 1954, every former Confederate state, plus West Virginia, Oklahoma, and Missouri, required public schools to be segregated by race. Three other states–Kansas, Wyoming, and Arizona–permitted local districts to choose segregation. Even as late as 1960, only 20 percent of all African Americans over age 25 had finished four years of high school. Just 3 percent over age 25 held a college degree.

By 1997, 86 percent of African Americans aged 25 to 29 were high school graduates, compared to 87 percent of whites of the same age. As of 1995, 13 percent of African Americans had completed four years of college, compared to 24 percent of whites. Such figures led one African American reporter to declare, "In sum, black Americans, in the face of massive social and legal barriers, have in a very few decades made enormous . . . educational gains."

Even so, the lack of educational equality in public schools such as Central High is a troubling issue. So is the concentration of a large number of African American children in inner–city schools. According to one

403

Marva Collins and students at her private academy

report, nearly 70 percent of African American children attend mostly African American schools. This is only a small drop from the 78 percent that attended such schools in 1968.

The recent backlash against affirmative action and the court decisions that limit busing have led some African Americans to rethink desegregation. The search for alternatives has triggered differences in opinion, such as those in the Points of View section on this page.

Alveda King, the niece of Martin Luther King, Jr., favors "school choice," or the right of parents to send their children to whatever school they choose. To achieve this goal, she supports the use of **school vouchers**—tax-funded certificates issued by a government for use in paying for a private school or public school in another district. Those in favor of vouchers say their use will let parents place their children in better schools. They believe that vouchers

Are integrated schools still needed to educate African American students? That was the question that the editors of *Jet* magazine put to leading educators, civil rights leaders, and journalists in the summer of 1997. Here are two of the many responses. One comes from Elaine R. Jones, president of the NAACP's Legal Defense and Education Fund (LDF). The other comes from Michael Eric Dyson, professor of African American studies and author of many books, including *Race Rules: Navigating the Color Line.*

Elaine R. Jones

LDF remains committed to the belief that racially segregated public school education is destructive for our nation and its people. . . . We believe that in 21st Century America, where our increasing diversity will obliterate [wipe out] the majority/minority distinctions that have framed race relations throughout American history, racially integrated education is essential.

We cannot expect to educate students in racially segregated public schools for 12 years or more and then throw them together in our work force, in our armed forces and in our communities in the belief that they will function harmoniously.

Michael Eric Dyson

It's been proven that students who attend integrated schools find more white-collar work, have higher wages, and complete more years of schooling. . . . [However], Black students in integrated schools are put on lower academic tracks, . . . are put in remedial classes, and are suspended at a higher rate than White students. It can be a tough way to go for young Black kids.

I'm with the people who say if we can direct resources to Black schools in the Black community, that would be a powerful step toward educational equity. . . .

There are many Black and White people who believe in the idea that just being near White children automatically gives Black children educational equality; that just isn't so. Just being near some White folks does not mean your child gets a better education.

Taking Another Look

1. Why does Jones oppose racially segregated schools?

2. What does Dyson feel are some of the shortcomings of integration?

3. **Critical Thinking** Do you agree that integration is the best method for improving the quality of education in public schools? Explain.

will make poorer schools improve by forcing them to compete for students.

The NAACP opposes vouchers. Officials argue that low-income families will be unable to pay for tuition costs left uncovered by a voucher. They also feel vouchers will lead to a further decline of inner-city schools. This is no time to give up, argues one NAACP lawyer. "The alternative is to consign a whole generation of kids to racially segregated opportunities." The challenge for the 21st century, as you will see in Chapter 35, is to extend equal opportunities to young people wherever they live.

Taking Another Look

1. What educational gains have African Americans made in the last 50 years?

2. What obstacles to equal educational opportunity still remain?

3. **Critical Thinking** Would you favor or oppose a program allowing the use of school vouchers? Explain.

LOOKING AHEAD

As the 21st century unfolds, African Americans in all walks of life are working to ensure a better future for themselves and their children. As in the past, they are finding strength in unity and a common heritage. As African Americans struggle to preserve cultural traditions and to win still greater equality, they will leave an imprint on the United States—just as they have done since the founding of the nation.

"This is a business where one day you might be in and the next day you're out. So it's up to you to take it to the next level." The next level for Lamont Hawkins, better known as U-God of the Wu-Tang Clan, means going from the recording studio into the boardroom.

The Wu-Tang Clan has diversified its business investments. Most members of the group have cut solo deals, giving Wu-Tang ties to nearly every major record label in the music industry. The Clan has also launched a clothing line that is made in China and in Massachusetts.

Other enterprising hip-hop artists are also turning a profit through smart investments. Deidra Roper, Salt N' Pepa's Spindarella, has put money into a skin-care line and a spa. "In the rap industry," says Roper, "we have the opportunity to do things with our money. It should be about putting some money away and starting something of your own, so you won't be dependent on people."

Vernon Slaughter, an entertainment lawyer, describes the ingredients for success beyond the music world. The artists who succeed, thinks Slaughter, are those who combine "the enthusiasm and creativity of hip-hop with the wisdom and experience of . . . the business sector." By doing this, those artists provide exciting new models of success in the African American community.

CLOSE UP: CHAPTER 3

The Who, What, Where of History

1. **Who** is Bob Lanier?
2. **What** is affirmative action?
3. **What** is meant by the term *poverty level?*
4. **Who** is Douglas Glasgow?
5. **What** was *Bakke v. University of California?*
6. **Where** was Proposition 209 passed?
7. **Who** is Ward Connerly?
8. **What** was *Adarand Constructors, Inc. v. Pena?*
9. **Who** Is Rodney King?
10. **Who** is Myrlie Evers-Williams?
11. **Who** is John Hope Franklin?
12. **What** are school vouchers?

Making the Connection

1. What is the connection between the growth of the suburbs and the decline of many inner-city neighborhoods?
2. What was the connection between the verdict in the Rodney King trial and the disturbances in Los Angeles?

Time Check

1. How many years separated the murder of Medgar Evers and the conviction of his killer?
2. How many years after Proposition 209 was passed did Houston voters support affirmative action?

What Would You Have Done?

1. Someone comes to you with a petition to put a measure opposing affirmative action on your state's ballot in the next election. She explains that affirmative action lables minorities and women as inferior. Will you sign the petition? Why or why not?

2. You are the parent of two children in a mostly African American school district. You want to provide them with the best education possible. What action would you take: **(a)** use school vouchers to send your children to a private school outside the neighborhood; **(b)** work to increase the resources of your local school; **(c)** ask the courts to desegregate the schools that your children attend. Explain your choice.

Thinking and Writing About History

1. Imagine that you work for a magazine that is going to publish a special issue entitled "The 1990s—A Time of Justice or Injustice for African Americans?" Write a brief essay answering the question in the title by referring to key issues and events of the 1990s.

2. The President's national panel on race relations has arranged a town meeting in your community. You have been asked to draft a plan for the meeting. The agenda should include a list of issues for discussion and a set of guidelines for talking about these issues. Your guidelines should include suggestions for the presentation of conflicting points of view.

Building Skills: Interpreting Statistics

You probably use **statistics**, or sets of numerical data, all the time. You might talk about the batting averages of your favorite baseball players, the rising prices of CDs, or the grades you receive in school.

Statistics help you to identify trends, or patterns of change over time. They also help you to recognize connections between facts or related trends. Finally, statistics are often used as evidence to support an opinion.

Answer the following questions about the graph on a separate sheet of paper.

1. What is the subject of this graph?

2. What data are being compared?

3. How could you use figures in this graph to support or oppose continuation of affirmative action in education?

▶▶ **% OF AFRICAN AMERICANS WHO GRADUATED COLLEGE, 1960–1996**

Source: *U.S. Bureau of the Census*

Toni Morrison receiving Nobel Prize in Oslo, Norway

Preserving the Legacy
(1972–Present)

THINKING ABOUT THE CHAPTER

How have African Americans influenced present-day United States society and culture?

The sound of the ringing telephone startled Toni Morrison. She had a sudden feeling that it must be terrible news. At first, she hesitated to reach for the phone. When she finally picked it up, a friend's voice on the other end asked: "Did you hear?" The news left Morrison speechless for a few minutes. She had just become the first African American woman to win the Nobel Prize in Literature. A few days later, in early October 1993, Henry Louis Gates, Jr., the chairman of Afro-American studies at Harvard exclaimed:

This is a great day for African Americans and for Americans in general. Just two centuries ago, the African American literary tradition was born in slave narratives [stories]. Now our greatest writer has won the Nobel Prize.

Reasons for the award become clear as soon as a reader picks up one of Morrison's books. The master storyteller pulls no punches when exposing the price that slavery and prejudice has exacted upon African Americans. Yet her words are so beautiful and so musical that people from all backgrounds read her works. When they put down her books, brilliant images of the struggles and triumphs of the African American people remain in their minds.

Though her case was special, Morrison was just one of countless African Americans who have built upon their heritage to create a better future for themselves and their children. In doing so, they have enriched the lives of all Americans.

1 ▼ AFRICAN AMERICANS ON THE MOVE

Why have African Americans started returning to the South?

For millions of African Americans, the South is their American homeland—the place where their grandparents lived. Racial hatreds pushed a flood of African Americans from the region. The coming of peace—the end of the violence unleashed against African Americans who sought their civil rights—is now pulling many African Americans back.

Reversing a Trend. After the end of the Civil War, there was a steady exodus of African Americans from the South. From 1900 to 1980, the percentage of the African American population that lived in the South dropped from 90 percent to 53 percent. Starting around 1980, however, African Americans began returning to the region. In the 1980s, for example, the South gained 368,800 African American residents.

How many states have an African American population of more than one million? In what two regions are most of these states?

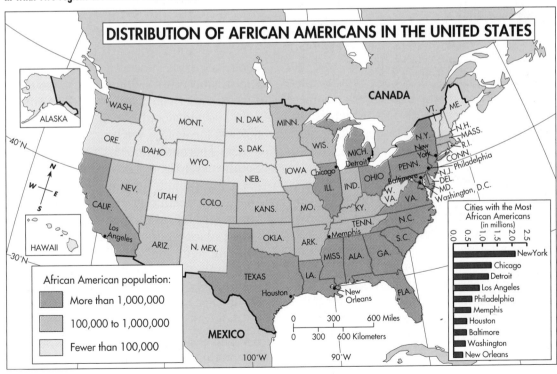

DISTRIBUTION OF AFRICAN AMERICANS IN THE UNITED STATES

African American population:
- More than 1,000,000
- 100,000 to 1,000,000
- Fewer than 100,000

Cities with the Most African Americans (in millions)
New York, Chicago, Detroit, Los Angeles, Philadelphia, Memphis, Houston, Baltimore, Washington, New Orleans

►► AVERAGE INCOME OF AFRICAN AMERICAN AND WHITE FAMILIES BY REGION, 1994

Region	African American	White
Northeast	$ 26,414	$ 45,169
Midwest	$ 21,844	$ 41,453
South	$ 24,322	$ 37,790
West*	$ 20,977	$ 40,833

* Includes Alaska and Hawaii

Source: *1997 Statistical Abstract of the U.S.*

In which region is average income for African Americans highest? In which is it lowest?

Two reasons account for the movement. First, manufacturing in Northern cities has declined in recent years. This decline reduced the economic opportunities that once lured African Americans out of the South. Second, the South's hostile racial climate has lessened.

In studying the United States in the 1990s, population expert Reynolds Farley found that the best integrated cities were in the South. Eight of these cities included military bases where the integration of the armed forces has spilled over into the military towns around the bases. Farley named Jacksonville, North Carolina, which is the site of Camp Lejeune, the best integrated metropolitan area in the country.

A New South. Today many African Americans find that the South has fewer barriers based on skin color than does the North. Andrew Young, an African American who is a former mayor of Atlanta, Georgia, credits this change to the Civil Rights Movement. Says Young: "We dealt with race overtly [openly]. I don't think they had to in the North. I mean, we really had to *struggle.*"

Statistics seem to support Young. As the 1990s began, more than two-thirds of all African American elected officials—68.8 percent—were found in the South. This change reflects the far-reaching effects of the voter registration drives of the 1960s. Today African Americans can vote freely in a region where racism once kept nearly 97 percent of African Americans off the voting rolls.

Today almost half of all African Americans in the South own their own homes, compared to a little more than 30 percent in the Northeast. Large economic gaps still exist, however, between African Americans and whites. For example, African American families in the South in 1994 earned about $24,332, compared to $37,790 for whites.

The African Americans moving into the South may help to reduce such economic gaps. In profiling the migrants, William H. Frey, a sociology professor at the University of Michigan, wrote in 1998: "Most black migrants to the South are of working age, and about one-fifth are college graduates." Frey believes that these migrants will bolster the African American middle class in the region.

Many of the middle-class migrants are moving into prosperous suburbs, such as the areas around Atlanta, Georgia, and

Charleston, South Carolina. This movement is increasing integration. Not all migrants, however, are looking for well-integrated neighborhoods. Instead, some have chosen heavily African American communities, such as those found in Prince George's County, Maryland. Explained Barron Harvey, a Howard University Professor:

> We always wanted to make sure our child had many African American children to play with, not just one or two. We always wanted to be in a community with a large number of black professionals and to feel part of that community.

Unlike in the past, however, living in a largely African American neighborhood in the South today is a matter of choice rather than a requirement of Jim Crow law.

Taking Another Look

1. **(a)** How have migration patterns among African Americans changed in recent years? **(b)** What are the causes of these changes?

2. How is the South of the 1990s different from the South of the civil rights era?

3. **Critical Thinking** If you were an African American whose ancestors had left the South, do you think you would be interested in returning to the South? Explain your answer and the factors that might influence it.

2 BUILDING ON TRADITION
▼ How are African Americans continuing
▼ a tradition of self-help?

The children came from all over the country. They stood with their parents near the sparkling pool at the foot of the Lincoln Memorial. In a march more than 200,000 strong, they had come to take part in a demonstration called Stand for Children.

The march, held in 1996, was the idea of Marian Wright Edelman, the African American founder and president of the Children's Defense Fund. Edelman wanted to put children on the nation's agenda. She had reminded Americans that, "As tough as times are and as hard as families are struggling for children, each and every one of us can do better."

Edelman did not look to government to bring about change. She looked to families, neighbors, teachers, and community leaders. "The key," said Edelman in a speech at the march, "is for people to go one-on-one and to make things happen for children at the local level."

Lending a Helping Hand. Edelman's call for action forms part of a long tradition of self-help among African Americans. As Earl G. Graves, editor of *Black Enterprise,* explained:

> One of the untold stories of the black American community has been its history of generosity. Kind words and healing hands from our families, neighbors, and the clergy have always embraced us in the time of need.

Today, as more and more African Americans are entering the middle class or becoming successful entrepreneurs, they are continuing this tradition. Graves, for example, created the KIDpreneurs Konference in 1996. At this annual meeting, some of the nation's top African American businesspeople teach children as young as 4 to 6—the "Weepreneurs"—and as old as 17 the economic and leadership skills to succeed.

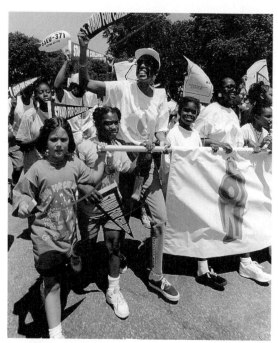

The Stand for Children rally

Other African Americans are helping in other ways. Entertainer Bill Cosby and Camille Cosby, his wife, have donated millions of dollars to such African American universities as Fisk and Spelman. Mel Blount, former star of the Pittsburgh Steelers, has set up two homes to help troubled boys. Retired General Colin Powell has dedicated himself to reviving volunteerism by chairing President Clinton's Summit for America's Future. In a 1997 speech, Powell issued a challenge to African Americans.

The challenge is for everybody who has been successful in Black America to stop, turn around, reach back, and reach down, and touch somebody who is wondering if the American dream is still there for them. And do it quickly because the gap is widening. . . . If we don't save these kids now, they're gone.

Long before Powell issued this call, 63-year-old Clara Hale came out of retirement in 1969 to touch some of the most helpless members of the inner cities—drug-addicted infants.

Clara McBride Hale, known today as "Mother Hale," was born in 1905. Hale's father died a short time after her birth, and her mother raised four children on her own. When Hale's own husband died at a young age, she too raised three children on her own. Instead of leaving her children to work outside the house, Hale began caring for other people's children. "The kids must have liked it," said Hale. "They didn't want to go home."

Hale raised a total of 40 foster children by the time she retired in 1968. Hale's retirement ended the next year when her daughter sent a drug-addicted mother and her drug-addicted infant to Hale. Within months, Hale had 22 drug-addicted babies in her five-room apartment. With the help of private donations, she went on to found Hale House—a program aimed at rebuilding families ravaged by drug abuse.

In 1985, President Reagan identified Hale as a "true American hero" in his State of the Union Address. Hale died in 1992, but her daughter, Dr. Lorraine Hale, has continued the work at Hale House. What is the doctor's prescription for healing the infants? The same one prescribed by her mother: hugs and kisses, laughter and hope.

412

African American Churches. Many African Americans who want to help youth in the nation's cities are turning to one of their oldest resources—the African American churches. Explained Reverend Alicia Byrd of the Congress of National Black Churches, "If you want to deal effectively with the black community, you have to deal with the churches."

Across the nation, African American churches are continuing their tradition of reaching out to their communities. "We've been watching the neighborhood crumble all around us. We couldn't stand by and do nothing," said Linda Perkins of Detroit's Greater Christ Baptist Church.

Because education is often the ticket out of the inner city, many African American churches are teaching their children. "Reach one, teach one, we'll make a difference." That's how the Reverend William Gable describes the educational programs offered by the New Orleans Progressive Baptist Church.

With the help of donations from individuals, foundations, and some government agencies, African American churches are offering a whole range of educational services. They provide tutorial programs, computer-literacy projects, science learning centers, and much more. The success of these programs was perhaps best described by one ten-year-old as he rushed into a church school in Chicago. "I can't wait to get to school," he told a reporter, "so I can get A's." These church schools are also receiving A's from many of the nation's top educators.

The Importance of Families. "It takes a village to raise a child." In the mid-1990s, First Lady Hillary Rodham Clinton popularized this African proverb with a book entitled *It Takes a Village.* African Americans have embraced this concept for centuries. Long before the invention of day-care, the raising of children belonged to the entire African American community. This concept helped African Americans survive the brutalities of slavery, which tore biological families apart.

Today, changes such as migration, two-career couples, and a growing number of single-parent households have created strains in child-rearing among nearly all American families. African Americans, who have always placed a high value on extended families, find it harder to keep close ties with relatives. To solve the problems facing many youth, African American sociologists are urging a return to the idea of a village. Explains Dr. Niara Sudarkasa (soo-DAR-kah-suh), president of Lincoln University:

> It is absolutely vital for us to return to [the extended family] for the basis of our self-help. . . . As we move into the 21st century, . . . we have to build on our kinship and our friendship ties if we are to succeed during the next century and the next millennium.

The Million Man March. In 1995, Louis Farrakhan (fah-rah-KHAN), the leader of the Nation of Islam, offered his solution for rebuilding unity in the African American community. He called for a massive march of African American men on Washington, D.C. This Million Man March was organized to foster a sense of family responsibility among African American men.

The Nation of Islam had long sought to further African American solidarity through programs of self-help. Louis Farrakhan was a strong supporter of this viewpoint. Farrakhan had often noted that white racism was a primary cause of the problems faced by African Americans. For the march, however, he stressed ideas of atonement, acceptance of responsibility, and unity.

▲▽

Berry Gordy (1929–) As a child, Gordy won a talent contest singing his own song, "Berry's Boogie." As an adult, he worked in a Detroit automotive plant, writing songs in his spare time for soul artists like Smokey Robinson. In 1960, Gordy used $800 to found Motown Records. Motown put soul at the top of the charts—and earned Gordy a place in the Rock 'n' Roll Hall of Fame.

Earl Graves (1935–) Graves served with distinction in the Army's elite Green Berets and worked as an assistant to Senator Robert F. Kennedy, a supporter of civil rights. Graves committed himself to winning equal economic opportunity for African Americans. One result of his efforts is *Black Enterprise*, a magazine championing African American economic empowerment.

Earvin "Magic" Johnson (1959–) Johnson led the Los Angeles Lakers to five NBA titles and played on the 1992 Olympic Gold Medal "Dream Team." He later became vice president of the Lakers and a successful investor in entertainment businesses. One of his proudest achievements is the Magic Johnson Foundation, which funds the fight against AIDS, especially through the education of young people.

John H. Johnson (1918–) In 1942, Johnson borrowed $500 to start the *Negro Digest*. That magazine grew into *Ebony*. With profits from *Ebony*, Johnson built a publishing empire. He expanded into books, producing titles such as *Before the Mayflower*, by African American historian and journalist Lerone Bennett. Johnson's many awards include the 1996 Presidential Medal of Freedom.

Margie Lewis (1958–) After spending hours reading science-fiction stories as a child, said Lewis in a 1996 interview, "it was only natural that I would develop an interest in space and nuclear power." In 1993, the nuclear engineer used her savings to start Parallax Inc., an environmental management firm. By 1998, the company boasted annual revenues of more than $23 million and employed 160 people.

Reginald Lewis (1942–1998) Lewis earned his first profits at age 10, delivering copies of an African American newspaper. As an adult, he made Beatrice International Holdings into the largest U.S. business owned by an African American. Lewis gave millions of dollars to colleges and universities, including Howard, Virginia State, and Harvard. In gratitude, Harvard named its international school of law after him.

Oprah Winfrey (1954-) In 1984, Winfrey, a radio and TV news reporter, began hosting Chicago's lowest-rated TV "talk show." She built it into *The Oprah Winfrey Show*, the first nationally syndicated TV talk show hosted by an African American woman. She also started her own television and film company, Harpo Studios, becoming one of the most powerful women in the entertainment industry.

Deborah Wright (1958–) Trained as a lawyer and an investment banker, Wright brought her financial skills to New York City government. In 1996, she became head of the Upper Manhattan Empowerment Zone Development Corporation. Armed with $300 million in government funds, Wright worked to attract businesses to Harlem, pledging to turn it into the "urban capital of the world."

Participants in the Million Man March in Washington, D.C. What was a result of this march?

The idea of a march struck a chord within the hearts of many African American men. It acknowledged publicly the problems that concerned the African American community: higher than average unemployment; the cycle of drug abuse, crime, and violence among inner-city youth; attacks on welfare and affirmative action; and what many African Americans saw as an unfair justice system.

The march took place on October 16, 1995. The crowd was striking in its diversity. There were investment bankers and welfare recipients. There were old men in overalls and young men in baggy jeans. There were Christians and Muslims. It was, in short, a cross-section of the African American community.

One of the people asked to inspire unity in this mass of people was 12-year-old Ayinde Shomari Jean-Baptiste. On the day of the march, the Chicago youth gave a speech that rivaled some of the most powerful African American speakers in the country. Facing the crowd, Ayinde declared:

> My fathers, you must shape the vision of tomorrow. But in order for the vision to become a reality, you must rededicate yourselves to a new beginning. Go back to your families, go raise and teach your children, go back and organize throughout this nation to bring about a better day for our people.

The march had an impact. In its wake, a biracial group of members of Congress approached President Clinton, urging him to take action on racial issues confronting the nation. The President then agreed to form the panel whose discussion would promote "racial healing." The march also inspired African American women to organize their own march for unity.

The Million Woman March. The Million Woman March was the brainchild of Phile Chionesu (SHE-oh-nay-soo), a business owner in Philadelphia. "I made a promise in having my daughter," explained Chionesu, "that I would do something before leaving this world that I could give to her . . . that would help her to become a better black woman."

The march had none of the backing that Louis Farrakhan commanded as the head of the Nation of Islam. It started instead at the grassroots level, with African American women holding yard sales and car washes

416

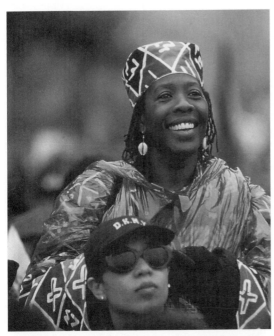

African American women made their voices heard at the 1997 Million Woman March. What was the purpose of the march?

to raise some of the more than $2 million to pay for the event. Chionesu and other organizers worked their way up to wealthier sponsors.

During two years of planning, Chionesu set the date of the march for October 25, 1997. Right up to the last minute, many women worried about the march's success.

"I [wanted this march] to be as soul-stirring as the 1995 march that had hardened brothers . . . confessing in the streets," recalled Donna Britt, a columnist for the Washington Post. The grassroots effort did not fail. Women from all walks of life showed up at the march. "We need to use our collective power," declared keynote speaker Maxine Waters, "to shape public policy, fight discrimination, racism, favoritism, and old-boy networkism."

Did ordinary women have the power to bring about such sweeping changes? Bernestine Singley, a marcher from Texas, thought so. The march showed, said

Singley, "that we have *everything* that we need, to do what we need to do now!"

Taking Another Look

1. What are some of the ways in which African Americans are building on the tradition of self-help?

2. What were some of the goals of the Million Man March?

3. **Critical Thinking** Explain what you think Reverend Alicia Byrd meant by her statement, "If you want to deal effectively with the black community, you have to deal with the churches."

3 ENRICHING AMERICAN ▼ CULTURE

How are African Americans enriching the culture of the nation as a whole?

Where can you find a cowry shell bracelet from Tanzania, a piece of kente cloth from Ghana, or a tightly woven basket from South Africa? If you live in New York City, the answer is the African Market in the heart of Harlem.

The market is a living example of the diversity of the African Diaspora. Goods from all over Africa and the African-influenced Caribbean are sold in open-air stalls. The variety of dress and hairstyles worn by shoppers and merchants rivals the variety of goods sold in the market. Haggling over prices at the stalls are people from all over New York City—African Americans, Haitians, Dominicans, Puerto Ricans, Asian Americans, whites, and more. Such scenes highlight the cultural interactions that have taken place in the United States because of the presence of more than 34 million people who trace their descent to Africa.

The African Influence.

Many African Americans refer to Africa as Mother Africa—the continent that gave birth to their culture. That culture has been deeply affected by the experience of African Americans on this continent. But ties to Africa remain strong.

The spirit of Africa can be seen in the clothing styles worn by some African Americans today—kente-cloth crowns, robe-like dashikis, or T-shirts emblazoned with the word *Africa*. Some parents give their children African names. Twins, for example, might be Taiwo (first born) and Kehinde (second born). Women tightly braid their hair in beaded cornrows, similar to the hairstyles worn in West Africa. Young men and women wear dreadlocks similar to those worn in the Caribbean, another region influenced by Africa.

The outpouring of black pride during the 1970s boosted the African spirit to new heights. Historian Robert Weisbord described the period as "Afro-America's African Renaissance." This rebirth of African culture cut across color lines.

The spirit of Africa can be seen in the clothing styles worn by some African Americans today.

Larger numbers of whites than ever before became—and still are—keenly aware of African American creativity.

Dancing to an African Beat.

African American dance caught public attention as a new generation of choreographers came of age. They built on the work of African American pioneers in modern dance, such as Katherine Dunham. African American dance troops, such as the Alvin Ailey American Dance Theater and Arthur Mitchell's Dance Theatre of Harlem, performed classical ballet. But they also introduced serious African American choreography to the public. Mitchell called it "ballet with soul."

Popular dance also reflects the influence of African Americans. Across the nation today, people dance to an African beat just as they did in the 1890s with the cakewalk, in the 1920s with the Charleston, in the 1930s and 1940s with the jitterbug, and in the 1950s with jive. In the 1960s white Americans were quick to move to Chubby Checker's Twist. They learned to Moonwalk with Michael Jackson. They picked up the high-energy hip-hop moves from rappers. "To put it very simply," explained Arthur Mitchell, "Black dance got everybody dancing."

Artists and Writers.

The explosion of African American culture in the closing years of this decade brought well-deserved attention to African American artists. Many of their works have been exhibited in Latin America, Europe, Asia, and Africa. White Americans paid greater notice to home-grown African American talent. Galleries across the nation showed the works of painters such as Jacob Lawrence, Romare Bearden, Lois Mailou Jones, and Faith Ringgold. The photographs of Gordon

Djimon Hounsou, from the African nation of Benin, played the role of Cinqué, the African who led the takeover of the slave ship *Amistad* in the 1997 film.

Parks and the sculptures of Elizabeth Catlett went on tour, too.

The names of African American writers also became familiar to the American public in the 1970s and later. Alex Haley published *Roots*, the story of the search for his ancestors both in this country and in Africa. Appearing in 1976, the year of the U.S. bicentennial, it was what Haley called "a birthday offering to my country." African Americans saw reason to be proud of their culture. Whites saw reason to respect it.

African American writers and poets such as Ntozake Shange, Alice Walker, and Terry McMillan climbed to the top of the best-seller lists or received major awards. In 1993, Toni Morrison, as you read, won the Nobel Prize for Literature—one of the highest honors awarded to any writer in the world (see Gallery, pages 384–385).

Popular Entertainment. By the 1980s and 1990s, African American talent had gone mainstream. Superstar Bill Cosby earned top TV ratings with his sitcom "The Cosby Show." Oprah Winfrey's Emmy Award-winning "The Oprah Winfrey Show" long held the title of the nation's No. 1 daytime talk show.

In popular music, African American influence had never been stronger. Great stars of the earlier days of rhythm and blues and rock 'n' roll remained popular—Tina Turner, James Brown, and Aretha Franklin. A new generation of jazz musicians appeared, including Wynton Marsalis. Artists such as Queen Latifah, Missy "Misdemeanor" Elliott, and Sean "Puffy" Combs took rap and funk to new levels of popularity. Meanwhile, other new performers like Tamia claimed Grammy nominations.

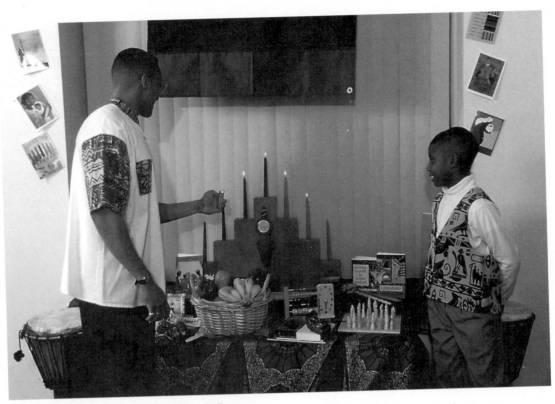

Kwanzaa is celebrated by a growing number of African Americans to honor their African heritage.

African American directors and actors have steadily turned out a series of box-office hits. Directors such as Spike Lee, John Singleton, Carl Franklin, and Charles Burnett earned places in Hollywood. So did stars such as Eddie Murphy, Whoopi Goldberg, Whitney Houston, Denzel Washington, Morgan Freeman, and Will Smith. In 1996, for example, Will Smith's blockbuster movie *Independence Day* pulled in a record $306.1 million. In 1997, Smith followed with another smash hit, *Men in Black.*

The increased media presence of African Americans has led Hollywood filmmakers to produce movies exploring the subjects of racism and slavery. *Ghosts of Mississippi* took as its central story the assassination of Medgar Evers. *Amistad* followed the rebellion and trial of Cinqué, the African who dared fight against the brutality of the Middle Passage. (For more on Cinqué, see page 132.) The effects of such movies were powerful on both actors and the people who watched them. Said Debbie Allen, one of the producers of *Amistad,*

When we shot that scene with the African mother clutching her child, choosing the freedom of death over slavery, I could not hide or hold back the tears as I watched her jump overboard into the ocean. It was as if I had jumped with her—and we both landed on the wings of an invisible bird called freedom.

Celebrating a Living Heritage. As the nation heads into the 21st century, African Americans are ensuring the survival of their

The Black American West Museum in Denver honors the contributions of African Americans to that region.

to keep the legacy alive. The Detroit Public Schools have created the African Heritage Cultural Center, which highlights African contributions to world civilizations. In Denver, Colorado, African Americans set up the Black American West Museum. This museum honors the African American pioneers who helped push back the nation's frontiers. Other museums honor African American artists. Still others collect artifacts from the past. "Years ago, people used to say there's no history; there's no record," explains one African American museum director. "Our goal, ideally, is . . . [to] tell that story."

heritage. Pressure from African American educators and parents has helped write the contributions of people of African descent into history. "If you learn more about your past," said one fifth-grader after studying about her African American ancestors, "you learn about who you are."

Every year, a growing number of African Americans celebrate their heritage through the observance of Kwanzaa (KWAN-zuh). This holiday runs from December 26 through January 1. Each night's celebration begins with the Swahili question *Habari gani?* (What's the news?) The answer is a discussion of one of the seven principles around which the holiday is organized: unity, self-determination, collective work and responsibility, cooperative economics, purpose, creativity, and faith. Each night ends with the cry, *Harambee!* ("Let's pull together.")

More than 100 African American museums around the country are also working

Taking Another Look

1. How have African Americans preserved and encouraged awareness of the African and African American heritage?

2. How has African American culture influenced white Americans?

3. **Critical Thinking** What do you think are some of the best ways to keep the African American heritage alive in the 21st century?

LOOKING AHEAD

This chapter has shown some of the ways that African Americans have tried to create a strong and living culture that their children can inherit. Evidence of the African heritage and the contributions of people of African descent can be found throughout the United States. It will be up to you, the first generation to reach adulthood in the 21st century, to keep the legacy alive for the next millennium.

FOCUS ON JUNETEENTH DAY

When is Independence Day? If you're an African American, you might respond, "June 19, 1865." That was the day that Union General Gordon Granger landed in Galveston, Texas. Nearly one month after the end of the Civil War, he announced the Emancipation Proclamation, which Texans had kept hidden from enslaved African Americans. "The people of Texas," declared Granger, "are informed that in accordance with a Proclamation from the Executive of the United States all slaves are free."

Free—the word spread like wildfire as African Americans in Texas celebrated their freedom. Each year thereafter, they honored Juneteenth Day with parades, picnics, and other events. As African Americans moved out of Texas, especially during the Great Migration of 1915-1930, they carried the tradition with them. Today more than 130 cities in the United States and Canada celebrate this holiday.

In the 1990s, members of the Congressional Black Caucus worked to put this special event on the nation's calendar. On April 10, 1997, the U.S. Senate approved a resolution recognizing June 19 as "Juneteenth Independence Day," the day that the last enslaved African Americans won their freedom. The date honors the start of the African American march toward full equality. It is a march that continues today.

CLOSE UP: CHAPTER 35

The Who, What, Where of History

1. **Who** is Toni Morrison?
2. **What** was the Stand for Children rally?
3. **What** is the purpose of the KIDpreneurs Konference?
4. **Who** was Clara McBride Hale?
5. **What** was the Million Man March?
6. **What** was the Million Woman March?
7. **Who** is Ayinde Shomari Jean-Baptiste?
8. **Where** is New York City's African Market?
9. **Who** is Katherine Dunham?
10. **What** is *Amistad?*

Making the Connection

1. Explain the connection between the Civil Rights Movement of the 1960s and the increase in the percentage of African Americans living in the South today.
2. What was the connection between attacks on affirmative action and the Million Man March?

Time Check

1. In what decade did African Americans begin returning to the South?
2. In what year did the Million Woman March take place?

What Would You Have Done?

1. Imagine that you want to spend a year being useful to other African Americans. What would you choose to do? Explain your choice, and tell how you would go about doing it.

2. Suppose you had the chance to make a major Hollywood film about some event in African American history. Which event would you choose, and which actors would you select to play the major roles? Explain.

Thinking and Writing About History

1. Imagine you had been asked to give a speech for either the Million Man March or the Million Woman March. Write what you would say in a two-minute address.

2. Suppose you could interview any one of the dancers, artists, writers, or musicians mentioned in the chapter. Decide which one you would choose to interview. Then write three questions you would like to ask that person.

Building Skills: Making Predictions

Every ten years, at the start of a decade, the government conducts a major census, or count, of the American people. It counts all kinds of things—for example, the number of people from various racial, ethnic, or national groups.

The Bureau of the Census—the agency that collects all the data—compiles its findings into a report. **Demographers,** or population experts, then take a general look at the U.S. population. Based on comparisons, they identify trends over time.

Government planners use these trends to make predictions. Predictions are forecasts of expected outcomes, or results. These predictions help officials make decisions on how governments might best serve the people.

The table on this page includes some predictions about the African American population in the 21st century. Study this data. Then answer the following questions on a separate piece of paper.

1. What is the subject of this table?

2. Find your current age group on the chart. What predictions have been made for the size of this age group between 2000 and 2016?

3. **(a)** How old will you be in 2016? Find this age group on the chart. How large is the group expected to be at that time? **(b)** Would you expect that age group to grow larger or smaller in the future? Explain.

▶▶ AFRICAN AMERICAN POPULATION BY AGE, 2000–2016 (in thousands)

Age Group	2000	2006	2010	2016
under 5	3,127	3,244	3,454	3,964
5–13	5,757	5,813	5,962	6,990
14–17	2,414	2,735	2,737	3,104
18–24	3,966	4,233	4,674	5,053
25–34	5,172	5,212	5,489	6,514
35–44	5,649	5,499	5,236	6,017
45–54	4,111	4,909	5,326	5,007
55–64	2,406	2,995	3,801	4,865
65–74	1,675	1,781	2,033	3,901
75–84	890	959	1,002	1,582
85+	317	354	396	541

Source: *U.S. Department of Commerce, Bureau of Census*

THE UNITED STATES TODAY

THE AFRICAN DIASPORA

→   Routes of slave traders

●   Major places of origin and destination of enslaved Africans

Hausa   African ethnic groups

Source: "Historical and Cultural Atlas of African Americans": Based on research by Joseph E. Harris

Map labels

ATLANTIC OCEAN

PACIFIC OCEAN

SOUTH AMERICA

UNITED STATES

NOVA SCOTIA

WEST INDIES

AFRICA

EUROPE

DENMARK

ENGLAND
- Liverpool
- London
- Bristol

FRANCE
- Paris
- Marseille
- Genoa

ITALY
- Venice
- Rome
- Naples

SPAIN
- Barcelona
- Seville
- Granada

CANARY IS.

Quebec
Montreal
New York
Richmond
Charlestown
Mobile
New Orleans
Mexico City
Veracruz
Cartagena
Callao
Lima
Valparaiso
Santiago
Buenos Aires
Montevideo
Rio de Janeiro
Salvador
Pernambuco

Arguin
Goree
Elmina
Lagos
Calabar
Cabin
Lua
Cape To

African ethnic groups
Berber
Moor
Fulani
Mandingo
Hausa/Fulani
Susu
Baule
Yoruba
Val
Asante
Ewe
Fante
Ibo
Ibibio
Awikam
Seke
Gal

105°W   90°W   75°W   60°W   45°W   30°W   15°W   0°   15°E

75°N

60°N

45°N

ASIA

ntinople
atolia
xandria

Baghdad

Basra

Shiraz

Bandar Abbas
Hormuz

Karachi

Mecca

Muscat

Jamnagor

Bombay

Jedda
uakin
assawa

Aden

Goa

Zella
Berbera

CEYLON

Mogadishu

MALAYSIA

NAIS

ombasa
anzibar
Kilwa

30°N

Tropic of Cancer

*PACIFIC
OCEAN*

PHILIPPINES

15°N

TERNATE

0°

Ibo

INDONESIA

JAVA

15°S

nane

MADAGASCAR

MAURITIUS

INDIAN OCEAN

REUNION

Tropic of Capricorn

30°S

45°S

0   1500   3000 Miles

0   1500   3000 Kilometers

45°E   60°E   75°E   90°E   105°E   120°E   135°E   150°E

40°N

20°W   10°W   0°   10°E   20°E   30°E   40°E   50°E   60°E

E U R O P E

Strait of
Gibraltar   *Tunis   *Tunis   *Algiers
Tangiers*   *Oran   *Algiers
Madeira   *Rabat
*(Portugal)   Casablanca

Mediterranean Sea   SOUTHWEST
ASIA

30°N

MOROCCO   *Tripoli

Alexandria*   *Cairo

Canary Islands   *Giza
(Spain)

Tropic of   Western   ALGERIA   LIBYA   EGYPT
Cancer   Sahara
(to Morocco)

20°N

MAURITANIA   *Timbuktu   NIGER   CHAD   Khartoum*   ERITREA
Nouakchott*   MALI   Lake   SUDAN   *Asmara
Chad

Dakar*   *Niamey   N'Djamena*   Djibouti*   DJIBOUTI   Gulf of Aden
GAMBIA   SENEGAL   BURKINA   Kano*
Banjul*   Bamako*   FASO   Addis
GUINEA-   Ouagadougou*   NIGERIA   CENTRAL   Ababa*
BISSAU   Bissau*   Ibadan*   AFRICAN   ETHIOPIA
GUINEA   CÔTE   *Lagos   REPUBLIC
Conakry*   D'IVOIRE   GHANA   Porto-   CAMEROON   Bangui*   SOMALIA
Freetown*   Yamoussoukro*   Accra*   Novo   Yaoundé*   Mogadishu*
SIERRA   Monrovia*   Lomé*   Douala*   UGANDA
LEONE   LIBERIA   Malabo*   Libreville*   DEMOCRATIC   Kampala*   KENYA
SAO TOME AND   Gulf of Guinea   CONGO   REPUBLIC   RWANDA   Nairobi*
PRINCIPE   Sao Tome*   EQUATORIAL   GABON   OF THE CONGO   Kigali*   L. Nyanza   INDIAN
GUINEA   Brazzaville*   Bujumbura*   OCEAN
Kinshasa*   BURUNDI   Mombasa*   Victoria*
L. Tanganyika   Dodoma*   SEYCHELLES
Luanda*   TANZANIA

ATLANTIC
OCEAN

ANGOLA   Lake   Moroni*
Nyasa
MALAWI   COMORO
Lilongwe*   ISLANDS
ZAMBIA
NAMIBIA   Lusaka*   MOZAMBIQUE   MADAGASCAR

AFRICA TODAY   ZIMBABWE   Antananarivo*   Reunion
BOTSWANA   Harare*   (France)

Windhoek*   Gaborone*

Pretoria*   Maputo*
Johannesburg*   Mbabane*   SWAZILAND
SOUTH   Durban*
AFRICA   Maseru*   LESOTHO

Cape Town*

0°Equator

10°S

Tropic of Capricorn

20°S

30°S

Nile River   Red Sea
White Nile   Blue Nile
Congo River
Zambezi River
Niger River

N
W   E
S

0   500   1000 Miles
0   500   1000 Kilometers

GLOSSARY

This glossary defines important terms used in this book. The page on which a term first appears is given in parentheses at the end of the definition.

abolition   act of ending something, such as slavery (79)

abolitionist   person who worked for an end to slavery in the United States (138)

affirmative action   policy designed to compensate for past discrimination in hiring practices and education and to increase opportunities for minorities and women (393)

African Diaspora   forced scattering of Africans to other parts of the world (25)

African National Congress (ANC)   major anti-apartheid organization in South Africa (387)

almanac   book that contains weather forecasts and astronomical information (93)

amendment   change made in the U.S. Constitution, or in a bill or law (82)

ancestor worship   belief that one's ancestors survive death and can be reached through prayers and offerings (32)

annex   to take over territory of another country or state (102)

anthropologists   scientists who study the origins of human beings and the development of their ways of life (3)

apartheid   former South African policy of strict segregation of races (387)

archipelago   string of islands (42)

Articles of Confederation   plan of government drawn up during the Revolutionary War (94)

artifacts   objects fashioned by humans (4)

artisans   skilled workers (28)

Atlanta Compromise   name given to speech made by Booker T. Washington in Atlanta, Georgia, in 1895 (239)

Black Cabinet   African American advisers in Franklin D. Roosevelt's administration (307)

Black Codes   laws passed by Southern states after the Civil War to limit the rights of African Americans (178)

Black Muslim   informal term for a member of the Nation of Islam (350)

black nationalism   belief that people of African descent share a common world view and have a common destiny (283)

Black Panther party   radical political party of the 1960s and 1970s, stressing self-defense by African Americans and, later, violent revolution (355)

Black Power   movement of African Americans beginning in the 1960s emphasizing control of their communities according to their own values (354)

Bleeding Kansas   nickname given to Kansas territory in 1856 because there was so much violence there over slavery (176)

blues   form of music that developed in the United States, probably from African American work songs; often expresses loneliness or sorrow, but sometimes reflects on life's problems with humor (252)

border states   four slave-holding states—Missouri, Kentucky, Maryland, Delaware—that remained loyal to the Union during the Civil War (177)

Boston Massacre   incident in which British soldiers killed five people, including Crispus Attucks (86)

boycott   organized refusal to buy or use a certain product or service in order to achieve certain aims (80)

bridewealth   gifts of money or goods made by a groom to the family of his bride (31)

bronze   metal forged from copper and tin (13)

cakewalk   high-stepping promenade, begun by enslaved African Americans as a way to poke fun at the manners of plantation owners (252)

call-and-response   music pattern from West Africa in which a leader sings a short bit and people sing it back, accompanied by percussion instruments (33)

cash crop   crop raised for sale rather than for a farmer's personal use (50)

cataract   strong rapids and waterfalls along a river (10)

chattel   a movable piece of property that can be bought and sold; way in which slaveholders viewed enslaved Africans (52)

checks and balances   system by which each of the three branches of government (executive, legislative, judicial) checks the power of the other branches to ensure that no one branch has too much power (94)

city states   self-ruling states made up of a city and its surrounding territory (27)

civil rights those rights given to all citizens of the United States by the Constitution and its amendments (232)

Civil Rights Movement movement of the 1950s and 1960s to win equal rights for all African Americans (317)

Civil War war between the United States of America and the secessionist Confederate States of America (175)

clans groups of people related to one another (39)

Cold War conflict between the United States and the Soviet Union, stopping short of actual warfare, which lasted from the end of World War II to 1990 (315)

collective bargaining negotiation between union workers and management to reach an agreement on wages, hours, and working conditions (260)

colony settlement of people living in a land outside their home country, but under the power of the home country (50)

compromise agreement in which each side agrees to give up some demands in order to reach a settlement (82)

Compromise of 1850 agreement under which Congress admitted California to the Union as a free state, left the slavery question in other former Mexican lands up to the settlers, and passed the Fugitive Slave Law (176)

Confederacy Confederate States of America; states that withdrew from the Union, or the United States, in the 1860s (177)

congregation group of people gathered together for religious worship (168)

Congressional Black Caucus informal organization of African American members of Congress (378)

conquistadors Spanish conquerors sent to the Americas in the 16th century (49)

conscientious objector someone who, because of moral or religious objections, refuses to fight in wars (362)

constitution basic laws and principles of a nation (79)

Constitutional Convention meeting called in 1787 to revise the Articles of Confederation (82)

Continental Army the colonists' military force (88)

contraband term used during the Civil War to describe an enslaved African American who fled behind Union lines (195)

convict-lease system hiring out of convicts to private employers (228)

Cotton Belt band of cotton-growing states that stretched from Georgia to Texas (110)

cotton gin machine for separating cotton fibers from the seeds of the plant (110)

credit promise to pay in the future for goods or borrowed money (206)

Declaration of Sentiments statement of liberation for the 2 million African Americans living under slavery (149)

de facto segregation separation of people by racial groups that results from customs rather than from laws (330)

delta low-lying plain at the mouth of a river (11)

denomination religious group called by the same name, such as Baptists (167)

depression period marked by a drastic decline in production and sale of goods and services and by a severe increase in unemployment (260)

dialect variations of a language spoken in a particular region or community (113)

discrimination unjust treatment based on race, religion, or sex (135)

disfranchise to deny people their rights of citizenship, especially the right to vote (229)

domesticate tame; as in to tame wild plants or animals for cultivation or stock (6)

dynasty series of rulers who are members of the same family (10)

economic sanctions refusal to trade or do business with another country until that country changes certain policies (387)

economy system of producing, distributing, and using goods and services (50)

Emancipation Proclamation January 1, 1863, declaration freeing all enslaved African Americans in parts of the South that were in rebellion (178)

embalm method of preserving the dead with chemicals (19)

entrepreneur person who risks money organizing a business to earn a profit (137)

escarpment steep cliff (6)

ethnic group people who share a culture and, often, a geographical location (275)

Exodusters African Americans who fled the South in large groups in 1879 and 1880, heading west (214)

extended family family that includes other relatives as well as parents and children (31)

federal system system of government that

divides power between the national government and state governments (94)

folk hero an admired person, or a legendary figure (217)

folktale traditional story handed down from generation to generation (33)

Free African society civic and religious organization founded in Philadelphia in the 1790s by Richard Allen (93)

Freedmen's Bureau federal agency set up in 1865 to help African Americans freed from slavery in the South; provided food and medicine, helped with jobs and housing, and started schools (178)

freedom ride any of a series of trips taken by groups to defy segregation of trains, buses, and bus stations in the South during the 1960s (343)

Free-Soil party pre-Civil War antislavery political party (146)

free state a state of the United States in which slavery was not permitted (175)

Fugitive Slave Law an 1850 law that required runaway enslaved African Americans to be returned to slaveholders (176)

geometry branch of math that studies the relationship of points, lines, planes, and surfaces of figures in space (19)

gerrymandering redrawing of a voting district to win an election advantage (381)

ghetto section of a city in which many members of the same ethnic group live (275)

grandfather clauses device in some Southern states designed to exclude African American men from voting; it exempted from literacy and property tests those men whose grandfathers had voted before 1867 (229)

Great Migration movement of African Americans in large numbers from the South to cities of the Northeast and Midwest during and after World War I (259)

Great Rift Valley deep cut in earth's surface in Africa, which extends more than 3,700 miles, from Syria to Mozambique (5)

Great Society social and economic policies and programs of President Lyndon B. Johnson in the 1960s (318)

griot in West Africa, a person who recites the important events of a society so that they can be passed down through the generations (33)

gross national product the total value of all goods and services produced in a country; also known as the gross domestic product (221)

hajj pilgrimage to the Muslim holy city of Mecca (25)

Harlem Renaissance period in the 1920s when literature and arts by African Americans flourished in Harlem, a section of New York City (260)

hieroglyphics an ancient system of writing that uses symbols and pictures to represent words (11)

immigrant person who comes to a new country, usually to settle there (50)

indentured servant person in colonial times who worked for a specific amount of time in return for passage to the colonies (51)

industrialization development of an economy based on large industries and machine production (221)

inflation a general increase in prices over time (374)

integrate to abolish separation of groups so that people of all races and ethnic groups can associate freely (204)

Islam religion based on the teachings of Muhammad (18)

jazz highly rhythmic music, often using improvisation that was originated by African Americans in the late 1800s (280)

jihad a holy war waged to spread the religion of Islam (24)

Jim Crow system of laws put into effect in the South after 1877 that discriminated against African Americans and provided for segregated public facilities (227)

Kansas-Nebraska Act law that organized Kansas and Nebraska as territories, repealing the Missouri Compromise and letting settlers there decide whether or not to allow slavery (176)

kente brilliantly colored woven cotton cloth, originally produced by the Ashanti of what is now Ghana (33)

Koran Muslim holy book (25)

labor union an association of workers formed to protect their rights (223)

latitudes imaginary lines running east and west on both sides of the equator (4)

Liberty party first antislavery political organization formed in the United States (146)

Louisiana Purchase territory stretching from the Mississippi River to the Rocky Mountains, purchased from France in 1803 (83)

lynch to hang or otherwise murder by mob action for supposed crimes (179)

Maroon in Jamaica, a runaway enslaved African or a descendent of such a person (60)

Middle Passage passage across the Atlantic Ocean from West Africa to the Americas that was the route for carrying enslaved Africans to the Americas (47)

migrant person forced to move in search of work (275)

migration an act of moving from one country or region to another (often in a group) (3)

militant aggressively active in support of a cause (149)

Minuteman Patriot who was ready to fight on a minute's notice (80)

Missouri Compromise agreement made in 1820 by which Missouri was admitted to the Union as a slave-holding state (175)

monopoly the complete or nearly complete control of an industry by one company (86, 222)

Moors Muslim Africans, mostly from North Africa; participated in the Muslim conquest of Spain (24)

mosque Muslim house of worship (25)

Mountain Men fur trappers who helped open the lands beyond the Mississippi in the early 1800s (103)

mummy dead body preserved by embalming or some similar practice; most commonly associated with the Egyptians (12)

Muslim believer in the religion of Islam (24)

NAACP National Association for the Advancement of Colored People (258)

National Urban League organization, founded in 1910, that works to increase the economic and political power of African Americans and to end racial discrimination (276)

Nation of Islam organization of African Americans who followed the religious principles of Islam and emphasized separation from white people; now, a group that split from the preceding, retaining the principles of racial separation (276)

New Deal political, economic, and social policies and practices of President Franklin D. Roosevelt in the 1930s (260)

Niagara Movement group that called for equality for African Americans; first met at Niagara Falls in 1905 (265)

nonviolence policy of not using violence or any physical force when protesting unjust laws (341)

Northwest Ordinance law passed in 1787 barring slavery in the Northwest Territory (83)

overseer person who supervised the work of enslaved Africans on a plantation (119)

Pan-Africanism belief that people of African descent have common interests and should join in a common struggle for freedom (284)

papyrus writing material made from the papyrus plant, used in ancient Egypt (11)

Patriot colonist who favored independence (80)

personal liberty laws laws passed by some Northern states forbidding anyone from helping to enforce the Fugitive Slave Law (183)

pharaoh title of the rulers of ancient Egypt (14)

plantation large farm that grew cash crops and was worked by enslaved African Americans (49)

planter plantation owner (61)

plateau an elevated piece of level land (6)

poll tax fee that a person had to pay in order to vote; instituted in the South to prevent African Americans from voting (229)

popular sovereignty principle that the people who lived in a territory should decide whether or not to allow slavery there (176)

poverty level an officially defined level of income below which a family cannot afford its basic needs (394)

prejudice intolerance of racial or ethnic groups other than one's own (93)

Progressivism reform movements of the early 20th century (257)

public opinion collective beliefs of the people in a given community or nation (143)

pyramid huge structure with square base and four triangular sides used as a royal tomb by Egyptian and Nubian civilizations (10)

racism the unjust treatment of a people by others who falsely believe that their race is superior and who have the power to enforce their attitude (63)

ragtime type of music that uses a strongly accented melody (252)

rain forest thick evergreen forest that grows in hot, wet climates near the equator (5)

recession general decrease in business activity, including production and employment (374)

Reconstruction period after the Civil War, from 1865 to 1877, during which former Confederate states rejoined the Union (175)

Redcoat name for a British soldier during the Revolutionary War (85)

regions areas with similar physical features and/or similar ways of life (7)

savanna sweeping grasslands (3)

school vouchers certificates issued by government to pay for private or public schools in another school district (404)

scribes record keepers; in ancient Egypt, people who recorded writings on papyrus (11)

secede to withdraw officially from a country or organization (177)

segregation separation by law or custom of racial groups on public transportation and in public facilities and residential areas (230)

sharecropping system of farm labor under which a person farms someone else's land in return for a share of the crop (206)

sit-in form of protest during the Civil Rights Movement in which African Americans tried to integrate segregated public facilities by refusing to leave until they were served (342)

slave codes harsh restrictive laws designed to limit the activities of enslaved African Americans (75)

slave driver a person, often an enslaved worker, who directed the work of enslaved laborers (119)

slave factory name for one of the slave-trading centers built by Europeans along the West African coast (54)

slave-holding state state in which slavery was legal before the Civil War (175)

slave raider person who raided villages in Africa for captives (48)

slum poor, overcrowded area of a city (257)

sodbusters name given to farmers on the Great Plains (215)

spiritual type of song that originated among enslaved African Americans, usually dealing with Biblical themes (121)

strike an organized refusal by employees to do work in an attempt to gain better pay and working conditions (228)

subsistence farmer farmer who produces crops for personal use only (31)

sultans Muslim rulers of the Swahili coastal towns of East Africa (40)

surname family name or last name (203)

Talented Tenth the well-educated upper 10 percent of the African American population who, according to W.E.B. Du Bois, have a duty to become leaders (264)

triangular trades name for a number of three-legged routes that were part of the sugar–slave trade of the 1600s and 1700s (62)

tributaries small rivers or streams that flow into a larger river (37)

tribute forced payment, usually from a weaker nation or people to a stronger nation or people (13)

unconstitutional not permitted by the Constitution (185)

underclass group of people with incomes below poverty level (356)

Underground Railroad system to help enslaved African Americans escape to the free states of the North and other places in North America (160)

Union the Northern and border states in the Civil War (176)

women's rights equal rights for women (143)

SOURCES

UNIT 1

THE BIG PICTURE

(3) Lerone Bennett, Jr., *Before the Mayflower: A History of the Negro in America 1619-1964,* p. 5.

CHAPTER 1

(12) Hieroglyphics, translated in *Timeframe 3000-1500 B.C.: The Age of God-Kings,* p. 60. (15) Punt official, quoted in *What Life Was Like on the Banks of the Nile,* p. 120. (15) Kasta, quoted in Basil Davidson, *The African Past,* p. 51. (16) Esarhaddon, quoted in A. Adu Boahen, *et. al., The Horizon History of Africa,* p. 80. (18) W.E.B. Du Bois, quoted in Maulana Karenga, *Introduction to Black Studies,* p. 57. Mary McLeod Bethune, quoted in Deirdre Mullane, ed., *Words to Make My Dream Children Live,* p. 43. (21) Greek sailor, quoted in A. Adu Boahen, *et. al.,* p. 80.

CHAPTER 2

(22) Arab writers, quoted in Leon E. Clark, *Through African Eyes,* pp. 28-29. (26) Muslim traveler, quoted in Basil Davidson, *A History of West Africa 1000-1800,* p. 172. (27) Muslim observer, quoted in Daniel Chu and Elliot Skinner, *A Glorious Age in Africa,* p. 112. (29) Benin chief, quoted in Basil Davidson, *A History of West Africa 1000-1800,* p. 131. (30) R.H. Stone, quoted in Robert Farris Thompson, *Flash of the Spirit,* p. 3. (30) Yoruba poem, quoted in Boahen et. al, p. 206. (31) Olaudah Equiano, quoted in Henry L. Gates, Jr., ed., *The Classic Slave Narratives,* p. 25. (34) African proverb, quoted in Kamuyu-wa-Kangethe and Maina-wa-Kinyatti, *What Is Your African Name?*

CHAPTER 3

(41) Ibn Battuta, John E.G. Sutton, *A Thousand Years of East Africa,* p. 81. (42) Swahili proverb, quoted in Jean-Denis Joubert, *Zanzibar Magic Islands,* p. 78. (43) Joubert, *Ibid.,* p. 75.

UNIT 2

THE BIG PICTURE

(47) Slave, quoted in Julius Lester, *To Be A Slave,* p. 24. (51) British critic quoted in Gary Nash, *Red, White, and Black: The Peoples of Early America,* p. 151.

CHAPTER 4

(53) Bartolome de las Casas, quoted in Daniel J. Boorstin, *The Discoverers,* p. 631. (54) African survivor of the Middle Passage, quoted in Lester, p. 25. (56) Sailor, quoted William Loren Katz, *Eyewitness: The Negro in American History,* p. 6. (57) Lord Chesterfield, quoted in E. Jefferson Murphy, *History of African Civilization,* p. 294.

CHAPTER 5

(62) Olaudah Equiano, quoted in Henry Louis Gates, Jr., ed: *The Classic Slave Narratives,* p. 37. (63) Olaudah Equiano, *Ibid.,* pp. 37-38. (51) Benjamin Quarles, *The Negro in the Making of America,* Revised Edition, p. 28.

CHAPTER 6

(68) 1667 law, quoted in Lerone Bennett, Jr., *Before the Mayflower: A History of the Negro in America 1619-1964,* p. 46. (69) African farmer, quoted in Robert A. Devine, *America Past and Present.* (71) Georgian leader, quoted in Katz (1967 ed.), p. 21. (72) Council of New Netherlands, quoted in Bennett, p. 442; Colony's Director, quoted in George Williams, *History of the Negro Race in America,* 1619-1880, p. 135. (73) German Quakers, quoted in Katz (1967 ed.), p. 35. (76) Alex Haley, quoted in "Why Roots Hit Home" *Time,* Feb. 14, 1977.

UNIT 3

THE BIG PICTURE

(79) Jupiter Hammon, quoted in Benjamin Quarles, *The Negro in the American Revolution,* p. 27. (81) Lord Dunmore, quoted in John Hope Franklin and Alfred A. Moss, Jr., *From Slavery to Freedom: A History of Negro Americans* 6th ed., p.69.

CHAPTER 7

(85) Prince Whipple, quoted in Benjamin Quarles, *Black Mosaic,* p. 48; Passersby, quoted in Quarles, *The Negro in the American Revolution,* p. 3; Boston Massacre participants and witnesses, quoted in Nell, p. 15; Crispus Attucks, quoted in Lerone Bennett, Jr., *Before the Mayflower: A History of the Negro in America 1619-1964,* p. 61; (88) White soldier, quoted in Bennett, p. 67. (89) British official and slave-ship owner, quoted in Quarles, *The Negro in the American Revolution,* p. 165; Slave-ship owner, quoted in Nell, p. 244; George Washington, quoted in Robert Goldston, *The Negro Revolution,* p. 53.

CHAPTER 8

(93) Benjamin Banneker, quoted in Milton Meltzer, ed. *In Their Own Words: A History of the American Negro 1619-1865,* pp. 14-15; Free African Society, quoted in August Meier and Elliot Rudwick, *From Plantation to Ghetto,* 3rd ed., p. 106. (95) Mr. Ellsworth, quoted in George Williams, *History of the Negro Race in America 1619-1880,* p. 418; Free African Society, quoted in Quarles, *Black Mosaic,* p. 63. (96) Lord Chief Justice Mansfield, quoted in Josephine Kamm, *The Slave Trade,* p. 25.

CHAPTER 9

(101) John Johnson and ship captain, quoted in Williams, p. 30; Commodore Chauncey, quoted in Katz (1967 ed.), p. 53; Oliver Hazard Perry, quoted in Franklin and Moss, p. 100. (88) Andrew Jackson, quoted in Bennett, p. 452.

UNIT 4

THE BIG PICTURE

(107) Ralph Ellison, quoted in Herbert George Gutman, *The Black Family in Slavery and Freedom,* p. 360.

CHAPTER 10

(112) Harriet Jacobs, quoted in Henry L. Gates, Jr., *The Classic Slave Narratives* pp. 353, 354. (113) White New England minister, quoted in George Williams, *History of the Negro Race in America 1619-1880,* (114) South Carolina law, quoted in William Loren Katz, Eyewitness: *The Negro in American History,* 3rd ed., p. 34. (115) Song, Millie Williams, former African American slave, quoted in George P. Rawick, ed., *The American Slave: A Composite Autobiography,* p. 172. (116) Uncle Silas, quoted in Saunders Redding, *They Came in Chains,* pp. 35-36. (117) Stephen (an African American child) quoted in James Mellon, ed., *Bullwhip Days,* p. 290; (119) Solomon Northup, quoted in Milton Meltzer, ed., *In Their Own Words: A History of the American Negro 1619-1983,* p. 24, 25. (121) Harriet Jacobs, quoted in Gates, p. xviii; Henry "Box" Brown, quoted in Charles Stearns, *Narrative of Henry Box Brown,* p. 57; (122) One American on slave literature, quoted in, R.J.M. Blackett, *Building an Antislavery Wall: Black Americans in the Atlantic Abolitionist Movement, 1830-1860,* p. 25.

CHAPTER 11

(124) David Walker, quoted in Lerone Bennett, Jr., *Before the Mayflower: A History of the Negro America 1619-1964,* p. 148. (125) David Walker, quoted in Milton Meltzer, ed. *The Black Americans: A History in Their Own Words 1619-1983,* p. 16. (126) Observer of Stone uprising, Nat Turner, quoted in Herbert Aptheker, *Nat Turner's Slave Rebellion,* p. 136. (128) Gabriel Prosser, quoted Bennett, p. 126. (129) Frederick Douglass, *Ibid.,* p. 170. (130) Nat Turner, quoted in Blassingame (1979 ed.); p. 219. (131) Nat Turner, quoted in Katz (1974 ed.), p. 121; judge, quoted in Bennett, p. 139. (118) Grave marker, quoted in Milton C. McFarlane, *Cudjoe the Maroon.*

CHAPTER 12

(134) Nancy Gardner Prince, quoted in Mary Frances Berry and John W. Blassingame, *Long Memory: The Black Experience in America,* p. 50. (135) Nancy Gardner Prince, Ibid. (137) Frederick Douglass, quoted in Bennett, p. 180. (139) Free African American statement, quoted in Bennett, p. 147. (156) Sojourner Truth, quoted in Diane Ravitch, *The American Reader: Words That Moved a Nation,* p. 86.

UNIT 5

THE BIG PICTURE

(143) Frederick Douglass, quoted in Lerone Bennett, Jr., *Before the Mayflower, A History of the Negro in America 1619-1964,* p. 160. (131) William Lloyd Garrison, *Ibid.,* p. 153.

CHAPTER 13

(149) Women abolitionists' statement, quoted in Dorothy Sterling, ed., *We Are Your Sisters,* p. 115. (151) Frederick Douglass, quoted in Benjamin Quarles, *Black Abolitionists,* p. 63; Henry Highland Garnet, quoted in Bennett, p. 155. (152) Henry Highland Garnet, quoted in Mary Frances Berry and John W. Blassingame, *Long Memory: The Black Experience in America,* p. 62; Frederick Douglass, quoted in Quarles, p. 66. (154) Frederick Douglass and Elizabeth Cady Stanton, quoted in Sarah M. Evans, *Born for Liberty,* p. 122. (157) Merchant, quoted in Katz (1974 ed.), p. 173.

CHAPTER 14

(159) William Still, quoted in Quarles, p. 156. (160) Edward Lycurgas, quoted in James Mellon, ed., *Bullwhip Days,* p. 302. (162) Thomas Cole, *Ibid.,* p. 65; Harriet Tubman, quoted in Sterling, p. 66. (163) Harriet Tubman, quoted in Bennett, p. 166; Harriet Tubman, quoted in Sterling, p. 69; Harriet Tubman, quoted in Linden, *et al., Legacy of Freedom: A History of the United States,* p. 298; Harriet Tubman, quoted in Bennett, (165) John Hope Franklin and Alfred A. Moss, *From Slavery to Freedom,* 6th ed., pp. 168-69; Charles Blockson, *"The Underground Railroad," National Geographic,* July, 1984, p. 9.

CHAPTER 15

(166) Thomas James, quoted in William S. McFeeley, *Frederick Douglass,* p. 82. (167) Richard Allen, quoted in Katz, p. 59. (168) New York, *Colored American,* quoted in August Meier and Elliot Rudwick, *From Plantation to Ghetto,* 3rd ed., p. 105. (170) Samuel Ringgold Ward, quoted in Quarles, p. 72. (171) Samuel Ringgold Ward, quoted in Bennett, p. 183.

UNIT 6

THE BIG PICTURE

(175) Frederick Douglass, quoted in Milton Meltzer, ed., *A History in Their Own Words 1619-1983.* (177) Abraham Lincoln, quoted in Daniel J. Boorstin and Brooks Mather Kelley, *A History of the United States,* p. 289.

CHAPTER 16

(180) Frederick Douglass, quoted in Lerone Bennett, Jr., *Before the Mayflower: A History of the Negro in America,* p.149; (181) Martin Robison Delaney, quoted in William Loren Katz, *Eyewitness: The Negro in American History,* p. 189. (182) African Americans, white abolitionists, and President Franklin Pierce, quoted in James McPherson, *Battle Cry of Freedom,* p. 119. (183) Anthony Burns, quoted in Herbert Aptheker, ed. *A Documentary History of the Negro People in the United States, Vol. I,* p. 371. (185) Newspaper, quoted in McPherson, Battle Cry, p. 176; Frederick Douglass, quoted in John Hope Franklin, *From Slavery to Freedom: A History of Negro Americans,* 3rd ed., p. 179; John Brown and Frederick Douglass, quoted in McPherson, *Battle Cry,* p. 203. (186) John Brown and Frederick Douglass, *Ibid.,* p. 205. (187) African American

women in Brooklyn, quoted in Herbert Aptheker, ed., *A Documentary History of theNegro People in the United States,* p. 441; Baltimore newspaper, quoted in McPherson, *Battle Cry,* p. 211.

CHAPTER 17

(191) *Atlantic Monthly,* quoted in McPherson, *Battle Cry,* p. 686; Frederick Douglass, quoted in James McPherson, *The Negro's Civil War,* pp. 39-40; Abraham Lincoln, quoted in Boortin and Kelley, eds, p. 281. (192) Frederick Douglass, quoted in McPherson, *Battle Cry,* p. 558; Henry M. Turner, quoted in McPherson, *Civil War,* p. 50. (193) Linton Stephens, (Southern leader) quoted in Peter J. Parish, *Slavery; History and Historians,* p. 153. (195) Frederick Douglass, quoted in McPherson, *Civil War,* p. 164; Cincinnati whites, quoted in Jack Fincher, "I Felt Freedom in My Bones," *The Smithsonian,* October 1990, p. 48. (198) African American soldier, *Ibid.;* Lorenzo Thomas (Adjutant general), quoted in Franklin, p. 197. James A. Seddon, quoted in McPherson, *Battle Cry,* p. 793. (200) Peter Burchard, "Heroes of 'Glory' Fought Bigotry Before All Else," quoted in *New York Times,* December 17, 1989. (201) Edwin Stanton, quoted in Benjamin Quarles, *The Negro in the Making of America, Revised Edition,* p. 119.

CHAPTER 18

(202) Freed African American, quoted in Milton Meltzer, ed., *In Their Own Words: A History of the American Negro 1865-1916,* p. 3. (204) Northern white woman, quoted in Gerda Lerner, *Black Women in White America,* pp. 102-103; Resident of Selma, quoted in Eric Foner, *Reconstruction: America's Unfinished Revolution 1863-1877,* p. 98. (206) John Solomon Lewis, quoted in Nell Irvin Painter, *Exodusters,* p. 3. (208) Blanche K. Bruce and white Democrat, quoted in *American Adventures, Vol. 2, Old Hate-New Hope,* p. 65. (209) Former African American slave, quoted in Meltzer, (1965 ed.), pp. 34-35. (210) W.E.B. Du Bois, quoted in Foner, p. 602.

CHAPTER 19

(212) John Solomon Lewis (African American sharecropper), quoted in Painter, p. 3. (215) Henry Adams, *Ibid.,* p. 87. (217) Nat Love, quoted in William Loren Katz, *The Black West,* p. 152.

UNIT 7

THE BIG PICTURE

(224) Thomas E. Miller, quoted in William Loren Katz, *Eyewitness: The Negro in American History,* p. 334.

CHAPTER 20

(226) "Jim Crow" song, quoted in Lerone Bennett, Jr., *Before the Mayflower: A History of the Negro in America,* p. 255. (227) T. Thomas Fortune, *Black and White,* p. 29. (228) African American fireman, quoted in Katz (1974 ed.), p. 305. (231) Editor of white newspaper, quoted in C. Vann

Woodward, *The Strange Career of Jim Crow,* p. 68. (232) T. Thomas Fortune, quoted in Katz (1974 ed.), p. 343; *Savannah Tribune,* quoted in Katz (1969 ed.), p. 378. (233) Ida B. Wells, quoted in Dorothy Sterling, *Black Foremothers,* p. 79. (234) Delegate and George White, quoted in Katz, (1974 ed.), 318.

CHAPTER 21

(236) New York *World,* quoted in Bennett, p. 204. (238) Booker T. Washington, *Up From Slavery,* p. 80. (225) Booker T. Washington, quoted in Emma Low Thornbrough, ed., *Booker T. Washington,* pp. 34, 35. (240) T. Thomas Fortune, *Ibid.,* p. 113; William Monroe Trotter, Ibid., p. 118; Charles W. Chestnutt, Ibid., p. 117; Ida B. Wells-Barnett, *Ibid.,* p. 121; Booker T. Washington, *Ibid.,* p. 35; Andrew Carnegie and Theodore Roosevelt, *Ibid.,* p. 17. (244) Booker T. Washington, courtesy of Tuskegee University.

CHAPTER 22

(254) George Washington Carver, quoted in Gene Adair, *George Washington Carver,* p. 83. (241) Paul Laurence Dunbar, *Lyrics of Lowly Life: The Poetry of Paul Laurence Dunbar,* p. 167.

UNIT 8

THE BIG PICTURE

(257) W.E.B. Du Bois, quoted in William Loren Katz, *Eyewitness: The Negro in American History,* p. 421.

CHAPTER 23

(263) Samuel Courtney (Washington supporter), quoted in Stephen R. Fox, *The Guardian of Boston: William Monroe Trotter,* p. 52. (264) W.E.B. Du Bois, quoted in August Meier, Elliott Rudwick and Francis L. Broderick, *Black Protest Thought in the Twentieth Century,* pp. 67-68; **Points of View:** Booker T. Washington, quoted in *American Reader: Words that Moved a Nation,* p. 187; W.E.B. De Bois, *The Souls of Black Folk,* p. 42. (265) W.E.B. Du Bois, quoted in Herbert Aptheker, ed. *A Documentary History of the United States, Volume II,* pp. 907, 909. (266) W.E.B. William English Walling, quoted in Lerone Bennett, Jr., *Before the Mayflower: A History of the Negro in America,* p. 337. (267) W.E.B. Du Bois, quoted in Bennett, p. 383; National Negro Committee, quoted in Patricia W. Romero, ed., *I, Too, Am America: Documents from 1619 to the Present,* p. 182. NAACP, *Ibid.,* p. 183; Deputy, quoted in Katz (1974 ed.), p. 350. (268) NAACP, quoted Meier, Rudwick and Broderick, p. 66. (269) W.E.B. Du Bois, quoted in Katz (1974 ed.), p. 420-421, (270) Benjamin Hooks, quoted in "Called Complacent, NAACP Looks to Future," *New York Times,* June 10, 1991. (271) W.E.B. Du Bois, quoted in *The Souls of Black Folk,* p. 37.

CHAPTER 24

(272) Hattiesburg, Mississippi man, quoted in Leslie H. Fishel, Jr. and Benjamin Quarles, *The Negro American,* p. 399. (274) Lonely voice, quoted in Milton Meltzer, ed.,

In Their Own Words: A History of the American Negro 1916-1965, pp. 4-5; African American newspapers, quoted in Emmet J. Scott, *Negro Migration During the War,* p. 31. (279) W.E.B. Du Bois, quoted in Meltzer, (1916-1965), p. 27.

CHAPTER 25

(283) Marcus Mosiah Garvey, quoted in E. David Cronon, Marcus Garvey, p.8; Hugh Mulzac (meeting participant), quoted in David L. Lewis, *When Harlem Was in Vogue,* p. 39: W.E.B. Du Bois, *Ibid.,* p. 15. (284) *Kansas City Call, Ibid.,* p. 24; Claude McKay, quoted in Mary Ellison, *The Black Experience: American Blacks Since 1865,* p. 106. (285) Marcus Garvey, quoted in E. David Cronon, *Black Moses: The Story of Marcus Garvey and the Universal Negro Improvement Association,* p. 189; Marcus Garvey, quoted in John H. Bracey, Jr., August Meier, Elliot Rudwick, *Black Nationalism in America,* p. 191. (286) Marcus Garvey, quoted in Maulana Karenga, *Introduction to Black Studies,* p. 118; (288) Kwame Nkrumah, quoted in David Lamb, *The Africans,* p. 286. (275) Cronon, *Black Moses.*

CHAPTER 26

(291) African American newspaper, quoted in Lewis , p. 24; African American poet, quoted in Milton Meltzer, ed., *The Black Americans: A History in Their Own Words 1619-1983,* p. 202; African American writer, quoted in Lewis, p. 96. (297) Sargent Johnson, quoted in *The Negro Almanac,* p. 765. (301) Langston Hughes, reprinted in *The American Experience,* p. 965.

CHAPTER 27

(302) Crowd member, quoted in Meltzer, *In Their Own Words,* p. 98. (303) Langston Hughes, *The Big Sea,* Arnold Y. Hill, (Urban League member), quoted in Howard Sitkoff, *A New Deal for Blacks: The Emergence of Civil Rights as a National Issue, Volume I,* p. 35. (305) Robert Vann, quoted in Strickland and Reich, p. 74; Man, quoted in Studs Terkel, *Hard Times: An Oral History of the Great Depression,* p. 499. (306) African American woman, quoted in Katz, (1969 ed.), p. 435; Franklin D. Roosevelt, quoted in Stikoff, p. 44; NAACP member, *Ibid.,* p. 55. (307) African American newspaper, Ibid., p. 65; Eleanor Roosevelt, Ibid., p. 63; Mary McLeod Bethune, quoted in Paula Giddings, *When and Where I Enter: The Impact of Black Women on Race and Sex in America,* p. 222. (308) New Deal program, quoted in Sitkoff, p. 69; Paul Robeson, Ibid., p. 328. (309) Frances Perkins, quoted in Katz, (1974 ed.), p. 430; Union organizer, *Ibid.,* p. 423. (310) Thurgood Marshall, quoted in Bracey, Meier, and Rudwick; A. Phillip Randolph, quoted in Edgar Toppin, *The Black American in U.S. History,* p. 233. (298) Ernest Critchlow, quoted in Katz (1974 ed.), p. 428.

UNIT 9

THE BIG PICTURE

(315) Martin Luther King, Jr., quoted in Diane Ravitch, ed. *The American Reader: Words That Moved a Nation,* p. 333.

CHAPTER 28

(321) Leslie Lee, quoted in "World War II's Black Pilots Fought on Two Fronts," *New York Times,* April 21, 1991. (322) African American soldier, quoted in William Loren Katz, *Eyewitness: The Negro in American History,* p. 466. (323) Sybil Lewis, quoted in Mark Jonathan Harris, Franklin D. Mitchell, and Steven J. Schechter, *The Homefront: America During World War II,* p. 119. (327) Geoffrey Perrett, *Days of Sadness, Years of Triumph,* p. 323; James Baldwin, quoted in J. Milton Yinger, *A Minority Group in American Society,* (New York; McGraw -Hill, 1965), p. 52.

CHAPTER 29

(332) John Birks "Dizzy" Gillespie, quoted in Studs Terkel, *Giant of Jazz,* p. 192. (334) John H. Johnson, "Publishers Statement" *Ebony,* Nov. 1990. (335) Ralph Ellison, "Flying Home," quoted in Edgar V. Roberts and Henry E. Jacobs, *Literature: An Introduction to Reading and Writing,* pp. 357-358.

CHAPTER 30

(337) Thurgood Marshall, quoted in William H. Chaffe, *The Unfinished Journey.* (339) Earl Warren, quoted in Chaffe, p. 152. (340) Rosa Parks and white bus driver, quoted in Henry Hampton and Steve Fayer, *Voices of Freedom: An Oral History of the Civil Rights Movement From the 1950s Through the 1960s,* p. 20; Leaflet , quoted in Anna Kosoff, *The Civil Rights Movement and Its Legacy,* pp. 31, 33. (341) Elderly African American woman, quoted in Robert Weisbrot, *Freedom Bound,* p. 17; Martin Luther King, Jr., quoted in J.W. Davidson, *et al, Nation of Nations: A Narrative History,* p. 1167. (342) Ezell Blair, Jr., quoted in Chaffe, p. 168; (343) James Farmer and Diane Nash, quoted in Pete Seeger and Bob Reiser, *Everybody Says Freedom,* p. 52. Freedom Rider's song, *Ibid.,* p. 61. (344) Martin Luther King, Jr., quoted in Lerone Bennett Jr., *Before the Mayflower: A History of the Negro in America 1619-1964,* p. 388; "Bull" Connor, quoted in Katz, p. 484; Martin Luther King, Jr., quoted in Seeger and Reiser, p. 109. (345) John F. Kennedy, Jr., quoted in Chaffe, p. 214; Martin Luther King, Jr., quoted in Ravitch, *The American Reader,* p. 332. (346) School Board member, quoted in "Historic Battleground, Old Battle: School Bias," *New York Times,* December 22, 1989.

CHAPTER 31

(347) Martin Luther King, Jr., quoted in Paul Sann, *The Angry Decade: The Sixties,* p. 140. (350) Fannie Lou Hamer, quoted in Hampton and Fayer, p. 178; (351) Malcolm X, quoted in Meier, Bracey, and Rudwick, p. 41. (352) Malcolm X, quoted in Seeger and Reiser p. 190. (353) Commentator, quoted in Rhoda Lois Blumberg, *Civil Rights: The 1960s Freedom Struggle,* p. 41. (354) James Meredith, quoted in Sann, p. 181; Stokely Carmichael and Willie Ricks, quoted in Seeger and Reiser, p. 218; (355) Martin Luther King, Jr., quoted in Chaffe, p. 367. (356) Lyndon B. Johnson, quoted in Sann. p. 229; Martin Luther King, Jr., *Ibid.,* p. 231; Kerner Commission report, quoted in Anna Kosof, *The Civil Rights Movement*

and Its Legacy, p. 91. (357) Barbara Jordan, quoted in Kosof, p. 91. (358) C. Eric Lincoln and Lawrence Mamiya, *The Black Church in the African American Experience,* p. 369. (359) Marian Wright Edelman, quoted in Hampton and Fayer, p. 244; Alex Haley, *Ibid.,* p. 250.

CHAPTER 32

(362) Robin Mannock (reporter) and Clide Brown (soldier), quoted in "The Negro in Vietnam," *Time,* May 26, 1967, p. 15. (363) Martin Luther King, Jr., quoted in Weisbrot, p. 247; African American soldier, quoted in Mary Frances Berry and John W. Blassingame, *Long Memory: The Black Experience in America,* p. 333. (364) Martin Luther King, Jr., quoted in Weisbort, p. 247; Viet Cong leaflets and African American medic, quoted in *Time,* Jan. 19, 1968, p. 21. (365) From an interview with John Wilkins, Aug. 1991. (367) African American soldier, quoted in "The Negro in Vietnam," *Time,* May 26, 1967, p. 18. (368) Visitor to "the Wall", quoted in Wallace Terry, *Bloods* (New York: Ballantine Books, 1984), p. 331. (369) "Siege of Khesahn Lifted; Troops Hunt Foe," *New York Times,* April 6, 1968.

UNIT 10

THE BIG PICTURE

(371) Carter G. Woodson, quoted in Deirdre Mullane, ed., *Words to Make My Dream Children Live,* p. 489. (374) Clarence Thomas, quoted in "Thomas Caught Up in the Conflict," *The Washington Post,* June 7, 1996. (376) Shirley Chisholm, quoted in Mullane, p. 81.

CHAPTER 33

(376) Chuck E. Burris, quoted in "Birthplace of Klan Chooses a Black Mayor," *The New York Times,* Nov. 22, 1997. (377) Stone Mountain citizen, *Ibid.* (377) Jesse Jackson, Jr., quoted in "Introducing Jesse L. Jackson, Jr.," *Ebony,* Feb. 1996, p. 157. (378) Jesse Jackson, Sr., quoted in Diane Ravitch, ed., *The American Reader: Words that Moved a Nation,* p. 368. (381) Jesse Jackson, Sr., "Analysts Differ on Ruling's Wider Effect," *The Washington Post,* June 14, 1996. (381) Clarence Thomas, quoted in "Thomas Caught Up in Conflict," *The Washington Post,* June 7, 1996. (381) Cynthia McKinney, "A Product of the Voting Rights Act," *The Washington Post,* Nov. 26, 1996. (382) Joseph Lowery, quoted in "Arson at Black Churches Echoes Bigotry of Past," *USA Today,* Feb. 8, 1996. (383) Kweisi Mfume, quoted in "Can Kweisi Mfume Turn the NAACP Around?" *Ebony,* Jan. 1997, p. 93. (386) Jesse Jackson, Sr., quoted in "Jesse Goes to Africa," *Black Enterprise,* Feb. 1998, p. 28. (p. 387) Nelson Mandela, quoted in "Free," *Newsweek,* Feb. 19, 1990, p. 44. (389) Nelson Mandela, quoted in "Mandela," *Newsweek,* July 2, 1990. (389) Leon H. Sullivan, quoted in

"A Meeting Place for Africans and U.S. Blacks," *The New York Times,* April 18, 1991.

CHAPTER 34

(392) Bob Lanier, quoted in "Bucking the Trend," *Black Enterprise,* Feb. 1996, p. 195. (393) Bob Lanier, *Ibid,* p. 198. (395) Douglas Glasgow, *The Black Underclass,* p. 274. (395) Ward Connerly, quoted in "Black University of CA Regents Member Fostered Move to Review Affirmative Action There," *Jet,* Aug. 7, 1995, p. 13. (398) Earl Graves, quoted in "Publisher's Page," *Black Enterprise,* Jan. 1998. (401) Rodney King, quoted in "What He Said," *Poughkeepsie Journal,* May 2, 1992. (401) Merlie Evers, quoted in "A Hot Summer of Bloodshed and Change," *The New York Times,* Feb. 4, 1994. (401) Merlie Evers, quoted in "NAACP Convenes 88th Convention in Pittsburgh," *Jet,* Aug. 4, 1997, p. 4. (401) Martin Luther King, Jr., quoted in Deirdre Mullane, *Words to Make My Dream Children Live,* p. 281. (404) Jean Brown Trickey, quoted in "The Right of Passage," *People,* Sept. 29, 1997, p. 170. (404) Editorial, "King Day: Signs of Progress," *Detroit News,* Jan. 19, 1996. (404-405) **Points of View:** Elaine R. Jones and Michael Eric Dyson, quoted in "Are Integrated Schools Still Needed?" *Jet,* Aug. 4, 1997, pp. 12-14, 16. (405) NAACP lawyer, quoted in "Look Who's Saying Separate Is Equal," *The New York Times,* Oct. 1, 1995. (406) Lamont Hawkins, Diedra Roper, and Vernon Slaughter, quoted in "hip-hoppreneurs," *Black Enterprise,* Dec. 1997

CHAPTER 35

(408) Henry Louis Gates, quoted in "Toni Morrison Is '93 Winner of Nobel Prize in Literature," *The New York Times,* Oct. 8. 1993. (411) Andrew Young, quoted in "Race and the South," *U.S. News and World Report,* July 23, 1990. (412) Colin Powell, quoted in "Reach Back and Reach Down," *Ebony,* June 1997, p. 23. (412) Clara McBride Hale, quoted in *Notable Black Women,* (Detroit: Gale Research, 1992) p. 434. (413) Ten-year-old student, *Ibid.* (413) Dr. Niara Sudarkasa, quoted in "Extended Families of the '90s," *Ebony,* Nov. 1996, p. 178. (414) Ayinde Shomari Jean-Baptiste, quoted in "Ayinde Jean-Baptiste: Superstudent," *Ebony,* Feb. 1997, p. 152. (415) Phile Chionesu, quoted in "Saw a Need, Went to Work," *Philadelphia Daily News,* Oct. 24, 1997. (415) Alicia Byrd, quoted in "Black Churches Turn to Teaching Their Young," *The New York Times,* Aug. 17, 1991. (418) Arthur Mitchell, quoted in "There's No Business Like Black Show Business," *Ebony,* August 1991. (420) Debbie Allen, quoted in "My Journey: The Making of Amistad," *Essence,* Dec. 1997, p. 140. (421) Museum director, quoted in "Black Museums: Keeping the Legacy Alive," *Ebony,* Mar. 1994, p. 42. (422) Gordon Granger, quoted in "Jubilee," *Time,* May 26, 1997, p. 117.

INDEX

Note: Pages in **boldface** type indicate photographs, maps, charts, and graphs; pages in *italics* indicate incorporated biographies and galleries.

PHOTO CREDITS

Iwasaki/Life Magazine c. Time Inc.; (bottom right) Culver Pictures, Inc. 318: UPI Bettmann. 320: The Schomberg Center. 321: Culver Pictures, Inc. 322: Bettmann Archive. 324: Wide World Photos. 325: Bettmann Archive. 326: Courtesy of the National Cotton Council. 329: Courtesy of the Chicago Housing Department. 331: Bettmann Archive. 332: Bettmann Archive. 333: Bettmann Archive. 336: Bettmann Archive. 337: Library of Congress. 339: Bettmann Archive. 340: Bettmann Archive. 341: Bettmann Archive. 342: Wide World Photos. 343: Bettmann Archive. 335: Bettmann Archive. 348: Magnum Photos. 350: Bettmann Archive. 351: Bettmann Archive. 353: Bettmann Archive. 355: Wide World Photos. 356: Bettmann Archive. 357: Magnum Photos. 360: John Wilkins. 362: Bettmann Archive. 373: Granger Collection. 365: Wide World Photos. 366: Wide World Photos.

UNIT 10

370: (top left) A. Ramey Stock Boston; (top right) Sotographs, Liaison International; (bottom right) Hazel Hankin/Impact Visuals. 375: Stock Boston. 376: Reuters/Tami L. Chappell/Archive Photos. 377: Rob Nelson, Black Star. 378: SIPA Press. 380: Bob Daemmrich, Stock Boston. 381: Courtesy of Congressional Black Caucus. 382: SIPA Press. 383: Jay Mallin, Impact Visuals. 384: (top to bottom) Sarah Putnam,

Courtesy of Henry Louis Gates, Jr.; Courtesy of Maya Angelou; Doug Hicks, Ithaca, New York; AP/Wideworld Photo. 385: (top to bottom) Reuters/Corbis-Bettmann; Archive Photos; AP/Wideworld Photos; Benno Friedman, Outline. 386: Jim Bourg, The Gamma Liaison Network. 387: AP/Wideworld. 388: Hazel Hankin, Stock Boston. 392: Liaison International. 393: Michael Springer, Gamma Liaison. 397: Alain Mclaughlin, Impact Visuals. 398: (top to bottom) Paul Hosefros/New York Times; UPI Bettmann; Rick Reinhard, Courtesy of The Children's Defense Fund; C. Brown, SIPA Press. 399: (top to bottom) Courtesy of United States Senate; Corbis-Bettmann; Evan Agosti, Gamma Liaison; Courtesy of the Mayor, Detroit, Michigan. 400: Reuters/Lou Dematteis/Archive Photos. 401: Gregory Pace, Sygma. 402: Johnson/Liaison. 403: The Washington Post. 404: Courtesy of Marva Collins. 408: Guner, SIPA Press. 412: Jerome Friar, Impact Visuals; UPI/Corbis-Bettmann. 414: (top to bottom) Daryl Estrine, Outline; The Schomberg Center; Alain Morvan, Gamma Liaison; Courtesy of Johnson Publishing. 415: (top to bottom) Jeff Slocomb, Outline; Ron Caesar; Ken Schles; Pete Souza, Gamma Liaison. 417: Bill Biggart, Impact Visuals; 418: Lawrence Migdale, Stock Boston. 419: Photofest. 420: Lawrence Migdale, Stock Boston. 421: Sherri Stewart O'Hara.

ACKNOWLEDGMENTS

Grateful acknowledgment is made to the following for permission to reprint copyrighted material:

AYER COMPANY—p. 113 from *History of the Negro Race in America 1619–1880,* by George Washington Williams. Reprinted by permission of Ayer Company Publishers, Box 958, Salem, N.H. 03102

BANTAM DOUBLEDAY DELL PUBLISHING GROUP INC.— pp. 265, 271: from *The Souls of Black Folk,* by W. E. B. Du Bois. Courtesy of Bantam Doubleday Dell Publishing Group Inc.— pp. 340, 350, 359: from *Voices of Freedom: An Oral History of the Civil Rights Movement from the 1950s Through the 1980s,* by Henry Hampton and Steve Fayer. Copyright (c) 1990. Reprinted by permission of Bantam Books.

THE JOAN DAVES AGENCY—p. 344: from "Letter from Birmingham Jail," Copyright (c) 1963 by Martin Luther King, Jr., copyright renewed 1991 by Coretta Scott King. Reprinted by permission of The Joan Daves Agency.—p. 349: from "Nobel Acceptance Speech," Copyright (c) 1964, 1965, The Nobel Foundation. Reprinted by permission of The Joan Daves Agency.—p. 355: from "I've Been to the Mountaintop," Copyright (c) 1968, the Estate of Martin Luther King, Jr. Reprinted by permission of The Joan Daves Agency.—pp. 315, 344: from "I Have a Dream," Copyright (c) 1963 by Martin Luther King, Jr., copyright renewed 1991 by Coretta Scott King. Reprinted by permission of The Joan Daves Agency.

JOHNSON PUBLISHING COMPANY—pp. 68, 72, 85, 88, 102, 124–125, 128, 131, 137, 139, 143, 145, 151, 163, 171, 180, 266, 267: from *Before the Mayflower: A History of Black America,* Fifth Edition, by Lerone Bennett Jr. Copyright (c) Johnson Publishing Company, Inc. 1961, 1962, 1964, 1969, 1982.

WILLIAM MORRIS AGENCY INC.—p. 335: from "Flying Home" by Ralph Ellison. Copyright (c) 1944 (renewed) by Ralph Ellison. Reprinted by permission of the William Morris Agency, Inc.

OXFORD UNIVERSITY PRESS, INC.—pp. 182, 185, 186, 187, 191, 192, 198: from *Battle Cry of Freedom: The Civil War Era* by James M. McPherson. Copyright (c) 1988 by Oxford University Press, Inc. pp. 134–135, 152, 154: from *Long Memory: The Black Experience in America* by Mary Frances Berry and John W. Blassingame. Copyright (c) 1982 by Oxford University Press, Inc. Reprinted by permission.—pp. 151, 152, 159, 170: from *Black Abolitionists* by Benjamin Quarles. Copyright (c) 1969 by Oxford University Press, Inc. Reprinted by permission.

PENGUIN USA—pp. 62, 63, 107, 112–113, 121: from *The Classic Slave Narratives,* edited by Henry Louis Gates, Jr. Courtesy of Penguin USA.

PRENTICE HALL—pp. 239–240: from the book, *Booker T. Washington,* by E.L. Thornbrough, Copyright (c) 1969. Used by permission of the publisher, Prentice Hall, Upper Saddle River, NJ

RANDOM HOUSE, INC./ALFRED A. KNOPF, INC.—pp. 191, 192, 194, 195, 196: from *The Negro's Civil War,* by James McPherson. Copyright (c) 1965 by James McPherson. Reprinted by permission of Pantheon Books, a Division of Random House, Inc.—pp. 82, 87, 101, 185, 194, 198, 371, 393: from *From Slavery to Freedom,* by John Hope Franklin. Copyright (c) 1980 by Alfred A. Knopf, Inc. Reprinted by permission of the publisher.

UNIVERSITY OF NORTH CAROLINA PRESS—pp. 79, 87, 89: from *The Negro and the American Revolution,* by Benjamin Quarles. Copyright (c) 1961 by The University of North Carolina Press. Reprinted by permission of The University of North Carolina Press.

UNIVERSITY OF WISCONSIN PRESS—pp. 283, 285, 286, 287: from *Black Moses: Marcus Garvey and the Universal Negro Improvement Association,* by E. David Cronon. Copyright (c) 1969, The University of Wisconsin Press. Reprinted by permission of The University of Wisconsin Press.